THE RISE OF THE UNCORPORATION

THE RISE OF THE UNCORPORATION

LARRY E. RIBSTEIN

Oxford University Press, Inc., publishes works that further Oxford University's objective of excellence in research, scholarship, and education.

Oxford   New York
Auckland   Cape Town   Dar es Salaam   Hong Kong   Karachi   Kuala Lumpur   Madrid   Melbourne
Mexico City   Nairobi   New Delhi   Shanghai   Taipei   Toronto

With offices in
Argentina   Austria   Brazil   Chile   Czech Republic   France   Greece   Guatemala   Hungary   Italy
Japan   Poland   Portugal   Singapore   South Korea   Switzerland   Thailand   Turkey   Ukraine
Vietnam

Copyright © 2010 by Oxford University Press, Inc.

Published by Oxford University Press, Inc.
198 Madison Avenue, New York, New York 10016

Oxford is a registered trademark of Oxford University Press
Oxford University Press is a registered trademark of Oxford University Press, Inc.

All rights reserved. No part of this publication may be reproduced, stored in a retrieval system, or transmitted, in any form or by any means, electronic, mechanical, photocopying, recording, or otherwise, without the prior permission of Oxford University Press, Inc.

Library of Congress Cataloging-in-Publication Data

Ribstein, Larry E.
  The rise of the uncorporation / Larry E. Ribstein.
    p. cm.
  Includes bibliographical references and index.
  ISBN 978-0-19-537709-5 ((hardback) : alk. paper)
  1. Associations, institutions, etc—Law and legislation—United States. 2. Partnership—United States.
  3. Private companies—United States. 4. Business enterprises—Law and legislation—United States.
  5. Corporation law—United States. I. Title.
    KF1361.R53 2009
    346.73'0668—dc22   2009021954

1 2 3 4 5 6 7 8 9
Printed in the United States of America on acid-free paper

Note to Readers
This publication is designed to provide accurate and authoritative information in regard to the subject matter covered. It is based upon sources believed to be accurate and reliable and is intended to be current as of the time it was written. It is sold with the understanding that the publisher is not engaged in rendering legal, accounting, or other professional services. If legal advice or other expert assistance is required, the services of a competent professional person should be sought. Also, to confirm that the information has not been affected or changed by recent developments, traditional legal research techniques should be used, including checking primary sources where appropriate.

(Based on the Declaration of Principles jointly adopted by a Committee of the American Bar Association and a Committee of Publishers and Associations.)

You may order this or any other Oxford University Press publication by visiting the Oxford University Press website at www.oup.com

To Henry Manne, who blazed the trail that brought me here.

CONTENTS

Acknowledgments xv

CHAPTER 1. INTRODUCTION 1

    A. Why Study Uncorporations? 1

        1. The Uncorporate Solution to Governance Problems 1
        2. The Uncorporation and Contracts 2
        3. The Uncorporation Today 2

    B. Uncorporations in the Economy 2

    C. Do Business Associations Matter? 3

    D. Theories of the Uncorporation 4

        1. Structure 4
        2. Contracts 6
        3. Flexibility 7

    E. Competition and Business Forms 9

    F. The United States and Around the World 9

    G. The Plot of the Book 10

CHAPTER 2. THEORETICAL CONSIDERATIONS 15

    A. Why Firms? 15

    B. Governing Firms 17

        1. Specialization of Management and Ownership 18
        2. Managers and Agency Costs 18
        3. Owners and Opportunism 19
        4. Owners vs. Creditors 20
        5. Firms and Non-firms 20
        6. Governance and Underlying Business Conditions 21

    C. Why Business Associations? 21

        1. Formation 22
        2. Property Ownership 22
        3. Firm's Relationships with Creditors 22

4. Management and Control   23
5. Financial Rights   23
6. Transferability   23
7. Fiduciary Duties and Remedies   23
8. Exit   24
9. The Role of Standard Forms   24

D. Why Business Association *Law*   25

E. Why *Different* Business Associations?   26

F. The Architecture of Business Association Statutes   28
1. Short All-purpose Statute   29
2. Chinese Menu Approach   29
3. Hub-and-Spokes   30
4. Flexibility   31

G. The Evolution of Business Associations   31
1. Choice and Design of Contracts   31
2. Government Constraints: Regulation and Tax   32
3. Jurisdictional Competition and the Common Law   34
4. Background Factors: Business Environment, Technology, and Culture   35

H. The Corporation and Uncorporation   36
1. History and the Regulation of Governance   36
2. Type of Contracts   37
3. Type of Governance   38

CHAPTER 3. PARTNERSHIP   39

A. Early History   40

B. The Nature of Partnership: Entity or Aggregate?   41

C. Vicarious Liability   43

D. Owners' Financial Rights   44

E. Management   46

F. Fiduciary Duties and Remedies   48

G. Transferring Rights   51

H. Exit   53

I. Formation   55

J. Limited Partnerships   60

K. Joint Stock Companies and Limited Partnership Associations   62

CHAPTER 4. THE RISE OF THE CORPORATION   65

   A. Corporate Features and Large Firms   67
- 1. Centralized Management and Corporate Boards   67
- 2. Fiduciary Duties and Remedies   68
- 3. Owner Voting   69
- 4. Capital Lock-in   71
- 5. Limited Liability   72
- 6. Transferable Shares   72
- 7. Entities and Aggregates   73

   B. Could Partnerships Have Adopted Corporate Features?   76
- 1. Capital-lock-in: In General   76
- 2. Entity Shielding   77
- 3. Partnership Break-up   77
- 4. Centralized Management   78
- 5. Transferability   79
- 6. Limited Liability   79

   C. Limited Liability without Incorporation   80
- 1. Non-recourse Contracts   81
- 2. Unintentional Partnerships   81
- 3. Undisclosed Principals   81
- 4. Promoter Liability   82
- 5. Corporation by Estoppel   83
- 6. Limited Tort Liability   84
- 7. Formal Noncorporate Limited Liability Firms   84

   D. The Corporation and the Regulation of Governance   85
- 1. Why Regulate Corporate Governance?   86
- 2. How Do Lawmakers Regulate Governance?   87

   E. International Comparisons   90
- 1. The United Kingdom   90
- 2. European and Latin American Developments   93

CHAPTER 5. THE PROBLEMS OF THE CLOSE CORPORATION 95

A. Limited Liability and the Closely Held Firm 96

B. Lock-in 97

C. Other Corporate Rules 98

D. The Corporate Tax: The Price of Limited Liability 99

E. Other Roadblocks to Partnerships with Limited Liability 101

F. The Close Corporation as Evolutionary Dead End 102

G. Denial 103

H. Judicial Acceptance 104
1. Director Control Agreements 106
2. Shareholder Voting Arrangements 106
3. Share Transfer Restrictions 107
4. Breakdown and Exit 108

I. Tax Accommodation of the Closely Held Corporation 112

J. Full Statutory Authorization of Close Corporations 113

K. Failure 116

CHAPTER 6. THE EVOLUTION OF THE MODERN UNCORPORATION 119

A. The LLC Revolution 119

B. The Uncorporation Develops 123

C. The Importance of Non-Organization Law 124

D. The Rest of the Uncorporation Menagerie 125
1. General Partnership 126
2. LLP 127
3. Limited Partnership 128
4. LLLP 130

E. The Evolving LLC 131

F. European Developments 133

CHAPTER 7. THE MODERN UNCORPORATION 137

A. Member Shielding: Limited Liability 138
1. Corporate Limited liability 139

2. The Evolution of Uncorporate Limited Liability   139
3. General Partnership: Entity Aspects of Unlimited Liability   140
4. Limited Liability Partnership   142
5. Limited Partnership   143
6. Limited Liability Company   143

B. Management   147

1. Corporation: Standardized Hierarchy   149
2. General Partnership: Direct Member Management   150
3. Limited Liability Partnerships   151
4. Limited Partnership: Uncorporate Centralized Management   152
5. Limited Liability Company: Chameleon Approach   153

C. Members' Financial Rights   156

1. Non-economic Members   156
2. One-owner Firms   158
3. No-owner and Nonprofit Firms   160
4. Contributions   161
5. Profits, Losses, and Distributions   163

D. Fiduciary Duties: General Principles   165

1. Fiduciaries vs. Non-fiduciaries   166
2. Due Care   166
3. Misappropriation   167
4. Business Opportunities   167
5. Good Faith   167
6. Opt-out   168
7. Remedy   168

E. Fiduciary Duties in Specific Business Associations   169

1. Corporation   169
2. General Partnership   171
3. Limited Partnership   174
4. Limited Liability Company   177

F. Dissociation and Dissolution   179

G. Transferring Interests   182

H. Taxes, Regulation, and Business Association Design   184

1. Securities Regulation   186

xii CONTENTS

      2. Employment Discrimination   189
      3. General Thoughts on Tax and Regulation   192

CHAPTER 8. UNCORPORATING THE LARGE FIRM   193

  A. The Troubles with Corporate Governance   195

      1. Shareholder Voting   195
      2. Board of Directors   199
      3. Fiduciary Duties   203
      4. Takeovers   205

  B. Incentives and Discipline in the Large Uncorporation   207

      1. Managerial Compensation   208
      2. Distributions   209
      3. Buyout and Liquidation   212
      4. Supplementary Monitoring Mechanisms   213

  C. Uncorporate Ungovernance   214

      1. Undirectors   214
      2. Undemocracy   215
      3. Takeover Proofing   217
      4. Fiduciary Unduties   219

  D. Examples of Uncorporate Governance of Large Firms   222

      1. Private Equity   222
      2. Venture Capital   226
      3. Activist Hedge Funds   228
      4. Publicly Traded Partnerships   231

  E. Why Uncorporate Now?   234

      1. The Demand for Capital Lock-In   234
      2. New Governance Technologies   235
      3. Fleeing Sarbanes-Oxley   235
      4. Credit Costs and the Role of Debt   236

  F. The Future of the Large Uncorporation   237

      1. Financial Engineering   238
      2. Financial Regulation   240
      3. Regulation of Uncorporations   241
      4. The Corporate Tax   243
      5. The Future of Publicly Held Uncorporations   245
      6. The Corporate/Uncorporate Partnership   246

CHAPTER 9. NEW DIRECTIONS 247

    A. Convergence or Divergence of Business Forms 247

    B. The Long-Term Future of the Uncorporation 249

    C. The Uncorporation and Mandatory Rules 250

    D. Toward the Disappearance of the Close Corporation? 252

    E. The Socially Responsible Uncorporation 254

    F. Small vs. Large Firms? 255

    G. The Future of the Business Association 256

    H. Why the Uncorporation Matters 256

TABLE OF CASES 259
INDEX 265

ACKNOWLEDGMENTS

Like the uncorporation itself, this book evolved over a long period of time and owes debts to many people who contributed to its ideas along the way.

One of the earliest and most important contributors is Alan Bromberg, who was the leading authority on partnership when I first became interested in the subject. Alan was my colleague at Southern Methodist University when I visited there in 1980–1981. He was gracious enough to take me on as a co-author for the revision of his single-volume *Crane & Bromberg on Partnership* into what became the four-volume treatise, *Bromberg & Ribstein on Partnership*. Alan's thoughtful, exhaustive and meticulous work set a high standard for this revision.

Later in the 1980s I became involved in the revision of the Uniform Partnership Act as a member of the ABA Committee on Partnerships and Unincorporated Business Organizations and its Subcommittee on the Revised Uniform Partnership Act. Through that committee that I met a bright and hardworking group of lawyers with whom I have interacted over many years and from whom I have learned a lot about the on-the-ground production of business entity law.

One of the lawyers I met on the partnership project was Bob Keatinge, a Denver lawyer. Keatinge later collaborated with me on Ribstein & Keatinge on Limited Liability Companies. His energy and willingness to contemplate the deeper implications of alternative business entities have helped inspire the law of LLCs and my own work in the area.

My work with the bar and on my partnership and LLC treatises has fueled my scholarly theoretical and empirical work on unincorporated business associations. This work owes a lot to my former colleague and frequent co-author Bruce Kobayashi.

Interactions with generations of law students also have been an important part of the evolution of my thinking on the uncorporation. Since the mid-1990s I have taught a course on unincorporated business entities at George Mason University School of Law and later at the University of Illinois College of Law and New York University School of Law. This teaching led to four editions (the most recent with Jeff Lipshaw of Suffolk University) of my Unincorporated Business Entities casebook. My teaching and casebook writing helped me develop an approach to this area that combines substantive law, policy analysis and business planning.

And thanks to Northwestern's Searle Center on Law, Regulation, and Economic Growth and its director Henry Butler for organizing a Research

Roundtable on a draft version of the book, and to the Roundtable participants whose very helpful comments contributed significantly to the book.

This book reflects the wisdom of all of these lawyers, scholars and students from whom I have learned so much over the years.

Last but far from least, I'm grateful once again to my wife Ann for her usual help and support.

Larry Ribstein
July 19, 2009

1. INTRODUCTION

A. WHY STUDY UNCORPORATIONS?

You have probably seen firm names with strange letters after them—not the familiar *Inc.* but *LLC* or *LP* or the ambiguous *Co.* The letters are not just on cleaning company vans but more familiar firms, including Chrysler LLC and Sears Brands LLC (aka Sears Roebuck). You may have wondered whether the difference in initials signifies anything of importance. This book answers that question: Yes.

This book concerns a particular *form* of business—what it calls an *uncorporation*. The term presently includes general and limited partnerships, limited liability companies (LLCs), and variations on these entities. This is *not* a book about a particular *type* of business (i.e., big, small, closely held, or public) or a particular industry.

Uncorporations come in all shapes and sizes and are increasingly encroaching on traditionally "corporate" domains. The thesis is that form matters.

This book shows that the differences between corporations and uncorporations not only have practical consequences for businesspeople and lawyers, but go to the heart of public debates about all types of business regulation. This is the first general theoretical and practical overview of alternatives to incorporation. Prior works on partnerships and other unincorporated firms have been intended mainly for practitioners. This work seeks to bring uncorporations into both the popular and academic debates that have previously focused on corporations. It covers the history, law, and finance of unincorporated firms; ancillary concepts connected with the evolution of these firms; and analyses of likely future trends in business organization.

1. The uncorporate solution to governance problems

Uncorporations provide a fundamental alternative to the corporation in addressing the central problems of business organization: how to minimize the costs of delegating power over investments to non-owner managers and controlling owners. Corporations and uncorporations are not just variations spread across a continuous spectrum of business organizations, but rather discrete alternatives to the basic business association features. Focusing on these basic alternatives provides a new perspective on the governance of firms that illuminates previously obscured policy choices.

Uncorporations can be big or small. For small firms, business association standard forms can be a significant factor in promoting entrepreneurship. These firms' governance problems are as daunting as those of the biggest ones. They include: How can control be delegated to expert managers without risking giving away the store? How can entrepreneurs be protected from the investors—and vice versa? How can resolution be facilitated of disputes that might tear the firm apart? Although the problems are big, the firms may lack the resources to deal expertly with multidimensional long-term contracting problems. The availability of sets of default rules that fill the contracting gaps can be critical to these firms' success.

As for big firms, corporate governance rules have been the plaything of regulators for nearly a century. The monitoring board, shareholder voting rights, fiduciary duties, mandatory disclosure, securities litigation, and much more are all areas that have been worked over by waves of reformers. Yet Enron and the financial meltdown of 2008–09, in which huge apparently sturdy firms suddenly imploded from hidden risks, all suggest that corporate governance reform has left us no closer to solving the fundamental agency problems in large firms. The uncorporation provides an opportunity for meaningful and constructive change.

2. The uncorporation and contracts

Regulation and standard forms are not the only avenues to good governance as uncorporations also help effectuate contractual approaches to governance problems. The corporation was born as a vehicle for linking government and business. This link persisted in the background even after purely private ventures incorporated. As government has been thought to create corporations, it needs no special justification to regulate the "privilege" of incorporation. Conversely, with uncorporate governance, the government must clear the same hurdles it faces when trying to regulate other contracts. The flexibility afforded by the lesser governmental role enables uncorporations to deal with a rapidly changing business environment.

3. The uncorporation today

As its title suggests, this book tells a dynamic story. Although lawmakers have sought to regulate firm governance by channeling entities into the corporate form, competition between the states and among business forms helps constrain regulatory excesses. This competition has enabled flexible uncorporate forms to supplant the corporation as the dominant form for closely held firms, then to move into large firms' corporate domain.

B. UNCORPORATIONS IN THE ECONOMY

Tax data provide a snapshot of the uncorporation's role in the economy. According to the most recent data available for incorporated and unincorporated business entities,[1] 1,630,161 limited liability companies filed returns in 2006. There were 718,765 general partnership and 432,550 limited partnership returns, for a total of 2,781,366 uncorporations. For the same period, 5,840,799 corporations filed returns. Uncorporations therefore were a little less than a third of all tax-reporting entities.

All types of firms and businesses employ uncorporate forms. General partnerships long have been used both for small firms among family and friends and much larger professional firms (usually as "limited liability partnerships"). Limited-purpose joint ventures between firms of all sizes often are organized as general partnerships and limited liability companies. Limited partnerships can be used for estate planning and for various kinds of investment vehicles, including venture capital, hedge funds, private equity funds, real estate, or natural resource firms. LLCs are ubiquitous, ranging from sole proprietorships through mom-and-pop operations to publicly held firms with thousands of investors.

C. DO BUSINESS ASSOCIATIONS MATTER?

Most people who are neither lawyers nor academics would probably see the distinctions between the corporation and uncorporation as a lot of technical nuances with little payoff. Economists and other social scientists might argue that it is the parties' basic deals that matter, not the formats they use for packaging them. Although lawyers might understand why differences among business associations matter, they tend to see these differences as mainly ways to accomplish specific tax and regulatory goals.

Skeptics of this project might pose three specific questions. First, why should we care about different types of business associations? After all, economists tell us that the heart of the business organization is the *firm*. As discussed in Chapter 2, firms can reduce parties' transaction costs by offering an alternative in the form of simpler contracts and transactions in spot markets. Given the many different arrangements parties make in the real world, it is very difficult to find clear lines between firms and market transactions or among types of firms. Myriad contracts provide for a bewildering variety of management and economic rights, fiduciary duties, and exit rights. It is not clear why packaging these terms into distinct standard forms should matter, particularly as the parties can tear these packages apart and contract for their own combinations. If the parties

---

1. The partnership data are from Statistics of Income Bulletin, Partnership Returns 2006 at 216 (Fall 2008) at 137–39, Figure H, http://www.irs.gov/pub/irs-soi/08fallbulpr.pdf. The corporate data are from 2006 Corporation Source Book, Statistics of Income, http://www.irs.gov/taxstats/article/oid=165716,00.html. Corporations reported about four times the net income of partnerships. However, income comparisons may be skewed by the fact that many partnerships are tax shelters operated to maximize tax losses.

can turn what has been formed under a corporation statute into something virtually identical to a partnership, why should it matter that they started with a corporation?

Second, assuming business associations matter, is there any point in general to distinguishing between corporations on the one hand and unincorporated firms on the other? In other words, even if there are important differences between specific business associations, it is not clear that there are also important differences between *categories* of business associations. Do the distinctions between an uncorporation and a corporation categorically differ from those between one type of uncorporation and another?

Third, even if we accept the importance of the above distinctions, this book's title suggests an evolution of business associations away from the corporate form seems to defy accepted wisdom. The corporation undeniably has driven business growth in the United States since the Industrial Revolution. As discussed in Chapter 4, it improved on traditional partnership forms as a vehicle for enabling the efficient management of large firms. The corporate form has proved capable of adapting to modern business problems. To the extent that the partnership form has remained viable, it is arguably only because partnerships have adopted such "corporate" features as centralized management and limited liability. So should this book be called instead *The Rise of the Unpartnership*?

This book responds to these questions and makes a case for paying more attention to alternatives to the corporation. It is a case worth making, especially in light of the failures of corporate governance exposed by the 2008–09 financial crisis. Managers of the largest and oldest financial firms apparently bet their companies' futures on financial instruments of dubious value. Accordingly, many people would agree that accepted approaches to corporate governance have proved inadequate and need to be fixed.

The uncorporate route to meaningful change clearly is worth exploring. Hedge and private equity funds have been instrumental in improving the governance of large corporations, and venture capital funds have been vital in funding entrepreneurs. Insights from the governance of these firms could point the way to reshaping the "corporate" world.

D. THEORIES OF THE UNCORPORATION

Several important concepts are useful in understanding the basic differences between corporations and uncorporations.

1. Structure
A firm can be seen as a set of contractual provisions among the owners and between the owners and managers intended to accomplish particular objectives. These provisions need to complement each other rather than working redundantly

or at cross-purposes. In other words, as discussed in Chapter 2, the statute needs to be *coherent*. The terms bundled into uncorporations provide a distinct approach to addressing the two main problems with which all business associations have to deal: delegating discretion to agents and allocating decision-making power among the owners.

Business associations all face the same general issues and share many substantive similarities, particularly regarding provisions relating to creditors and other non-owner third parties. They once differed significantly as to whether the firm's creditors could reach the owners' individual assets. This difference became less important after the "LLC Revolution" discussed in Chapter 6, which broke down tax and regulatory barriers to insulating owners from firms' debts. Owners' limited or vicarious liability to creditors is no longer a central basis for distinguishing corporations and uncorporations.

This book aims to identify the important differences between modern (post-LLC Revolution) uncorporations and corporations. These differences focus on the relationships among the owners and between the owners and the managers of the firm.

General partnership law assumes a close horizontal relationship among the owners and involvement of all of the owners in managing the firm. This follows from the partners' individual liability to the firm's creditors. If owners are going to have their entire personal fortunes on the line, they had better be intensely involved in the firm. General partnership law and contracts also have to deal with controlling owners' incentive to gang up on a minority and appropriate an unfair share of the firm's earnings and property. Unlike in a publicly held corporation, minority owners cannot flee by selling their stock in the open market. The owners' recourse in the classic partnership is to force dissolution of the firm, or at least a buyout of their interests. This power to cash out of the firm is, in effect, a powerful control mechanism that augments the minority's voting rights.

In modern uncorporations, the owners' limited liability lets them be passive, delegate control to managers, and hold their interests as part of a diversified portfolio of investments. These passive uncorporate owners have concerns about agency costs similar to those of public corporation shareholders. The difference between the firms is how they deal with these costs, with corporations relying primarily on the stock market, owner voting, and courts to discipline managers.

In contrast, modern uncorporations borrow tricks from traditional partnerships. Uncorporate managers are, like partners, full-fledged owners of the firm, with strong incentives to act in the firm's interests. Also like partners, uncorporate owners can exit by getting cash directly out of the firm. This can be a more effective type of exit than the stock market because the exit price is not depressed by bad management. It is also an effective disciplinary device because it directly removes assets from the bad managers' control.

Although the modern uncorporation is the product of various business, tax, and regulatory forces, it is not a sharp break with the past. As discussed in Chapter 3, uncorporations with centralized management or limited liability (or both), particularly the limited partnership and joint stock company, have been around since before the rise of the modern corporation. The rise of the uncorporation is *not* the modern evolution of the corporation, but the re-emergence of uncorporate forms after a relatively brief period of corporate dominance.

2. Contracts

Uncorporations are characterized by their reliance on contracts. This is an aspect of uncorporations' partnership heritage, as partnerships are contracts among the owners. The Uniform Partnership Act mainly provides default rules that apply to partners only in the absence of a contrary agreement. The statute's few mandatory rules apply mostly to those who are not parties to the partnership agreement, including creditors of the firm or of the individual members. Partners can vary even these rules, but they would need the creditors' consent.

The Revised Uniform Partnership Act provides for a few additional mandatory rules among the partners, mostly relating to fiduciary duties. However, the statute spells these out at the beginning and explicitly makes them exceptions to the general rule of enforcement of the partnership agreement.[2] Other uncorporation statutes (including those for limited liability companies and limited partnerships) follow the partnership model in this important respect.

In contrast, corporate law is mainly couched in mandatory terms. As discussed in Chapter 4, the corporation's special regulatory nature emerged from its historical roots. The corporation initially was a vehicle for government enterprises, monopolies, or franchises. When government gives firms special deals, it is only natural that regulation would be part of the quid pro quo. This is as true of the bailouts of today as it was of the corporations of three hundred years ago.

The problem is that when these government-related entities evolved into purely private operations, they retained the corporate form's entanglement with government regulation. Rather than being a contract solely among the owners, incorporation was regarded as a privilege that firms had to beg or buy from the state. Even after the states widely adopted *general incorporation* statutes that removed state permission from the formation process, states remained involved by issuing the certificate that gave life to the separate corporate entity. The owners could agree among themselves to operate the firm as a partnership, but they could receive corporate entity features only through the state. The vestige of state involvement in creation in turn supports an argument for the state

---

2. *See* Revised Uniform Partnership Act, § 103 (1997) ("RUPA").

being able to regulate corporate governance without having the same justifications required for regulation of other types of contracts.[3]

History alone cannot explain the different susceptibilities of corporations and uncorporations to regulation. Even if corporations *started* as creatures of the state, they did not have to *remain* in captivity. But legislators have a lot to gain from guarding access to the governance levers of large, publicly held firms. For example, managers want laws that help them retain power while workers want to protect their jobs and pay. Federal and state legislators can earn campaign support and other benefits by favoring particular groups. In a purely contractual regime, the contracting parties get to keep all of the gain from their contracts rather than giving some of it to legislators. The lawmaking stakes are big not just for the parties to the firm, but also for society. Large firms exercise significant economic power, and they can use their economic clout to seek political favors. Accordingly, lawmakers have an incentive to try to manipulate the governance of big firms so that they are not aggressive competitors for power.

Uncorporations not only explicitly permit, but also indirectly facilitate contracts. A firm's contractual freedom should be evaluated not only in terms of the flexibility permitted by a given business association statute, but in light of the alternative available standard forms. Uncorporations' contribution to contractual freedom is a reason the proper design of these statutes is so important. The more distinct and coherent are the sets of terms these statutes offer, the more viable is a firm's choice of form, which becomes merely a Hobson's choice if all standard forms are unsatisfactory.

Lawmakers have been well aware of the implications of choice of form for freedom of contract. Chapters 4 and 5 discuss how lawmakers facilitated the rise of the corporation by blocking the exits to uncorporate business forms. However, the opening up of the limited liability company alternative discussed in Chapter 6 had the important effect of creating contracting space for all firms—not just those that organize as LLCs.

3. Flexibility

Uncorporations differ from corporations in terms of their ability both to choose contract terms that suit the particular firm and to modify terms to adjust to changes in the firm or its business environment. This is obviously a by-product of the uncorporation's reliance on contracting. However, flexibility deserves a separate discussion because rigidity is not necessarily inconsistent with contracting.

The corporate form is designed for larger firms with many owners. These firms, particularly if they are publicly held, have a lot to gain from standardizing terms.

---

3. *See* Henry N. Butler & Larry E. Ribstein, *Opting Out of Fiduciary Duties: A Response to the Anti-Contractarians*, 65 Wash. L. Rev. 1 (1990).

Investors have to incur costs to learn about different governance mechanisms. Firms can reduce their cost of capital by saving investors these costs.

Firms with many owners also face obstacles in modifying their terms after they are formed. Individual shareholders have little incentive to initiate changes because they must incur the costs while sharing the benefits with thousands of others taking a "free ride" on the first mover's efforts. Managers easily can initiate changes, but the free-rider problem makes it hard for shareholders to protect themselves from changes favoring the managers.

Thus, in standard publicly held corporations, flexibility may be more of a benefit for powerful corporate managers than for passive shareholders. Investors might instead prefer to delegate to state lawmakers the power to modify their contracts to take account of business developments.[4] Lawmakers would exercise this power subject to discipline by the market for state corporation law. In other words, corporations would choose their incorporating state not only for its current law, but for its reputation for making changes that are in firms' interests. If the leading state of Delaware failed to keep up with conditions or made changes that were not in firms' interests, it would lose litigation business and franchise taxes.

By contrast, uncorporations are designed mostly for closely held firms. Because they do not need standardization, and because their owners can easily make changes, uncorporations can take full advantage of the ability to customize their contracts to suit particular firms' needs.

Given the different needs of uncorporations and corporations, the different approaches can be rationalized as enhancing a firm's contracting options. Larger firms select the corporate form for standardization while smaller firms choose the uncorporate form for flexibility. However, as discussed in the preceding section, the different standard forms are not designed entirely to enhance contracting. As corporations are a mechanism for regulating governance, we would not expect firms to be able to choose freely whether to organize as a corporation or an uncorporation. In fact, as discussed throughout this book, government has used the tax laws and regulation of limited liability to "charge" firms for exercising corporate "privileges." This has had the effect of limiting parties' options as compared to a world of free contracting.

This discussion focuses on the classic types of uncorporations and corporations for which the respective standard forms are designed. But corporations and uncorporations do not neatly sort by type—there are many closely held corporations and some large and even publicly held uncorporations. The two types of "crossovers" have different degrees of success. As we will see in Chapter 5, corporate rigidity is a curse for close corporations. By contrast, Chapter 8 shows that uncorporate flexibility can be a benefit for large uncorporations.

---

4. *See* Henry Hansmann, *Corporations and Contracts*, 8 Am L. Econ. Rev. 1 (2006).

E. COMPETITION AND BUSINESS FORMS

Theories of the uncorporation have a dynamic aspect that inheres in the tension between lawmakers' incentives to overregulate governance (as discussed above) and competitive forces that constrain these regulatory tendencies. Firms can avoid restrictions on contracting by exploiting "horizontal" variations across jurisdictions, "vertical" variations within jurisdictions between different types of business associations, and potentially near-infinite variations among private contracts.

As we will see throughout the book, contracts and competing laws have driven the continuous evolution of business association law and broken down barriers to contracting. A corporation need not obey a state's mandatory rules if it can easily choose another state's (say, Delaware's) enabling statute. Indeed, the mere existence of the "Delaware option" essentially makes all business association law optional.[5] Also, parties to firms have proven quite ingenious in designing terms to exploit gaps in the rules. For example, if a state statute mandates cumulative voting for directors to ensure that minority shareholders have seats on the board, firms can reduce the minority's seats just by electing fewer directors each year. Lawmakers might regulate this particular end run, but creative firms can come up with another one.

Horizontal and vertical competition and contracting thus mitigate the risks of overregulation. However, they also can erode beneficial regulation. Accordingly, there is some need for regulation that reduces these evasions by crossing vertical, horizontal, and contracting borders. By analyzing the functions of business forms, this book provides some insight into both when regulation is appropriate and how the regulation should be designed to avoid undermining the benefits of choice among different business associations.

F. THE UNITED STATES AND AROUND THE WORLD

This book focuses on U.S. business associations. Its basic plot and themes draw primarily from recent U.S. business history and institutions, particularly U.S. federal and common law systems, along with business association, tax, and regulatory laws. However, as the uncorporation is a worldwide phenomenon, the book also discusses developments in other countries. There is reason to believe a similar process involving tension between regulated and flexible business forms is occurring throughout the world. Commentators and practitioners outside the United States therefore will find this book of interest not just because

---

5. *See* Larry E. Ribstein, *Unlimited Contracting in the Delaware Limited Partnership and Its Implications for Corporate Law*, 17 J. CORP. L. 299 (1991).

G. THE PLOT OF THE BOOK

the U.S. developments are themselves significant, but because they illuminate what is happening in other countries.

As indicated by its title, this book has a sort of a plot in tracking the increasing importance of uncorporations in modern business. *Rise* describes the current trend, but the overall history looks more like two humps than a straight-line trajectory. From the beginning of business associations until the latter part of the nineteenth century, the partnership and its offshoots dominated as the basic form of business. Corporate-type firms during this period were government-run or government-associated firms; they did not play a role in the purely private sector.

The nineteenth century saw the Rise of the Corporation. The corporate form dominated because it was designed to deal with business demand for centralized management. Business structures forked off into corporations for large and ultimately publicly held firms and partnerships for smaller, closely held firms. Commentators have viewed the adaptation of the corporation for use by private firms as a watershed event which, among other things, created the basis for the Industrial Revolution.[6] Financial engineering and new business structures clearly were an important part of this revolution.

A big reason the corporation was so important for the industrial firm was that it enabled firms to be entities separate from their owners.[7] The corporate entity concept has several facets. First, owners have no hard-core right to leave and cash out of the firm. This strengthens managers' power to control the firm's assets. Conversely, partners' ability to cash out gives them control and commensurately loosens manager control. Shareholders' lack of such a right is consistent with their passivity and the corporate separation of management and control.

Second, *shareholders' creditors* have no direct right to the firm's assets. This increases the *firm's* creditors' ability to rely on the firm's assets and follows from the owners' own lack of direct access to the firm's cash.

Third, the *corporation's* creditors can look only to the firm and not to the individual owners for payment of their debts, thus limiting the liability of the firm's owners to their investments in the firm. This enables corporations to separate ownership and control functions. The owners are specialized risk bearers who can reduce the cost of risk by holding diversified portfolios of shares. (Shareholders cannot do this if their entire portfolios might be called on to pay the debts of a

---

6. *See* Margaret M. Blair, *Locking in Capital: What Corporate Law Achieved for Business Organizers in the Nineteenth Century*, 51 UCLA L. REV. 387 (2003).

7. *See* Henry Hansmann & Reinier Kraakman, *The Essential Role of Organizational Law*, 110 YALE L.J. 387 (2000).

single firm in the portfolio.) Specialization of risk bearing also enables the creation of public securities markets that can cheaply disseminate information about the firm.

The corporate form eventually spread even to small, closely held firms. This reflects the fact that partnerships could not contract for the critical "corporate" feature of owners' limited liability to tort creditors. Thus, firms that wanted limited liability had to incorporate. The twentieth-century tort revolution increased firms' demand for both limited liability and incorporation.

Federal tax law reinforced small firms' incentive to incorporate through classification rules that made it difficult for limited liability firms to avoid the double corporate tax. State laws did, however, increasingly recognize closely held corporations. Federal tax law furthered this recognition by letting simple closely held corporations avoid the corporate tax through Subchapter S of the Internal Revenue Code. These developments pushed the partnership form to the margins occupied mainly by professional firms and contracts that included features the courts classified as unintentional partnerships. At this point, one could speak of the "death of partnership."[8]

The story so far seems to be one of an outmoded governance technology—partnership—being pushed aside by a sleeker model: the corporation. But there is an alternative narrative in which legal rules share the stage with business needs. Partnership default rules, particularly including partners' vicarious liability for partnership debts, made the partnership relationship awkward for all but a relatively small niche of very closely held firms. Though partners could contract around most of these default rules, they always ran into the stone wall of vicarious liability that drove the rest of the partnership contract. Partnership vicarious liability in effect channeled modern firms into the corporate form that government had set aside for them.

The law, however, was not immutable. Out of the death of partnership and the rise of the corporation rose the new and improved uncorporation. The process began with closely held firms. The corporate entity features that had suited large, publicly held firms did not fit closely held ones. Locked-in owners could not effectively discipline managers and majority shareholders by withdrawing their investments, and corporate monitoring devices were either unavailable or too costly to be effective.

Therefore, business people began pushing the legal barriers to limited liability in the partnership form. Regulators could be expected to resist this development because adding limited liability to the contractual and flexible partnership form would complicate government efforts to tax and regulate this valuable feature. However, jurisdictional competition eroded state barriers to contracting

---

8. *See* Larry E. Ribstein, *The Deregulation of Limited Liability and the Death of Partnership*, 70 WASH. U. L.Q. 417 (1992).

for corporate features in partnerships. This in turn undermined the federal tax distinction between partnerships and corporations, which purported to rest on the corporate and partnership features of state business association law.

The closely held firms that emerged from this process are the first "uncorporations." This label is admittedly vague because it only says what the firms are not, not what they are. The firms might more descriptively be called "incorporated partnerships" on the theory that the firms had adopted the key corporate feature of limited liability.

So which feature is more important—*incorporated* or *partnership*? Some commentators suggest that partnerships with limited liability really represented the natural evolution of the corporate form, free from the prior constraints on entity features.[9] In contrast, this book argues that uncorporations' critical features are those borrowed from partnerships: the reliance on managerial incentives and owners' access to the cash to deal with agency costs, and majority oppression of minority owners. From this perspective, recent history is one of the rise of uncorporate-type business forms rather than increased dominance of the corporate form.

One might suppose that with the rise of closely held uncorporations, business association law had reached a stable equilibrium with large, publicly traded firms taking the corporate form and small, closely held firms taking the uncorporate form. Indeed, federal tax law reinforced this equilibrium by applying the corporate tax to the vast majority of publicly traded firms.[10]

As it turned out, the equilibrium was not so stable. Corporate features were proving costly and unwieldy even for the large firms for which they were developed. Uncorporate incentives and disciplinary devices provided an important alternative to corporate-style monitoring. The demand for alternatives to corporate-style governance of large firms fueled competition among contracts and jurisdictions and paved the way for uncorporate governance of large firms. In particular, Delaware has actively promoted the freedom to contract out of corporate-type duties—and therefore the flexibility that is an important aspect of the uncorporation. Thus, as the story comes to the present, there is a real chance that uncorporate business forms will occupy a significant portion of the contract space once filled by the corporation.

This book proceeds as follows: Chapter 2 provides theoretical background for the issues discussed in the book, including the theory of the firm, the nature and function of business association statutes, and the more general distinctions between corporate-type and partnership-type statutes.

Chapter 3 discusses the classic general partnership form. Partnerships have "aggregate" features emphasizing the power and responsibility of individual

---

9. *See* Henry Hansmann et al., *Law and the Rise of the Firm*, 119 HARV. L. REV. 1333 (2006).

10. *See* Internal Revenue Code, § 7704, 26 U.S.C. § 7704 ("IRC").

members, including owners' personal liability for the firm's debts and power to cash out of (and perhaps unilaterally destroy) the firm. But even the classical general partnership had entity features that enabled owners to keep the assets together in an effective business enterprise, including the firm's primary responsibility for its debts, members' power to bind the firm (and the fiduciary duties that accompanied this power), and default rules that kept the firm together long enough to accomplish its intended purpose. Overarching the specific aggregate and entity features in the statutory default rules was the partners' power to contract for virtually any combination of features they wanted, including terms that closely approximated the corporate form. This analysis of the classical partnership forms shows how the seeds of the modern uncorporation were planted long ago. However, the classical partnership was so focused on closely held firms that investors in larger firms had a strong need for an alternative to partnership.

Chapter 4 discusses the rise of the corporation, focusing on the evolution of the corporate form for use by the modern publicly held firm. This chapter emphasizes that the rise of the corporation was not as inevitable as some commentators have claimed. Although the classical partnership was unsuited to governing larger firms, it was flexible enough to have been adapted for this use. This adaptation arguably would have been no more of a stretch than was the borrowing of the corporate form from the public sphere for use by private firms. In fact, the rise of the corporation had as much to do with regulation of alternatives to incorporation as with market forces. This analysis sets the stage for the story in Chapter 6 of the way contracts and vertical and horizontal competition enabled the uncorporation to break through the regulatory protection of the corporate form.

Chapter 5 discusses the extension of the corporate form to closely held firms. Again, government-imposed constraints had a lot to do with this development. Firms wanted to combine partnership features with limited liability and avoidance of the double-level corporate tax. However, state statutes refused to open up limited liability to partnerships, and the tax laws made it hard for limited liability firms' to avoid the corporate tax. The close corporation form evolved under the pressure of contracts and jurisdictional competition to provide the features closely held firms needed. But the close corporation was fundamentally infected by its still being a corporation.

Chapter 6 discusses the response to the problems of the close corporation—what might be called the LLC Revolution. LLCs enabled firms to contract for both limited liability and partnership features. The LLC spread across the vast majority of states in only a little more than a decade. By the time the revolution ended in the late 1990s, all states fully recognized the LLC form. Moreover, the federal government decided to allow firms to choose partnership-type taxation regardless of their business structure. Thus, the uncorporation reasserted its dominance at least for closely held firms.

Chapter 7 examines in detail the modern closely held uncorporations that have emerged from the LLC Revolution. The chapter's main point is to demonstrate the value of viewing the features of statutory standard forms as *coherent sets* of terms. This analysis makes sense of the distinctions both between corporations and uncorporations and among different uncorporations. The analysis indicates that state statutes generally have evolved toward providing efficient terms.

Chapter 8 discusses the uncorporation's modern extension into large and publicly held firms. Some of these firms are organized as uncorporations, while many others are owned and controlled by such uncorporations as private equity, hedge, and venture capital funds. This story ends with the financial crisis that prevails at the time this book was written, which presents significant opportunities for the expansion of uncorporations into the large firm realm. At the same time, such expansion might be accompanied by regulation of the uncorporation and convergence of the corporate and uncorporate forms that would undermine firms' ability to choose among these contracting options. This book's analysis of the importance of preserving the corporate-uncorporate distinction can help guide these policy decisions.

Chapter 9 concludes by analyzing the implications of the analysis for emerging issues in uncorporations. These issues include the future of separate business association statutes, the survival of the close corporation, and the potential demise of the whole concept of the business association.

In general, several themes recur through the book: the dynamic nature of business and regulation, the force of private contracting and jurisdictional competition in breaking down regulatory barriers, and the extent to which regulation has resisted this erosion. The story of the *Rise of the Uncorporation* is, in part, a tool for examining the basic forces at work in the evolution of business and of business law.

2. THEORETICAL CONSIDERATIONS

This chapter introduces the specific issues concerning the uncorporation and frames them theoretically. The chapter's goal is to provide an understanding of the concept of the uncorporation in the general context of the functions of economic firms, the legal constructs known as business associations, and the processes that drive the evolution of these structures.

A. WHY FIRMS?

A business association is basically a set of contracts among individuals or other entities to supply various types of inputs, including capital, goods, and services. Consider a farmer who borrows from a bank to finance the purchase of a field, machinery, and seed, then hires workers to grow corn. These labor, purchase, and loan agreements could be viewed as a firm or business association. How does the farmer's set of contracts differ from each of the component contracts or any other type of contract?

In his seminal 1937 article, "The Nature of the Firm," Ronald Coase asked how transactions within firms differed from those in markets, and why some transactions happened within firms while others occurred in markets. His answer focused on transaction costs. A firm such as General Motors (which Coase studied in the 1920s) turns inputs into outputs through many steps. Each step theoretically could be handled as a sale by one firm and a purchase by a separate firm, but this would involve many negotiations of prices and terms. So it might be cheaper to organize all of the transactions into one business that owns all the equipment and employs all of the workers necessary for producing cars. Coase saw evidence of his theory of the firm in the law of agency, which provides for a *principal* to direct an *agent* by fiat rather than negotiating each of the agent's acts at arm's length as in the open market.

Coase also wondered why, if fiat is cheaper than negotiating transactions, there is not one big firm. Why not eliminate *all* of those pesky transactions, including the ones between firms? Coase thought the answer was that at some size, the costs of running the firm exceed the benefits of reducing market transactions, though he did not articulate what these costs might be.

Many economists have followed in Coase's footsteps thinking about the distinct nature and functions of firms. Some theories seek a fuller explanation of why firms bring transactions together by giving one party the power to organize transactions. Parties alternatively could reduce the transaction costs of separate transactions by laying out specific rights and obligations in a single long-term contract. For example, a party may agree to deliver its output or the other party's requirements over several years at prices determined by an agreed formula.

Armen Alchian and Harold Demsetz explained the use of firm-type contracts via a theory of *team production,* in which a team produces more value than the members could by working separately.[11] For example, a team of movers may make more than the members working individually because customers pay extra for speed.

A more important example of team production is reputation. Transactions often require parties to trust each other's expertise or reliability or that the goods are as represented. A law firm, for example, may provide a basis for trust by developing a reputation for fair dealing. A reputable firm can charge more than one with a bad or no reputation. The extra charge helps ensure that the firm will continue to be trustworthy because a firm revealed as a cheat cannot charge a reputational premium in future transactions. The firm's reputation thus serves as a kind of bond it posts to ensure future performance.[12]

Team production enters the picture because a firm's reputation is worth more than those of individuals. The firm "rents" its reputation to lawyers just starting out with no reputation and to those near retirement whose reputations offer little comfort because they will not need them much longer.

Now consider the problem team production poses for firms. Because the team as a whole produces extra value, it may be very hard to determine how much the firm should pay each team member. If members do not get paid the value of their contributions, they have an incentive to shirk and let their colleagues pick up the slack. As a result, everybody shirks, nothing gets done, and nobody gets paid.

For example, a law firm has to figure out how to get its lawyers to contribute to building the firm's reputation. This is based not only on individual lawyers' success in transactions or the courtroom, but also on their work in writing, engaging in law reform, representing clients pro bono, engaging in continuing legal education, and mentoring junior associates. These efforts combine to help the firm attract clients and charge more for its services. However, it still may be difficult to determine the value of each member's contribution to the firm's reputation. Without the right incentives, lawyers might try to free ride off of their colleagues' reputation-building efforts. Then as noted above, everybody shirks and what is left is simply a collection of individual lawyers rather than a firm with its own reputation.

---

11. *See* Armen Alchian & Harold Demsetz, *Production, Information Costs, and Economic Organization,* 62 AM. ECON. REV. 777 (1972).

12. *See* Benjamin Klein & Keith B. Leffler, *The Role of Market Forces in Assuring Contractual Performance,* 89 J. POL. ECON. 615 (1981).

Alchian and Demsetz theorized that the shirking problem in these situations was solved by the firm's having a *monitor* who identifies slackers and high achievers and administers appropriate punishments and rewards. This explains the agent-principal relationship that Coase saw as the foundation of the firm. A conventional long-term contract does not work because to draft it, the firm has to know each party's contribution, which gets back to the team production problem. The monitor can be motivated by sharing the enterprise's gain after subtracting payments such as wages and interest to the team members. The more value the monitor can extract from the team members and the firm's other resources, the higher the monitor's reward. The monitor is thus the firm's *owner* in the sense of getting all of the firm's benefits and taking all of its risks.

Other theories besides team production explain why firms are organized. In particular, conventional non-firm contracts cannot fully deal with the parties' temptation to be "opportunistic"—that is, to take selfish advantage of each other in ways that are permitted by the literal terms of the contract or tolerated by gaps or costs of the legal system.[13] No matter how detailed their contract, the parties cannot foresee everything. Moreover, a contract's obligations may not be fully enforceable because it takes time and money for the parties to hire lawyers and go to court. A party may exploit the other party's short-term need for a good or service by deliberately violating the contract. Express deliverers therefore own their airplanes and integrated manufacturers once owned parts suppliers so a recalcitrant supplier could not hold up an entire assembly process.[14]

The point of this discussion is that there is real economic value in forming firms. Yet firms also involve costs (as discussed below). Unless contracts and legal rules can mitigate these costs, some firms may not be formed and value will be lost. As we will see, business associations are critical in minimizing the costs of governing firms.

B. GOVERNING FIRMS

Once firms are formed, the parties have to solve other problems in their governance contracts. These include not only the shirking problem Alchian and Demsetz described, but agency costs between owners and managers and opportunism among owners. In general, there is a tension between the centripetal forces that bring firms together and the centrifugal governance problems that pull them apart. These problems have no obvious single solution. That is one

---

13. *See* Oliver Williamson, Markets and Hierarchies: Analysis and Antitrust Implications 26–30 (1975).
14. *See* Benjamin Klein et al., *Vertical Integration, Appropriable Rents, and the Competitive Contracting Process*, 21 J.L. & Econ. 297 (1978).

reason it is helpful to offer contracting parties a variety of different statutory forms.

1. Specialization of management and ownership

Alchian and Demsetz's theory of solving team production problems with a monitor works best if there is just one owner who reaps all of the rewards from monitoring. There are in fact many such "sole proprietorships." The bigger the firm, the more it needs to separate ownership and management functions. There is no reason to assume the person who contributes management skills is the best source of money to operate the business. Also, larger firms are likely to have many owners. Investors can reduce their risk by holding diversified portfolios of assets that produce offsetting gains and losses in unpredictable future situations. However, they can do so only if they do not try to manage every firm in which they invest. Another reason for financing firms with many small investments is that these investments can be traded in a market at prices that provide valuable and timely information as to how the firm is doing.

2. Managers and agency costs

Although there are significant benefits to specializing management and ownership, specialization has its costs. Unless the monitor gets all of the profits, she has an incentive to sacrifice the firm's welfare for her own. That is because each dollar the *firm* loses from the monitor's shirking or self-dealing costs the *monitor* less than a dollar. Jensen and Meckling explored this problem, which they termed agency costs—that is, the costs of delegating control to an agent to exercise on behalf of the owners.[15] The owners can monitor the agent or insist that the agent pay a bond which she forfeits if she slacks off or steals. However, bonding and monitoring may be expensive, and close monitoring may interfere with the agent's ability to do her job. Therefore, the firm may have to accept some residual loss as the cost of hiring the agent.

The parties might be able to avoid some agency costs by specifying all obligations and penalties for an up-front breach in a detailed contract. But such a contract is obviously very difficult to write and (because nobody can foresee the future) necessarily incomplete. A complex business therefore must find some way to delegate open-ended discretion to managers without having all the gains of this delegation eaten up in agency costs. The more power the agent has, the more effectively the agent can run the business for the owners' benefit—but also possibly, his own separate benefit. Thus, there is a tradeoff between the need to delegate power to the agent and the need to make the agent accountable in exercising the power through monitoring as well as incentive and disciplinary devices.

---

15. *See* Michael Jensen & William Meckling, *Theory of the Firm: Managerial Behavior, Agency Costs and Ownership Structure*, 3 J. FIN. ECON. 305 (1976).

As we will see, the corporation and the uncorporation represent alternative mechanisms for dealing with this trade-off.

3. Owners and opportunism

One way to constrain agents' power is for the owners to exercise control over the managers. Even where the owners delegate management power, they still usually reserve the power to vote on economically significant firm actions and on election and removal of managers. This vote has been rationalized as an *error correction* mechanism.[16] Owners may have other powers that they can exercise unilaterally, particularly the power to force dissolution of the firm or to demand the return of their investments. These are control powers in the sense they constrain managers by reducing the resources the managers control.

Just as managers can abuse their power by acting self-interestedly, so can owners. This potential abuse is analogous to owner-manager agency costs in that it arises from the imperfect alignment of the interests of the power holder and the firm. When a majority of the firm's owners can decide an issue, they may take value from the minority rather than increasing the value of the firm.[17] On the other hand, if the members must make decisions unanimously, a single member may seek a personal payoff as the price of not blocking a transaction that would benefit the firm. Also, an owner may try to appropriate some of the firm's value by leaving and taking some of the value of the business with her.

The difference between owner-to-owner and managerial abuse of power is that although managers are supposed to act in the *firm's* interests rather than their own, the whole point of owners' powers is to let them act in their *own interests* to constrain managers. This suggests owners should be freer than managers to act selfishly. The big question is when owners' conduct crosses the line from permissible self-interest to abuse. The line that owners should not cross is similar to that applying to all contracting parties. This is the concept of *opportunism* we met above as an explanation for forming firms. Firms can give rise to opportunism as well as mitigate it because (as with other types of contracts), firms give the parties powers they can exploit selfishly.

Through their governance contract, the parties can try to minimize opportunism. But this as with everything else in governance involves trade-offs. The parties could avoid intra-firm opportunism by using extra-firm contracts, but then they would be back in the same situation that led to the formation of the firm. The parties could stay in the firm and eliminate the majority owner problem by dividing ownership among many smaller owners. But then the firm runs into a

---

16. *See* Robert B. Thompson & Paul H. Edelman, *Corporate Voting*, 62 Vand. L. Rev. 129 (2009).

17. For a discussion of strategies for dealing with this problem in a variety of different contexts, see Reinier R. Kraakman et al., The Anatomy of Corporate Law: A Comparative and Functional Approach (2004).

free-rider problem: if the shareholders all hold small interests in the firm, no owner has an incentive to take a strong interest in governance because an activist would have to bear the whole expense of taking action while sharing any gain with all the other owners.

4. Owners vs. creditors

Anybody who loans money or provides services to a firm trusts the owners to ensure that the firm can pay. These contracts therefore involve agency costs, just as do contracts between owners and managers. The difference is that creditors contract only for a fixed payment rather than (as with owners) a right to what is left after paying off the other claimants. However, the various contracts can blend at the edges, particularly in uncorporations, some of whose owners may resemble glorified creditors.

5. Firms and non-firms

A question that has bedeviled commentators ever since Coase is where to draw the line between firms and non-firms. Coase theorized that firms involve principals directing the work of agents while contracts outside the firm involve exchanges in markets. But Alchian and Demsetz noted that there is fiat in a general sense in all contracts, as the whole point of the contract is to bind the parties to rights and obligations.

Professor Daniel Spulber has defined the firm as existing when its objectives are separate from those of its owners.[18] When a firm has distinct objectives, it has to devise ways to achieve them rather than being merely an extension of the owners. For example, consumer organizations differ from firms because they seek to achieve the goals of their consumer members rather than the separate goals of the organization.

But as with all attempts to define the firm, this proposal breaks down at the margins. For example, Spulber distinguishes *basic partnerships* from firms because the former maximize the owners' interests.[19] But the owners of even the simplest partnership must figure out how to achieve their *joint* objectives, which are likely to differ from those of each owner individually. The mere fact that the partners directly own and manage a partnership does not make it a non-firm as long as its ownership and the owners' objectives are joint rather than individual. In any event, even if basic partnerships are not firms, this would just set up the next problem of trying to distinguish between a basic partnership and a firm.

Another possible place to locate the firm/non-firm boundary is in the idea of legal personhood. As we will see below, a distinct function of business association law is creation of property rights in artificial persons whose debts are not

---

18. *See* DANIEL F. SPULBER, THE THEORY OF THE FIRM: MICROECONOMICS WITH ENDOGENOUS ENTREPRENEURS, FIRMS, MARKETS AND ORGANIZATIONS, 64–76 (2009).

19. *Id.* at 51.

payable out of the owners' property and whose property is not subject to the owners' debts. This definition of the firm has special value for the corporate/uncorporate distinction emphasized in this book because the contract-based uncorporation traditionally has had less legal help than corporations in creating property rights in the entity.

6. Governance and underlying business conditions

Many governance problems (including agency costs and opportunism) stem from the fact that firms need to own a lot of property, and therefore have to raise money from multiple investors. As discussed in the next chapter, classic early partnerships were simple traders, and then later, professional firms. Firms got bigger because, among other reasons, their operations became more far-flung and riskier as trade expanded. Firms could mitigate their business risks by diversifying their operations and assets, buying competitors, and developing long-term reputations for trustworthy behavior, all of which required significant capitalization.[20] Also, improvements in transportation, communications, and manufacturing technologies made it worthwhile to have large integrated firms that coordinated production and distribution.[21] The benefits of scale and size outweighed the agency and opportunism costs entailed in financing expansion.

The broader point is that firms' governance structures respond to underlying business conditions, such as the level of trade or manufacturing activity. Also, the development of markets, contracting mechanisms, and information and transportation technologies affects firm structure. The relevance of business conditions creates a need for flexible business structures that can adapt to the times. Therefore, the law's ability to provide and enforce legal standard forms and to change these forms over time can significantly contribute to economic growth.

C. WHY BUSINESS ASSOCIATIONS?

Here we move from the economic concept of the *firm* to the legal concept of the *business association*. Although this is a shift to law, the economic idea of the firm remains important because business associations are designed to help the parties create the economic relationships just discussed.

A business association is a special type of contract that is distinguished in part by its longevity—and therefore a need to adapt to unknowable future conditions. Because the parties to a business association cannot know each eventuality they

---

20. *See* Meir G. Kohn, *Business Organization in Pre-Industrial Europe*, (http://papers.ssrn.com/paper.taf?abstract_id=427744) (July 2003).
21. *See* ALFRED D. CHANDLER, JR., THE VISIBLE HAND: THE MANAGERIAL REVOLUTION IN AMERICAN BUSINESS (1977).

may face, they have to set up decision-making structures to deal with events as they arrive. Business associations also have to provide *coherent* sets of rules that deal efficiently with the various agency problems arising from these decisions.

These problems of longevity and coherence make business associations costly to construct. Without the right business association standard forms, some efficient contracts will not get made, some firms may not be formed, and some firms may incur higher transaction costs than if the right form were available. Consider the following list of some of the issues business association statutes need to cover and the default rules they provide, which are usually subject to a contrary agreement.

1. Formation
The firm needs a way for the parties to the firm to declare their relationship to the rest of the world. This could be a formal written contract, a filing with the state, or a definition of the elements of a contract that trigger the application of the business association law.

2. Property ownership
Firms need to control the property important to the functioning of the business. They therefore need rules blocking the firm's owners and the owners' creditors from exercising direct rights over the firm's property. This so-called *entity shielding* enables the firm's managers to serve the firm's objectives rather than responding to demands for cash from owners and their creditors.[22]

Business associations also need to separate owners' property from the firm. *Owner shielding*, or what is commonly referred to as *limited liability* protects owners' assets from the firm's creditors.[23] This enables owners to invest in diversified portfolios of companies without each investment exposing their whole portfolio to ruinous liability. However, limited liability may increase a firm's credit costs. Although all firms need some entity shielding to function as firms, some might reject owner shielding because its public market and diversification benefits may be less than the credit costs the owners will save if they personally back the firm's debts.

3. Firm's relationships with creditors
Business association law protects the firm's creditors against some of the owners' actions, particularly including excessive distributions to the owners. These rules are designed to address potential agency costs between owners (who control the firm's assets) and creditors (who depend on the assets for repayment of their debts). These rights can be provided for in contracts between owners and creditors.

---

22. *See* Hansmann et al., *supra* note 9.
23. *Id.*

Business association statutes also provide a minimal backup protection for creditors who deal in frequent small transactions where it would be costly to spell out the creditors' rights in each contract.

4. Management and control

Owners may delegate to managers the power to run the firm. This entails rules that allocate rights and powers among the members and managers and empower managers to bind the firm in transactions with third parties. The owners generally can vote on particular transactions and on election and removal of managers. The statutes include rules allocating voting rights among the members (generally either by financial contribution or equally) and establishing the total votes (generally either majority or unanimous) necessary to make particular decisions.

5. Financial rights

Business association law determines the default allocation of profits, losses, and distributions among the members. As with control rights, default financial rights are allocated either equally or by financial contribution. The key right in this category is the one to distributions from the firm. Rights (if any) to ongoing distributions complement the owners' rights to exit the firm by buyout or liquidation (as discussed below). As noted throughout the book, owners' rights to get cash out of the firm can be an important mechanism for reducing agency costs between managers and owners. However, owners' access to the cash also can increase the potential for agency costs between owners and creditors by increasing the creditors' risk that the firm will not be able to pay its debts.

6. Transferability

Partners can transfer only their financial rights, but corporate shareholders can transfer both management and financial rights. Transferability of management rights in corporations reflects the fact that corporate shares are designed to be freely traded among dispersed and anonymous owners. By contrast, partners generally have no market for their shares and care deeply about the identity of their comanagers. Whether management rights are transferable helps determine whether the owners need some other form of exit via buyout or dissolution. Transferability also increases the value of owners' management rights by enabling dispersed holders to convey these rights to bidders for control who can then aggregate them into an effective control block.

7. Fiduciary duties and remedies

One way to deal with agency costs between managers and owners is by giving the owners a judicially enforced fiduciary duty. Here it is important to highlight nomenclature that will be discussed throughout the book. *Fiduciary* duties are owed by the firm's *managers* to the owners. By contrast, weaker duties, sometimes referred to as *good faith*, deal with opportunism by non-fiduciaries, including by shareholders to each other. Although the fiduciary duty is intended to curb all selfish behavior, weaker opportunism duties permit selfish behavior as long as it is within the owners' express or implied agreement.

8. Exit

The owners may be able to compel either the firm's liquidation or purchase of their interests by the firm or other owners. These exit rights differ from the owners' ability to exit via transfer of shares to a third party (as discussed above). As transfer generally occurs at the current market value of the owners' shares, it reflects any market discount due to inefficient management. Moreover, transfer rights are not very important in the absence of a liquid market for the firm's shares—the usual situation for uncorporations. Rather, it is buyout or liquidation that enables the owners of closely held firms to escape bad managers.

In addition to providing liquidity for the exiting owners, the owners' right to dissolve or cash out of the firm can discipline managers either as or more effectively than a voting right. As discussed throughout the book, this discipline contrasts with the monitoring mechanisms such as voting, directors, or fiduciary duties on which corporations rely.

9. The role of standard forms

Owners, managers, and creditors can and do choose any combination of rights, powers, and duties they wish along the above dimensions. But for the reasons discussed below, business associations group these rights into a limited number of standard-form contracts: corporations, partnerships, limited liability companies, and so forth.

As with any other type of standard form, a business association contract is designed to reduce the parties' costs of contracting. These costs can be high for business associations because of the long-term nature of the contract and the complexities of coordinating its various elements into a *coherent* set of rules that work well together in minimizing firms' agency and other governance costs. Indeed, in very small businesses the costs of customized contracting may be high enough to prevent the parties from reaching any kind of deal or to leave important issues undecided and ripe for costly litigation. A standard form business association also may create benefits by serving as a sort of magnet for a network of judicial decisions, business practices, and customs that help to clarify the deal terms.[24] The more users join the network, the greater is the incentive to produce information for the users and the more valuable are the contracts.[25]

---

24. Michael Klausner, *Corporations, Corporate Law, and Networks of Contracts*, 81 VA. L. REV. (1995).

25. *See* Charles J. Goetz & Robert E. Scott, *The Limits of Expanded Choice: An Analysis of Express and Implied Contract Terms*, 73 CAL. L. REV. 261 (1985).

D. WHY BUSINESS ASSOCIATION *LAW*

The functions of business associations discussed in the previous section could be performed by private contract, enforced by contract law, and supplemented by various other areas of the law, including trust and agency. Private organizations could produce standard forms, just as the realtor associations produce standard form leases and franchisors devise standard forms for all of their franchisees. Why do we need business association *statutes*?

First, some rules are effective only if adopted by statute because otherwise they cannot fully bind all of the relevant parties. This particularly applies to the property rights aspects of business association statutes as discussed above. For example, without the entity shielding rule, each owner could unilaterally offer her creditors priority in the firm's assets, creating a mess of conflicting priorities. With respect to owner shielding, the firm could contract with voluntary creditors to bar recourse against the owners' assets, but this would not work against involuntary tort creditors. Business association law operates in these respects against the world. This is like property law generally, except that business association law deals with the special problem of multiple owners joining and leaving over time. Creation of these rights has been referred to as the *essential* function of business organization law that is not accomplished by other types of law such as contract or property.[26]

Second, a statutory standard form has the advantage of the publicity created by public acts, including state publication of the statutes, and greater willingness by lawyers and others to comment on the law than might be the case for privately promulgated standard forms.

Third, statutes may be useful in creating the network effect described in the previous section. As already noted, the more people use a form, the more interpreters it will have and the clearer it will become. Although any standard form can create a network, users will be more likely to be drawn to a new statutory form because it is more likely than a privately promulgated one to attract a critical mass of users.

Fourth, government can craft mandatory rules and penalties that can reduce private enforcement costs. Effective penalties are not only costly to design, but also may not be enforceable in private contracts.[27] One such penalty provision is the limited partnership *control rule*, which holds limited partners liable for the debts of the business if they participate in controlling it, thereby ensuring that only those who have personal liability will be involved in management.[28]

---

26. *See* Henry Hansmann & Reinier Kraakman, *The Essential Role of Organization Law*, 110 YALE L.J. 387 (2000).

27. For a leading case on enforceability of liquidated damage clauses, see Lake River Corp. v. Carborundum Co., 769 F.2d 1284, 1290 (7th Cir. 1985).

28. *See* REVISED UNIFORM LIMITED PARTNERSHIP ACT, § 303 (1985) (RULPA).

Creditors theoretically could insert a covenant in their agreements with debtors binding any members who actively participate in management. But courts might hesitate to enforce these agreements against members who did not sign the agreement or who joined the firm after the agreement was entered into.

A general question regarding the role of law in business associations is whether the law itself affects the structure of firms or whether legal rules are elicited in response to changes in firm and business needs.[29] For example (as discussed below in Chapter 5), some commentators argue that rules such as *capital lock-in* barring dissolution by individual owners helped promote the Industrial Revolution. On the other hand, at least some contracts, statutes, and court decisions might have arisen because firms' business needs made them worthwhile. The law's ability to respond to business needs depends significantly on the flexibility and adaptability of the legal system. We would expect more responsiveness in a dynamic system that encourages free contracting and jurisdictional competition. As discussed in Chapter 1 and below in this chapter, these elements are an important part of this book's theory of the uncorporation.

E. WHY *DIFFERENT* BUSINESS ASSOCIATIONS?

A final issue concerning statutory standard business association forms is how many different ones there should be. Although there are many different types of firms, it is not clear there needs to be a separate statute for each type of firm.

An important factor in determining the optimal number of business association statutes is the concept of *coherence* discussed throughout this book. As indicated above, the various features of business associations need to be coordinated so that they efficiently meet firms' needs, particularly in responding to agency costs and opportunism. For example, a firm with a strong majority shareholder may need less protection from manager agency costs but more protection against owner-owner opportunism than a firm with weak, dispersed owners. Business associations that offer members strong rights to exit the firm when they are dissatisfied with its performance may not also need to offer them strong rights to sue the managers for breach of fiduciary duties.

The coherence attribute means that some statutory combinations of terms are more efficient than others despite the fact the parties usually can contract out of most of the default rules of a particular business association. The availability of multiple coherent business association statutes gives firms alternative sets of rules that fit their needs and that they can opt into without incurring extensive planning and drafting costs. The more choices firms have, the easier it will be for

---

29. This is a continuing theme in RON HARRIS, INDUSTRIALIZING ENGLISH LAW: ENTREPRENEURSHIP AND BUSINESS ORGANIZATION, 1720–1844 (2000).

them to find sets of terms they can use without customized drafting to make the standard form fit. The better able firms are to pull business associations "off the rack" as it were, the lower their contracting costs.

Apart from reducing contracting costs, coherent business association statutes create a good basis for gap filling and interpretation by clearly signaling to courts the structure whose gaps are being filled. For example, a limited partnership signals that it wants strong managers and passive owners, while a general partnership likely wants strong owner participation in management. A court accordingly should be less willing to interpret an ambiguous contract to eliminate member voting rights in a general partnership than it would the same contract in a limited partnership. Also, a court may be more likely in the absence of explicit exit provisions to lock a member into a corporation than into a partnership on the theory that the parties' choice of the partnership form indicates that they want an easier exit than if they had selected the corporate form. A general partnership or a member-managed LLC can contract for the same terms as, say, a limited partnership, but contracting for these terms via other standard forms would send the courts mixed weaker signals and get back less predictable results.

A firm's choice of form also signals courts and regulators on how to apply regulatory statutes. For example, a court arguably should be less willing to apply a securities or employment discrimination statute to protect owners in a general partnership than it would in a corporation because partners' managerial role suggests they need less legal protection from managers than do corporate employees or investors.

In short, having distinct and coherent business association statutes offers firms contracting opportunities they would not have if they could just draft individual terms. Firms not only have lower initial contracting costs than they would with a smaller set of forms, but also can expect lower litigation and regulatory costs and greater certainty through the life of the firm. This can make a critical difference for smaller firms that may have higher drafting, planning, and litigation costs per dollar of capitalization than do larger ones.

But we can always have too much of a good thing: some practitioners and academics argue that business associations have unduly proliferated, creating confusion for courts, owners, and third parties dealing with firms. They wonder how many different business associations we really need.[30] There is certainly a limit to the number of different business forms the market can handle. The more different business associations firms and those they deal with them need to learn about, the higher will be the information costs incurred. At some point the costs of sorting out the differences will exceed the benefits of having a form for every use. Moreover, the benefit discussed above of coherent business forms involves

---

30. For a discussion and analysis of these arguments, see Larry E. Ribstein, *Making Sense of Entity Rationalization*, 58 BUS. LAW. 1023 (2003).

the development of cases, forms, and other interpretive tools. The existence of more types of business associations for the same number of firms may dissipate the body of interpretive materials available to each particular type of business association.

However, this concern with having too many different business associations does not tell us precisely how many there should be. Even if we think we already have enough, the next new business association might prove to be better suited for many firms than any of the existing forms. Chapter 6 shows how the limited liability company started inauspiciously in the 1970s as an obscure experiment by private parties in the state of Wyoming, far from the commercial centers. We might have asked why we needed this when we already had partnerships, corporations, and limited partnerships. There was every reason to dismiss the LLC as an oddity or example of the excessive proliferation of business forms. But LLCs ultimately became the leading business form in terms of number of new formations as a result of a combination of circumstances that would have been impossible to predict with confidence when the form was invented.

As another example, almost twenty years after the invention of the LLC, the limited liability partnership (LLP) was invented by lawyers in the major commercial center of Dallas, Texas. The LLP was designed to piggy back on the widely used general partnership form and to facilitate conversion by existing firms. It quickly swept through all fifty-one U.S. jurisdictions. Yet today the LLP is just a niche entity, used only by some professional firms. A business association czar might rationally have nixed the LLC and slated the LLP for success. Yet the market for business forms has led everyone to decide otherwise—and it is not clear this decision is a bad one.[31]

Perhaps the best response to the question of what is the right number of business associations is to encourage experimentation through interjurisdictional competition. As discussed below, business association statutes largely are developed by lawyers who have little incentive to waste their time. Indeed, lawyers tend to be conservative on these matters and wait until new forms have been tested. This suggests that we are more likely to get too few new business associations than too many. In any event, the failed experiments will not attract many users and probably will have little negative impact on successful business associations.

F. THE ARCHITECTURE OF BUSINESS ASSOCIATION STATUTES

Determining the number of different business associations is more complex than just counting the statutes because the business associations provided for

---

31. For a theoretical and empirical comparison of LLCs and LLPs, see Bruce H. Kobayashi & Larry E. Ribstein, *Choice of Form and Network Externalities*, 43 WM. & MARY L. REV. 79 (2001).

under a given jurisdiction's laws may interrelate in a variety of ways. This section considers some of these alternatives. In evaluating firms' choices, keep in mind that in addition to their vertical choice of form *within* given states, firms also have horizontal choice of statutes available *across* different states. (Chapter 7 discusses this overall framework in more detail.)

1. Short all-purpose statute

The legislature could enact an all-purpose business association statute that includes a few basic provisions difficult to replicate by contract, such as those regarding relationships with creditors. However, this model may scrimp on default rules which (as discussed above) can significantly reduce contracting costs. A supposedly stripped-down statute therefore may have to include a surprising number of terms. Moreover, the more terms the all-purpose statute must include, the less likely it will be to suit all the firms that would adopt it. For example, although service-of-process or creditor remedy provisions may fit all firms, once the statute starts adding voting and fiduciary rules, the need arises for variation—and therefore for one of the other alternatives.

2. Chinese menu approach

A legislature seeking to offer more help via default rules could enact a sort of "Chinese menu" that proposes alternative rules within categories. For example, the statute could let firms choose a transfer provision from Category A and a dissolution provision from Category B.

However, although this approach better assists the parties on drafting than the stripped-down one, it fails to provide coherent sets of terms. Under a Chinese menu approach, firms would have to figure out for themselves how the terms work together. For example, the discussion above identifies eight types of business association provisions. If there are five alternatives within each "menu category, the parties would potentially have 390,625 combinations (5 to the eighth power)." Firms would then have to choose which combination best suits their needs. Thus, while a Chinese menu statute may reduce the burden of *drafting* individual provisions, it leaves firms with the burden of *choosing* the combination of provisions that works best for them. Business association statutes could be constructed to guide the parties to the right trade-offs for particular types of firms while freeing them to customize individual terms for their particular needs.

All-inclusive statutes have other advantages over Chinese menus. First, as discussed above in explaining the rationale for different business associations, a distinct business association statute provides a general structure that helps courts interpret the parties' deal and apply regulatory statutes.

Second, all-inclusive standard forms enable the parties to choose a particular mix of mandatory and enabling rules, thereby offering assurances to all of the members and third parties that the deal will not be changed unless certain procedures are followed. Some rules in each statute may be mandatory in the sense that they can only be contracted around at some cost—that is, the cost of opting into a completely different form. But these rules are enabling in the alternative sense that this cost of choosing another form does not altogether prevent firms from contracting. For example, firms could bind themselves to the limited partnership control rule and effectively lock limited partners out of management roles by choosing the limited partnership, or they could opt for more flexible management via the LLC form. A Chinese menu offers choice on a rule-by-rule basis, which closely resembles a purely optional regime.

3. Hub-and-spokes

The statute could provide for a "hub-and-spokes" arrangement that includes provisions common to all business associations in the spokes and provisions for specific business associations in the hubs that cross-reference the spoke provisions. The Texas multiple entity statute[32] is the most ambitious effort along these lines. Uniform lawmakers have drafted or are working on specific modules such as the Model Registered Agents Act.[33]

Links between statutes provides a modified version of hub-and-spokes. For example, until the 2001 version of the Uniform Limited Partnership Act, the standard format for limited partnership statutes provided only for some terms (including those relating to the limited partners) in the limited partnership statute while linking to others in the general partnership statute. The general partnership statute was, in effect, the hub while the limited partnership statute was a spoke.[34]

Hub-and-spokes might be considered a *modular* approach to constructing business associations. People employ modularity in different contexts to economize on information and decision-making costs. For example, in object-oriented computing, programmers plug in modules rather than custom coding each program; contract drafters plug in standardized boilerplate provisions; and those creating choice-of-law clauses designate one state's law to minimize the number of applicable-law decisions the drafters need to make.[35] The Texas statute cited above is an example of modularity in which the Texas legislature has identified particular rules that can be applied in the same way within different business associations.

---

32. Tex. Bus. Orgs. Code Ann. (Vernon 2006).

33. *See* Model Registered Agents Act and Amendments to Entity Acts to Rationalize Annual Filings, National Conference of Commissioners of Uniform State Laws (2006), http://www.law.upenn.edu/bll/archives/ulc/mraa/2006act_final.pdf.

34. For an analysis of linkage between statutes, *see* Larry E. Ribstein, *Linking Statutory Forms*, 58 J. Law & Contemp. Prob. 187 (Spring 1995).

35. *See* Henry E. Smith, *Modularity in Contracts: Boilerplate and Information Flow*, 104 Mich. L. Rev. 1175 (2006).

However, modular approaches are probably not very useful for business associations because firms need coherence. Each type of provision must be designed for a particular statute rather than for being "dropped into" multiple statutes. Statutory drafters may underestimate this need for coherence. For example, the limited partnership form might seem to simply add passive, limited liability members to a general partnership, making it appropriate to link general partnership provisions. However, this addition of passive members may affect the need for devices to ensure the accountability of the general partners—something that is not necessary when all of the members are active and involved in the firm. So perhaps drafters should put fiduciary duty provisions in the spoke and not in the hub. After carefully applying a coherence analysis, drafters might conclude that only the most plain vanilla housekeeping sort of provisions (such as who may be a registered agent) belong in the spokes, while everything else needs to be in the hub.

4. Flexibility

In addition to the coherence issues discussed above, legislatures need to choose an overall drafting strategy as to flexibility or rigidity. A flexible statute would have mostly or even exclusively optional rules designed to serve as a basis for customized drafting. By contrast, a rigid statute would have a lot of mandatory rules designed for firms who cannot be expected to do much customized drafting. As we will see in Chapter 7, there is just such a strategy spectrum with respect to LLC statutes. States' choices depend on the expected market for their laws. Delaware, for example, attracts more sophisticated firms that do a lot of customized drafting.

G. THE EVOLUTION OF BUSINESS ASSOCIATIONS

In order to understand the history and role of the uncorporation, it is important to understand the *forces* that shape business associations. Business associations are not brought forth fully formed by a deity, economists, or other theorists. Rather, they are the product of market forces, political pressures, and parties' ability to shop for the applicable law. This may make them messier than theory would predict.

1. Choice and design of contracts

The basic source of business association rules is the contracts firms make. Firms have an incentive to draft contracts and choose standard-form terms so as to minimize their costs of doing business. Just as firms shop for parts, property, and people that serve their needs at the lowest cost, so they will try to choose or design contracts that help ensure the business is run efficiently. For example, a restaurant franchise whose employees take too long producing hamburgers and filch money from the till will have higher costs and lower revenues than an outlet with better controls. The same is true if the firm has lax or self-dealing managers or bickering owners who cannot agree on important business decisions.

The availability of different business associations shapes parties' contracts. This is an application of Coase's intuition that the relevance of law depends on transaction costs,[36] which include not only the costs of making customized contracts rather than opting into standard forms, but those of choosing the standard form or state law. Business association law can determine the efficiency of firms' contracts. If a firm can choose a business association that offers an appropriate coherent set of rules, it may have a better opportunity for success than if suitable business associations are not available. A firm's ability to choose the applicable standard form or state law creates a market for law that determines to some extent what rules are available and which are successful.

Skeptics may insist that there is no orderly market for business forms and therefore that it is futile to try to isolate the factors that guide their evolution, as this book attempts to do. Under this skeptical view, instead of making a careful or informed choice of business form, parties are simply blindly following what others are doing, or more often, relying on lawyers or accountants who do not understand what needs to be considered. However, this book's analysis of the evolution of business associations does not require that businesspeople fully understand what they are doing when they make their choice. Whatever individual businesspeople know or intend, in a functioning economic system the survivors of the competition among alternative forms are those that were best adapted to their environment. This implies that we can sensibly hypothesize what factors are likely to determine the outcome—and test our hypotheses by examining these outcomes.[37]

2. Government constraints: regulation and tax

Firms may try to minimize their regulatory and tax costs by drafting and selecting appropriate contract terms. We will see throughout the book how tax law in particular has affected the structure of firms and choice of form. As discussed in Chapters 5 and 6, the rules for distinguishing between firms that are and are not subject to the corporate tax has profoundly influenced the evolution of the

---

36. *See* Ronald H. Coase, *The Problem of Social Cost*, 3 J.L. & ECON. 1 (1960).

37. *See* Armen A. Alchian, *Uncertainty, Evolution, and Economic Theory*, 58 J. POL. ECON. 211, 217 (1950) (noting that "individual motivation and foresight, while sufficient, are not necessary. All that is needed by economists is their own awareness of the survival conditions and criteria of the economic system and a group of participants who submit various combinations and organizations for the system's selection and adoption"). For an application to the competition among business forms, see Bruce H. Kobayashi & Larry E. Ribstein, *Evolution and Uniformity*, 34 ECON. INQ., 464 (July 1996), *reprinted in* UNCERTAINTY AND ECONOMIC EVOLUTION (John Lott, ed., 1997).

uncorporation and the dominance of the corporation. Chapter 7 discusses other rules that may be affecting business form, including estate and gift tax, federal diversity jurisdiction, debtor-creditor law, and professional regulation.

These tax and regulatory laws can perversely affect business form. If courts or legislatures are too rigid in using business associations as the basis for regulatory classifications, the parties may use the business associations to, in effect, contract out of regulatory requirements that arguably should apply. When that happens, the regulation rather than the firm's basic agency-cost-control needs might perversely drive a firm's choice of form. In other words, the tax or regulatory tail may wag the business association dog.

Laws may not only have a perverse indirect effect on business form, but also might be designed to encourage inefficient business structures and discourage efficient ones. As discussed throughout the book, the uncorporation can be a powerful alternative to the corporation for disciplining managers and constraining owner-manager agency costs. Therefore, taxes and regulation may be unfriendly to the uncorporation. Just as managers have been able to shape corporate governance in their favor,[38] so have they been able to maintain the corporation's dominance against competition from uncorporations. As discussed in Chapter 8, this leads to corporate tax laws whose effect is to discourage distributions that might weaken managers' hold on the firm's cash.

The law may not only discourage socially beneficial uncorporate structures, but also encourage socially inefficient structures. This, too, is the result of interest groups. Lawyers in particular have a lot of say in drafting business association statutes—and they have an incentive to draft statutes that appeal to firms' owners and managers, who are the ones actually choosing the statutes under which to form their firms. Creditors have little role in this choice and therefore generally are not a big presence at the legislative bargaining table. To be sure, firms have to take their creditors' preferences into account in choosing their form of business to minimize their cost of credit. But some firms may not care about the preferences of involuntary tort creditors. We will see in Chapter 7 how this dynamic has encouraged the development of asset protection features of uncorporation statutes.

As we will see below, the law can influence business associations in a passive as well as affirmative way by slowing the move to more efficient arrangements. The evolution of business associations depends on the development of case law and interstate acceptance of new terms. Even if firms can choose from among statutes in any state, the firms' use of the statutes depends on whether the states in which they do business will recognize and enforce them. These circumstances enable courts and legislators to block efficient contracts. In other words (and to

---

38. *See* MARK J. ROE, STRONG MANAGERS, WEAK OWNERS: THE POLITICAL ROOTS OF AMERICAN CORPORATE FINANCE (1996).

put this in the Coasian framework), high transaction costs increase the effect of law and reduce its efficiency. Firms can try to lobby lawmakers to accept the new provisions, but because firms have diverse needs, it may be difficult for them to coordinate around specific law changes. In general, if the costs of change exceed the benefits of having new rules, firms may have to live with unsatisfactory laws.

3. Jurisdictional competition and the common law

Firms that do not like the rules in a particular jurisdiction may be able to take advantage of the rules in another jurisdiction. As we will see throughout this book, the potential for jurisdictional competition in business law has been an important force shaping business associations and driving the rise of the uncorporation.

Diverse laws and mobile capital enable firms to decide which laws apply to them either by contracting for the applicable law or by physically moving to a place that has the laws they want.[39] In the United States (and increasingly also in Europe), jurisdictions apply their laws regulating firms' internal governance only to firms that choose the law by incorporating in the regulating state or country, irrespective of where the firms do business or are located physically.[40] This *internal affairs* choice-of-law rule obviously makes it easy for firms to choose their governance rules. Firms' ability to choose the applicable law creates, in effect, a market for business association law in which the law is selected by firms rather than imposed by regulators.

The market for law can be an important force driving legal change. Jurisdictions experiment with different legal approaches that may or may not succeed. A dominant national or regional supplier of law may emerge (as has Delaware in the United States) that commits resources to developing high-quality laws. Other jurisdictions have some incentive to participate in the law market in order to encourage local firms to choose their laws and courts and to be attractive legal environments for firms to locate their business.

The mere existence of multiple jurisdictions cannot, however, create a market for law. States need to have the incentives to compete. Politicians respond to numerous interest groups, not all of whom care about jurisdictional competition. Lawyers exert much of the pressure for competitive state laws because they want to attract clients to the jurisdictions and courts in which they are licensed.[41]

---

39. *See generally*, ERIN A. O'HARA & LARRY E. RIBSTEIN, THE LAW MARKET (2008).
40. *Id.* Chapter 6.
41. *See* Larry E. Ribstein, *Lawyers as Lawmakers: A Theory of Lawyer Licensing*, 69 Mo. L. REV. 299, 355–62 (2004). Thus, the Delaware bar is responsible for making Delaware corporate law competitive. Larry E. Ribstein, *Delaware, Lawyers, and Contractual Choice of Law*, 19 DEL. J. CORP. L. 999, 1009–10 (1994). State bar associations have been instrumental in creating and promoting new unincorporated business forms. *See* Carol R. Goforth, *The Rise of the Limited Liability Company: Evidence of a Race Between the States, but Heading Where?*, 45 SYRACUSE L. REV. 1193 (1995).

Bar groups and individual lawyers also provide a sort of "after-market support" by writing treatises and other explanatory material and providing advice, opinion letters, and continuing legal education programs. This not only helps lawyers sell their home jurisdiction's laws, but also builds their individual reputations and clientele. We have already seen how these materials help increase the value of business association statutes.

More fundamentally, the nature of the legal system may or may not affect how firms evolve. As discussed in Chapters 4 and 5, common law courts in the United States have helped entrench the corporate form by impeding acceptance of uncorporations. By contrast, civil law systems (particularly those in France and Germany) apparently have been more responsive than common law systems to business needs for uncorporate forms of business.[42] However, a common law system eventually may produce higher quality law than a civil law system. This conclusion is at least suggested by cross-country evaluations of legal systems in the so-called *law and finance* literature.[43]

Whether a country has a federal system of states and a federal government also may affect development of its business associations. A federal system may make evolution of business forms both easier and harder. We have seen that jurisdictional competition (which is aided by a federal system) encourages innovation and competition. However, a firm may be reluctant to adopt a new type of business association if the new form may not be recognized everywhere it does business. A federal system accordingly can enhance the conservatism of the common law.[44]

It is difficult to reach any clear conclusions about the quantity and quality of legal evolution in different legal systems. One fact does emerge: the corporation has done better in the leading common law federal jurisdiction (the United States), than elsewhere in the world.

4. Background factors: business environment, technology, and culture

The evolution of business forms depends on a host of extralegal factors, particularly business conditions, technology, and culture.

Technology drives the development of business generally. As discussed in Chapter 4, the rise of the corporation was largely attributable to the development of new forms of manufacturing, communications, and transportation, all of which created a need for a business association that could accommodate large firms. Chapter 8 discusses the important role of the innovation of private equity, hedge fund, and venture capital structures in the rise of the large uncorporation. But there is a sort of chicken-and-egg problem as to whether the technologies

---

42. *See* Timothy Guinnane et al., *Putting the Corporation in Its Place*, Working Paper 13109, http://www.nber.org/papers/w13109.
43. *See* Rafael La Porta et al., *Law and Finance*, 106 J. POL. ECON. 1113 (1998).
44. *See* Guinnane et al., *supra* note 42.

developed in response to business needs or were an autonomous factor in creating these needs. Clearly it was a combination in the sense that firms could not create all of the necessary technologies until business conditions had made gains from these technologies possible.

Culture also plays a role. Business forms evolve and develop because firms have incentives to increase profits by reducing agency and transaction costs. This may explain why business forms have developed more rapidly in cultures that have a robust profit motive than in those that deemphasize competition. For example, it has been argued that elements of Islam may have played a role in reducing incentives to innovate, therefore slowing the evolution of business in the Middle East.[45]

Finally, general business and economic conditions are important. Factors such as the cost of credit, tax rates, and business sentiment determine firms' costs and benefits from adopting particular business forms and general willingness to experiment with new forms. For example, Chapter 6 shows how a significant change in relative corporate and individual tax rates had a significant effect in spurring the *LLC Revolution*. Chapter 8 discusses the role of credit availability in the rise of the large uncorporation.

H. THE CORPORATION AND UNCORPORATION

We now come to the question that is the focus of this book: are there meaningful differences between *uncorporations* and *corporations*? In other words, does it help our understanding of the governance of firms to focus on overarching distinctions between these types of business associations? Here we consider some fundamental distinctions.

1. History and the regulation of governance

The partnership could be considered the original and basic form of business association. As discussed more fully in Chapter 3, the partnership could have been the basis for the complete range of business associations. However, the invention and spread of the corporation introduced discontinuity in the spectrum of business associations. As discussed in Chapter 4, scholars have argued that the corporation became the dominant business form in the United States during the nineteenth century because it enabled development of large-scale firms and thereby helped facilitate the Industrial Revolution in the United States. In this view, history turned the partnership from the main business association into an anachronism.

---

45. *See* Timur Kuran, *The Scale of Entrepreneurship in Middle Eastern History: Inhibitive Roles of Islamic Institutions* (Mar. 2008) ERID Working Paper Number 10, http://ssrn.com/abstract=1265117.

However, the corporation's rise is not as easy to explain as it might appear. Why did firms seeking a better business form not just tweak the flexible contract-based partnership? One answer is that the development of the corporation was less a matter of need than of politics. Although the parties to firms might have wanted to adjust the partnership form, the law would not let them add the critical feature of limiting owner liability for the firm's contracts and torts. This feature became increasingly important with the expansion of tort liability in the twentieth century. The parties could not cheaply create limited liability for torts simply by private contract, and even limited liability for contracts presented logistical problems that required more than just contract enforcement. Returning to Coase, these transaction costs left a role for law. Government cooperated, but at the price of regulating corporate features and barring the use of uncorporations as an end run around this regulation.

Firms' demand for limited liability coupled with its being available only to corporations led to the corporation's dominance for closely held as well as publicly traded firms. The partnership form was left for use mainly by very small and informal firms and by professional firms that sought to borrow the partnership's aura of collegiality. It was not until the latter part of the twentieth century that both large and small firms started to reject the trade they had been forced to make of the single level of partnership tax for personal liability of owners and default rules suited mainly to smaller, closely held firms.

Thus, the invention and spread of the corporate form coupled with its regulatory basis created the fundamental dichotomy between the corporation and the uncorporation that is a major theme of this book. Uncorporations share the significant attribute that they are flexible, contractually based entities. If business associations were animals, uncorporations would be cats, multiplying in unseemly fashion, running all over the place, refusing to fall into a mold, and defying regulators' efforts to bring them to heel. By contrast, corporations would be dogs, slotting comfortably into a particular structure that lends itself to regulation. This book will explore this dichotomy and its implications.

2. Type of contracts

Uncorporations differ from corporations not only in terms of the degree of regulation, but in the nature of their contracts. Uncorporations have real contracts; corporations have hypothetical ones. Corporations are designed for publicly held firms. Dispersed owners cannot easily coordinate over specific terms or modifications so they accept the state-provided standard form along with judicial interpretations and statutory modifications. When filling gaps in the corporate contract, courts cannot look to the actual intent of thousands of parties so they make up a hypothetical "intent" based on what the courts view as reasonable.[46]

---

46. *See* JONATHAN R. MACEY, PROMISES KEPT, PROMISES BROKEN 20 (2008).

This resembles a real contract only in the loose sense that the parties accept the hypothetical bargain when they do not contract around the hypotheses the courts have provided.

The courts may get even further from any notion of contract in corporate cases to the extent that their results are based on norms of good governance that may or may not be subject to contractual variation.[47] By contrast, courts in uncorporation cases look closely at the actual language of real agreements. The court may impose liability based on an implied covenant of good faith, but as discussed in Chapter 7, this is essentially a mechanism of contract construction in the sense of building on what the parties have actually agreed to.

3. Type of governance

Finally, we will see throughout the book that corporations and uncorporations differ regarding their approaches to governance. Corporations try to control agency costs through various types of monitoring by shareholders, directors, and courts. This emphasizes the monitors' scrutiny of decision-making inputs and procedures. Partnerships may use the same types of mechanisms, but they involve much closer scrutiny than is feasible in publicly held corporations.

However, uncorporations that separate ownership and control tend to drop monitoring and instead focus on the owners' power to exit by demanding buyout, dissolution, or distribution of the cash. This essentially uses the market to judge management because the owners leave if they think they can get a better return on their investments outside the firm. The market's judgment in turn depends on what the firm is actually producing rather than on how the firm makes its decisions. Unless the owners are closely involved in management, this may be a much more reliable approach. Although it may not work better in every case, at least it gives investors a distinct alternative to the corporation.

---

47. *See* Edward B. Rock, *Norms & Corporate Law*, 149 U. Pa. L. Rev. 1607 (2001); Edward B. Rock, *Saints and Sinners: How Does Delaware Corporate Law Work?*, 44 U.C.L.A. L. Rev. 1009 (1997); David A. Skeel, Jr., *Shaming in Corporate Law*, 149 U. Pa. L. Rev. 1811 (2001).

3. PARTNERSHIP

This chapter discusses the basic uncorporate form—the partnership. The chapter has three objectives. First, it describes how the modern general partnership (as it took shape in the United States and the United Kingdom in the nineteenth century) provides a coherent contractual framework for the governance problems discussed in Chapter 2. General partnership law provides rules designed for a particular type of relationship among multiple owners who, as the statutes say, are "carrying on a business for profit." This distinguishes partnerships both from sole proprietorships and from nonbusiness and nonprofit relationships such as the tenancy in common. More importantly for present purposes, general partnership provides for a *specific type* of business co-ownership that differs from centrally managed firms—that is, a relationship among active owners.

Second, the chapter discusses key variations on the partnership form: the limited partnership and the joint stock company. The point is to show that by the time of the modern corporation's emergence in the nineteenth century, partnership had provided the basis for the governance needs of large firms with passive investors. This poses the question discussed in Chapter 4: why did the corporate form have to be adapted for private use from its origin as a vehicle for public-sector business? As we will see, the corporation was not the only business structure suited to the Industrial Revolution; rather, it was the best way for government to hold the reins of large firms.

Third, this chapter shows the role played by the traditional general partnership in the rise of the corporation. The general partnership suits only a narrow and rather primitive type of firm featuring equal management and financial rights combined with vicarious liability of all owners for the firm's debts. These default rules are not even remotely suited to the specialization of ownership and management rights that characterizes most modern firms. And yet this is the business association with which investors are stuck if they have profit and management rights and do not form a limited liability firm. In other words, general partnership is a trap business people fall into if they are not careful.

At the same time, lawmakers traditionally were not receptive to noncorporate limited liability alternatives to the general partnership—the limited partnership and the joint stock company. The next two chapters show how the combination of the partnership trap and restrictions on partnership-type alternatives channeled firms into the rigid corporate form where they could be most easily taxed and regulated.

A. EARLY HISTORY

The general partnership originated in *societas*—that is, a family or household organization.[48] They were also referred to as *compagnia*, which means "those sharing bread," thus reflecting their origins in households.[49] These family-based precursors differed significantly from today's partnerships. Initially only the *pater* could enter into debts that bound the family. The firms were cemented by kinship and lasted only as long as those ties. As Kerim Bey told James Bond in *From Russia with Love*, "All of my key employees are my sons. Blood is the best security in this business." Before the development of modern technologies for controlling agency costs, all business was as dangerous as Bey's spy business and the family was the only feasible way to bind agents. The Roman societas was more like a Mafia family than a modern partnership.

Partnerships evolved from families to firms in response to the globalization of trade and development of more sophisticated contracts and business technology. Rules developed through contracts and mercantile usage for imposing liability on investors for the firm's debts and permitting each partner to bind the firm.[50] Partners' personal liability for the firm's debts was a key aspect of general partnership by the fourteenth century. Indeed, when the leading financial center of Siena changed the rule to one of limited liability in 1310, businesses fled the city, and it had to reverse itself.[51] Partners' vicarious liability motivated them to figure out how to ensure the responsibility of agents serving far from the home office. Compensation became more precisely related to performance. This partly reflected the development of sophisticated double-entry bookkeeping which itself may have developed in response to business needs.[52]

Partnership law meanwhile had been developing in the English mercantile courts from the late thirteenth century, as officially recognized in the Statute of the Staple.[53] The common law of partnership began to absorb mercantile law while the English Partnership Act of 1890 clarified the law.[54] In the United States, the National Conference of Commissioners on Uniform State Laws built on this law with the Uniform Partnership Act (UPA) begun in 1902 under

---

48. William Mitchell, *Early Forms of Partnership*, 3 SELECT ESSAYS IN ANGLO-AMERICAN LEGAL HISTORY 183 (1909).

49. *See* Avner Greif, *The Study of Organizations and Evolving Organizational Forms through History: Reflections from the Late Medieval Family Firm*, 5 INDUSTRIAL AND CORPORATE CHANGE, n.2, 473 (1996); Meir G. Kohn, *Business Organization in Pre-Industrial Europe*, Dartmouth College Department of Economics, http://papers.ssrn.com/paper.taf?abstract_id=427744 (July 2003).

50. *See* Mitchell, *supra* note 48, at 188–91.

51. *See* Greif, *supra* note 49.

52. *Id.* at 497, note 38.

53. 27 Edward III, Statute 2 (1353).

54. 53–54 Vict. c. 39 (1890), *reprinted in* 7 U.L.A. 249 (1949).

Harvard's Dean James Barr Ames, completed by the University of Pennsylvania's Dean William Draper Lewis in 1914, and ultimately adopted by every U.S. state.

B. THE NATURE OF PARTNERSHIP: ENTITY OR AGGREGATE?

The idea that the partnership is an aggregate of the individual owners rather than a separate entity has served as a conceptual basis for the development and legal protection of the corporation, which U.S. law has always regarded as a separate legal entity. However, the aggregate concept of partnership never quite matched the reality of the modern partnership. Partnerships had evolved by the nineteenth century from extended families to business entities separate from their partners. In particular (as discussed below), partnership property rules preserve owners' and creditors' joint rights in the firm's assets from interference by individual owners and their creditors. This enables the owners to commit common property to a collective business strategy without concern that an individual owner might divert the firm's property to some personal use or other business. Indeed (as discussed in Chapter 2), creating these distinct firm rights is a critical function of business association law.

Although partnerships have long had some critical entity features, those drafting or construing the law have balked at explicitly characterizing them as entities. The explanation can be found in a recurring theme of this book: preserving corporate privileges as a legislative prerogative. As discussed in the next chapter, state legislatures once sold corporate features, and the characterization of these features as privileges controlled by lawmakers has lingered as a justification for taxation and regulation. Official entity status conceptually supports several of these privileges, including limited liability and the choice-of-law rule that lets firms select the state that supplies their governance rules. Provisions in some state constitutions that all legal persons were corporations supported the rejection of entity characterization in an initial draft of the UPA.[55] The aggregate-entity distinction between corporations and partnerships was reinforced just prior to the adoption of the UPA by the adoption of the Sixteenth Amendment authorizing federal income taxation of persons, arguably including legal persons. If partnerships were going to be denied critical entity features, they wanted at least to avoid having to pay for them.[56]

---

55. See William Draper Lewis, *The Uniform Partnership Act–A Reply to Mr. Crane's Criticism*, 29 HARV. L. REV. 158, 165 (1915).

56. See A. Ladru Jensen, *Is a Partnership Under the Uniform Partnership Act an Aggregate or an Entity?* 16 VAND. L. REV. 377, 387 (1963) (noting that "[t]he recognition of the Internal Revenue laws of partnerships as an aggregate for purposes of income taxation will most surely long continue * * * because small unincorporated businesses need the economic

The aggregate characterization of partnership was far from clear in the various bodies of law that contributed to the creation of partnership law.[57] Civil law, which survived in Louisiana,[58] favored entity characterization. However, the common law resisted the entity concept,[59] treating all of the partners as owners as tenants in common,[60] thereby enabling each partner to possess and transfer the property for personal purposes. Yet common law rules mitigated the harshest effects of these rules as the courts introduced a doctrine of *partners' equities* that provided for copartner rights against the other partners and their transferees. This illustrates the common law's capacity to adjust over time to pressing business needs. However, along with this adjustment came jurisdictional variation and unpredictability.

The drafters of the original UPA tried to find order in this chaos. The UPA's first drafter, Dean James Barr Ames, would have defined a partnership as "a legal person."[61] But Ames died before completing the project, and his successor, Dean William Draper Lewis, rejected the legal person theory and its application to partnerships.[62] The final act was a compromise:[63] it substantively characterized partnerships in many respects as legal entities, defined *partnership* as a "person,"[64] and explicitly embraced the law merchant, which recognized partnerships as entities.[65] On the other hand, the UPA takes an aggregate slant in defining partnership as an "association of two or more persons."[66]

The UPA's treatment of partnership property is the clearest illustration of the Act's schizophrenic approach to the aggregate-entity issue. Indeed, an examination of the UPA's property provisions makes us think of Steve Martin in the film *All of Me* in which he has to share a single body with Lily Tomlin. The Act starts out by providing that the partnership can acquire property in its name, which sounds entity-like.[67] But things get confusing in § 25, which provides for *individual* partner rights in partnership property. Although individual partners own the property as "tenants in partnership," they cannot do anything important

---

advantage of a single tax on the income allocated to the members to grant them much needed aid in the competition of the market place") (footnote omitted).

57. *See* Gary Rosin, *The Entity-Aggregate Dispute: Conceptualism and Functionalism in Partnership Law*, 42 Ark. L. Rev. 395 (1989).

58. *See* State v. Morales, 256 La. 940, 240 So. 2d 714 (1970).

59. *See* 1 Lindley, Partnership 61 (5th ed. 1891).

60. *See* Bloodworth v. Bloodworth, 226 Ga. 898, 178 S.E.2d 198 (1970).

61. *See* UPA, Second Tentative Draft, § 1(1).

62. *See* Lewis, *supra* note 55 at 191.

63. *See* Jensen, *supra* note 56; Rosin, *supra* note 57.

64. *See* UPA § 2.

65. *Id.* § 5; Arthur Jacobson, *The Private Use of Public Authority: Sovereignty and Associations in the Common Law*, 29 Buff. L. Rev. 599, 639–51 (1980).

66. UPA § 6(1) (1914).

67. *Id.* § 8.

with it—they cannot possess the property for individual purposes, assign it individually, pass it to heirs, or subject it to attachment or execution on an individual claim. Moreover, the Act provides that an individual partner possesses only the interest a corporate shareholder has in the corporation: an interest in the firm's profits, without a default right to access this cash until dissolution.[68]

The schizophrenic nature of partnership property rights manifests itself in the gaps left open by the specific statutory rights of tenants in partnership. For example, can a partner be guilty of the crime of embezzlement when he takes partnership property without copartner consent? Although the partner has no right to possess the property for individual purposes, is she really stealing it if she has individual rights to it? Indeed, as we will see in Chapter 7, even today some statutes distinguish partnerships from other business associations in this respect.

These issues still are not completely clear. The Revised Uniform Partnership Act (RUPA) at least provides that a "partnership is an entity distinct from its partners"[69] and that "property acquired by a partnership is property of the partnership and not of the partners individually."[70] This Act, which was first promulgated in 1994, has been passed in about three-fourths of the states. But the issue may be in doubt in the remaining states, and even RUPA states still have pre-RUPA case law.

Thus, while partnerships had all of the substantive legal qualities they needed to carry on business as legal entities, the corporation's lock on the official entity privilege left a residue of confusion. This is important because it preserved a special advantage for the corporation just at the time the corporate form was rising to prominence. As we will see in Chapter 4, such legally created advantages cumulatively left an important opening for the rise of the corporation.

C. VICARIOUS LIABILITY

Business association statutes address the extent to which the firm's creditors can proceed against the assets of both the firm and the individual partners. A key partnership feature long has been the potential liability of each partner for *all* of the partnership's debts (not merely the partner's share of the partnership's losses as discussed in the next section).[71]

Although vicarious liability might be seen as an *aggregate* feature, it has entity aspects. The owners' vicarious liability is based on debts contracted or incurred on the firm's behalf by people acting as agents of the firm. The owners may be

---

68. *Id.* §§ 26–27.
69. RUPA § 201.
70. *Id.* § 203.
71. *See* UPA § 15; RUPA § 306.

liable even to people they have never met and who have never heard of them.[72] The liability therefore is created through the firm and is administered through the creditor's obligation to proceed first against the firm (as discussed in this section) and the rules regarding indemnification and contribution among the partners (discussed in the next section).

Partners' vicarious liability is arguably the single most important and distinctive feature of partnership. Unlike the other partnership features discussed below, partnerships cannot fully avoid vicarious liability solely by contracting among themselves. It therefore makes sense to think about the other default rules of partnership as following from the basic design choice of vicarious liability rather than vice versa. As discussed throughout the remainder of this chapter, partners' commitment to back all of the firm's debts drives many other partnership rules, including partners' equal financial rights, equal and active participation in management, and right to exit an onerous partnership relationship by compelling dissolution of the firm.

What may seem somewhat surprising in the following discussion is the narrow application of the partnership standard form to real-world firms. Firms in which owners are all active and to which they contribute fairly equally are unusual in a business world increasingly dominated by specialization of investment and management functions. Yet as we will see below in this chapter, partners' individual liability for all partnership debts and the default rules that follow from this liability potentially apply to *any* relationship of co-ownership, defined broadly in terms of sharing profits and control.

However, one could imagine a different set of default rules that suits a broader swath of firms. These rules might start with limited liability of owners, or a less onerous form of vicarious liability that applies only to active managers, or liability proportioned to partners' financial contributions. The joint and several liability provided for by partnership law gives firms a powerful incentive to choose the corporate form in which they get limited liability—but with regulatory strings attached.

D. OWNERS' FINANCIAL RIGHTS

In the absence of an agreement to the contrary, partners share profits and losses equally regardless of the partners' contributions to the firm.[73] To take an extreme example, suppose Partner A will contribute all of the funding, Partner B has the bright idea on which the business is based and will work full time as manager, and Partner C will be sales manager. Though C's contribution might seem to be

---

72. *See* WILLIAM HOLDSWORTH, A HISTORY OF ENGLISH LAW 198 (2d ed. London 1937).
73. UPA § 18(a); RUPA § 401(b).

worth less than those of A and B, unless they agree to the contrary, the partners will share profits and losses equally. A does not get interest on his contribution and B does not get paid for being manager.

The equal sharing rule might seem odd to those who are used to the corporate scheme in which shareholders who contribute the most money get the most votes and the biggest piece of the profits and dividends. However, equal sharing makes sense as a default rule given that anyone who decides to be a partner has potentially exposed all of her wealth to payment of the firm's debts.

Should courts apply a different default rule if the parties' financial and labor contributions are unequal, but they have not explicitly contracted around the statutory default rule? Even if the contract does not seem to match the deal, courts should not make up contracts for the parties. Not only might a court get the particular case wrong, but it could muddy the default rules for later partnerships.

The equal-sharing default rule also can play a role in the firm's dealings with third parties. In service partnerships such as law firms in which clients rely on the firm to give high quality service, the partners' equal sharing in effect *bonds* this assurance. When this rule is in effect, third parties know that each new partner the firm hires will reduce the existing partners' earnings shares unless the new partner brings in enough additional profits to offset the equal share the firm pays the member. This gives the firm a strong incentive always to hire the best people it can. But if instead the firm pays the new partner just enough to cover the fees the partner generates, the firm stands to gain by hiring low-quality professionals and then charging what the market will bear. This increases the likelihood that the firm will try to get away with hiring low-quality professionals. Third parties therefore can judge the reliability of the firm's services by how it pays its members.[74]

Although this theory makes sense for equal-sharing firms, it does not account for all the other firms formed under the general partnership statutes. The rest of the partnership world is best explained as a set of default rules that provide the best (albeit rough) statutory standard form for firms that choose to adopt partnership-type joint and several liability.

So far we have been discussing profits and losses as if it is clear what they mean. However, the partnership statutes do not define these terms. From an accounting standpoint, profits and losses commonly refer to the positive or negative difference between revenues and expenses. They also might refer to the positive or negative difference between the firm's assets and liabilities when these are divided up among the partners, usually on dissolution or partner dissociation. This is the more important context for determining profits and

---

74. *See* Jonathan D. Levin & Steven Tadelis, A *Theory of Partnerships* (Oct. 2002), Stanford Law and Economics Olin Working Paper No. 244, http://ssrn.com/abstract=311159.

losses in *default* partnerships, which often do not have very precise accounting for revenues and expenses when they are ongoing.

A partner's share of the losses differs from his potential personal liability to partnership creditors for all of a partnership's debts. The partners try to adjust their internal sharing with their external payments through indemnification and contribution. They get *indemnified* by the *partnership* for what they pay third parties.[75] The partnership's liability for indemnification, as with other liabilities, may produce a loss in the sense of an excess of liabilities over assets. The partners are supposed to *contribute* their shares of the loss to the firm to make up the shortfall.[76] The creditors must first try to recover their debts from the firm out of the firm's property, which includes these contributions. The partners' joint and several liability therefore is really a backup to the partnership's liability rather than a primary source of creditors' recovery.

E. MANAGEMENT

Just as partners' vicarious liability justifies their equal financial rights in the firm, so it underlies their significant say in the partnership's business and its use of the property. Partnership default rules provide that the partners vote equally on all ordinary matters connected with the partnership business and that all partners must consent on extraordinary matters and amendments to the agreement.[77] As with financial rights, these rules apply in the absence of an agreement to the contrary even if some partners have made larger contributions of property or time than others.

Different rules apply to transactions with third parties. Many firms like the convenience of letting one person bind the firm rather than making all the owners sign off on each transaction. Partners have that power. Partnership statutes provide that a single partner's act binds the firm if it is "for apparently carrying on in the usual way (ordinary course) the partnership business" unless the third party knows (or receives notification) that the partner lacked authority.[78]

Partnership, however, is a special application of agency rules. In general, an agent's job limits her power to bind the firm. Thus, a janitor of a firm engaged in the plumbing business cannot bind the firm to a major plumbing contract. But a *partner can* bind the firm to ordinary transactions solely because she is a partner unless the third party knows of a limit on the partner's authority.

Partners' agency power is yet another implication of vicarious liability. Given that every partner has committed to vicarious liability for the firm's debts, it

---

75. UPA § 18(b); RUPA § 401(c).
76. UPA § 40(d); RUPA § 807(b).
77. UPA § 18(e) and (h); RUPA 401(f) and (j).
78. UPA § 9; RUPA § 301.

logically follows that every partner would be empowered as such to act for the firm regardless of other aspects of the partners' status. To be sure, it might also be argued that all of the vicariously liable partners would want to be able to sign off on every transaction. However, the partners need to be able to carry on the business efficiently. They therefore empower individual members to bind the firm while using their substantial management power and power to dissolve the firm at will to keep their copartners in check.

Joint management such as that provided for in a standard-form partnership can be very costly to maintain. As the partners may have different ideas about how to run the firm, they may have to negotiate every issue. Partners also may try to use their veto power to renegotiate their economic rights in the firm. As discussed in Chapter 2, this potential for opportunism is a basic problem of allocating power among joint owners.

The partners might even argue about what triggers the veto power. Suppose the partners have decided on a particular course of action for operating the firm, but circumstances change. Does the change make carrying on as before a new decision that calls for a majority, or even a unanimous vote? For example, three partners agree to race a horse. The horse develops a problem that might cripple it the next time it races. The trainer-partner does not want to race, while the other two partners favor risking the horse for a big purse. Who decides? (A court basically punted on this issue after a long opinion by dissolving the firm without deciding who had the power to wind it up.)[79]

These problems of joint decision making could be resolved by delegating power to one or a couple of people. But as discussed in Chapter 2, separation of ownership and control creates potential agency costs. In general, the fewer the number of owners who have to sign off on a decision, the lower the costs of reaching it, but the higher the potential costs that the decision makers can impose on the other owners. Crafting decision-making rules requires balancing the costs of reaching a decision against the costs the empowered can impose on the unempowered.[80]

Most ongoing firms want to centralize power more than is provided for in partnership default rules. Firms usually make many decisions and have to be able to continually adjust to changing business conditions. Also, as the owners of most firms ought to be able to agree on a strategy of maximizing profits, delegating power to properly disciplined and incentivized managers may not impose heavy costs on noncontrolling owners. However, where partners have unlimited liability for the firm's debts, group decisions can impose very significant risks on individual members, as where the firm decides to engage in speculative new business, borrow a lot of money, or enter into a long-term lease.

---

79. Paciaroni v. Crane, 408 A.2d 946 (Del. Ch. 1979).
80. *See* JAMES M. BUCHANAN & GORDON TULLOCK, THE CALCULUS OF CONSENT: LOGICAL FOUNDATIONS OF CONSTITUTIONAL DEMOCRACY (1962).

As discussed below, one way to deal with these problems is to centralize management but give the members exit rights. However, these rights may threaten the firm's continuity and stability.

In short, partnership management rules can be costly on balance for many firms. Yet the rules fit with other aspects of the partnership standard form, particularly partners' vicarious liability. The point again is to show how vicarious liability forces partnerships into a governance corner from which they have a strong incentive to escape to the limited liability haven of incorporation.

F. FIDUCIARY DUTIES AND REMEDIES

Many lawyers and commentators think of a general partnership as the epitome of a fiduciary relationship. Certainly this idea is reinforced by the most famous partnership case, Justice Cardozo's opinion in *Meinhard v. Salmon*.[81] The famous jurist pulled out all of the linguistic stops in describing the partner's duty as the "punctilio of an honor the most sensitive" and holding that a partner could not appropriate an opportunity from his copartner.

Justice Cardozo was on solid economic ground in holding that a fiduciary must act in the firm's interest rather than his own. The constraint on self-interested conduct solves a practical problem of judicial supervision of agents. Courts understand that they have a limited ability to second-guess business judgments and that owner-managers have ample incentives to do a good job so as to get a raise, promotion, or new job; keep their jobs; or increase the value of their interests in the firm. These bets are off when managers' and the firm's interests conflict. So a strict duty of unselfishness should apply where a property owner delegates significant power over the property to another party. However, when the parties are not exercising this managerial power, there is no need for a heavy-duty constraint on their conduct, and they ought to be able to act in their self-interest, just as they can in other commercial dealings.[82]

Justice Cardozo's opinion should not, however, be taken as describing the duties between all partners in a standard-form partnership. It is true that a partner may hold significant power, whether through a majority vote or a power to effectively destroy the firm by triggering dissolution. But the partner has contracted for these powers not as a fiduciary watching over the property of others but to enable the partner to protect her own property rights in the firm. It follows that partners normally should be able to exercise these powers selfishly.

Although partners in a standard form partnership do have some obligation to their copartners in exercising their contractual powers, it is not a *fiduciary* obligation.

---

81. Meinhard v. Salmon, 249 N.Y. 458, 164 N.E. 545 (1928).
82. *See* Larry E. Ribstein, *Are Partners Fiduciaries?* 2005 U. Ill. L. Rev. 209.

Rather, it is a duty to wield their contractual powers in *good faith*. As discussed in more detail in Chapter 7, the good faith duty is actually a judicially implied contractual covenant that when a situation arises the contract does not explicitly cover, the court should consider whether the parties, in light of their explicit agreement, would have permitted the conduct at issue if they had foreseen it at the time of the contract. If the court concludes that the parties would have prohibited the conduct at the time of contracting, it interprets the contract as if it included the prohibition. The covenant facilitates contracting by freeing the parties from having to draft provisions in execruciating detail that anticipate every eventuality.

The *Meinhard* case itself arguably did involve the classic fiduciary relationship between an active manager (Salmon) and a passive financier (Meinhard), co-venturers in managing a building in midtown Manhattan. The court held that as manager, Salmon owed Meinhard a strict duty to disclose that he had been offered the opportunity to manage the building that would be constructed on the property after the conclusion of the lease that was the basis of the partnership. As Salmon was a manager, Justice Cardozo is arguably justified in saying:

> Salmon had put himself in a position in which thought of self was to be renounced, however hard the abnegation. He was much more than a coadventurer. He was a managing coadventurer. . . . For him and for those like him the rule of undivided loyalty is relentless and supreme.[83]

In other words, because Salmon as manager had taken on the responsibility of actively promoting the interests of the venture with Meinhard, he could not selfishly appropriate the opportunity for himself. Although Cardozo did not expressly limit his rule to managers, it is Salmon's managerial status that justifies the result.

Although Salmon had a strict fiduciary duty, he may not have breached it. This seems clear from the extensive background research Professor Geoffrey Miller has done into the case.[84] Miller shows that Meinhard and Salmon each made ten times their $52,000 investments. The new project the court obliged Salmon to disclose was vastly bigger than the one Salmon managed for Meinhard—not a mere eight-story office building, but a twenty-story building that was eventually expanded to fifty-nine stories following the conclusion of the case, thereby becoming one of the largest construction projects to date in New York. The property owner offered this opportunity to Salmon because of his

---

83. *Meinhard*, 249 N.Y. at 468; 164 N.E. at 548.

84. Geoffrey P. Miller, *Meinhard v. Salmon, in* THE ICONIC CASES IN CORPORATE LAW (Jonathan R. Macey, ed., 2008). For another detailed discussion of the background of *Meinhard, see* Robert B. Thompson, *The Story of Meinhard v. Salmon, in* CORPORATE LAW STORIES, Chapter 4, 105–33 (J. Mark Ramseyer, ed., 2009). Among other things, Thompson details the expansion of the project discussed in the text immediately following this note.

unique talents as a developer, not because of his role in the prior partnership. Salmon agreed to inform Meinhard about developments, but only if Meinhard asked about them, which he did not.

Despite these facts, the court saddled Salmon with an unwanted partner for an indefinite period on top of the twenty-year term of the partnership. Thus, there is considerable doubt that Salmon's opportunity to manage the new development could by any stretch be considered something that Salmon, even as a fiduciary, was bound to share with Meinhard. In his dissenting opinion, Justice Andrews stressed facts such as these in arguing that Salmon had not breached his duty.

Miller suggests that Justice Cardozo's colorful language was intended to bridge the apparent chasm between the facts and the result. Cardozo pulled out the stops in referring to concepts of chivalry and honor, loyalty and comradeship of soldiers under fire, and religion. But this begs the question of *why* Cardozo wanted to bridge this gap. Why not simply hold that Salmon had not breached his duty? One answer may be that Cardozo concluded that the fiduciary duty works best if fiduciaries err on the side of foregoing self-interest. In other words, they should keep in mind Cardozo's colorful language and his holding in favor of breach in a close case when they find themselves in a borderline situation. They should not be encouraged by the reasoning Justice Andrews used to conjure excuses for acting selfishly.

Perhaps most importantly for present purposes, *Meinhard* is explicitly a case involving a "managing *co-adventurer*," even if Cardozo's reasoning is not necessarily limited to that situation. Although Salmon's *fiduciary duty* stems from his status as a manager, the partnership or joint venture facts may have been decisive in determining that Salmon's conduct was a *breach* of this duty. The partnership context matters because of the special nature of the partnership standard form discussed above. Partners are vicariously liable for the firm's debts and therefore have a default right to an equal share of profits. An investment in a standard-form partnership is more likely to be a livelihood than a part of a diversified portfolio of thousands of stocks. Accordingly, the partners likely have especially high expectations from the people they have entrusted with management responsibilities. These strict duties are yet another consequence of partnership that might push parties into the official state-sanctioned form of business association—the corporation.

Although partnership default fiduciary duties are strict, the partners can contractually modify them. That was at least as true at the time of *Meinhard* as it is today. The UPA captures the rule in effect around Cardozo's time that a partner must account for benefits "derived by him *without the consent* of the other partners."[85] Cardozo's stern admonitions nevertheless carry over to the waiver

---

85. UPA § 21 (emphasis added).

context by supporting a requirement that agreements opting out of fiduciary duties be explicit.[86] RUPA qualifies modifiability by forcing partners to "identify specific types or categories of activities that do not violate the duty of loyalty, if not manifestly unreasonable" or to specify a "number or percentage [that] . . . may authorize or ratify, after full disclosure of all material facts, a specific act or transaction that otherwise would violate the duty of loyalty."[87]

Overall, general partnership law provides a framework both for default fiduciary duties and for contracting out of these duties that suits small vicarious liability relationships in which fiduciary breach can have particularly serious consequences for each member. As with other general partnership default rules, it is easy to see why less intimate firms would have been anxious to escape the general partnership's fiduciary framework to the haven of incorporation. However, we would expect some mitigation of these rules as partnerships adopt limited liability and the wall of corporate privilege crumbles. Indeed, Chapter 7 discusses how modern uncorporations have moved toward complete freedom regarding contracting for fiduciary duties.

G. TRANSFERRING RIGHTS

Partners have only a limited ability to transfer their rights in the firm to third parties. The default rules balance the partners' need for liquidity against transfers' potential harm to copartners. As with other firms, the owners cannot unilaterally transfer the firm's property.[88] This rule protects the firm's need to conduct an operating business from the owners' unilateral action in pursuing their separate interests. The owners can transfer their economic rights in the partnership—that is, their rights to distributions.[89] Partners' creditors can access the partners' economic rights in the firm through a garnishment-like proceeding called a *charging order*.[90] The partners' power to unilaterally transfer economic rights and lack of power to transfer rights in the firm's specific property are both consistent with the rights of corporate shareholders.

The critical distinction between partnerships and corporations with respect to transferability is that partners cannot unilaterally transfer their rights to manage the firm. This obviously limits the liquidity of partnership interests, as economic rights may not be very valuable without the power to protect those rights. For example, a court held that an assignee had no right to question the

---

86. *See* Thompson, *supra* note 84, at 133 (suggesting that Cardozo would have taken a restrictive view of contracting out of fiduciary duty).
87. RUPA § 103(b).
88. *See* UPA § 25; RUPA § 502.
89. *See* UPA § 26, and 27; RUPA § 503.
90. UPA § 28; RUPA § 504.

nontransferring partners' decision to pay one of them a large commission even though that had the effect of stopping payments to the assignee.[91] Indeed, the transferee is worse off than a mere creditor of the firm because he has no fixed claim to debt repayment or interest—just to a share in whatever distributions the firm makes. The selling partner retains management and control rights, but no longer has an economic interest to protect. The transfer, in effect, nullifies the seller's power and disconnects control and economic power in the firm. By contrast, corporate shareholders can transfer both economic and management rights. Shareholders thereby get both greater liquidity and the ability to sell control to someone who can use it more effectively.

As with the other rights discussed above, nontransferability of management rights follows naturally from the other default partnership terms also discussed above, particularly vicarious liability. Because of this liability and the strong management rights that follow from it, partners would expect to be able to control who can exercise governance rights. Moreover, vicarious liability inherently limits transferability even apart from restrictions on transfer of management. Partners probably will not want to transfer their management rights if they have to keep the liabilities—and they should not be allowed to transfer their liabilities as this could frustrate the firm's existing creditors. Imposition of fiduciary duties to transferees on the nontransferring partners is no solution because the inherent conflicts between the two groups could breed litigation. The best the law can do is to empower transferees to get a court to dissolve a firm that has no unexpired term,[92] at least where this would not enable transferees to disrupt the firm.[93]

Special issues concern partners' creditors. As noted above, the creditors can get a charging order allowing them to access distributions that would otherwise go to the debtor partner. The creditor also can become an actual transferee of the interest by foreclosing on it (in much the same way that a bank forecloses on a mortgage). This entitles the creditor, as with other transferees of partnership interests, to sue for judicial dissolution.

But the creditors are in a potentially worse predicament than other transferees because although partners' voluntary transferees can bargain with the transferor for protection, partners may have little concern for their creditors. Creditors must bargain at the time of the debt with their debtors—and perhaps also with the debtors' partners—for rights to collect their debts out of the partnership property. We will see in Chapter 7 that creditors' limited access to

---

91. Bauer v. The Blomfield Company/Holden Joint Venture, 849 P.2d 1365 (Alaska 1993).

92. See UPA § 32(2) and RUPA § 801(6).

93. *Id.* (providing that dissolution on application by a transferee is subject to "a judicial determination that it is equitable to wind up the partnership business").

debtor partners' interests makes uncorporations a potentially valuable asset protection mechanism.

In general, transfer is simply not much of an option for partners seeking to exit the firm. This is yet another implication of vicarious liability. The problems with transfer make important the exit rules discussed next.

H. EXIT

We have seen that partnership involves a heavy commitment—partners are personally liable for partnership debts, and therefore have a strong incentive to participate actively in management, but cannot easily exit their investments by selling them to third parties. This leaves only one exit route: cashing out. Partners can unilaterally dissolve the firm or compel the firm to buy them out.

Under the Uniform Partnership Act, a partner's ceasing to be "associated in the carrying on of the business" *by definition* constitutes a dissolution of the partnership.[94] The partnership is dissolved by the "express will" of any partner, *even if* dissolution is "in contravention of the agreement between the partners," as well as by a partner's death or bankruptcy, among other causes.[95] On dissolution, each partner has the power and right to compel a sale of the partnership assets and distribution of the proceeds unless the partnership is for an unexpired term or undertaking (in which case liquidation can still be forced by any partner who did not wrongfully cause the premature dissolution).[96] If the partnership does not liquidate because the partner's departure is wrongful or the partnership agreement provides for continuation, the leaving partner at least gets to be bought out by the partnership.[97]

The Revised Uniform Partnership Act slightly mitigates the threat to the partnership's continuity by providing that partner dissociation prior to an agreed term or undertaking does not dissolve the firm unless half or more of the partners agree.[98] But in other circumstances RUPA continues the UPA rule of automatic dissolution by dissociation of a partner.

Dissolution is not only a form of exit: it also drives dispute resolution in partnerships. The traditional rule in partnerships is that partners cannot sue each other or the partnership other than in a special proceeding called an *accounting*, which resolves all pending disputes among the partners.[99] The accounting

---

94. UPA § 29.
95. *Id.* § 31.
96. *Id.* § 38.
97. *Id.* § 42.
98. RUPA § 801.
99. The accounting is provided for in UPA § 28. The rule that the accounting is the exclusive remedy is a case law development. *See* 2 ALAN R. BROMBERG & LARRY E. RIBSTEIN, BROMBERG & RIBSTEIN ON PARTNERSHIP, § 6.08(c) (2009) ("BROMBERG & RIBSTEIN").

remedy and the modern erosion of the remedy are discussed further in Chapter 7. For present purposes, it is worth emphasizing that an accounting normally occurs on dissolution—in other words, that partnership law bundles litigation with exit. This recognizes that the law does not expect the close-knit partnership relationship and its heavy mutual obligations to survive contentious disputes among the members.

Although these rules solve the problem of getting partners out from under their onerous obligations, they raise other problems. The dissolution breaks up the business and sacrifices possible going concern value unless the partners who want to continue can come up with the money to buy the firm. Because a very closely held business may have only a speculative value, its owners may not easily be able to persuade a bank or other financier to lend against the assets. Each partner therefore can "hold up" her copartners for more money or perks by threatening to leave. Also, partnerships that are based on the partners' skills are vulnerable to partners' walking off and taking with them not only those skills, but the clients, contacts, and knowledge they gained while at the firm—a problem that especially plagues large law firms today. Indeed, there is evidence that early partners dealt with these problems by forming firms only with those who were least likely to take advantage of them, as by joining with those of similar age and skill.[100]

A California case illustrates the problem.[101] Two brothers partnered to establish a laundry business in Santa Maria, California, in 1949, contributing their resources and losing money for the first eight years of the business. The area at the time was noted mainly for cattle and sheep grazing. Then in October 1957, the Soviets launched Sputnik, which in turn caused the laundry's business to take off. As it happened, the local World War II Army base, Camp Cooke, was a great place to put ICBMs, so it became Vandenberg Air Force Base—a major source of laundry.

Plaintiff chose this particular time to dissolve the business, bringing this case seeking a judgment declaring his right to do so. Defendant argued that granting the judgment would enable his brother to effectively steal the business in that the brother had all the expertise needed to run it and indirectly held a $47,000 note he could call at any time. All plaintiff had to do to pull off the heist was to pay a minimal price for the used equipment and he would own the substantial going concern value of the business that his brother helped pay for. The court's opinion noted that "[d]efendant charges that plaintiff has been content to share

---

100. *See* Howard Bodenhorn, *Partnership and Hold-Up in Early America*, NBER Working Paper No. W8814 (Mar. 2002), http://papers.ssrn.com/paper.taf?abstract_id=302575.

101. Page v. Page, 55 Cal. 2d 192, 359 P.2d 41, 10 Cal. Rptr. 643 (1961).

the losses but now that the business has become profitable he wishes to keep all the gains."[102]

Despite these suspicious circumstances, the UPA compelled the court to dissolve the firm, leaving the court to mutter about the possibility that plaintiff had engaged in bad faith by opportunistically taking advantage of the law to injure his brother. But bad faith is a tricky proposition. As discussed above, it requires abuse of a contract. Here there was no contract other than the default provisions of the partnership statute, and plaintiff seemingly was doing precisely what these provisions allowed him to do.

Partnership law might solve this problem by making it harder for partners to dissolve the firm. Indeed, partners can do this for themselves by drafting around the default partnership rules and providing for more continuity. But the harder it is for partners to leave, the more they confront the problem that dissolution was designed to solve the problem of locking the partners into a burdensome relationship.

In other words, the basic problem with dissolution comes back to the partnership relationship that dissolution at will is designed to address. As we have seen, this relationship is driven by the partners' vicarious liability, which in turn entails direct and equal management rights, equal financial rights, strict fiduciary duties, and inability to leave the firm simply by selling shares. These partnership rights and obligations necessitate an exit right, which somehow must temper the threat of opportunism by dissolving partners. So partnership law defines a Hobbesian relationship that is not only nasty and brutish but potentially short. Firms seeking a better world had to accept the one that government prescribed for them: the corporation.

I. FORMATION

Partnership default rules obviously apply to those who have decided to create a partnership. That decision may be obvious if the parties have embodied their relationship in something called a partnership agreement. But partnership law does not require either a written agreement or the formal filing of a certificate with a state agency, as does a corporation. If the parties have agreed to a particular type of relationship, partnership law fills in its terms except to the extent that the parties otherwise agree. Specifically, partnership statutes define *partnership* as "an association of two or more persons to carry on as co-owners a business for profit."[103] The statutes also provide that the relationship is presumed from

---

102. *Id.* at 646.
103. UPA § 6, RUPA § 101(6) and 202(a).

sharing of profits, except when the profit sharing occurs in one of several specified relationships that are *protected* from being partnerships.[104]

The most straightforward explanation of these rules is that they prescribe a sort of *hypothetical bargain* for the parties.[105] If the parties have agreed to particular terms, the law hypothesizes that they would want the other terms that partnership law associates with co-ownership unless they agree otherwise.

The trick under this approach is determining when the parties to a business relationship have decided to become co-owners. The parties may just have an ordinary non-"firm" contractual relationship such as a loan or long-term supply or requirements contract that should not subject them to the heavier consequences of partnership law. These contract terms may vary along an infinite spectrum from arms' length to co-ownership. If the statute identifies certain relationships as being partnerships, it needs to be clear about which terms are key so the parties know what they are (and are not) getting into. But clarity necessarily entails arbitrariness at the margins.

What specific elements of a relationship clearly signal that the parties wanted to be partners? We might think from the discussion so far that the clearest signal would be the parties' agreeing to be personally liable for the debts of the business. As we have seen, personal liability is a critical element of a general partnership in the sense that it brings along the other elements of the relationship. However, vicarious liability is not really an appropriate subject of the contract solely among the partners. Courts accordingly need to consider what elements of that agreement justify holding them personally liable to third parties.

The statutory emphasis on profit sharing is, in fact, a good place to begin. Profits are a positive difference between revenues and expenses while losses are a negative one. Those who have decided to share profits have incentives also to share management responsibilities to maximize profit's revenue *and* expense components. These people would be the co-monitors of the business from the perspective of the theory of the firm discussed in Chapter 2. Profit sharers have an incentive to choose and motivate the other participants to maximize their share of what is left after paying off the parties to the firm's other contracts.

Note that if *one* person gets all the profits, that person would be the sole monitor, the only one with the incentive to minimize shirking. The law characterizes this as an agency relationship, generally defined as one where the *agent* works under the control of and for the benefit of the *principal*.[106]

---

104. UPA § 7, RUPA § 202.

105. For an analysis of this approach and its application to partnership law, see Stephen M. Bainbridge, *Contractarianism in the Business Associations Classroom: The Puzzling Case of Kovacik v. Reed and the Allocation of Capital Losses in Service Partnerships*, 34 GA. L. REV. 631 (2000).

106. AMERICAN LAW INSTITUTE, RESTATEMENT (THIRD) OF AGENCY, § 1.01 (2006).

Sharing *gross revenues* alone does not indicate partnership. Unlike a profit sharer, a gross sharer (such as a salesperson working on commission) is not concerned with the expense part of the equation and therefore has less need to participate in management to watch over his financial interest. The same reasoning applies to other types of gainsharing, as where a bank shares the gain on resale of the property that is the security for a loan, which usually depends more on the general market than on how the property is managed.[107]

The hypothetical bargain analysis also explains the statutory categories of *protected* relationships.[108] In relationships such as debtor-creditor or employer-employee, the parties may want to share profits without becoming full-fledged co-owners. For example, employees may get bonuses or stock options that reflect profits to motivate their effort, and creditors may get profits to compensate for risk, all without any intention of their being more involved in the business than other employees or creditors. Courts therefore have demanded more evidence of co-ownership in these situations, including the parties' active participation in control, which as we have seen is a hallmark of partnership and which would be rare in the typical debtor-creditor or employer-employee relationship.[109]

However, there may be more going on here than just making up a hypothetical bargain. Courts may have policy reasons for imposing the obligations of partnerships in particular situations even if that is not the likeliest inference about what the parties wanted. Suppose, for example, that the parties explicitly declare in writing that they are *not* partners, but agree to all of the trappings of partnership, including the important ones of profit sharing and control. A court might impose the default rules of partnership (particularly including vicarious liability) to protect creditors and others who have dealt with the business and did not agree to the disclaimer of partnership. This prevents parties who are in substance co-owners from running the business in their own interests and leaving the creditors out in the cold. Moreover, as discussed below (and consistent with a theme of this chapter), these rules channel parties who want to avoid vicarious liability into the officially protected zone of incorporation.

To see how all these rules work, consider two classic cases on the definition of partnership. In *Minute Maid Corp. v. United Foods, Inc.*,[110] United contracted with Minute Maid to buy a lot of orange juice. This contract was very favorable to United, perhaps because Minute Maid needed a reliable outlet for its perishable juice. Among other things, United received volume discounts, notice of pending and sometimes substantial price increases so it could stock up on juice before the increase went into effect, and protection against price declines.

---

107. For a discussion of what constitutes profit-sharing, see 1 BROMBERG & RIBSTEIN, *supra* note 99, § 2.07(b)(4).
108. These are discussed in *id.* at § 2.09.
109. Control sharing as an element of partnership is discussed in *id.* at § 2.07(c).
110. 291 F.2d 577 (5th Cir.), *cert. denied*, 368 U.S. 928 (1961).

The problem is that United could not take full advantage of these terms because it did not have the cash (and apparently could not get financing on ordinary terms), to maximize its purchase of orange juice. Unbeknownst to Minute Maid, United entered into a "Memorandum of Agreement" with Cold Storage to essentially speculate on Minute Maid's inventories at Minute Maid's expense—basically a "heads-I-win-tails-you-lose" deal for United in which Cold Storage provided both financing and storage space. In addition to standard credit and storage charges, the parties set up a "special account" that subtracted Cold Storage's credit and storage charges from the discounts and special deals United got from Minute Maid and paid half of any credit balance to Cold Storage. Though Cold Storage technically also was on the hook for half of any excess of charges over discounts, it was hard to see how it would end up owing anything because of the notice and price protection provisions in the United-Minute Maid agreement. Indeed, on termination of this agreement there was a $22,000 positive balance in the special account. United did not, however, pay Minute Maid despite its financing from Cold Storage.

Minute Maid sought to recover an unpaid $143,000 from Cold Storage, which Minute Maid argued was United's partner. The court agreed with Minute Maid, reasoning that the United and Cold Storage financing/storage arrangement amounted to a partnership over which they had joint control. This control was largely in the form of Cold Storage's right to determine whether the juice inventory securing its loans was "acceptable" and to agree on the volume to be purchased.

But contrast *Minute Maid* with *Martin v. Peyton*.[III] The securities firm of Knauth, Nachod & Kuhne (KNK) was headed down the tubes. One of the partners, Hall, got a loan of securities from his friends the Peytons (as well as from George W. Perkins, Jr. and Edward W. Freeman) to use as collateral for bank loans. The loan agreement specified that the parties did not intend a partnership and that the profit interest was merely additional compensation for the loan. Indeed, KNK had initially offered to make the Peyton group partners but they declined the offer. The lenders got a pile of speculative securities as collateral, 40 percent of the firm's profits up to $500,000 (but not less than $100,000) until the Peyton group got its securities back, and an option to join the firm.

There is much here that seems to cross the line into partnership. The terms are certainly closer to an equity investment than a pure loan. The parties evidently structured the agreement to avoid the usury laws (and therefore to avoid characterization as a loan). The agreement provides for a particular person (Hall) to manage the business, and gives the Peyton group partner-like rights to be informed, to be consulted on important matters, and to veto speculative or

---

III. 246 N.Y. 213, 158 N.E. 77 (1927).

injurious business. The court nevertheless held that the relationship was not a partnership, reasoning that the provisions conferring power on the Peyton group were simply understandable creditor protections designed in light of the speculation that had driven the firm to ruin.

At first blush the outcomes of these cases seem strikingly inconsistent. In both cases, the alleged partners shared profits. The control terms the court thought were important in *Minute Maid* seem even more like typical creditor protections than those in *Martin*. In both cases, the inside creditors appeared to be in a better position than the outside creditors to protect against the loss. To be sure, the outside creditors were probably aware of the Peyton group's involvement in *Martin*, while Minute Maid definitely did not know about Cold Storage. But this is not a particularly persuasive distinction as the outside creditors had already made their loans and could not do anything about the Peytons' role even if they knew about it. While the non-partnership provision in the *Martin* agreement clearly signals the partners' intent, remember that the agreement cannot control the rights of third party creditors. Moreover, Professor William Klein emphasizes that the *Martin* result does not comport with the policy of putting the loss on the party who is in the best position to protect against it.[112]

The cases might, however, be rationalized by focusing on the different roles in the cases played by the inside creditors. In *Martin*, the Peyton group was brought in to try to salvage an already difficult situation—an activity debtors seemingly would generally want to encourage. By contrast, as the court explicitly acknowledged, Cold Storage actually helped United run up a bigger debt to the uninformed Minute Maid than United could have done on its own. Indeed, Minute Maid might have pulled the plug on the venture had it known that United and Cold Storage had joined forces to take advantage of Minute Maid's generous terms.

The uncertainties in these cases illustrate the basic problem that contracting parties face when they seek to finance a business. How can the parties to arrangements such as those in *Minute Maid* and *Martin* know for sure whether they are on the hook for their borrower's debts? The only way would seem to be to form one of the official limited liability firms, particularly the corporation. Cases such as *Minute Maid*, which block informal limited liability, put pressure on the financiers to make it official.

This fits with this chapter's theme of showing how partnership law channels firms into the corporate form, which for many years was the leading limited liability option. The courts' willingness to impose the significant burdens of

---

112. *See* William A. Klein, *The Story of Martin v. Peyton: Rich Investors, Risky Investment, and the Line between Lenders and Undisclosed Partners*, CORPORATE LAW STORIES, *supra* note 84. Klein attributes the *Martin* court's focus on the disclaimer of partnership in the agreement to plaintiff's strategic mistake in imputing conspiratorial motives to the creditors, who were prominent members of the New York financial and social scene.

partnership even on those who did not explicitly want them gives the parties a strong incentive to incorporate.

The parties' problem is that going the corporate route can be costly and burdensome. Beyond the taxes and other costs of forming the firm, the parties may have to deal with default and mandatory rules that are not suited for their firm. For example, the strong fiduciary duties of cases such as *Meinhard* may not suit all relationships. *Meinhard* and *Martin* therefore can be seen as companion cases, with *Meinhard* showing the fiduciary duties that lurk if *Martin* had not allowed the financiers to remain creditors. Justice Andrews, dissenting in *Meinhard*, carried the day in *Martin*. But *Minute Maid* shows that this strategy will not always succeed.

The parties in both these cases did have an alternative both to unofficial limited liability and to incorporation: they could form a limited partnership (as discussed in the next section). Indeed, the arrangement in *Martin* resembled an unofficial limited partnership, with the outside investors as the limited partners and Hall and the others in KNK as the general partners. But as discussed immediately below, the courts of *Martin*'s time strictly interpreted the rules regarding formation of limited partnerships. Again, firms were channeled toward the corporation.

Professor Klein suggests that *Martin* is consistent with the modern trend toward limited liability.[113] However, given the ready availability of officially sanctioned limited liability, the question arises whether parties should have to clarify their relationship by adopting limited liability. *Martin* arguably made more sense in its time as a way of avoiding the high costs of official limited liability than it would today, given the broader availability of limited liability business forms.

J. LIMITED PARTNERSHIPS

The general partnership is not the only classic form of partnership. The limited partnership form offers both limited liability and centralized management. It enables the capitalists—the limited partners—to contribute funds to a business and exercise some power over the firm without falling into the *Minute Maid* trap of accidental partnership. As we will see in Chapters 6 and 7, the limited partnership form has been important in the United States as a basis for LLC statutes.

Despite its centralized management and limited liability, the limited partnership differs in basic ways from the corporation. It has always included many general partnership rules on such matters as lack of formal entity status, transfer of interests, rights of partners' creditors, and dissolution at will. These rules are modified to accommodate limited partners, particularly the limited partners'

---

113. *See* Klein, *supra* note 112.

lack of voting and management rights and lack of a right to dissolve the firm. But even these modifications differ from standard corporate rules. Thus (as we will see in Chapter 8), limited partnership has offered a significant alternative to the corporation in the governance of large and even publicly held firms.

It is important to keep in mind that the limited partnership is not some recently concocted answer to or variation on the corporation. Rather, it developed at the same time as (and alongside) the general partnership, long before the development of the modern corporation. The limited partnership evolved from the *commenda*, a form of business in which capitalists (*commendators*) could invest risky capital at high rates of return in roving traders (*tractators*) without violating usury laws. Commendas were common since the early twelfth century[114] and were established by statute in Pisa as early as 1156. The limited liability of commendators was provided for by statute in Florence in 1408. Commendas developed from even earlier origins in the Byzantium *chreokoinonia*, the Jewish *isqa*, and the Arabian *qirad*.[115]

Though long popular in Europe, the limited partnership did not catch on until relatively recently in the United States and the United Kingdom. Limited partnerships were first recognized in France in 1673. They were first introduced in the United States by New York in 1822, influenced by the version that was included in the 1807 French Commercial Code.[116] Limited partnerships were not introduced in the United Kingdom until 1907.[117]

The history of the limited partnership in the United States illustrates the general themes of the book and foreshadows the later development of limited liability as discussed in Chapter 6. Limited partnerships were promoted as a substitute for the special privileges and limitations of the corporate form.[118] However, to preserve the corporation's special status, the limited partnership had to be hemmed in, particularly by a firm being forced to strictly adhere to required formalities and to avoid any participation in control by the limited partners.[119] Notwithstanding these restrictions, the limited partnership form evidently offered enough advantages over other business associations that

---

114. See Kohn, *supra* note 49.

115. See J. H. Pryor, *The Origins of the Commenda Contract*, 52 SPECULUM 5–37 (1977).

116. For a discussion of early New York limited partnerships, see Eric Hilt & Katharine E. O'Banion, *The Limited Partnership in New York, 1822–1853: Partnerships without Kinship*, NBER Working Paper No. 14412, http://papers.nber.org/papers/w14412.

117. See HARRIS, *supra* note 29 at 19–21, 273–74.

118. See Hilt & O'Banion, *supra* note 116 at 9, n.36 (noting that New York had adopted general incorporation statutes eleven years before the limited partnership).

119. See EDWARD H. WARREN, CORPORATE ADVANTAGES WITHOUT INCORPORATION 306 (1929) (noting that "[t]he lurking danger that a special partner might be exposed to unlimited liability has seriously restricted the use of the limited partnership statutes").

firms were willing to accept the risks of noncompliance. Although early limited partnerships were few in number, they were relatively large in capitalization.[120]

The specific advantages of the limited partnership form were similar to the advantages of modern uncorporate forms, including the LLC. The limited liability of the limited (or special) partners offered a distinct advantage over general partnerships. This feature proved useful in attracting passive investments by experienced businessmen with entrepreneurs to whom they were not related. These wealthy and well-connected limited partners evidently were the nineteenth century equivalent of today's angel investors. Conversely, general partnerships were more likely to be formed among family members, reflecting the greater risk and joint commitment necessitated by vicarious liability—and therefore the greater need to rely on family ties.[121] By comparison with corporations, special partners were willing to forego any participation in control in exchange for not locking up their investments in the firm to the extent required in the more durable corporation.

The limited partnership's ability to compete against the better-recognized and politically protected corporate form can be attributed to some of the same factors that were later to prove important in the spread of the limited liability company. Recognition began in one state (New York) and spread to others.[122] The development in New York was encouraged by its embodiment in a well-publicized statute (thus indicating the role of statutes in developing standard forms, as discussed in Chapter 2), lawyers' efforts to explain and promote the new laws, and a sophisticated city bar in New York.[123]

It is interesting to consider why the United Kingdom did not recognize the limited partnership until 1907, almost a century later than it started to take hold in the United States, despite the many similarities between U.S. and UK partnership and corporate law. This may have had something to do with the different path taken in the United Kingdom to the regulatory corporate form. It also may owe something to the greater receptiveness of the U.S. federal system to innovations. (The UK history is discussed in more detail in Chapter 4.)

K. JOINT STOCK COMPANIES AND LIMITED PARTNERSHIP ASSOCIATIONS

A third variation on partnership-type firms, the joint stock company, offers several corporate elements that the limited partnership did not: tradable shares, long life, and a corporate-type board. The joint stock company evolved by

---

120. *See* Hilt & O'Banion, *supra* note 116.
121. *Id.* at 27.
122. *Id.* at 29.
123. *Id.* at 12.

the mid-sixteenth century out of the partnership.[124] Its main early use was in providing private capital for public-private ventures such as colonial projects in Italy, Holland, France, and England.[125] The joint stock company became a major governance form in England into the nineteenth century; it is the foundation of the English equivalent of the corporation.

The limited liability of joint stock members was at first not clear because members were subject to calls for additional capital. Mitchell notes that the "essence of a joint stock company" was really its durability, not limited liability.[126] Indeed, the joint stock company rose to prominence in England as the basis of the East India Company at least partly because it avoided the easy dissolvability of the partnership form.[127] (The development in England of the joint stock company and of limited liability is discussed in more detail in the next chapter.)

The joint stock company was significant in the United States into the twentieth century.[128] A prominent law professor, Edward Warren, wrote a treatise in 1929 that focused substantially on it.[129] One of America's largest and most important firms, American Express, was a joint stock company whose members had personal liability until 1963.[130] Warren argued that this form of business provided an important way to get many corporate attributes without high corporate fees, corporate-type regulation, or burdensome disclosures.[131]

The development of the joint stock company opens to question many commentators' view that the corporate form was necessary to provide the durability and other features essential for modern business enterprise. It confirms what is evident from this survey of partnership forms: that the partnership has always had significant flexibility and has been able to evolve in response to business needs. However, as we will see, the explanation for the rise of the corporation has more to do with politics and governments seeking to control capital than it does with business necessity.

Finally, we come to a peculiar business association that is of no importance today, but had its moment in the sun in the United States in the late nineteenth century: the limited partnership association. Pennsylvania passed the first statute in 1874, followed by Virginia (1874), Michigan (1877), New Jersey (1880), and

---

124. *See* William J. Carney, *Limited Liability Companies: Origins and Antecedents*, 66 U. COLO. R. REV. 855 (1995).

125. *See* Mitchell, *supra* note 48, at 192–94.

126. *Id.* at 192–93.

127. *See* Ron Harris, *The Formation of the East India Company as a Deal between Entrepreneurs and Outside Investors*, http://papers.ssrn.com/sol3/papers.cfm?abstract_id=567941.

128. *See* Carney, *supra* note 124.

129. *See* WARREN, *supra* note 72.

130. *See* Mark I. Weinstein, *Share Price Changes and the Arrival of Limited Liability in California*, 32 J. LEGAL STUD. 1 (2003).

131. *See* WARREN, *supra* note 119, at 383.

Ohio (1881). The Carnegie Steel Company was among the firms that adopted this form.

The limited partnership association had all of the advantages of the limited partnership and the joint stock company plus an important additional feature: limited liability for all members. It was, after all, an *association*, so the firm bore the debts. Indeed, as we will see, this strong corporate resemblance is what caused the trouble—it was seen as a way to get all of the advantages of incorporation without the burdens that government wanted to impose in exchange for recognizing corporate features.[132]

Why did the limited partnership association fail? One possible explanation is that the states resisted a partnership-type alternative that offered *everything* the corporation did, *including* limited liability. As we will see in the next chapter, the absence of such an alternative helps explain the rise of the corporation. The search for a successful version of the limited partnership association is a major theme of Chapters 5 and 6, with the search culminating in the limited liability company.

---

132. For discussions of the limited partnership association, see WARREN, *supra* note 119, at 508–25; Wayne M. Gazur & Neil M. Goff, *Assessing the Limited Liability Company*, 41 CASE W. RES. L. REV. 387, 393–94 (1991).

4. THE RISE OF THE CORPORATION

Chapter 3 showed that the general partnership was designed for the most intimate firms, in which parties were willing to be liable for the firm's debts and therefore wanted default rules such as equal management, financial rights, and easy dissolution. When the Industrial Revolution created a need for bigger firms, they needed a different legal structure, which turned out to be the corporation. The corporation has been said to have made the large firm possible,[133] and even to have enabled the West to outpace Eastern civilizations that were the first to develop advanced mercantile economies.[134] The conventional wisdom is that the Industrial Revolution displaced the partnership as the basic business structure.

This story seems plausible. The general partnership form was indeed unsuited to the emerging large firms. General partnerships tended to rely on their owners' reputations and did not need a fancy organizational setup that would survive the people or families that organized them. The Industrial Revolution made firms bigger than ever. The railroads, canals, and telegraph; Rockefeller's oil empire; Carnegie's steel; Ford's automobiles; great retailers such as Sears and Montgomery Ward; and manufacturers such as General Motors could shape rather than merely respond to markets.[135] These vast organizations transcended and survived their individual promoters and owners and needed to raise money in the capital markets that were developing during the nineteenth century. The dispersed passive investors who replaced hands-on partners could not shoulder the firm's liabilities.

The corporate form was not, however, as obvious an organizational choice at the time of the Industrial Revolution as it seems in retrospect. The corporation's desirable features came with thick strings attached. Corporations initially were created as the vehicle for government monopolies and franchises rather than purely private firms. Even after corporations started to be used for private purposes, entrepreneurs had to go to the state legislature to buy a charter, which enabled lawmakers to impose conditions and restraints.

States started enacting general incorporation laws in the early nineteenth century that let any firm organize a corporation as long as it made a state filing and

---

133. See Margaret M. Blair, *Locking in Capital: What Corporate Law Achieved for Business Organizers in the Nineteenth Century*, 51 UCLA L. REV. 387 (2003).

134. *See* JOHN MICKLETHWAIT & ADRIAN WOOLDRIDGE, THE COMPANY: A SHORT HISTORY OF A REVOLUTIONARY IDEA (2003).

135. ALFRED D. CHANDLER, JR., THE VISIBLE HAND: THE MANAGERIAL REVOLUTION IN AMERICAN BUSINESS (1977).

paid a filing fee.[136] Although general incorporation undercut the notion that states "created" corporations, corporate law continues to be influenced by this idea. For example, the Supreme Court barred corporations from making certain political expenditures while protecting other types of firms under the First Amendment, citing the "unique state-conferred corporate structure that facilitates the amassing of large treasuries."[137] Thus, the fiction of state-creation has outlasted its reality.

The corporation's history as a state-created vehicle endowed it with functional defects. Early corporations had monopoly privileges that insulated them from market risks. Like animals kept in captivity, these firms' structure was not especially appropriate for competitive markets. Shareholders needed more protection from managerial misconduct if they no longer had a government-conferred monopoly to fall back on. Efficient securities markets, which are today's powerful mechanism for evaluating managers and changing control, were less robust in the nineteenth century.

Another problem with attributing the corporation's dominance to its inherent superiority is that a lot of what the corporation could do, the partnership could do as well or better. Although the default partnership was suited for small, closely held firms, the partnership is also inherently contractual and adaptable to different uses. In particular (as discussed in Chapter 3), the contractually based joint stock company and limited partnership forms provided bases for evolving efficient governance for publicly held, centrally managed firms. Indeed (as discussed later in this chapter), the joint stock company played this role in the United Kingdom.

So why did large firms not adapt partnerships to serve their needs? As we will see, lawmakers got in the way, particularly with restrictions on noncorporate limited liability. The corporate form represents a quid pro quo: big firms get corporate features, and government gets an opportunity to regulate governance, just as it did when corporations were public-private partnerships. This was an offer firms could not refuse because government denied partnerships the key "corporate" feature of limited liability.

We begin with an analysis of why corporate features mattered to big firms. The discussion then shows that partnerships also had access to these features, with the critical exception of limited liability. The chapter ends with an examination of the politics of choice of form and some support for this story in the alternative histories that unfolded outside the United States.

---

136. The evolution of general incorporation laws as a product of state competition is discussed in Henry N. Butler, *Nineteenth Century Jurisdictional Competition in the Granting of Corporate Privileges*, 14 J. LEGAL STUD. 129 (1985).

137. Austin v. Michigan Chamber of Commerce, 494 U.S. 652 (1990). The Court referred to limited liability as one of these special state-conferred corporate advantages. *See also* FEC v. Mass. Citizens for Life, Inc., 489 U.S. 238, 257 (1986).

A. CORPORATE FEATURES AND LARGE FIRMS

This section describes features that make corporations suitable for large firms. Some, such as limited liability and capital lock-in, clearly have advantages for the large firms the corporate form is designed to accommodate. The main question concerning these features is whether they are reserved only for corporations and, if so, why. Others (such as the board of directors) are *available* to noncorporations, but *required* for corporations. These features constrain the governance of large firms. Lawmakers have made it hard for partnerships to adopt some corporate features to prevent them from getting the benefits of incorporation without its restrictions. The two types of corporate features combine to support a regulatory theory of the corporate form.

1. Centralized management and corporate boards

The feature that perhaps best characterizes the large-firm nature of the corporation is its centralized management. Shareholders control but do not manage corporations. Corporate executives handle day-to-day management and bear some responsibility for strategy. The managers are appointed, supervised, and removed by a board of directors, who, in turn, are elected and may be removed by the owners.

The board is one of the most distinctive features of the corporate form. To be sure, all large firms (including large partnerships) need to centralize management power in a small group that can operate quickly, efficiently, and expertly. Also (as discussed in Chapter 8), some large limited partnerships have directors that advise managers. But only a corporation *must* have a board of directors that is separate from the executives and appointed directly by the owners.

The traditional explanation of the board of directors is that it monitors the managers on behalf of the shareholders, thereby addressing potential agency costs inherent in the shareholders' delegation of control. This explanation is supported by shareholders' power to elect and remove directors. However, the directors are not strictly shareholders' agents. For example, as we will see in Chapter 5, the board traditionally was required even in closely held firms where the owners clearly do not need intermediaries to watch over their agents and where directors hardly can be counted on to protect the minority from the majority who elected them.

Some commentators theorize a non-monitoring role for the board of directors. In particular, Blair and Stout argue that the board does or should represent the interests of all of the constituencies that deal with the corporation, including workers, creditors, and suppliers.[138] Although shareholders have the exclusive

---

138. *See* Margaret M. Blair & Lynn A. Stout, *A Team Production Theory of Corporate Law*, 85 VA. L. REV. 247 (1999).

power to elect directors, they face significant practical limits in constraining directors' discretion, including the discretion to serve other constituencies. Theories such as Blair and Stout's seek to provide normative support for at least maintaining this status quo, and perhaps for even further reducing shareholder power.

Blair and Stout's theory meshes with Frank Gevurtz's historical account of the board's political legitimizing role.[139] Gevurtz traces the board of directors to the corporation's origins in the joint stock company, which in turn evolved out of merchant associations through which merchants conducted their own businesses and elected a board to pass ordinances to regulate the group. These merchants needed political representation on the ordinance-passing body, not monitors. Though corporations have moved far from their medieval guild roots, the board was a convenient institution to address lawmakers' concerns about corporate power. Gevurtz notes that when New York enacted its initial general incorporation law, it demonstrated its concern about corporate power by restricting the amount of capital these liberated corporations could raise.

If the board is supposed to provide political legitimacy rather than monitoring, perhaps it should represent all corporate constituencies as Blair and Stout suggest. Moreover, such a board would help constrain corporations to act consistently with the objectives of lawmakers rather than solely those of investors. A board attending to non-shareholder constituencies is unlikely to push too strongly against regulation. Not surprisingly, we will see in Chapters 5 and 8 that the board of directors is one of the corporate features that lawmakers have sought to protect from competition by partnerships.

2. Fiduciary duties and remedies

As discussed in Chapter 3, the fiduciary duty of loyalty constrains owners' costs of delegating power to agents. Rather than forcing judges to closely evaluate the costs and benefits of managers' decisions, fiduciary duties impinge mainly on managers whose interests conflict with those of the firm. Fiduciary duties are appropriate in any situation in which owners delegate to others substantial power to manage their property. From this perspective, they seem to fit the standard centrally managed corporation better than the member-managed partnership. However, fiduciary duties are appropriate for partnerships that contract for centralized management.

The important question is whether fiduciary duties differ between standard form corporations and centrally managed partnerships. *Meinhard v. Salmon* (discussed in Chapter 3) indicates that a managing partner's fiduciary duty is particularly strict, probably because of the partners' vicarious liability for the

---

139. See Franklin A. Gevurtz, *The Historical and Political Origins of the Corporate Board of Directors*, 33 HOFSTRA L. REV. 89 (2004).

firm's debts. However, while partnerships can contract out of the duty of loyalty, corporations can contract out of only the duty of care,[140] and the Delaware Supreme Court has qualified even this authorization by holding that failing to institute proper controls can constitute a breach of the non-waivable duty of good faith.[141] This restriction on contracting is another indication of the regulatory nature of the corporation.[142]

3. Owner voting

In the absence of an agreement to the contrary, partners vote equally rather than according to their financial contributions, have a say on all ordinary business matters, and have the power to veto important matters and amendments to the agreement. These powers reflect partners' close association with the firm and vicarious liability for its debts. By contrast, corporations are designed for large firms with many owners who have only limited liability.

This has important consequences for owner voting. Corporate shareholders vote according to their shares, and therefore capital contributions—one share, one vote. Ordinary decisions are delegated to the managers. Even on important matters, individual shareholders cannot block a decision. Shareholders have weaker powers not just because of the logistics of having large numbers of voters, but because disagreements are not likely to be very intense: shareholders are concerned only about how their portfolios are performing rather than fixating on individual investments. Also, shareholders who are dissatisfied with their investments easily can call their brokers and sell their shares at current market price. By contrast, partners often work full time in their firms and cannot easily sell their shares.

Corporate shareholder voting has been considered a very significant aspect of the legally mandated corporate governance structure. Though corporate managers and the board wield substantial power, the courts have been careful to preserve what has been called a "sacred space" for shareholder voting.[143] Although the business judgment rule broadly protects managerial decisions, special rules restrict managers' decisions that interfere unduly with shareholder voting rights. Moreover, shareholder power is protected by federal and state laws mandating disclosures in connection with shareholder votes and substantive shareholder rights. Shareholder voting seems like a logical constraint on exercise of control by powerful managers. The firm's owners, whose profit share gives them a big interest in the firm's success, would seem to be the best monitors of

---

140. *See, e.g.* Del. Gen. Corp. L. § 102(b)(7).

141. *See* Stone v. Ritter, 911 A.2d 362 (Del. 2006).

142. *See* Henry N. Butler & Larry E. Ribstein, *Opting Out of Fiduciary Duties: A Response to the Anti-Contractarians*, 65 WASH. L. REV. 1 (1990).

143. Robert B. Thompson & D. Gordon Smith, *Toward a New Theory of the Shareholder Role: "Sacred Space" in Corporate Takeovers*, 80 TEX. L. REV. 261, 326 (2001).

managerial performance. Thus, the shareholder vote has been theorized as a device for correcting managerial errors.[144]

Despite corporate law's emphasis on shareholder voting, shareholders generally do not seem very interested in it. Extensive proxy disclosures tend to land in the trash. Dispersed shareholders holding diversified portfolios (or even mutual funds owning hundreds or thousands of firms on their behalf) have little incentive to incur the costs of participating in governance when the benefits of these efforts will accrue to all of the shareholders to "free ride" on the activists' efforts.

The shareholder vote's monitoring function can be salvaged, at least in theory, by viewing it in conjunction with securities markets and the *market for control*.[145] When mismanagement drives the stock price down, this gives somebody an opportunity to buy control and make a change that brings the price back up. The market for control thus addresses the *free-rider* problem in exercising shareholders' voting rights. So even if shareholder voting has little meaning for ordinary transactions when the firm is functioning well, it has a sort of backup function, springing into action when things get bad enough to justify a control change.

However, this theory cannot explain the whole structure and function of corporate shareholder voting. For example, why distribute extensive proxy statements in connection with shareholder votes? Presumably a control purchaser easily can find this information as long as it is publicly available—and perhaps even if it is not. Why must these statements include minutiae about managerial compensation and other matters that are probably not of much interest to somebody considering making a change of control? As we will see in Chapter 8, the traditional monitoring theory of shareholder voting must contend with logistical problems with share voting and financial engineering that increasingly have separated voting power from share ownership.

The deeper explanation for shareholder voting in large firms is the same as that for other corporate rules, including the board of directors and mandatory fiduciary duties: political legitimacy mingles with monitoring. The shareholder meeting is not simply a way to ensure that managers are running the firm in the shareholders' interests, but also a mechanism for admitting vox populi into the running of these powerful institutions. As with the other corporate governance devices, the specific corporate approach to shareholder voting is less a tool of efficient governance than regulation that lawmakers must protect from erosion, including by non-corporate business associations.

---

144. *See* Robert B. Thompson & Paul H. Edelman, *Corporate Voting*, 62 VAND. L. REV. 129 (2009).

145. *See* Henry G. Manne, *Mergers and the Market for Corporate Control*, 73 J. POL. ECON. 110 (1967).

4. Capital lock-in

As discussed in Chapter 3, each partner by default can dissolve a partnership or seek a buyout by the firm. This feature long has been considered a significant cost of partnership as a basis for governing long-lived firms. By contrast, default corporate rules do not let a member (or his creditor or heir) force the corporation to liquidate or buy his interest. Only the board of directors and the owners acting as groups can dissolve the firm. These rules help keep the capital "locked-into" the firm against individual owners' efforts to remove it.

Chapter 3 discussed the practical problems the partnership rule of dissolution at will creates even for small firms. These problems are exponentially greater for larger firms, which need many years and much planning and capital to develop. Most importantly, a significant component of firm value often comes from its reputation or goodwill, which the firm builds over many years of advertising and being good to customers, workers, and suppliers. Much of this going concern value may be lost if the firm has to liquidate to pay off exiting owners. More importantly, the risk of having to liquidate may prevent large firms from developing in the first place.

As already noted, Blair has argued that this lock-in feature is essential to ensure the integrity of the immense and complex organizations that arose during the Industrial Revolution.[146] In these complex organizations, assets have extra value because of their bundling with other assets.[147] For example, Alfred Chandler demonstrated how the profits of an organization such as Sears depended on its capacity for *throughput*: integration of its purchasing, production, advertising, and sales so that it could sell what it had made and bought.[148] Throughput calls for long-term planning and therefore substantial continuity of management.

Partners' ability to dissociate from and possibly force liquidation of the firm empowers them to "hold up" the other owners for a share of the firm's going concern value as the price of letting it continue. The potential for holdup may be an acceptable trade-off in small firms for enabling partners to get their capital out of the firm and protect themselves from oppression by controlling owners. But it is too high a price for large firms, particularly when shareholders can exit by selling shares in the open market.

The question regarding capital lock-in is not whether it is an important governance feature for large firms, but whether it can explain the dominance of the

---

146. *See* Margaret M. Blair, *The Neglected Benefits of the Corporate Form: Entity Status and the Separation of Asset Ownership from Control*, in CORPORATE GOVERNANCE AND FIRM ORGANIZATION: MICROFOUNDATIONS AND STRUCTURAL FORMS 45–66 (Anna Grandon, ed., 2004); Blair, *supra* note 133.

147. *See* OLIVER E. WILLIAMSON, THE ECONOMIC INSTITUTIONS OF CAPITALISM: FIRMS, MARKETS, RELATIONAL CONTRACTING (1985); Benjamin Klein et al., *Vertical Integration, Appropriable Rents, and the Competitive Contracting Process*, 21 J. L. & ECON. 297 (1978).

148. *See* CHANDLER, *supra* note 135.

corporate form. As we will see below, nothing prevents *partners* from contracting for lock-in.

5. Limited liability

Corporate shareholders are not, like partners, personally liable for the firm's debts. This feature of limited liability supports centralized corporate management because shareholders can more safely trust managers and other owners when their personal wealth is not at stake. Limited liability has other advantages for large firms: it enables shareholders to own diversified portfolios of shares rather than concentrating on the single firm for whose debts they may be held to be personally liable, and it facilitates share markets because buyers do not have to worry about the wealth of their co-owners and shareholders do not have to be prevented from transferring their obligations to insolvent purchasers.[149] The Industrial Revolution triggered a need for a form of business that could accommodate raising large amounts of capital, which in turn required passive owners who could minimize their risk by investing in many different companies. Requiring owners to be personally liable for the all of firms' debts might have switched off the corporate engine of the Industrial Revolution and forced the economy to continue relying on small-scale firms.[150]

A critical question concerning limited liability does not concern its importance for large firms, but rather whether it is an exclusively *corporate* feature. As we will see, limited liability may have been associated with the corporation not because it is intrinsic to the corporate form, but because lawmakers refused to extend it beyond the corporation to which they could attach a regulatory quid pro quo.

6. Transferable shares

Corporate shareholders can freely transfer management as well as economic rights. By comparison (as discussed in Chapter 3), default partnership rules let partners freely transfer only economic rights. This reflects the fact that close-knit partners would not want to be stuck sharing control with strangers. Shareholders' ability to transfer management rights substitutes for a power to compel dissolution or buyout and bolsters shareholders' management rights by enabling them to transfer control to those who can make better use of it.

---

149. *See* Frank H. Easterbrook & Daniel R. Fischel, *Limited Liability and the Corporation,* 52 U. CHI. L. REV. 89 (1985).

150. To be sure, the law might have reached the compromise of imposing liability on shareholders proportional to their ownership in the firm—something that might have worked for large firms. *See* Henry Hansmann & Reinier Kraakman, *Toward Unlimited Shareholder Liability for Corporate Torts,* 100 YALE L.J. 1879 (1991). A full analysis of this alternative and why it was not adopted lies beyond the current discussion. For present purposes it is enough to show that the *partnership* approach to vicarious liability was unsuitable and it was necessary to find an alternative for large firms.

7. Entities and aggregates

The corporation has been regarded from its inception as a legal entity distinct from its owners. For example, corporations can own property, have fully transferable management rights, and be free of dissolution via unilateral member vote. By contrast (as discussed in Chapter 3), partnerships historically were considered to be aggregates of the partners. Indeed, this is often viewed as the most important difference between partnerships and corporations. Even the names of the business associations indicated the difference—*partnership* referring to the relationship among the individual members, and *corporate* referring to the separate body, or corpus, that the law created.

However (as discussed in Chapter 3 and below in this chapter), partnerships traditionally have had by default (or could obtain by contract) many entity features. Their difference from corporations therefore is less in some essential nature of the business form than in the lawmakers' decision to hold the line at the "entity" features they wanted to tax or regulate, particularly limited liability.

The corporation's entity nature has many direct and indirect legal implications. For example, the corporate entity can sue and be sued. Federal law further facilitates entity litigation involving corporations by providing that a corporation resides in a single state for purposes of federal diversity jurisdiction.[151] Therefore, a corporation can litigate in federal court as long as the entity's citizenship differs from that of all of the parties on the other side of the case. However, the U.S. Supreme Court again accepted the state law aggregate-entity distinction in holding that this is available only to corporations as unincorporated firms are deemed to reside for diversity jurisdiction purposes wherever their members reside.[152] Indeed, it gets even worse for unincorporated firms because this rule also applies to unincorporated firms that are members of other unincorporated firms, as well as members of members of members, and so forth.

The corporate entity characterization generally fits the large firms for which the corporate form was designed. The fact that at least the default rules of partnerships and corporations generally divide along aggregate-entity lines enables firms to choose the model that best suits their needs. It is important to keep in mind, however, that the aggregate-entity distinction is not really designed to enable free choice. Rather, the need to create an artificial entity has been a constraint on giving partnerships "entity" features such as limited liability. Thus, common law courts have long held that without legislative or royal authority, they *could not* recognize legal entities that held rights and duties separate from natural persons.[153] Lawmakers' decision to recognize the corporation—and only the corporation—as a separate entity is, of course, a legal and political decision

---

151. 28 U.S.C. § 1332.
152. *See* Carden v. Arkoma Associates, 494 U.S. 185 (1990).
153. *See* Paul G. Mahoney, *Contract or Concession? An Essay on the History of Corporate Law*, 34 Ga. L. Rev. 873, 882 (2000).

rather than a reflection of some law of the physical universe. In fact, lawmakers eventually decided to recognize partnerships as legal entities in virtually every relevant respect, including holding of property, durability, and liability.[154] In 1994 the drafters of the Revised Uniform Partnership Act (which has now been adopted in the vast majority of jurisdictions) took the logical step of officially declaring that the partnership was an "entity."[155]

The reason lawmakers refused initially to recognize some entity characteristics outside of corporations is because this recognition was part of the quid pro quo for the regulatory burdens that corporations have to bear. Corporate entity characteristics were first fixed in U.S. law by special legislative acts that endowed corporations with quasi-public functions and monopoly powers. As discussed throughout this chapter, this special privilege idea still underpins the regulatory theory of the corporation. Thus, it is not surprising that America's first great corporate case, *Trustees of Dartmouth College v. Woodward*,[156] bundles the privilege and entity concepts. Chief Justice John Marshall characterized the corporation as an:

> artificial being, invisible, intangible, and existing only in contemplation of law. Being the mere creature of law, it possesses only those properties which the charter of its creation confers upon it, either expressly, or as incidental to its very existence. These are such as are supposed best calculated to effect the object for which it was created.

In other words, it is the "artificial being" aspect of the corporation that exists "only in contemplation of law." Only the state, and not a mere private contract, can create a corporate entity.

The state-creation aspect of the corporate entity implies that the creating state's law must control the creature's internal governance. The entity theory therefore provides a conceptual basis for the *internal affairs* choice-of-law rule that permits a corporation to incorporate in a particular state (such as Delaware) and be sure that Delaware law will be applied wherever the corporation does business or its members are located.[157] This ability to choose the applicable law provides the backbone of jurisdictional competition for corporate law which (as discussed throughout this book) has been critical to the law's development. By contrast, partnerships traditionally are subject to standard choice-of-law rules

---

154. *See* 1 BROMBERG & RIBSTEIN, *supra* note 99, at § 1.03; Robert Hessen, *A New Concept of Corporations: A Contractual and Private Property Model*, 30 HASTINGS L.J. 1327, 1335 (1979).

155. RUPA § 201.

156. 17 U.S. (4 Wheat.) 518, 636 (1819).

157. The special choice-of-law rule for corporate governance is reflected in AMERICAN LAW INSTITUTE, RESTATEMENT (SECOND) OF CONFLICT OF LAWS §§ 304, 307 (1971).

giving courts significant leeway not to apply the law the parties designate in their contract.[158]

As discussed more fully elsewhere, the internal affairs doctrine ("IAD") turns on states' incentives to enforce choice of law, which in turn depends on firms' ability to physically exit nonenforcing states.[159] This reason the states had weaker incentives to enforce choice-of-law provisions for partnerships than for corporations probably has more to do with the courts' concern about containing the spread of limited liability to partnerships than with a conceptual difference between entities and aggregates. Nevertheless, the entity theory probably played at least a marginal role in encouraging states to accept the IAD for corporations.

The notion of the corporation's being a creature of its formation state has played a role in defining the federal and state roles in regulating corporate governance. In *CTS Corp. v. Dynamics Corp. of America*,[160] the Supreme Court held that Indiana's regulation of an interstate tender offer for the shares of an Indiana corporation was not preempted by federal takeover regulation and did not discriminate against interstate commerce under the commerce clause. This sharply contrasts with the Court's earlier decision in *Edgar v. MITE Corp.*,[161] which held that a *non-incorporating* state was barred on these grounds from regulating a national tender offer. The *CTS* Court specifically relied on the internal affairs rule, saying, "[n]o principle of corporation law and practice is more firmly established than a State's authority to regulate domestic corporations, including the authority to define the voting rights of shareholders."[162] The Delaware Supreme Court in turn has cited *CTS* as providing Constitutional authority for the corporate internal affairs choice-of-law rule.[163]

In short, if firms want corporate features such as limited liability they must seek state authorization to be entities. Ironically, the choice-of-law implication of entity status helped trigger state competition, which ended up making corporate advantages more widely available. At the same time (as we will see in Chapter 6), the entity-aggregate distinction could not completely prevent the internal affairs doctrine from spreading to unincorporated firms.

---

158. *See id.* § 187(2) (providing for grounds for not applying the contractually designated law).

159. *See generally*, O'Hara & Ribstein, *supra* note 39, Ch. 6; Larry E. Ribstein & Erin A. O'Hara, *Corporations and the Market for Law*, 2008 Ill. L. Rev. 661.

160. 481 U.S. 69 (1980).

161. 457 U.S. 624 (1982).

162. 481 U.S. at 89.

163. *See* Vantagepoint Venture Partners 1996 v. Examen, Inc., 871 A.2d 1108, 1116 (Del. 2005).

B. COULD PARTNERSHIPS HAVE ADOPTED CORPORATE FEATURES?

We have seen that special corporate characteristics come in two flavors. Some such as limited liability, durability of the entity, and the internal affairs rule clearly are advantages for large firms. Other rules are more of a mixed bag. Fiduciary duties and remedies, shareholder voting rules, and boards of directors are suited to large firms, but aspects of these rules and their mandatory nature are also costs. Corporations therefore must accept constraints as the price of their special advantages.[164]

This raises the question (discussed in this section) of why firms did not attempt to get corporate features through the less-regulated partnership route, as then they would not have had to accept regulation as the quid pro quo for the features they wanted. Indeed, as discussed in the following sections, partnerships long have been able to contract for such corporate-type features, with one critical exception—limited liability.

1. Capital-lock-in: in general

As noted above, an important corporate feature is durability, or what Blair has called "capital lock-in," which lets managers serve long-term corporate goals free from owners' personally motivated liquidation demands.[165] If, as Blair argues, the corporation brought us the Industrial Revolution, this implies we should be wary today about eroding the corporate features that have enabled such success.[166] Chapter 8 discusses the broader policy debate as to the merits of capital lock-in, focusing on the large firm context. This section shows that the lock-in idea, whatever its merits, cannot explain the corporation's dominance.

Understanding capital lock-in requires some unbundling of the concept. In its broadest sense, the term means that the firm rather than the individual members own the firm's property. But we have seen in Chapter 3 that by the time of the rise of the corporation in the nineteenth century, partnership law already had developed the basic idea that the partnership has rights in the firm's property separate from those of its owners. This section more precisely distinguishes property rules involving the rights of third parties claiming through the partners from those involving the partners' rights. The distinction is important because of the greater difficulty of contracting in the third-party scenario. The basic point is that at least from the nineteenth century forward, partnership property rights were safe from third party claims where contracting was difficult and could be contractually protected from claims by partners.

---

164. *See* MICKLETHWAIT & WOOLDRIDGE, *supra* note 134, at 53 (noting that government wants something in return for granting corporate privileges).

165. *See* Blair, *supra* note 133.

166. *See* Larry E. Ribstein, *Should History Lock in Lock-in?*, 41 TULSA L. REV. 525 (2006).

2. Entity shielding

Professors Hansmann, Kraakman, and Squire have identified *entity shielding*, which protects the business entity from the claims of owners' creditors, as a critical function of all business association law.[167] The authors distinguish this from *owner shielding*, or shielding the owners' assets from the claims of the entity's creditors. Entity shielding is of practical importance because complex firms could not exist without it. It would be hard to imagine how a firm could survive if it were vulnerable to being picked to pieces by owners' creditors who lacked any interest in the firm's welfare. The concept is legally important because only business association law creates the relevant legal rights. Non-business association property rules are not concerned with protecting an organization so that it can perform business functions. Conventional contracts can only bind each owner's creditors, not the creditors of owners who do not make these contracts. Not surprisingly in light of its basic importance to all firms, entity shielding is not a distinctive corporate feature. As discussed in Chapter 3, mercantile law had developed similar rights in partnerships by the time the modern corporation came on the scene in the nineteenth century.

3. Partnership breakup

In emphasizing the corporate feature of capital lock-in, Blair is actually focusing on the specific aspect of lock-in that denies individual corporate shareholders the power to compel dissolution of the firm or buyout of their interests. By contrast, as we have seen, the traditional partnership rule lets a single partner cause dissolution at will.

The problem with attributing the corporation's rise to partnership dissolution at will is that partnerships long have had significant continuity despite this rule.[168] Even under the traditional default rules, a partner could not freely dissolve a partnership prior to the expiration of an agreed term.[169] To be sure, on a partner's death the firm may have to wind up and pay off the deceased partner's heir.[170] Blair discusses specific situations illustrating the threat that partners' heirs might rip apart partnerships by claiming against partnership property.[171] But partners' heirs have no direct interest in partnership property[172]—only a right to the deceased partner's share of the partnership.

---

167. *See* Hansmann et al., *supra* note 9.

168. *See, e.g.,* Arthur J. Jacobson, *The Private Use of Public Authority: Sovereignty and Associations in the Common Law*, 29 BUFF. L. REV. 599, 648–51 (1980) (discussing various aspects of partnership law's recognition of the ongoing character of business).

169. *See* 2 BROMBERG & RIBSTEIN, *supra* note 99, at § 7.03(a); JOSEPH STORY, COMMENTARIES ON THE LAW OF PARTNERSHIP §§ 273–276, at 410–20 (2d ed. 1846).

170. *See* UPA §§ 38, 40; RUPA §§ 801, 807.

171. See Blair, *supra* note 133, at 420–23, 442–49, and 452–54.

172. *See* UPA § 25(2)(d); RUPA § 501. At worst, some states historically provided that heirs got legal title if the property was not needed for winding up. *See* 1 BROMBERG & RIBSTEIN, *supra* note 99, § 3.05(f)(1).

Apart from default rules, partners long have been able to agree that they will continue the business after a partner's dissociation by voluntary act or death[173] or to adjust the amount and terms of the buyout. For example, Blair cites two prominent examples of large nineteenth century partnerships, Baldwin Locomotive and Andrew Carnegie's steel company, that managed to draft for sufficient continuity through gradual buyout of exiting and deceased partners.[174] So traditional default rules understate partnership's potential to provide for the continuity that large firms need.

To be sure, default rules matter, as contracting around them may be costly. Firms might find it easier to take rules favoring durability from off the corporate shelf than to customize the partnership form to fit modern firms. But it is unclear this would have been harder than converting the corporation from government's partner to a standard form suitable for purely private firms. Moreover (as discussed in Chapter 7), even the default rules of partnership-type firms came to provide for significant durability. These rules probably were adopted in response to business practices and therefore might have developed much earlier but for the corporate detour.

The main distinction between corporations and partnerships regarding entity shielding is actually a fairly minor one. A partner's creditor, assignee, or heir can petition the court for a judicial dissolution.[175] However, this right exists only if the partnership is not for a term or the term has expired, and therefore can be limited by contract. Moreover, the court can protect the entity and avoid a sacrifice of going concern value by ordering purchase of the petitioner's interest instead of dissolution.

4. Centralized management

Although centralized management is important for large firms and has been traditionally identified with corporations, general partnerships traditionally have been able to contract to confer powers on centralized managers (as provided in the early twentieth century's Uniform Partnership Act).[176] The main management difference between partnerships and corporations is that general partnerships traditionally have found it hard to cut off nonmanagers' power to bind the firm. However, partnership-type firms such as the limited partnership and joint stock company discussed in Chapter 3 did centralize authority in the managers.

---

173. See BROMBERG & RIBSTEIN, § 7.11(e); STORY, *supra* note 169, at § 199, at 306–07 (discussing clauses for continuation notwithstanding partner death in order to be sure that the business is "steadily carried on"); *id.* § 207, at 318–19 (discussing clause providing for purchase of other partner "at a valuation" if "express stipulation").

174. See Blair, *supra* note 133, at 451–54.

175. See UPA § 31(2); RUPA § 801(6).

176. See UPA § 18 (providing that governance rights are "subject to any agreement between [the partners]").

Partnerships also could contract for corporate-type boards. The only difference between corporations and partnerships regarding the board is that (as discussed above) a corporation *must* have one. Chapter 5 discusses how this became a problem for close corporations.

5. Transferability

The default non-transferability of management rights is and always has been an important partnership feature. However, as with centralization of management, partners traditionally have been able to agree to permit full transferability of partnership rights.[177] Indeed, as discussed in Chapter 3, free transferability was a feature of the joint stock company, which developed out of the partnership.

6. Limited liability

Corporate shareholders have only limited liability for their firms' debts. By contrast, partnership creditors can claim against partners' individual assets. Limited liability seems at first glance to be a convincing explanation for the corporation's dominance, as only the corporate form provided for this default rule at the time corporations rose to prominence during the nineteenth century. We have seen how this corporate feature was reinforced by the corporation's entity status. A famous early treatise on the differences between corporations and partnerships captured the importance of limited liability in distinguishing between entities:

> Transferable shares and concentration of the powers of management and a small number of necessary parties in suits are minor advantages of incorporation. But limitation or elimination of liability of the shareholders is not merely the chief single advantage of a business corporation but it is the advantage which in the estimation of legislatures and also in the estimation of the public is of more importance than all the other advantages put together. It is the main thing.[178]

Limited liability is particularly important because, unlike the other corporate features discussed above, partnerships could not easily contract for it without lawmakers' cooperation as they have to include the creditors in these contracts. With many creditors this may be very costly, and with involuntary tort creditors it is impossible. As lawmakers could control access to limited liability, they could exact a quid pro quo for it by channeling limited liability firms into the corporate form and then taxing and regulating corporations. The normative basis for the quid pro quo is unclear. Limited liability could not be considered a subsidy to firms to the extent that creditors adjust their credit charges for the greater risk.

---

177. The partners' power to veto new members provided for in UPA § 18(g) is one of the internal rights that is subject to an agreement to the contrary per the introductory paragraph of that section.

178. *See* WARREN, *supra* note 119, at 399.

Even to the extent that limited liability shifts risks to tort creditors who cannot demand compensation for the additional risk, society arguably gains because investors are attracted to socially productive ventures.[179] However, it is not clear why limited liability firms should "pay" for this social benefit by being subjected to extra constraints on their operations.

Although limited liability is beneficial for large firms, its role in the corporation's initial ascent is not as obvious as it might first appear. To begin with, limited liability was not an urgent matter in the mid-nineteenth century. The corporation rose to prominence prior to the development of enterprise liability,[180] which made limited liability a critical corporate feature. Many early corporate statutes did not grant full-fledged limited liability,[181] but rather retained personal liability until owners had at least minimally capitalized the firm.[182] Even some large firms did not take advantage of limited liability when they could have done so. For example, a prominent financial company, American Express, had vicarious liability until the 1960s. When California finally became the last state to eliminate shareholder liability, the shares of California companies did not react positively.[183]

Limited liability clearly did become important when enterprise liability expanded at the turn of the twentieth century. As discussed in the next section, courts and legislatures could and did refuse to let unincorporated firms adopt corporate-type limited liability. As we will see in Chapter 5, this bar continued until well into the twentieth century. Limited liability accordingly was a significant reason for the rise of the corporation during that century.

C. LIMITED LIABILITY WITHOUT INCORPORATION

This section discusses various contractual mechanisms by which limited liability could have evolved in partnerships. It also shows that the law generally has not been receptive to these contractual approaches to limited liability. There are some policy arguments for these restrictions, including that forcing parties to deal through a formal firm would help clarify the fact of limited liability, the assets against which creditors can make their claims, and the rules protecting creditors from owners' manipulation of those assets. But owners and creditors arguably should be able to choose whether to rely on contractual protections.

---

179. *See* Herbert Hovenkamp, *The Classical Corporation in American Legal Thought*, 76 Geo. L.J. 1593, 1657–58 (1988).

180. *See* John Fabian Witt, *Speedy Fred Taylor and the Ironies of Enterprise Liability*, 103 Colum. L. Rev. 1 (2003) (discussing the history of enterprise liability).

181. *See* Blair, *supra* note 133, at 419.

182. *See* Hovenkamp, *supra* note 179, at 1654–56.

183. Weinstein, *supra* note 130.

Policy aside, lawmakers have incentives to protect their prerogatives to regulate corporate governance by blocking a contractual or partnership end run around incorporation. As we will see, the results of the cases seem to mingle these policy and political elements.

1. Non-recourse contracts

Modern courts enforce partners' contracts with their creditors by requiring the latter to look for payment to the firm's assets and not to the partner individually.[184] Unlike shareholders, partners cannot limit their liability just by publicly recording a limited liability agreement as third parties should not be bound by the public record unless they have some notice of the need to check it.[185] But courts have refused to bind even parties who knew about the limited liability agreement. For example, plaintiffs recovered against a business trust beneficiary though they knew about a publicly recorded trust instrument providing for the beneficiaries' limited liability,[186] and trustees of a business trust were liable for personal injury to an employee though he had expressly agreed to look only to the company's assets for any debts or damages.[187] These cases stressed that business association statutes provided the only route to limited liability. They are best viewed as blocking contractual end runs around the legislature's control over limited liability.

2. Unintentional partnerships

We saw in Chapter 3 that courts prevented parties from participating in firms with rights and powers similar to partners while avoiding partners' liability for the firm's debts. These cases are best understood in the context of the lawmakers' general effort to secure control over limited liability.

3. Undisclosed principals

Even if parties can insulate themselves from liability by getting third parties' agreement to that effect, they cannot do so simply by lurking in the background during the transaction. Supposethat A represents himself to be the owner of a business. T sells goods to A on that basis, but A fails to pay the debt. When T sues A, A reveals that he cannot pay, and that he was actually an agent for P, an undisclosed principal. T can recover from P if the latter authorized T to act for him—and possibly even if he did not.[188]

---

184. *See* Warren, *supra* note 119, at 367.
185. Allegheny Tank Car Co. v. Culbertson, 288 F. 406 (N.D.Tex. 1923).
186. Thompson v. Schmitt, 115 Tex. 53, 274 S.W. 554 (1925).
187. Fisheries Co. v. McCoy 202 S.W. 343 (1918),
188. *See* AMERICAN LAW INSTITUTE, RESTATEMENT (THIRD) OF AGENCY § 2.06 ("an undisclosed principal is subject to liability to a third party who is justifiably induced to make a detrimental change in position by an agent acting on the principal's behalf and without

Watteau v. Fenwick[189] illustrates this rule. Humble had sold his bar at the Victoria Hotel to a brewery, but stayed on as the brewery's manager. Humble's name stayed on the license and the door, but his agreement did not authorize him to bind defendants to the purchase of any goods except bottled ales and mineral waters. A creditor nevertheless was allowed to recover from the defendant for cigars, Bovril, and other articles the creditor sold relying only on Humble's credit.

This result is not straightforward on policy grounds. After all, plaintiff really is dealing just with Humble and relying on Humble's credit. The brewery, for its part, never consented to be bound to the creditor for this transaction. Perhaps plaintiff could argue that he was misled by the appearance (which the brewery helped to create) that Humble was still in business for himself. But should the plaintiff be able to rely on outward appearances without checking the true owner's credit? Whichever argument is most persuasive, it is at least clear that the court is seeking to punish an effort to obtain informally a benefit that only the legislature should be able to dispense.

4. Promoter liability

Suppose P, in organizing a business, contracts on behalf of the business with T, an architect, to draw up plans for the new firm's building. The contract provides that T shall collect solely from a corporation to be formed and not from P. Courts have held in this situation that, although the business eventually formed is liable if it assumes the contract, P is also liable unless T agrees to substitute the business as a party.[190]

As in the undisclosed principal case, T explicitly contracted to recover only from the new corporation. But here T understood exactly who or what he was dealing with—the new corporation was out front rather than undisclosed. So why hold P liable? Perhaps T was silly to agree to perform based on the assurance of payment by a corporation that had not even been created. This could lead the court to demand that the contract be more explicit before T is barred from recovering from the corporation-to-be.[191] On the other hand, we cannot be sure

---

actual authority if the principal, having notice of the agent's conduct and that it might induce others to change their positions, did not take reasonable steps to notify them of the facts."). Randy Barnett, *Squaring Undisclosed Agency Law with Contract Theory*, 75 CAL. L. REV. 1969 (1987); William Draper Lewis, *The Liability of the Undisclosed Principal in Contract*, 9 COLUM. L. REV. 116 (1909); Floyd R. Mechem, *The Liability of an Undisclosed Principal*, 23 HARV. L. REV. 513 (1913).

189. 1 Q.B. 346 (1892).

190. The facts are based on Stanley J. How & Assoc's v. Boss, 222 F.Supp. 936 (S.D.Iowa 1963). *See also*, Quaker Hill v. Parr, 148 Colo. 45, 364 P.2d 1056 (1961); Kessler, *Promoters' Contracts: A Statutory Solution*, 15 RUT. L. REV. 566 (1961).

191. RKO-Stanley Warner Theatres, Inc. v. Graziano, 67 Pa. 220, 355 A.2d 830 (1976) (enforcing an explicit agreement to that effect).

that P and T did not agree to speculate on the ultimate formation of the firm and to take the extra risk into account in negotiating their deal. Thus, the result cannot be fully understood without taking account of the courts' wariness with contractually creating corporate-type limited liability.

5. Corporation by estoppel

Suppose T contracts with P acting on behalf of X Corporation. T actually believes he is dealing with a limited liability firm and not with P individually. However, T does not know that X Corporation has not been officially formed at the time of the contract, though it was formed thereafter. Should the court create what has been called a *corporation by estoppel*—that is, force T to rely on the assets of the corporation he thought all along he was dealing with, and that now in fact exists? This would seem to be a logical result as unlike in the promoter cases, T clearly intended to contract only with a corporation.

Many older cases enforced the parties' likely expectations and applied this estoppel theory.[192] However, corporate statutes reversed the trend of the estoppel cases by holding those "assuming" or "purporting" to act in the name of an unformed corporation to be personally liable to their creditors.[193] Though it may make sense not to force T unwittingly into a contract with a nonexistent party, the rule operates harshly where the contract was entered into during a brief period of corporate noncompliance with statutory formalities.[194]

Lawmakers' rejection of corporation-by-estoppel seems even more clearly than the rules discussed above to be part of lawmakers' effort to protect their incorporation franchise. One court warned that recognizing limited liability in this situation would "threaten[] to undermine the incorporation process, since one then may obtain limited liability by consistently conducting business in the corporate name."[195] A commentator argued that the sole basis of the rule is that limited

---

192. *See* Alexander Hamilton Frey, *Legal Analysis and the "DeFacto" Doctrine*, 100 U. PA. L. REV. 1153 (1952) (finding that courts often refused to impose liability on owners of defective corporations where the parties dealt on a corporate basis, although they often rationalized this result in terms of the "de facto corporation" doctrine).

193. *See, e.g.,* REV. MOD. BUS. CORP. ACT § 2.04 (providing that "[a]ll persons purporting to act as or on behalf of a corporation, knowing there was no incorporation under this Act, are jointly and severally liable for all liabilities created while so acting").

194. *See* T-K Distributors, Inc. v. Soldevere, 704 P.2d 280 (Ariz. App. 1985)(defendants held personally liable for debt incurred during brief period of revocation of charter for failure to file a report and pay a fee, where neither party was aware of the revocation); Thompson & Green Machinery Co., Inc. v. Music City Lumber Co., 683 S.W.2d 340 (Tenn. App. 1984)(both parties believed the company was incorporated, and it was in fact incorporated the day after the promissory note was signed).

195. *See* Cranson v. International Business Machines Corp., 234 Md. 477, 200 A.2d 33 (1964).

liability is a jealously guarded privilege.[196] It is worth noting that the Model Act language is similar to language in the Bubble Act (discussed in Chapter 6), which similarly sought to prevent competition with officially sanctioned firms.

6. Limited tort liability

Even if courts were willing to enforce contracts between firms and their creditors providing for owners' limited liability, this would not protect owners from claims by tort victims. Limited tort liability therefore seems necessarily to be up to legislatures rather than a contractual phenomenon. However, broader recognition of contractual limited liability might have laid a foundation for limited liability in tort cases. If firms' voluntary creditors were willing not to hold owners personally liable, this supports the same result for tort creditors. Paul Mahoney notes that by the time courts started imposing tort liability on firms (around 1700), joint stock companies' charters had created contractual limited liability. At this point the rule of unlimited liability for torts was not inevitable. Mahoney observes:

> It would not have been a radical act for a court to declare, in an appropriate case, that an unincorporated joint-stock company was a separate legal entity, that its charter's declaration of limited liability (if any) was effective against contract creditors, and that the developing principle of respondeat superior was sufficient to give a tort creditor a claim against the assets of a joint-stock company but not its individual owners.[197]

7. Formal noncorporate limited liability firms

As discussed more fully in Chapter 5, state statutes now provide for several types of noncorporate limited liability firms, including limited partnerships, limited liability companies, limited liability partnerships, and business trusts. Indeed, as discussed in Chapter 3, limited partnerships (which offer limited liability to nonmanaging owners) have a history about as old as general partnerships. All of these statutes provide for formation of the firm via a state filing rather than solely by private contract. An evolutionary process driven both by private contracting and jurisdictional competition is gradually breaking down legislative barriers to noncorporate limited liability.

Why couldn't these developments have occurred in the nineteenth century or before and blunted the corporation's rise? In other words, assuming that limited liability was a significant feature of nineteenth-century firms and that it was initially available only to corporations and not to partnerships, why could lawmakers not have recognized limited liability in partnerships rather than turning to the corporation? Given that the law needed to change to accommodate the new firms,

---

196. *See* Calvert Magruder, *Comment*, 40 HARV. L. REV. 733 (1927).
197. *See* Mahoney, *supra* note, at 885.

why did the change come via the newfangled corporation rather than through the time-tested partnership? The partnership would not have had to change radically. Joint stock companies had every corporate feature *except* limited liability. Limited partnerships offered passive capital contributors the same limited liability as corporate shareholders. After all (as noted above), undisclosed agency and silent or unintentional partnerships could alone have taken the courts most of the way. This development would have hastened the rise of the uncorporation, which as we will see ended up happening at the end of the twentieth century.

One possible answer is that there were inherent problems with adding limited liability to noncorporate business forms. For example, Lamoreaux argues that limited partners could dissolve limited partnerships (thus sticking the general partners with responsibility for outside claims), while limited partners would have priority over general partners as to the return of their contributions.[198] However, these rights among the partners easily could be adjusted by contract and reflected in the standard form to accommodate the addition of limited liability. Indeed, limited partners today do not have the power to unilaterally dissolve the firm.

As discussed more fully in the next section, creating statutory noncorporate limited liability may have been impeded in the United States by the logistical problems with starting a new standard form imposed by a federal system and the common law. The internal affairs choice-of-law rule would save corporations from being subject to multiple laws.

However, as discussed above, uncorporations did not have the advantage of this rule. Chapter 6 shows how unincorporated limited liability firms finally arose in the United States because of state competition prodded by private contracting. State and federal lawmakers no longer could bottle up "corporate" features in the corporate form. Chapter 8 indicates that the main constraint on partnership governance for large firms is a tax rule based on tradability of shares rather than choice of business form. In the United Kingdom (as discussed below), regulation long has been based on number of owners rather than the form of organization. These developments indicate that regulation based on statutory standard forms is unstable. Government eventually must focus on firms' basic characteristics or activities rather than their choice of form. This is one of the factors spurring the rise of the uncorporation.

D. THE CORPORATION AND THE REGULATION OF GOVERNANCE

The above discussion shows that the rise of the corporation was not as necessary or inevitable an aspect of the Industrial Revolution as some commentators

---

198. *See* Naomi Lamoreaux, *Partnerships, Corporations, and the Theory of the Firm,* 88 AM. ECON. REV. 66, 68–69 (1998).

have suggested. The flexible partnership was at least an equally logical basis for the development of new business forms suitable for large firms. The corporation is best explained, not as *enabling* large firms, but as a way to *regulate* them. This section discusses why lawmakers sought to regulate corporate governance, and how the U.S. common law/federal system helped lawmakers channel large firms into the corporate form and away from alternative business entities. In light of the discussion so far in this chapter, it should not be surprising that both explanations focus on the one corporate feature that requires government involvement: shareholders' limited liability.

1. Why regulate corporate governance?

There are both policy and political explanations for the regulation of corporate governance. From a policy standpoint, there is arguably some justification for regulating firms whose owners are insulated by limited liability from direct responsibility for corporate conduct. Regulation or liability can tame firms' perverse incentives to impose harms on society. By reducing firms' profits and stock prices, regulation or liability directs resources to socially productive firms. But limited liability also sets a floor on owners' responsibility and distorts allocation of resources by letting owners ignore risks that can reduce the firm's value below zero.[199] This *moral hazard* problem arguably justifies special regulation of limited liability firms.

There are, however, problems with the moral hazard argument for regulation. On policy grounds, although limiting liability for torts may encourage socially productive business activities, restricting the activities of limited liability firms may discourage these activities. It is not easy for regulators to figure out precisely where to draw the line.

As a practical matter, even if some regulation of limited liability firms is appropriate, the regulation that has been applied to corporate governance is unlikely to effectively deal with moral hazard. Some regulation might work, such as restricting the activities of limited liability firms, requiring firms to maintain minimum capital or insurance, or assessing penalties on owners short of joint and several liability. Indeed, lawmakers have tried all of these approaches. But recall that corporations received an important advantage that helped free them from these constraints—the *internal affairs* choice-of-law rule. As noted above,[200] corporations might have gotten this advantage only because of a concern that applying the rule to uncorporations would lead to limited liability there as well. But the distinction did creditors little good. As long as corporate managers and the shareholders they answered to could choose the applicable governance rules,

---

199. The bankruptcy "fresh start" lets owners of all firms ignore risks that would reduce their wealth below zero. However, the discussion concerns choice of form, and therefore focuses on differences between corporations and partnerships.

200. *See supra* text accompanying note 159.

they could be sure to avoid rules that impinged too sharply on them. In other words, when imported into the choice-of-law rule, the very "entity" characterization that backed up limited tort liability undercut efforts to regulate firms that adopt this feature.

The laws constraining corporate governance that have survived jurisdictional competition impose features such as the board of directors and fiduciary duties that today mainly are intended to protect shareholders from managers or each other.[201] Even if these features are supposed to protect shareholders, as discussed below in Chapter 8 they are increasingly inefficient for many large firms. They have, however, been insulated somewhat from erosion by the systemic features discussed in the next subsection and the effects of the federal corporate tax (discussed in Chapter 8).

A second explanation for regulating governance is that lawmakers can earn political favors by making or blocking changes in general incorporation statutes as they did in early corporate history by selling special charters. Firms' ability to get corporate features such as limited liability conferred special advantages on companies for which they were willing to pay legislators. Legislators also can control tax burdens and benefits.

Third, lawmakers see firms as competitors for power. Paul Mahoney has described regulation of the corporation and blocking alternatives to incorporation as "part and parcel of the governmental unease with unfettered enterprise."[202] The success of lawmakers' general regulatory agenda depends to some extent on the intensity of corporate opposition. Corporations can be tamed not only by regulating their conduct and muting their political activities[203] but by adjusting their governance—for example, by including multiple constituencies on the corporate board and empowering social activist shareholders. Although it is not clear how effective these regulations have been,[204] this at least explains some attempts to regulate corporate governance.

2. How do lawmakers regulate governance?

Lawmakers' ability to regulate firms' governance depends on the systemic considerations discussed in Chapter 2: courts and the federal system. To begin with,

---

201. To some extent, as discussed above in this chapter, these rules (particularly those requiring a board of directors) may have been originally intended to force or permit governance in the interests of non-shareholder constituencies. However, the rules do not actually operate so as to fundamentally diverge from shareholder interests, taking into account managers' and directors' necessarily broad discretion to run the firm. *See* Larry E. Ribstein, *Accountability and Responsibility in Corporate Governance*, 81 N. D. L. REV. 1431 (2006).

202. *See* Mahoney, *supra* note 153, at 893.

203. *See* Larry E. Ribstein, *Corporate Political Speech*, 49 WASH. & LEE L. REV. 109 (1992).

204. *See supra* note 201.

flexibility is inherent in the contractual nature of governance. To regulate governance, lawmakers have to block contractual alternatives, particularly modifications of partnership to produce corporate equivalents. This is difficult because parties can combine and vary governance terms in innumerable ways to achieve regulatory arbitrage—that is, to avoid regulation through an unregulated alternative that has similar economic consequences. In particular, the parties can contractually vary the existing partnership, limited partnership, and corporate standard forms in ways that both loosen the shackles of the corporate form and introduce limited liability to the partnership.

A U.S.-style legal system enhances the flexibility inherent in contracting for governance. The common law gives judges significant discretion in applying legal rules. If a ruling blocks socially efficient contracts, the parties can keep litigating this issue in a variety of scenarios and with different contract terms until the courts ultimately authorize a close equivalent. The U.S. federal system also provides a potential exit from regulation. If a jurisdiction decides to impose an inflexible mandatory rule, firms can try to contract for the law of a more flexible jurisdiction—and to physically move if their local court refuses to enforce the contract.

On the other hand, common law and federal systems can inhibit flexibility. Parties may be reluctant to try new types of contracts or business associations that have not yet attracted a body of precedents that assures the parties that courts will sensibly enforce and interpret the arrangements. The common law arguably impedes new business forms.[205] Firms crave the certainty and predictability that only legislatures can bestow on private contracting.[206]

Firms might be able to cut through the chaos of the common law and multiple jurisdictions by contracting for a single jurisdiction's law. As we have seen, this has powerfully constrained the regulation of corporate governance. However, the corporation is protected from competition with noncorporate contracts, which traditionally have not been subject to the internal affairs rule. The enforceability of such contracts therefore depends on the judgments of all the courts that might have jurisdiction, which may be all of the courts of the states in which a firm does business or in which its owners reside.

Consider an illustration of the quandary multiple jurisdictions create for firms. Suppose a firm does business and has owners in ten states. Nine of these states allow the firm to organize as a limited liability association, but one insists on characterizing the firm as a general partnership even if it is recognized as a limited liability firm in the other nine. In this situation, it might be too risky for

---

205. *See* Timothy W. Guinnane et al., *Ownership and Control in the Entrepreneurial Firm: An International History of Private Limited Companies* (Dec. 2007), Yale University Economic Growth Center Discussion Paper No. 959, http://ssrn.com/abstract=1071007.

206. *See* J. WILLARD HURST, THE LEGITIMACY OF THE BUSINESS CORPORATION IN THE LAWS OF THE UNITED STATES, 1780–1970, at 116–18 (1973).

the firm to try for limited liability unless it can avoid the holdout state at reasonable cost. Even worse, there is a sort of chicken-and-egg problem in that states may not even bother passing a statute that firms will not use because they are not protected in the other states.

The common law adds further complications. The affected parties can contract for the corporate-specific features discussed above other than limited liability, including centralized management, transfer of management rights, owners' power to unilaterally dissolve, and fiduciary duties. The partners could litigate restrictions on these contracts until courts eroded them. Their success may vary depending on the type of restrictions. Although courts might not be very receptive to parties trying to disavow their own express agreements, they likely would find it hard to uphold firms' variations on limited liability against tort victims who were not even parties to the agreement. Even in contract cases involving undisclosed principals or unintentional partners, there may be no explicit creditor agreement. For example, in the promoter contract cases, it is not clear the creditor is agreeing to a contract in which there is no present obligor.

Limited partnerships provide a specific example of the problems of revising the partnership form in a common law federal system. As we have seen in Chapter 3, limited partnerships achieved some recognition after they were introduced in the early nineteenth century even though it was against a strong headwind of state resistance. The states enforced statutory requirements regarding formation and limited partner participation in control. These restrictions were finally overcome by the original Uniform Limited Partnership Act promulgated in 1916 and an important Supreme Court case applying this law.[207] This official statutory change encouraged formation of limited partnerships, which gave rise to case law, which in turn encouraged still more firms. But until the legislatures signaled their tolerance of the limited partnership, the courts were not receptive.

The limited partnership association had less success than the limited partnership. This statutory form took a step beyond the limited partnership in limiting the liability of managing as well as passive members.[208] However (as discussed in Chapter 3), the form never caught on. For example, Pennsylvania courts more strictly enforced accuracy requirements in registration documents for partnership associations than for corporations, revoking the liability shield in the former type of firms even for slight mistakes.[209] The courts evidently were uneasy with this new, noncorporate form of limited liability.

These examples illustrate the difficulties of getting new rules on limited liability accepted by lawmakers and courts in a common law federal system.

---

207. Giles v. Vette, 263 U.S. 553 (1924).
208. *See* Timothy Guinnane et al., *Putting the Corporation in its Place* (2007), NBER Working Paper 13109, http://www.nber.org/papers/w13109 (summarizing this history).
209. *Id.* at notes 79–80.

These difficulties enhance lawmakers' leverage in restricting partnership alternatives to the regulated corporate form. The rights that legislatures establish through corporate law (particularly limited liability to tort creditors) are like property rights that need to be established by laws because they cannot be cheaply contracted for. Lawmakers allocate in ways that benefit themselves and interest groups. Moreover, legislators and judges restrict private contract so as to enhance the value of state-created property rights.[210]

We will see in Chapter 6 that contracts and jurisdictional competition eventually broke down barriers to the uncorporation in the late twentieth century, but not before the corporate form had dominated for almost a hundred years.

E. INTERNATIONAL COMPARISONS

The above discussion focuses on the United States. However, to what extent are these developments the product of unique U.S. circumstances, including the country's particular history and common law and federal systems? We can get some insights by looking at UK, European, and Latin American developments.

1. The United Kingdom

The United Kingdom has taken a markedly different turn from the United States.[211] In the early eighteenth century, the South Sea Company was formed in 1711 as a chartered company (a type of quasi-public corporation) to trade with South America. A few years after the company's formation, a new need arose as the country had borrowed heavily to finance its war with Spain, increasing the national debt from five to fifty million pounds. When the war ended, interest rates dropped but the debt was non-redeemable. So the hard-pressed nation came up with a plan to allow public creditors to convert their bonds into South Sea Company tradable shares. The company would use the cash to pay off the debt, borrow at a lower interest rate, and leave the former bondholders as shareholders in the South American trade. The financing and peacetime economy triggered a stock market boom in which many smaller non-chartered companies tried to participate. This set off a wave of speculation, sopped up funding that otherwise would have gone to the South Sea Company (and eventually to the government), and generally eroded chartered companies' special privileges.

---

210. The author is indebted to Henry Manne for the property rights analogy. Another application of this point is family law, in which lawmakers restrict nonmarital sexual relationships in order to privilege marriage.

211. *See generally*, HARRIS, *supra* note 29 (discussing the history and development of modern business forms in the United Kingdom).

The government responded to the influx of these so-called "bubble" companies in 1720 with what has become known as the Bubble Act, which provided in part:

> [A]ll . . . publick undertakings . . . presuming to act as a corporate body . . . raising . . . transferable stock . . . transferring . . . shares in such stock . . . without legal authority, . . . and all acting . . . under any charter . . . for raising a capital stock . . . not intended . . . by such charter . . . and all acting . . . under any obsolete charter . . . for ever be deemed to be illegal and void. . . ."[212]

UK lawmakers thereby cut off private competition with the government for capital and the private threat to Parliament's power to dole out corporate privileges.[213] This is a direct example of lawmakers protecting their power to regulate business forms by blocking nonregulated alternatives. The Bubble Act, the lack of any general incorporation law, and the consequent high costs of the special privilege of incorporation throttled the British economy for more than a century until Britain adopted the equivalent of a general incorporation law in 1844.

Changing business conditions, including the growth of the share markets[214] and increased need for limited liability,[215] ultimately increased the demand for incorporation. Also, litigation involving joint stock companies during the first half of the nineteenth century in England eroded regulation of incorporation. These developments encouraged Parliament to adopt a general incorporation law in 1844.

Although the United Kingdom was similar to the United States in its initial protection of the corporate form, the eventual role of business conditions, and the common law in eroding regulatory protection of the corporation, the two countries differ regarding the roles of corporate and unincorporated business associations. The United Kingdom never obsessed over the difference between corporations and partnerships as did U.S. lawmakers. The U.S. law of business associations developed on its own from a time when there was no developed concept of private corporate law in the United Kingdom. The U.S. notion of private corporate law was linked to the traditional quasi-public concept of the corporation while UK law was based on the partnership-derived joint stock company.

This general difference between the United States and the United Kingdom is evident in several ways. First, the governance of large private firms in the United Kingdom until the early eighteenth century focused on noncorporate

---

212. 6 Geo. 1, ch. 18 (1720).
213. *See* Henry N. Butler, *General Incorporation in Nineteenth Century England: Interaction of Common Law and Legislative Processes*, 6 INT'L. REV. L. & ECON. 169, 172–73 (1986); HARRIS, *supra* note 29, at 64–79.
214. *Id.* at 119–20.
215. *Id.* at 128–30.

firms, namely joint stock companies. Although some of these firms were chartered, the basic form was derived from the joint stock company rather than it having a distinct corporate form as in the United States.

Second, it is not surprising in light of this history that the Bubble Act targeted transferability which, as discussed above, is available to partnerships as well as corporations. Indeed (as discussed in Chapter 3), transferability is a feature of the joint stock company that is derived from partnership. Although limited liability ultimately became associated with incorporated firms, it was not firmly established as a feature of incorporation until eleven years after the UK general incorporation law—the Limited Liability Act of 1855.[216]

Third, even after the Bubble Act, joint stock companies remained an important structure for large firms. Thus, the important distinction in the United Kingdom continued to be between chartered and non-chartered joint stock companies rather than between the distinct categories of corporation and partnership. By contrast, in the United States special charters were never as important as in the United Kingdom for granting monopoly status, perhaps because state competition whittled away state prerogatives in this respect. Thus, there was less need to develop the joint stock company alternative to incorporation.[217]

Fourth, the traditional partnership form was never viable as a potential framework for large firms in the United Kingdom because litigation within the firm had to be handled in chancery, "a place to be avoided if at all possible"[218] as any reader of *Bleak House* knows.

Fifth, the widespread use of the joint stock company made less necessary the adoption of the limited partnership form, which was discussed and rejected in favor of a general corporation law. Another factor in the United Kingdom's belated acceptance of the limited partnership may have been greater hostility in that country than in the United States to forms based on civil law. Accordingly, while the first limited partnership law was adopted in the United States in 1822, the United Kingdom did not officially recognize the limited partnership until 1907.[219]

Sixth, and perhaps most importantly, when general incorporation did come to the United Kingdom in 1844, it was accompanied by a general regulation of governance not tied to specific business forms. All firms with more than twenty-five owners (regardless of specific form) had to register and disclose.[220] The key

---

216. See L.C.B. Gower, *Some Contrasts Between British and American Corporation Law*, 69 HARV. L. REV. 1369, 1371 (1956).

217. *Id.* at 1372.

218. *See* HARRIS, *supra* note 29, at 164.

219. *See* Ron Harris, *Law, Finance and the First Corporations*, in GLOBAL PERSPECTIVES ON THE RULE OF LAW (James J. Heckman et al., eds., 2009) (noting that the United Kingdom developed the joint stock company to substitute for the continental limited partnership).

220. *See* HARRIS, *supra* note 29, at 283–84.

distinction in the United Kingdom, therefore, was between large and small firms rather than as in the United States between corporations and uncorporations. In the United Kingdom, the partnership has been by legislation confined to its classic version discussed in Chapter 3—the very small firm.

This history has significant implications for modern business associations in the United States and the United Kingdom. Gower notes that the English business corporation "evolved from the incorporated partnership, based on mutual agreement, rather than from the corporation, based on a grant from the state, and owes more to partnership principles than to rules based on corporate personality."[221] This has contributed to the default nature of British company law, pursuant to which (as in partnerships) the statute explicitly applies only to the extent the agreement does not provide to the contrary except in specified situations.[222] There is no comparable provision in modern U.S. corporation law.[223]

2. European and Latin American developments

Europe also presents a contrast with the United States regarding the roles of corporation and unincorporated firms. France and Germany long have had popular private limited liability company alternatives to incorporation (including the Belgian and French SARL and the German GMBH) that offer limited liability and flexible rules regarding dissolution.

Some commentators have stressed these forms' superiority to the corporation (such as their offering protection to minority shareholders), and have argued that this tends to rebut the so-called "law and finance" position that common law systems are more conducive to business development than civil law systems.[224] But these commentators do not clarify why a civil law system might have offered more suitable business associations than a common law system. Although as they argue, the common law system can resist change, as discussed above it also can provide opportunities for experimentation. Meanwhile, a civil law system relies on legislatures, which as we have seen have incentives to resist contractual alternatives to regulation.

The assumption that Europe has produced better business associations is also questionable. Although European unincorporated firms are more flexible than U.S. and UK corporations, European business governance is overall more regulated than in the United States.[225] In any event, we will see in Chapter 6 that the

---

221. *See* Gower, *supra* note 216, at 1371–72.
222. *See id.* at 1376.
223. *See* William J. Carney, *Limited Liability Companies: Origins and Antecedents*, 66 U. COLO. L. REV. 855, 871–72 (1995).
224. *See* Guinnane et al., *supra* note 42.
225. *See* Carney, *supra* note 124, at 862–67.

flexibility of the U.S. common law and federal systems ultimately prevailed, while Europe has been slower to offer a comparable choice of business forms.

With respect to the comparison with the United Kingdom, the above discussion shows that the governance of even large British firms is based on the contractual partnership model, and that regulation is generally by disclosure rather than by restrictions on capitalization or governance terms. Indeed, as discussed in Chapter 6, the introduction of an equivalent to the "internal affairs" choice of law rules in Europe enabled the United Kingdom to undermine some European regulation, particularly minimum capitalization requirements. As with the U.S. comparison, the increased importance of intermediate business forms in Europe is more likely attributable to greater overall regulation of business governance in Europe than to greater flexibility.

More generally, the regulatory version of the corporation (which has played such an important role in U.S. business association law) has been much less dominant in both the United Kingdom and Europe. In this sense, the dialectic between the corporation and the uncorporation that plays throughout this book appears to be mainly a U.S. phenomenon. Apart from the efficiency of these various systems, this dialectic at least has caused business history to follow a different course in the United States than elsewhere in the world. Had the United States not found the corporation in the nineteenth century, large firms might have followed the British path and relied on the contractual partnership model. But this does not mean that nineteenth century industrial firms would have been big versions of early partnerships. Rather, the United States might have moved earlier toward the modern uncorporation discussed below in Chapters 6 through 8 that has emerged in the last twenty years.

5. THE PROBLEMS OF THE CLOSE CORPORATION

We saw in Chapter 4 that the corporate form rose in popularity in the nineteenth century to accommodate the large firms that drove the Industrial Revolution. This development is supported by the superficial logic that the durable, centrally managed corporate entity is better suited to large firms than the more intimate and transient partnership.

However, as we probe more deeply, it is not clear why large firms did not take the alternative path of adapting to their needs the standard partnership form or partnership variants such as the joint stock company and limited partnership. The corporation was not the inevitable choice for these firms because of its origin as an arm of the state. In fact, the corporation's dominance may have less to do with its inherent advantages than with lawmakers' incentives and ability to use the corporation as a basis for regulating governance.

This chapter carries the story into the closely held firm, where the mystery posed in the last chapter deepens. Although the corporate form was at least a plausible choice for large firms, it seems illogical for closely held firms as they do not need such features as a board of directors or freely transferable shares. The corporate form not only has the wrong default rules for closely held firms, but makes it too hard for those firms to change the rules. As discussed in Chapter 4, U.S. corporations were historically regarded as concessions or privileges granted by the state. Even after states adopted general corporation laws that freed parties from having to pay the legislature for special charters, the terms of incorporation remained subject to state control and limitations.

The plight of closely held firms in the United States illustrates the implications of the corporate-partnership divide in that country and points up the distinction between UK and U.S. law discussed in Chapter 4. U.S. firms were stuck in a corporate trap that UK firms managed to avoid by skipping over the corporate form and relying on the partnership-based joint stock company. Because UK firms were not regulated through the corporate form, lawmakers did not need to channel firms away from partnership. Rather, all firms were subject mainly to default rules and to disclosure regulation based on the number of owners.

Despite the corporation's unsuitability for closely held firms, by the mid-twentieth century the corporate form dominated in this arena as well as for large firms. In both contexts, the government used its power over limited liability to limit its availability to corporations. Closely held firms' widespread use of the corporate form indicates that the benefits of limited liability outweighed firms' costs of having to accept the other aspects of the corporate form along with it.

This chapter shows that the story of the close corporation is characterized by firms' search for an organizational form combining corporate-type limited liability with other partnership features. The close corporation instead offered the *incorporated partnership*, which had the significant drawback of forcing partnership-type firms to accept or contract around corporate default rules as the price of limited liability.

Contracts and jurisdictional competition eventually eroded regulation of the governance of closely held firms to the point that these firms eventually could fully contract for partnership features. But even then they were stuck inside of the corporation. It took the LLC Revolution (discussed in Chapter 6) to enable closely held firms to escape into a form of their own.

A. LIMITED LIABILITY AND THE CLOSELY HELD FIRM

The last two chapters show that the partnership and corporation are well designed for closely held and publicly held firms, respectively. Both types of firms want limited liability, but there are also significant differences between the two contexts in this respect. The benefits of limited liability clearly outweigh the costs for publicly held firms. Limited liability facilitates passive investment and trading of shares, two of large firms' most important features. Also, publicly held firms seek the corporate form so that they can assemble large amounts of capital and lock up it up for an indefinite period.

Limited liability also potentially involves somewhat higher credit costs for close corporations than for publicly held firms. A smaller capital cushion increases the importance of owners' liability for debts. Creditors have more difficulty getting information about closely held firms whose shares do not trade in a public market. As small firm owners often rely on their businesses for income, they may want to take earnings or even capital investments out of the firm. The potential that a closely held firm's assets could flow into the owners' pockets at any time makes reliance on these assets particularly hazardous. Creditors also get little comfort from closely held firms' management structure. The managers are either the owners themselves or are closely controlled by the owners. The firm's managers therefore are much more likely to favor the owners' interests if the firm is closely held than if it is publicly held. That becomes a concern when the owners have limited liability—and therefore a temptation to leave too little money in the firm for its creditors. By contrast, publicly held firms' professional managers may be and act more like employees or creditors than owners.

Even if limited liability is riskier for creditors of closely held firms, it does not necessarily follow that it should be unavailable in this context. Contract creditors can charge the firm for the extra risk or get the protection of personal owner guarantees. The owners are not completely off the hook for tort liability as heavy tort risks can make contract liability more costly. Also, voluntary creditors might insist that the firm insure—and insurers can charge according to the firm's safety practices and whether it has limited liability.

Limited liability presents the biggest problems in the smallest firms, which may want it only because they have mostly tort creditors who cannot adjust their credit charges or terms. As small firms became increasingly responsible for harms attributable to their activities in the twentieth century, they had strong incentives to seek shelter from vicarious liability.

The logical way to meet small firms' rising demand for limited liability was to develop a limited liability form of partnership. However, government sought to confine limited liability to the corporate form where it could be more conveniently taxed and regulated. The challenge was to figure out a way to pound the square peg of the closely held firm into the round corporate hole.

B. LOCK-IN

The most important corporate feature for closely held firms other than limited liability is likely to be durability—that is, a member's inability to unilaterally trigger dissolution or buyout. As discussed in Chapter 3, an opportunistic partner could effectively appropriate much of the value of the business by dissolving it and forcing a sale, as with the laundry brothers in *Page v. Page*. The corporate form prevents this by requiring the owners to agree to any termination of the business.

Durability is not, however, a panacea for the very closely held firm because it can help controlling owners and managers treat locked-in owners opportunistically. Thus, closely held firms have to balance the costs of allowing owners to leave against those of forcing them to stay.[226] So although the continuity of the corporate entity is generally seen as a reason for incorporation, it may be more a cost than a benefit for at least some closely held firms.

Closely held firms theoretically can contract for their desired amount of continuity. However, the default rules of the standard form are particularly important regarding durability because the costs of negotiating and drafting these rules may be high in relation to the amount of capital. The parties may

---

226. It has been argued that durability of the firm was such an important feature that closely held firms chose to incorporate in the nineteenth and early twentieth centuries despite the greater risk of minority shareholder oppression. *See* Naomi R. Lamoreaux & Jean-Laurent Rosenthal, *Corporate Governance and the Plight of Minority Shareholders in the United States Before the Great Depression* (NBER Working Paper No. W10900, 2004), at 14, http://papers.ssrn.com/paper.taf?abstract_id=618582. However, as discussed below, the trade-off might actually have been between lack of durability and limited liability. For an analysis of the tradeoffs inherent in partnership exit provisions, see Larry E. Ribstein, *A Statutory Approach to Partner Dissociation*, 65 WASH. U. L.Q. 357 (1987).

have a hard time foreseeing whether and how their relationship might break down and what rules they would need to govern a smoothly functioning relationship. Also, the specific mechanisms for dealing with breakdown can be quite complex.

Partnership offers critical advantages over the corporate form for closely held firms seeking to balance the costs and benefits of durability. First, the partnership statute has a nuanced set of default rules that suit a variety of circumstances. For example, in the absence of a contrary agreement, partners can compel liquidation only if the firm is not for an unexpired agreed term or undertaking. Agreeing to a term or undertaking indicates that the partners expect significant costs if the firm breaks up before the expiration of the term or undertaking. (Like abandoning a cake before it is baked, all the preparation and ingredients will be wasted.) A partner therefore may be able to extract concessions from his copartners by threatening to leave before the firm is "out of the oven." It also matters under partnership default rules whether a partner is leaving voluntarily or because of death, disability, or bankruptcy (situations where there is little concern that the leaving partner is acting opportunistically).[227]

Second, even firms that wanted more or less durability than what was provided for under default partnership rules would still be better off as partnerships because they could contract for the precise rules they needed. However, they did not get a similar level of flexibility from the corporate form because (as discussed below) close corporations had to contend with entrenched corporate norms.

In short, closely held firms had to decide whether they wanted partnership default rules and flexibility on dissolution more than they wanted limited liability.

C. OTHER CORPORATE RULES

Closely held firms want corporate features other than lock-in and limited liability. For example, many small firms delegate management power to a subset of owners or to non-owner professional managers. They also may choose corporate-style owner voting by financial contribution rather than per capita, and decide even important matters by majority vote. Even firms that want corporate-type rules may not want the specific version of these rules that corporate statutes provide. For example, firms with centralized management might not want to bother with a board of directors or require formal shareholder meetings. In any event, it should be easy for closely held firms that are big enough to want corporate-type governance to contract for the precise rules they desire.

---

227. *See* Larry E. Ribstein, *Statutory Forms for Closely Held Firms: Theories and Evidence from LLCs*, 73 WASH. U. L.Q. 369, 395–401 (1995) (discussing these and other nuances in dissolution rules).

D. THE CORPORATE TAX: THE PRICE OF LIMITED LIABILITY

Government can influence firms' choice of form by determining the tax consequences of organizing in particular forms, particularly including the corporate income tax and the shareholder level tax on corporate dividends. As a corporation is essentially an artificial entity that stands in for the shareholders, this amounts to a *double* tax on the shareholders. A firm's willingness to incur this tax depends on the benefits of being incorporated. In other words, the extra tax is in a sense a fee for incorporating.

The impact of the corporate tax depends on various factors, including the tax rates for corporate income, personal income, and the capital gains shareholders realize when they sell their shares, as well as the corporation's tax deductions (including salaries to shareholder-owners).[228] If the personal tax rate is high, the corporate and capital gains rates are low, and the corporation can deduct amounts distributed to shareholders as wages and interest, individuals might want to let corporate income accumulate in the firm—and then in effect cash in on it by selling their stock. The corporate tax's impact also depends on whether firms have business incentives to retain earnings. The corporate form may enable growing firms to *shelter* their retained earnings from the shareholder-level tax on distributions. However, this will not work for the many closely held firms that are essentially vehicles for the owners to earn a living.

The impact of the double corporate tax on closely held firms was muted during the first half of the twentieth century when the closely held corporation rose to prominence. Personal income tax rates were higher than corporate tax rates, and the corporation could take some deductions for employee benefits that were not available to unincorporated firms. Thus, closely held firms could incorporate; take income out as deductible wages, interest, and rent; and shelter much of the rest in the corporation. Ironically, the corporate tax was advantageous for personal service firms, which would seem to be the classic partnerships. Conversely, partnership tax worked for some passive investment firms whose owners used depreciation rules to create tax losses that sheltered income earned in other activities.

The benefits and burdens of the corporate tax raise the question of what *corporate* features trigger the tax. After all, both the corporation and the partnership are merely standard forms under state law that parties have significant leeway to alter contractually. The federal government therefore had the daunting task of determining precisely which of the myriad variations provided for or

---

228. *See* John W. Lee, *A Populist Political Perspective of the Business Tax Entities Universe: "Hey the Stars Might Lie but the Numbers Never Do"*, 78 TEX. L. REV. 885, 921–22 (2000); Larry E. Ribstein & Bruce H. Kobayashi, *Choice of Form and Network Externalities*, 43 WM. & MARY L. REV. 79 (2001); Leandra Lederman, *The Entrepreneurship Effect: An Accidental Externality in the Federal Income Tax*, 65 OHIO ST. L.J. 1401, 1430–33 (2004).

authorized by state law got corporate tax treatment. The federal government might have approached this task in the simplest way by taxing only firms that were corporations under state law. However, this effectively would have left the determination in the hands of state legislators who had more reason to make their laws attractive for tax purposes than to care about the effect of these laws on federal revenues.

Congress applied the corporate tax to associations.[229] Treasury clarified that it was not relying on state-created categories by defining *association* in terms of what it deemed to be entity characteristics, including continuity of existence, centralized management, and limited liability. The Supreme Court held that a trust with these characteristics passed a "corporate resemblance" test for purposes of applying the corporate tax.[230] A federal appeals court in *Kintner v. United States*[231] applied these factors against the government in holding that a medical association was a corporation for purposes of getting a deduction for an employee benefit plan. The Treasury then passed the so-called Kintner Regulations.[232] This rule tweaked the definition with a slightly different set of factors that added free transferability to the above list and declared that firms needed more than half of these four main characteristics to be a tax corporation.

It has never been clear why the Kintner characteristics should define a tax corporation,[233] but for about thirty years, the Kintner test effectively emphasized limited liability. Indeed (as detailed in Chapter 6), the rules did not let a firm be taxed like a partnership if all members had limited liability (a limited partnership was taxed as a partnership because it had a general partner that had vicarious liability). Thus, the tax classification rules effectively forced firms to pay a tax to the federal government for complete limited liability. Firms would gain little from lobbying states to add limited liability to the partnership form because this would make them partnerships only for state and not federal tax purposes.

There are at least two reasons for focusing on limited liability as the basis of the corporate tax. First (as discussed in Chapter 3), there is a political explanation: limited liability gives government leverage in taxing as well as regulating because it is the feature firms have the most difficulty replicating contractually. In other words, firms' demand for limited liability enabled government to charge for it.

Second, imposition of a second-level tax on distributions in limited liability firms makes some sense from a policy standpoint. As discussed above, depending

---

229. See IRC § 7701(a)(3) ("[T]he term 'corporation' includes associations. . . ."); *id.* § 7701(a)(2) (definition of "partnership").

230. See Morrissey v. Comm'r, 296 U.S. 344 (1935).

231. 216 F. 1d 418 (9th Cir. 1954).

232. Treas. Reg. § 301.7701-2(a) (1996).

233. For a discussion of various potential theories, see Larry E. Ribstein, *The Deregulation of Limited Liability and the Death of Partnership*, 70 WASH. U. L.Q. 417 (1992).

on tax rates, the tax may encourage firms to retain earnings. Conversely, partnership taxation encourages firms to distribute earnings so that owners do not have to pay tax on earnings they do not receive. However, distributions leave creditors of limited liability firms more vulnerable to the risk the film will fail. The ultimate policy question turns on a variety of factors, including the costs of forcing closely held firms to accept corporate default rules. But the existence of a policy justification for the tax scheme helped prop up this increasingly awkward tax classification system.

Although the corporate tax is imposed on firms regardless of the business association form they choose, it is related to this choice of business form. Other things being equal, the corporate tax is necessarily more costly if the firm does not plan to retain earnings and thereby benefit from the "inside" tax shelter. Conversely, if the firm is going to retain earnings, it would want the more durable corporate form. So a firm that is taxed like a corporation has an incentive to adopt corporate features.

Tax reform in the 1980s abruptly changed the political equilibrium by increasing firms' demand to escape the corporate tax. At the same time, the expansion of tort liability was making vicarious liability a less desirable choice. Firms therefore had a significant incentive to ask state legislatures to manipulate state business association laws to test the margins of the Kintner regulation. As discussed in Chapter 6, this eventually caused the government to abandon the tax on limited liability and adopt a "check-the-box" rule that allowed even firms with corporate features to opt for partnership taxation as long as the firm did not have freely tradable interests. This was an important step away from the government's protection of the corporate form and toward the rise of the uncorporation.

E. OTHER ROADBLOCKS TO PARTNERSHIPS WITH LIMITED LIABILITY

As discussed in Chapter 4, transaction costs and the lawmaking process (particularly including the common law, the federal system, and the choice-of-law rules) affect the development of business associations. These factors clearly are part of the rocky road to the recognition of partnerships with limited liability. In particular, partnerships faced problems trying to contract around the default partnership rule of vicarious liability. The next section shows that corporations had similar problems contracting for partnership terms.

As firms could not rely on courts to enforce these contracts, they needed the cooperation of the legislature. But lawmakers were reluctant to loosen their grasp of limited liability. Moreover (as discussed in Chapter 4), unincorporated firms, which did not have the benefit of the corporate internal affairs choice of law rule, needed statutory and judicial recognition of their business association in every state in which they operated. This slowed acceptance of new business forms.

The supply of and demand for statutes providing for partnerships with limited liability was complicated by other factors. As long as the federal government was going to tax these firms as corporations, firms might rather form *as* corporations. Also (as discussed in Chapter 2) the value of business association statutes reflects the network consisting of materials such as cases, legal forms, treatises-that assists in interpretation and application of these statutes. Creating a new set of statutes providing for partnerships with limited liability would trigger the need for a whole new network to answer such questions as determining the scope of this new form of limited liability. Yet creation of such a network requires firms to form under the statute, which they may not do because of the absence of a network—a "chicken and egg" problem.

These problems left legislators with little incentive to experiment with new-fangled business association statutes. They would have to invest time and political capital in a new type of statute that they may not even understand and that few firms might adopt.[234] Practicing lawyers might provide guidance and statutory language, but even they might be unwilling to invest in a project with such a speculative payoff.

Thus, it is not surprising that closely held firms were locked into the ill-fitting corporate mold, and that closely held corporations were ubiquitous through the last quarter of the twentieth century. Eventually (as we will see in Chapter 6), the partnership with limited liability triumphed in the form of the limited liability company. It turned out that the key was freeing these firms from the corporate tax. But first, the close corporation had to fail. The following section tells that story.

F. THE CLOSE CORPORATION AS EVOLUTIONARY DEAD END

We have seen that closely held firms had the unsatisfactory choice between a partnership (which had the terms they needed except for limited liability), and a corporation (which had limited liability but also the corporate tax and default rules that were designed for large, publicly held, centrally managed firms). By the mid-twentieth century, most closely held firms were choosing the corporate form. Private contracting and jurisdictional competition drove the gradual evolution of a special type of corporation for closely held firms. But the close corporation was an evolutionary dead end because the corporate form could not be a satisfactory vehicle for closely held firms. The rest of this chapter discusses the

---

234. For discussions of state legislators' incentives (or lack of incentives) to innovate, see Brian D. Galle & Joseph Kieran Leahy, *Laboratories of Democracy? Policy Innovation in Decentralized Governments*, 58 EMORY L.J. 1333 (2009); *see also* Susan Rose-Ackerman, *Risk Taking & Re-Election: Does Federalism Promote Innovation?*, 9 J. LEG. STUD. 593 (1980).

four stages of close corporation history (modeled loosely on the four stages of grief): denial, partial acceptance, legislation, and failure.

G. DENIAL

By the late nineteenth century, the courts came to recognize that there was such a thing as a closely held corporation—that is, a firm with few owners that organized under the corporation statute. Courts then had to decide the extent to which they would allow private parties to use contracts to turn corporations into de facto partnerships.

The courts' first approach was to refuse to adjust corporate norms to accommodate these firms. A classic example is *Jackson v. Hooper*,[235] in which two men formed English and New York (later Illinois) corporations to sell the Encyclopedia Britannica in the United Kingdom and the United States. They allegedly agreed to operate the business as a coequal partnership notwithstanding the corporate form. The New York-cum-Illinois corporation had five directors: the two "partners" and three dummies allegedly under the copartners' control. When the partners fell out, the directors forgot they were dummies, joined with the defendant, and ousted the plaintiff from control.

The plaintiff then asked for the firm to be dissolved as if it were a partnership. The lower court found that the parties had created a joint venture, and decreed what the directors could and could not do in managing the business and transferring assets and shares. The appellate court refused to enforce a partnership in the corporate form. It also held that Illinois and New Jersey law required the corporation's business to be managed by directors, who could not abdicate their duty to exercise their independent judgment on behalf of the corporation.

This and similar cases have been analyzed as examples of how courts refused to let private contracts compromise inflexible corporate norms.[236] The refusal is somewhat understandable. After all, the parties *chose* the corporate form, thereby in effect making the applicable corporation statute part of the parties' agreement. Even if the parties said they were partners, it is not clear what they were. The courts can be forgiven for not wanting to create what might be called the *All of Me* problem referred to in Chapter 4—a firm whose background rules pull in two directions. So the court in *Jackson* sensibly applied the rules of the business association the parties explicitly had chosen, here including the directors' power and duty to control the corporation. The result is not so different from what the parties jointly agreed, even if it is not what the plaintiff wanted in the particular case.

---

235. 75 A. 568 (N.J.Err. & App. 1910).
236. *See* Harwell Wells, *The Rise of the Close Corporation and the Making of Corporation Law*, 5 BERK. BUS. L.J. 263 (2008).

After all, by incorporating the parties were arguably seeking durability. If the defendant had seized on the partnership form to dissolve the firm and take it over, effectively expelling the plaintiff, plaintiff presumably would have wanted the relationship to be a corporation. Courts need to provide clear rules that the parties know before disputes develop rather than characterizing the relationship on an ad hoc basis at the time of litigation.

The real problem here is that legislatures forced closely held firms such as the two-man firm in *Jackson* into the uncomfortable choice between limited liability and corporate inflexibility. This created a problem that the courts (as illustrated in *Jackson*) could not easily solve.

H. JUDICIAL ACCEPTANCE

Denying accommodation to the close corporation did not turn out to be a long-term solution. Firms wanted limited liability and, as of the mid-twentieth century, shelter from personal income taxes. As incorporating was the only way they were going to achieve these objectives, firms kept crafting agreements that gave them partnership-type governance in the corporate form.[237] Repeatedly confronted by cases involving increasingly sophisticated agreements, the courts gradually stopped insisting that firms formed like corporations act like corporations. The courts found it harder to ignore the parties' clear intentions despite the tension between partnership agreements and corporate statutes.

Another factor in the enforcement of these agreements is that states and their courts have an interest in providing a hospitable environment for businesses. If a state's courts barred valuable contracts, firms could choose the law of a more business-friendly state. States may have been willing to sacrifice some regulatory priorities to being a congenial home for profit- and fee-generating firms as long as the agreements did not blatantly thwart the corporate form.

Interestingly, the *Jackson* court criticized the lower court for interfering in the internal governance of foreign corporations. The opinion was written by James Dill, the father of New Jersey corporation law, who was instrumental in developing the internal affairs rule and for making New Jersey the first major beneficiary of this rule (before Delaware took over).[238] Although Dill was not about to let some encyclopedia salesmen kill the goose that laid New Jersey's golden eggs, the case might have come out differently if the firm had been incorporated in New Jersey.

As discussed at the end of this chapter, jurisdictional competition was not enough to save the close corporation because not many firms were interested in

---

237. See id.
238. See Frederick Tung, *Before Competition: The Origins of the Internal Affairs Doctrine*, 32 J. Corp. L. 33, 79–80 (2006).

this form. But Chapter 6 shows that jurisdictional competition ended up being critical to the development of the LLC.

Although courts were willing to enforce agreements that preserved at least a semblance of the corporate format, they stopped short of letting parties to incorporated firms act just as if they were partners. Thus, firms could empower shareholders out of proportion to their investment in the firm, enable some direct control by shareholders rather than directors, and impose share transfer restrictions. But they could not completely dispense with the board of directors, because that was the indispensable emblem of the corporate form.

For example, consider the case of *Clark v. Dodge*,[239] decided twenty-six years after *Jackson* in neighboring New York. Again, two men were quasi-partners in two corporations (this time formed in New Jersey). The passive financier, Dodge, was a 75 percent owner, while Clark, had the remaining 25 percent. Clark naturally wanted to be protected from Dodge's potential use of his controlling share position to fire Clark or appropriate corporate assets. Yet because the business took the corporate form (thereby getting the limited liability that a medicine manufacturer would need by this point in the twentieth century), it had to respect the corporate format, including a shareholder-elected board.

Clark and Dodge crafted an agreement giving Clark the partnership features of direct control he wanted that stayed close enough to the corporate outlines to satisfy the court. The parties agreed that Dodge would vote his stock for Clark as director, and would vote as director for Clark to continue to be general manager and to receive a quarter of the corporation's net income without having that share diluted by payment of excessive salaries to other officers or agents. This gave Clark some direct control over the business while (unlike in *Jackson*) respecting the directors' role. The question was whether a court would strike this down because it was substantively too close to a partnership.

The agreement was tested when Dodge used his voting power to expel Clark, who sought to use the agreement to get back into power. As in *Jackson,* the court cited the "statutory norm" that the business was to be managed by the board of directors. But this time the court relented:

> Are we committed . . . to the doctrine that there may be no variation, however slight or innocuous, from that norm, where salaries or policies or the retention of individuals in office are concerned? There is ample authority supporting that doctrine . . . and something may be said for it, since it furnishes a simple, if arbitrary, test. Apart from its practical administrative convenience, the reasons upon which it is said to rest are more or less nebulous. Public policy, the intention of the Legislature, detriment to the corporation, are phrases which in this connection mean little. Possible harm to *bona fide* purchasers of stock or to creditors or to stockholding minorities have more substance; but

---

239. 269 N.Y. 410, 199 N.E. 641 (1936).

such harms are absent in many instances. If the enforcement of a particular contract damages nobody—not even, in any perceptible degree, the public—one sees no reason for holding it illegal, even though it impinges slightly upon the broad provision of § 27 [providing for management by directors]. Damage suffered or threatened is a logical and practical test, and has come to be the one generally adopted by the courts. . . . Where the directors are the sole stockholders, there seems to be no objection to enforcing an agreement among them to vote for certain people as officers.

The last line of this passage suggests that the shareholders could do what they wanted if all of them were parties to the agreement. However, the court noted both that the agreement was signed by all the shareholders *and* that it only "impinge[d] slightly" on the statutory norm by preserving the board's role. Dodge had to vote as director for Clark as general manager only as long as Clark was "faithful, efficient, and competent," thereby preserving the exercise of board judgment. Similarly, Dodge vowed not to vote for excessive compensation to others—another reasonable requirement. The court added the finishing touch by construing Dodge's agreement to pay Clark a quarter of the "net income" to mean earnings left after the directors had "set aside whatever they deemed wise."

The combination of judicial flexibility and the parties' drafting ingenuity had created a temporarily workable compromise of partnership governance and corporate forms. The parties could contract for a variety of shareholder voting arrangements and could even surmount the problem of board control by staying within the lines like those drawn by *Clark v. Dodge*. However, things were far from simple, as cases such as *Clark* did not constitute a judicial license of free contracting for close corporations. Consider the discussion in the following subsections of some of the questions left to be resolved.

1. Director control agreements
The cases did not clarify how much the agreement could limit the directors' exercise of judgment before the board became substantively *Jackson*-type dummies. For example, would the *Clark* agreement have been enforceable if it had clearly specified the rules for what the directors could set aside before giving Clark his payout? This left critical questions about enforcement of the agreement that would make the parties uneasy about entering into these deals.

2. Shareholder voting arrangements
In deciding whether to enforce agreements on shareholder voting, the courts were concerned about unduly transgressing the corporate norm that shareholders vote according to their ownership in the firm rather than per capita as in partnerships. These agreements potentially created the risk of profligate management by separating ownership and control—a risk that might haunt creditors if the limited liability firm failed. This seemed clearly a problem if shareholders

delegated their voting power entirely to nonowners for long or indefinite periods. The court then might refuse to enforce the voting proxy against a shareholder who wanted to back out of the agreement, at least unless the proxy was accompanied by the transfer to the holder of an "interest" in the corporation that would mitigate the separation of ownership and control.

Again the courts were willing to meet the parties halfway, this time by letting shareholders (who presumably had the firm's interests at heart) agree with each other how to vote. The statutes explicitly accommodated this by permitting voting agreements. Thus, in the famous case of *Ringling v. Ringling Brothers-Barnum & Bailey Combined Shows, Inc.*,[240] the great Delaware Vice Chancellor (later Chancellor) Seitz upheld a voting agreement that let a non-shareholder arbiter control the parties' vote in the event they disagreed. Statutes also provided for voting trusts, which officially separated the vote from the economic rights in the corporation but covered this up a bit by lodging legal title to the stock in the voting trustee. (This somewhat resembled the ploy by Jack Nicholson's character in *Five Easy Pieces* when a waitress refused to serve him toast of ordering a chicken salad sandwich on toast without the chicken salad.) Finally, the statutes let the parties allocate voting rights through the corporate charter, which made the rights part of the corporate structure and provided notice to shareholders and third parties.

But as with the director control agreements, these voting agreements also raised questions as to what the courts would tolerate. When did a voting agreement so separate ownership and control that it impermissibly attempted what was permitted only via a voting trust or charter provision? While *Ringling* upheld the carefully crafted agreement in that case, the Delaware Supreme Court later refused in the case of *Abercrombie v. Davies* to enforce a voting agreement among the shareholders in an oil company that looked exactly like a voting trust except its failure to comply with the voting trust statute and its taking the name *agreement*.[241]

3. Share transfer restrictions

The courts limited the parties' power to restrict the owners' ability to sell their shares—obviously an important type of agreement in a firm that was meant to be managed and controlled directly by close-knit owners. Recall from Chapter 3 that restrictions on selling partnership management rights are part of the partnership standard form and safeguard the parties' right to choose their associates. By contrast, restrictions on shares of artificial corporate entities implicated the different norm against undue inhibition of alienation of property. Thus, for example, a New York court refused to enforce an agreement prohibiting transfers

---

240. 49 A. 2d 603 (1946).
241. 130 A. 2d 338 (1957).

by members of a two-man real estate firm,[242] though this is the same rule that would have applied by default in a partnership.

4. Breakdown and exit

Because courts *did* enforce arrangements such as those described above, they had to deal with the consequences of the breakdown of the relationship with which the agreements often failed to deal. Indeed, concern with these potential consequences might at least partly explain the courts' reticence about enforcing the deals.

This is where the *All of Me* problem of trying to reconcile the partnership and corporate aspects of the agreement comes home to roost. Suppose the parties firmly lock control in two owners or ownership factions, bypass the board as a potential arbiter of disagreements, and block the exits through share transfer restrictions. Then an ownership faction uses its control to injure the other frozen-in owner, or the parties' deadlock freezes the business. A partnership might readily resolve these problems by empowering each partner to dissolve the firm and force its liquidation. But the distinctive feature of the corporation is its durability. Thus, default corporate rules provide for dissolution only with director and majority shareholder approval.

Although a close corporation might contract for partnership-type dissolution by a single owner, a court might not enforce such an agreement because the board is supposed to be able to decide when the corporation dissolves. In any event, close corporation owners often either lacked the foresight to plan for the breakdown of their relationship, or could not easily figure out how to balance the dangers of freeze-in against the risk that a member would use a power to dissolve the corporation to oust a comember. Recall from Chapter 3 that partnership statutes deal with this problem by providing nuanced default rules that balance the costs and benefits of dissolution, as by penalizing partners for departure before the expiration of an agreed term.

The close corporation form really falls apart in dealing with breakup. The parties are stuck with a relationship that is clearly not functioning as intended—and there are no remedies either in the parties' agreement or the statute's default rules. This clearly shows why (as discussed in Chapter 2) statutes need to be coherent. Partnership-type direct control necessitates a partnership-type mechanism for settling inevitable disputes. Yet the durability of the corporate entity forces the parties into an eternal dance of death.

As with other close corporation issues, the courts began dealing with this problem by rigorously enforcing the durability of the parties' chosen entity and

---

242. Rafe v. Hindin, 29 A.D.2d 481, 288 N.Y.S. 2d 662, *aff'd mem.* 23 N.Y.2d 759, 244, N. E.2d 469, 296 N.Y.S.2d 955 (1968).

holding that the courts had no inherent power to dissolve.[243] Some statutes provided for judicial dissolution for deadlock, and there was prominent commentary supporting liberal use of this power.[244] But these statutes and decisions were not a panacea. The statutes initially extended only to the deadlock situation, leaving little recourse for squeeze-outs and other misconduct, and it was not clear how far the courts should go even if they had the power. As often discussed above, there is a trade-off between the need to allow parties to exit the relationship and the opportunism that such an exit opportunity might entail.

These trade-offs were brought home in a famous 1960 *Harvard Law Review* article by Abram Chayes arguing that courts should be ready—but not overly anxious—to slaughter the "sacred cow" of corporate existence.[245] Chayes used as the text for his sermon the case of *Matter of Radom & Neidorff, Inc.*,[246] in which the court denied dissolution of a corporation owned by feuding siblings. The sister, who inherited her interest on her husband's death, imposed on her brother the burden of running the business while refusing to cooperate in its management and suing him for breach of fiduciary duty. When the brother tried to rid himself of his troublesome sister by suing to dissolve the business, the court refused the request. Chayes sympathized with this result. The brother was evidently seeking to take over the business for its liquidating value, which was only a fraction of what it was worth as a going concern. Yet only the brother had the skills and contacts to continue the business. Thus, allowing dissolution would have enabled the brother to take the business from his sister for much less than it was worth.

The case calls to mind *Page v. Page* (discussed in Chapter 3) about the two brothers who owned the laundry. There partnership law allowed the managing brother to do what the brother in *Radom* sought—to take the business for its liquidating value. The critical difference is that this result was plainly allowed by the default agreement provided by the partnership statute. By contrast, corporate law requires a shareholder and director vote on dissolution. So Chayes correctly observes that "[s]urely, when they organized the business the two men [the plaintiff and his brother-in-law] did not contemplate this kind of bet on survivorship."[247] Instead, it is more consistent with the corporate statute to force the brother to negotiate with his sister over the price of her departure.

States eventually went beyond these judicial and legislative deadlock remedies and empowered courts to dissolve on the basis of oppression of locked-in minority

---

243. *See* Carlos Israels, *The Sacred Cow of Corporate Existence, Problems of Deadlock and Dissolution*, 19 U. CHI. L. REV. 778 (1952) (surveying cases).
244. *Id.*
245. *Madame Wagner and the Close Corporation*, 73 HARV. L. REV. 1532 (1960).
246. 307 N.Y. 1, 119 N.E.2d 563 (1954).
247. Chayes, *supra* note 245, at 1547.

owners by controlling shareholders.[248] For example, New York lets holders of 20 percent or more of the corporation's shares petition for dissolution if:

(1) The directors or those in control of the corporation have been guilty of illegal, fraudulent or oppressive actions toward the complaining shareholders;
(2) The property or assets of the corporation are being looted, wasted, or diverted for non-corporate purposes by its directors, officers or those in control of the corporation.[249]

These provisions left for courts what constitutes "illegal, fraudulent or oppressive actions." For example, in *Gardstein v. Kemp & Beatley*,[250] the New York Court of Appeals permitted dissolution on these grounds where close corporation managers cut off distributions that had formerly been given to non-employee shareholders. In applying a test used by many other courts under similar statutory language, the *Gardstein* court held that cutting off the distributions to petitioners frustrated their "reasonable expectations." But it is not clear why this test was satisfied in the case. Though the plaintiffs would have no return on their shares without dissolution, should they reasonably have expected such a return?

Although petitioners received distributions when they were employees, at that point all of the shareholders were employees. When the petitioners left the firm's employ, this was the first time the firm had to deal with non-employee shareholders. So the petitioners had neither a contract nor a clear expectation that they would continue to receive distributions after they left. Even if the employees might have expected the company to buy their shares when they left, this would still require the court to determine the value, which in turn would depend on whether the employees were entitled to distributions. Note that the firm arguably had a business purpose for not continuing distributions to non-employees: Salary bonuses are tax-deductible by the corporation, but dividends are not, and payments made to non-employees look more like dividends than salary.

Decisions such as *Gardstein* seem to involve courts making up contract provisions for close corporation shareholders as they go along. Recall that long before *Gardstein*, the New York case of *Clark v. Dodge* enforced a contract that assured continued compensation to a close corporation employee-shareholder. Why should the court provide a contract for parties who have not made one for themselves? To be sure, it is easy to sympathize with plaintiffs in cases such as *Gardstein* in which they were essentially partners, but without partners' usual

---

248. For a comprehensive analysis of these problems, see F. HODGE O'NEAL & ROBERT B. THOMPSON, O'NEAL AND THOMPSON'S OPPRESSION OF MINORITY SHAREHOLDERS AND LLC MEMBERS, (Rev. 2d ed, 1999–2009).
249. N.Y. BUS. CORP. L., § 1104–a.
250. 64 N.Y.2d 63, 484 N.Y.S.2d 799, 473 N.E.2d 1173 (1984).

recourse of dissolving the firm at will when they want to cash out. Partnership default rules are designed for this type of firm. But while applying these rules to corporations arguably does justice in the individual case, combining corporate and partnership default rules leaves the law quite unpredictable.

A possible compromise for cases such as this (which Chayes proposed[251] and which New York eventually built into its close corporation dissolution statute)[252] is to let the party opposing dissolution avoid this drastic remedy by buying out the plaintiff at fair value. However, this remedy raises almost as many problems and issues as it resolves. It does not necessarily achieve the right balance of the need for exit against the potential for opportunism because it is not clear the plaintiff is entitled to any kind of exit.

Also, what is the *fair value* of an interest in a close corporation? The term implies something other than market value, such as a pro rata share of the firm rather than the price plaintiff could get for her noncontrolling interest. Yet why treat someone who was content to buy and own a noncontrolling share as an equal holder just because she decided to sue, given that no determination of wrongdoing is necessary to trigger the provision? Perhaps most troubling, how does the buyout remedy link with the parties' express agreement? For example, the court in Pace Photographers[253] gave the plaintiff the fair value of his shares rather than the lower price provided for in the agreement's share transfer restriction. The court made no determination that the defendants had engaged in wrongdoing while there was some evidence the plaintiff had done so. In a case such as this, why should the plaintiff not be bound by his express agreement?

At least in Pace or Gardstein it can be said that the parties had deliberately chosen the statute, and therefore implicitly opted into the remedies the statute provided. But even that saving grace does not apply in the famous case of *Donahue v. Rodd Electrotype Co.*[254] It involved two owners of a business—Harry, who had invested his life savings, ran the business, and had an 80 percent share, and Joseph, who was content to work in the company and had refused an opportunity to invest along with the dominant owner. Nearing retirement, Harry engaged in some estate planning by selling many of his shares to the company and giving some to his children with the ultimate view of passing control to them.

However, the court ordered that Harry's sale to the company should either be rescinded or Joseph should be given an "equal opportunity" to sell his otherwise locked-in interest to the company for the same price Harry received. Here there was *neither* an agreement *nor* a statutory provision that entitled Joseph to this

---

251. See Chayes, *supra* note 245.
252. See N.Y. B.C.L. § 1118.
253. In re Pace Photographers, 71 N.Y.2d 737, 530 N.Y.S. 2d 67, 525 N.E.2d 713 (1988).
254. 367 Mass. 578, 328 N.E. 2d 505 (1975).

valuable right of being able to "tag along" with Harry's decision to sell his stock to the company. Joseph seems to have gotten a windfall from the court's willingness to make up a buy-sell agreement for the parties.

What should be done about the problem of close corporations? Professors Hetherington and Dooley provocatively suggest a statutory provision allowing a close corporation minority shareholder to require the firm to purchase her stock at any time for fair value as long as the purchase would not make the corporation insolvent.[255] This proposal received a lot of attention, but no state adopted it. And it is no wonder: even if the proposal would make sense in the context of a partnership statute (and not even partnership statutes provide for anything quite like this), the remedy would apply to firms that deliberately elected to be *corporations*, not partnerships. That election suggests that the parties wanted a particular set of rules, arguably including corporate-type durability.

Thus, the courts and legislatures never fully accommodated closely held firms regarding the corporate form. As long as the parties are operating in the corporate form, there is an inevitable mismatch between their agreement and the default agreement the law supplied. No statute can deal with all of the variations that can arise. Courts may fill the inevitable gaps by relying on the norms of the statute the parties have chosen to govern their business, but this does not necessarily provide a clear or coherent solution if the statute is a mélange of corporate and partnership norms. The inherent problem is not that the parties could not figure out what kind of agreement they wanted, but that the law did not provide the agreement many clearly desired: a partnership with limited liability. The parties were willing to compromise and accept the extra governance costs of an ill-fitting agreement as long as the corporate form gave them limited liability and the tax costs of incorporation were not too high. As discussed in the next section, the problem is that the tax costs did get too high.

I. TAX ACCOMMODATION OF THE CLOSELY HELD CORPORATION

By the late 1950s, pressures were building on the closely held corporation. The problems of the ill-fitting corporate form were becoming clearer, and as personal tax rates started falling, the disadvantages of corporate double taxation increased. Against this background, Congress in 1958 first adopted Subchapter S of the Internal Revenue Code[256] (later substantially liberalized by the Subchapter S Revision Act of 1982),[257] which allowed closely held corporations to get many of the tax advantages of partnership. A Subchapter S corporation's income and losses

---

255. John A.C. Hetherington & Michael Dooley, *Illiquidity and Exploitation: A Proposed Statutory Solution to the Remaining Close Corporation Problem*, 63 VA. L. REV. 1 (1977).
256. IRC §§ 1361–1379.
257. *See* Subchapter S Revision Act of 1982, Pub. L. No. 97-354, 96 Stat. 1669.

"flow through" to the shareholders like they do in a partnership. However, the Code restricts the availability of Subchapter S by, among other things, limiting the number of shareholders (now seventy-five) and letting the firm have only "one class of stock."

Subchapter S could be considered a kind of political safety valve by which Congress hoped to head off both demands to eliminate the corporate tax and state efforts to provide for the partnership with limited liability by lifting the tax from smaller corporations who most wanted to be partnerships and for which the corporate tax would be particularly burdensome.[258] The 1982 revision to Subchapter S served a similar purpose as states were making the limited partnership a more viable alternative to incorporation, as did the 1996 increase of maximum owners from thirty-five to seventy-five just as the limited liability company was taking hold.[259] The enforced simplicity of the one-class-of-stock requirement protects against revenue loss by discouraging fancy structures that shift income from high tax to low tax bracket owners. The complexity of partnership taxation—and the danger posed by tax law's anti-abuse rules[260]—encourages parties to embrace this simplicity.

What Subchapter S does not do is give firms a reliable way to get limited liability without the corporate tax *outside* the corporate form.[261] Subchapter S mainly provided more firms that should be partnerships the opportunity to muddy their governance by becoming corporations while failing to solve the underlying problem with incorporation of small firms.

J. FULL STATUTORY AUTHORIZATION OF CLOSE CORPORATIONS

As discussed above, corporation statutes long have explicitly permitted some of the devices that close corporations rely on, including authorization of shareholder voting agreements and voting trusts, broad authority to vary share voting rights, and dissolution provisions. Many of these provisions apply to all corporations while others (particularly the oppression remedies) applied only to close corporations.

---

258. *See* Jennifer Arlen & Deborah M. Weiss, *A Political Theory of Corporate Taxation*, 105 YALE L.J. 325 (1995); Steven A. Bank, *A Capital Lock-In Theory of the Corporate Income Tax*, 94 GEO. L.J. (forthcoming 2006) (noting that Subchapter S "narrowed the base of companies subject to the separate corporate tax rather than threatening the system itself").

259. *See* Small Business Job Protection Act of 1996, Pub. L. No. 104-188, § 1301, 110 Stat. 1777 (codified at IRC § 1361(b)(1)).

260. Treas. Reg. § 1.701–2 (2004); LARRY E. RIBSTEIN & ROBERT R. KEATINGE, RIBSTEIN & KEATINGE ON LIMITED LIABILITY COMPANIES § 17:3 (2d ed., 2005–08).

261. Subchapter S applies only to a "domestic corporation." *See* IRC § 1361(b).

In 1955, North Carolina pioneered very broad authorization of corporate modifications in closely held corporations, including permitting share transfer restrictions and agreements restricting the authority of or eliminating the board. The North Carolina statute clarified that no written agreement among all owners of a corporation whose shares are not generally traded "shall be invalid as between the parties thereto, on the ground that it is an attempt by the parties thereto to treat the corporation as if it were a partnership or to arrange their relationships in a manner that would be appropriate only between partners."[262] This authorizes a corporation to operate exactly like a partnership.

The new generation of close corporation provisions that followed North Carolina's path-breaking statute recognized the distinctness of closely held corporations by making the provisions available only to a special class of firms, defined in terms of number of shareholders, absence of a public offering or listing on a securities exchange, use of stock transfer restrictions, and election of coverage.[263] Some of these special provisions are in the general corporation statute, while others (including the Delaware provisions) are isolated in a special close corporation subchapter. Limiting the provisions to closely held firms appears designed to ensure that the courts will develop a special jurisprudence that does not apply to the very different public corporations covered by the statute's general provisions.[264]

These provisions seemingly gave closely held firms exactly what they had always needed—the ability to operate as partnerships, yet with corporate-type limited liability and a form of partnership-type taxation. What more could they want? The answer is that despite even these advanced legislative efforts to adapt the corporate form to the closely held firm, closely held firms wanted to be real partnerships rather than ersatz partnerships in corporate form. Even a relaxed corporate form still impinged on them because close corporation provisions were still lodged within the corporate code. The statutes mainly just let close corporations make their own contracts, or at most added a few special default rules dealing with such things as share transfer restrictions and buyouts.[265] Special close corporation provisions fit uneasily with the general corporation law that still applied to close corporations. Even with broad freedom of contract, the attempt to wrap the closely held firm up in the corporate form still was not working.

---

262. N.C. Gen. Stat. § 55–73(b)(1955).
263. See, e.g., 8 Del. Code §§ 341–356 ("Del. G.C.L."); Mod. Bus. Corp. Act § 7.32; Maryland Corps. & Ass'ns Code §§ 4–101 to 4–603; N.Y. Bus. Corp. L. § 1104–a (providing for remedy for corporation whose shares are not listed on a national securities exchange or regularly quoted in an over-the-counter market); Tex. Bus. Corp. Act Arts. 12.01 et seq.
264. See Ian Ayres, *Judging Close Corporations*, 70 Wash. U. L.Q. 365 (1992).
265. See, e.g., the Maryland provisions cited in *supra* note 263.

Consider the following questions, among others, these statutes raised:

(1) Assuming a firm elects and qualifies under the close corporation provisions, what sorts of agreements does the statute let it adopt? For example, the Model Business Corporation Act precludes agreements that are "contrary to public policy."[266] The Official Comment suggests that the provision does not authorize agreements that eliminate dissenters' rights, derivative actions, or inspection rights. But it is not clear why these provisions should be essential for forms that are not standard form corporations.[267]

(2) Would a minor formal glitch in the procedure for becoming a "close corporation" throw the corporation into the general rules for corporations? *Zion v. Kurtz*[268] held that a corporation could still qualify for Delaware's special close corporation treatment although there was no election in the certificate as the statute required. The court reasoned that there were "no intervening rights of third persons, the agreement requires nothing that is not permitted by statute, and all of the stockholders of the corporation assented to it." But this would seem to contravene the express provisions of the statute requiring a charter provision. Also, what other minor glitches would this case allow? May a corporation that does not qualify as a close corporation under the statute (as where its shares are freely tradable though closely held) use the statutory close corporation provisions? Uncertainty as to which statute applies to a firm makes planning and litigation more costly On the other hand, the courts understandably hesitate to be too rigid with often informal closely held firms.

(3) *Zion* raised the issue of the formalities necessary to opt out of statutory constraints. There is an additional question of what remedies are available to a firm that has rejected treatment as a statutory close corporation. Does such a firm qualify for judicial protection as would have been the case if there had been no statutory close corporation provisions? For example, the court in *Toner v. The Baltimore Envelope Co.*[269] refused to give a shareholder in a standard corporation an equal opportunity to be bought out, along the lines of the *Donahue* case and as provided for in Maryland's close corporation provisions. The court reasoned that giving this remedy to the plaintiff would be inconsistent with the legislature's decision to apply the remedy only to firms that had elected close corporation status. *Nixon v. Blackwell*[270] similarly held that non-employee

---

266. *See* Mod. Bus. Corp. Act § 7.32(a)(8).
267. For example, as discussed in Chapter 7, the application of the corporate derivative suit to closely held firms may be particularly inappropriate.
268. 50 N.Y.2d 92, 428 N.Y.S.2d 199, 405 N.E.2d 681 (1980).
269. 498 A.2d 642 (Md. 1985)
270. 626 A.2d 1366, 1379–81 (Del. 1993).

minority shareholders of a closely held firm that was not covered by Delaware's special close corporation provisions were not entitled to an equal opportunity to receive stock options awarded to key employees. The court noted the non-application of Delaware's special provisions, the fact that even shareholders of a corporation covered by these provisions would not be entitled to protection, and the shareholders' failure to negotiate for protection. The court therefore suggested that if Delaware close corporation shareholders did not take advantage of their freedom to draft for protection or invest in firms that did, they could not expect to get help from the court.

(4) Even if the firm were fully formed as a close corporation, it still might not be clear what remedies are appropriate if the relationship breaks down and the parties have not fully agreed as to the consequences. Should the firm be dissolved as if it were a partnership, or should a court respect the fact that parties chose to be a corporation, albeit a closely held one? In other words, all of the questions in cases such as *Gardstein* and *Pace* remain.

In short, the fundamental problem of the close corporation form is that it fails to carry out the basic function of a business association statute described in Chapter 2 of providing a coherent framework for filling gaps in inevitably incomplete contracts. This is most obvious for closely held firms that form as standard corporations. The double formation process imposed by the close corporation provisions—that is, requiring both incorporation and qualification and election to become a close corporation—answers some of these questions, but poses others. What if the firm does not complete the second stage of the process? Even if it does, should the gaps be filled with the default rules of the corporate form the firm chose, or those of the partnership form (which seem more appropriate)?

K. FAILURE

The discussion so far shows that none of the judicial and legislative approaches to close corporations solved the basic problem of attempting to insert partnerships into the corporate form. The combination of corporate default rules and partnership contracts proved awkward for closely held firms. Moreover, there is a good chance that smaller and more informal firms generally did not even know about the special close corporation option. In any event, few firms opted for special close corporation status.[271] The close corporation ultimately was an

---

271. *See* F. Hodge O'Neal & Robert B. Thompson, O'Neal and Thompson's Close Corporations and LLCs: Law and Practice, § 1.20 (2008); Wells, *supra* note 236. O'Neal & Thompson, *supra*, compiled data on close corporation filings in states with special close corporation provisions. The following are the 1992 ratios of close corporations to total

unsatisfactory byproduct of the regulation of limited liability. The close corporation form dominated as long as it did only because the exclusive corporate route to limited liability was worth the cost for many firms. The next chapter shows that when the tax costs of incorporation increased to the point that the close corporation was no longer viable, firms moved toward a better solution. The uncorporation broke the shackles of the corporate form, then proceeded to evolve rapidly from the early 1990s through the present.

---

corporations: Alabama, 5,324/155,198; Wisconsin 5,101/98,602; Pennsylvania 24,000/580,000; Kansas "a lot less" than 5% of total corporations; Missouri 863/82,694; Montana 828/97,009; Nevada 742/63,172; and Wyoming 753/12,422. Delaware had no close corporation data in 1992, but reported 16,684 close corporations in 1985 and 202,115 total corporations in 1992. Texas reported that of all corporate filings, 3.71% were statutory close corporations in 1978 and 5.59% in 1979. Two 1985 Texas studies based on different data showed 5.91% and 6.09% electing close corporation status. Only California showed significant percentages of close corporations—28% in 1978 and 19% in 1985—but the attorney conducting the study thought those numbers "misleading" because most filings were by nonlawyers who did not understand the consequences of close corporation status.

6. THE EVOLUTION OF THE MODERN UNCORPORATION

Chapters 4 and 5 traced the corporation's rise to embrace both the large firms that arguably fit into the corporate mold and the closely held firms that do not. Lawmakers could channel firms into the corporate form (where they could be regulated and taxed) by blocking alternative routes to corporate features, particularly including limited liability.

Chapter 5 ended with the failure of the close corporation. Closely held firms had sought to combine limited liability with partnership features and had pressed for changes in the corporate form to accommodate this need. Though the close corporation was an unwieldy contraption, it dominated closely held firms for much of the twentieth century. The close corporation increasingly accommodated contracting for partnership governance, but still left corporate default rules in place to bite would-be partners who had not fully contracted around them. Partnership-type firms needed partnership default rules. Yet despite the demand for a partnership with limited liability, the corporate form was locked into place by concerns about deregulating limited liability and eroding the corporate tax, as well as the inherent difficulty of coordinating courts and lawmakers in a common law federal system.

This chapter shows how the partnership with limited liability overcame these obstacles. Within a very short period in the late 1980s and early 1990s, the LLC Revolution broke the corporation's hold on the closely held firm. The unleashing of the LLC began the second phase of the evolution of uncorporate business forms largely free of the tax and regulatory constraints on limited liability that had previously bound them. The first three subparts discuss the general forces at work during this period. The chapter then takes a closer look at the evolution of specific uncorporations.

A. THE LLC REVOLUTION

The revolution that unseated the corporation began modestly with the Wyoming LLC statute.[272] An oil company wanted a form of business that it was used to

---

272. *See* William J. Carney, *Limited Liability Companies: Origins and Antecedents*, 66 U. COLO. L. REV. 855, 857 (1995) (briefly recounting this history).

working with in Panama. After first hitting a dry legal well in Alaska, the firm got a statute passed in 1975 in Wyoming.

William Carney, who observed this development as a young law professor in Wyoming, reflected twenty years later that the statute seemed to be just a special vehicle for oil and gas companies, so unheralded that he heard about it only after it was passed.[273] Carney first wrote about the new statute as barely more than a footnote to a much longer article about the Wyoming corporation law, dismissing it as an amalgam of corporate, limited partnership, and general partnership provisions that "leaves more questions unanswered than it solves, and for that reason alone does not represent a viable alternative for most enterprises."[274] But Carney did note that the entity "may be a viable alternative to the limited partnership if it receives favorable treatment from the Internal Revenue Service."[275] In any event, the initial Wyoming statute could not have been more than a first step as the new form awaited acceptance by the Internal Revenue Service and the other states. By 1988 only one other state (Florida in 1982) had adopted an LLC statute.

However, the floodgates opened in 1988, and by 1994 all but three states had adopted LLC statutes. This LLC Revolution occurred despite the reluctance of courts, state lawmakers, and federal tax authorities to sanction a new business form. It resulted from several factors that had been brewing change prior to 1988 beneath a seemingly placid status quo. First, because of the Tax Reform Act of 1986, top corporate tax rates came to exceed top individual rates, and sales of stock no longer received favorable capital gains treatment. This made the corporate tax costly for more firms because they could no longer benefit from the "inside" tax shelter on retained earnings.[276] Firms now had more incentive than ever to be tax partnerships.

Second, it was getting harder for the IRS to maintain a distinction between tax partnerships and tax corporations. Recall from Chapter 4 that the Kintner Rules applied a multifactor test that nominally required at least two corporate characteristics in addition to limited liability for a court to hold that a firm was a

---

273. *Id.*

274. William J. Carney, *Close Corporations and the Wyoming Business Corporation Act: Time for a Change?* 12 LAND & WATER L. REV. 537, 581 (1977). Many of the questions that concerned Carney related to issues like authorization of a complex capital structure, meetings, indemnification, removal of managers, and mergers that mattered more to formal corporations than to unincorporated firms. Carney analyzed the statute as mostly drawn from the Wyoming Business Corporation Act, with a few sections from Wyoming's versions of the uniform partnership and limited partnership acts. *Id.* at 581–82.

275. *Id.* at 582, n.232.

276. *See* Merton H. Miller, *The Modigliani-Miller Propositions After 30 Years*, J. ECON. PERSP. (Fall 1988) at 99, 117–18.

"tax corporation." The IRS also had signaled irrespective of the other factors, any firm would be classed as a corporation if all members had limited liability.[277]

But the states kept passing statutes that put pressure on the IRS definition. For example, in 1988 Georgia passed a new limited partnership act that for the first time allowed limited partners to fully participate in control without having personal liability. Limited partnerships had been eligible for partnership tax treatment under the Kintner test because the general partners had personal liability. The Georgia statute forced the IRS to decide whether a limited partnership with managing limited partners could be a tax partnership while a firm with no general partners could not. (The IRS also had to ask, what will they think of next?) Although the IRS put the LLC Revolution in abeyance by delaying a ruling on the tax status of the Georgia statute,[278] it would ultimately have to confront the tax status of partnerships with limited liability.

Third, Congress reduced some of the IRS's concern about loosening tax classification by adopting a statute characterizing most publicly traded partnerships as corporations.[279] This liberated the IRS from the revenue worry that large firms might use liberal tax classification rules to become tax partnerships. It also reduced the need to distinguish between partnerships and corporations for tax purposes. Maybe these entities could all be allowed to avoid the corporate tax as long as they did not get too big, as measured by trading of their shares.

All of this set the stage for a 1988 IRS ruling classifying a Wyoming LLC as a partnership for tax purposes.[280] This unleashed the passage of LLC statutes and set in motion state tinkering with the provisions of these statutes. The IRS valiantly struggled to rule on these variations. But by the end of the 1990s, by which time all states had adopted LLC statutes, the IRS had to give up the ghost and adopt a "check-the-box" rule that allowed firms essentially to decide whether they wanted to be taxed as partnerships or corporations.[281]

The LLC Revolution indicates that many of the theoretical impediments to the development of new limited liability partnership forms discussed in Chapter 5—conservatism of the common law courts, lawmakers' lack of incentives to experiment, and firms' concerns about interstate acceptance of new forms—were actually mirages. By tinkering with agreements and provoking

---

277. See 45 Fed. Reg. 75,709 (1980). The IRS withdrew this regulation in 1982 (I.R.S. News Release IR-82-145 (Dec. 16, 1982); I.R.S. Announcement 83-4, 1983-2 I.R.B. 30 (Jan. 14, 1983). But at around the same time if both issued a private letter ruling classifying an LLC as a corporation (Priv. Ltr. Rul. 83-04-138 (Oct. 29, 1982)) and then announced that it would not issue further private rulings concerning LLC classification (Rev. Proc. 83-15, 1983-1 C.B. 676).

278. Georgia's statute did not receive the IRS ruling ensuring partnership classification until 1991. See Rev. Rul. 91-51, 1991-2 C.B. 434.

279. See IRC § 7704.

280. Rev. Rul. 88-76, 1988-2 C.B. 360.

281. See Treas. Reg. § 301.7701-1-3 (2004).

court decisions, lawyers could drive the development of business forms. The big impediment to change all along was federal tax law, which effectively imposed a tax on limited liability and thereby discouraged firms from adopting (and states from developing) business associations that combined limited liability and partnership features. Firms and their lawyers had to work within the tax classification framework and weaken it from within. Once the old framework based on limited liability fell and the IRS gave its imprimatur to the LLC, the full evolutionary force of the common law and federal system was unleashed. The IRS, left with no clear, policy-based distinction between corporate and partnership characteristics to fall back on, ultimately had to surrender to the onslaught of statutes.

This story differs from an alternative account by Hansmann, Kraakman, and Squire (HKS) in which they view the evolution of the incorporated partnership in terms of the increasing importance of a particular characteristic of firms—that is, "entity shielding."[282] HKS saw partnership as converging with the corporate form by offering more protection from potential liquidation by owners (which they call *strong* entity shielding) and creditors (which they call *weak* entity shielding). HKS attribute this development to more sophisticated valuation and disclosure mechanisms and judicial remedies that protected owners of closely held firms from oppression by controlling owners.[283] They reasoned that, given this protection, owners of closely held firms could get an adequate exit route through buyout, and therefore did not need to compel liquidation of the firm. Notably, HKS minimize the role of limited liability as neither crucial nor even desirable.

The HKS story helps explain the rise of the close corporation, which in fact offered greater entity shielding than the uncorporation. HKS's account cannot, however, explain the LLC Revolution. Though HKS find evidence for the increasing continuity of partnerships in RUPA's eliminating mandatory dissolution of the partnership on partner dissociation,[284] RUPA merely clarified the buyout versus liquidation situations that had existed since before the UPA. More importantly, the LLC, which was the key innovation of the period, offered *less* entity shielding than close corporations. Given the problems of member lock-in in

---

282. *See* Hansmann et al., *supra* note 9.
283. *Id.* at 1398–99.
284. The authors also cite UPA and RUPA mechanisms for delaying payment to the wrongful partner and RUPA's provision that dissociation for a partner's personal bankruptcy is wrongful. However, the absence of decided cases suggests that the former rule has never been significant. The latter rule applies only to a narrow category of partner dissociations and may be invalid under bankruptcy law to the extent that it penalizes bankrupt partners and interferes with reorganization of the bankruptcy estate. *See generally*, Larry E. Ribstein, *Partner Bankruptcy and the Federalization of Partnership Law*, 33 Wake For. L. Rev. 795 (1998).

close corporations (as discussed in Chapter 5), this feature of LLCs was actually a benefit rather than a cost of the uncorporate structure. Though HKS note that LLCs ultimately provided for greater default continuity than partnerships, we will see in the next chapter that this change is better explained as the unexpected effect of a federal estate tax rule than by the improved technologies HKS stress.

In short, the LLC Revolution was produced by a combination of private contracting, state experimentation in a federal system, and tax considerations that increased the payoff from new contracts and experiments. The revolution demonstrates that the corporation's dominance for closely held firms during much of the twentieth century is best explained by taxation of the "corporate" feature of limited liability rather than by any inherent benefits of the corporate form for closely held firms or impediments to the law's ability to evolve in a federal common law system. The corporate form was primarily a tool of the state that was blunted by contracts and jurisdictional competition.

B. THE UNCORPORATION DEVELOPS

The development of the uncorporation during the LLC Revolution reflects many of the general influences on the law of business associations discussed in Chapter 2. First, state competition is important. Although initially only corporations could choose the state law that would apply to their governance, a byproduct of the LLC Revolution discussed further in Chapter 7 is that this choice of law rule now also applies to unincorporated firms. Unincorporated firms therefore can keep their operations in one state while forming in (and thereby choosing) the governance law of another state. States and countries compete to supply the law to firms based elsewhere while keeping locally based firms home.[285]

Second, there are practical limits on variation among business association statutes. Firms and parties dealing with them incur costs of keeping informed about the differences. Also, other things being equal, the more different types of statutes and forms there are, the less interpretive material (such as cases, treatises, forms, and legal advice) there will be for each form. The result may be a formal or informal process of achieving uniformity across different state laws and standardization among business associations.[286]

Third, the potential benefits of uniformity suggest that there may be some value in having a mechanism for coordinating state law. The main coordinating mechanism for U.S. state law is the National Conference of Commissioners for Uniform State Laws (NCCUSL). Though NCCUSL has been very active regarding

---

285. *See* Bruce H. Kobayashi & Larry E. Ribstein, *Jurisdictional Competition for LLCs* (working paper, 2009).
286. *See infra* text accompanying notes 304–305.

uncorporation statutes, the results have been questionable.[287] Also, the states can observe each other and coordinate on their own by adopting provisions that have been adopted elsewhere. While this process may be slow and hit-or-miss, it may get better and quicker results than a politically driven uniform lawmaking process.

Fourth, business associations are shaped not only by general business needs, but by regulatory and tax statutes, particularly those adopted at the federal level that aretherefore beyond the direct influence of state legislatures. Federal laws may influence the demand for variation across states and among standard forms. These effects occur when federal or other regulatory statutes prohibit or attach costs to certain types of terms. As discussed in the next section, tax rules and regulations may lead firms to adopt governance terms that would not make sense from a pure transaction cost standpoint in the absence of the tax or regulation.

C. THE IMPORTANCE OF NON-ORGANIZATION LAW

The above discussion indicates that business organization law is more a product of firms' business and general legal environment than a constraint. Indeed, one scholar has referred to business association law as "trivial."[288] On the other hand, *non*business organization law is a *nontrivial* part of the environment that shapes the evolution of business associations.[289]

A regulation's effect on business associations depends on whether the application of the regulation is determined by the state law business association statute the firm has chosen. If a regulation turns on choice of form, it may be formally mandatory but trivial in substance because firms can avoid the regulation by choosing the applicable form and contracting out of the standard form's default rules. A regulation therefore has greater mandatory effect if it disregards the chosen state law form and applies based on how the firm's characteristics fit with the regulatory intent. In general, there is a trade-off between regulators' use of rules to achieve clarity and predictability and standards to ensure fit with regulatory objectives.

The relationship between non-organization and business association law is complex and dynamic. On the one hand, business associations adapt to and develop in the shadow of non-organization law. The success of this adaptation helps determine the efficiency of business organization law in minimizing firms'

---

287. See *infra* text accompanying note 305.
288. See Bernard S. Black, *Is Corporate Law Trivial?: A Political and Economic Analysis*, 84 Nw. U. L. Rev. 542 (1990).
289. See Larry E. Ribstein, *Important Role of Non-Organization Law*, 40 Wake For. L. Rev. 751 (2005).

transaction costs. However, business organization law may undermine non-organization law's objectives by enabling parties to reduce the effect of regulation by choosing their business form or formation state. Indeed, uncorporations' ability to facilitate this regulatory "arbitrage" is one of their attractions and a reason government may prefer to channel firms into the more rigid corporate form.

Non-organization law clearly has left its mark on business organizations, particularly uncorporations. Business forms have developed to give firms ways to escape vicarious liability and the corporate tax. At the same time, non-organization law may have constrained developments that would have happened in the absence of this law. The next chapter discusses the effect of these laws in more detail, focusing on the period following the emergence of the LLC in the early 1990s.

Tax is the most obvious non-organization law influence on business associations. Chapter 5 and the beginning of this chapter discuss in detail the role of the corporate tax in driving firms first to incorporate, then to the uncorporation. Chapters 7 and 8 show how federal estate and income tax have profoundly influenced the evolution of uncorporate law.

Tax rules can influence not only choice of business form but also the choice of specific governance rules within forms. For example, following the IRS ruling clarifying that LLCs could qualify for partnership tax treatment, LLCs had an incentive to avoid corporate characteristics other than limited liability—that is, centralized management, free transferability, and continuity of life. This prodded lawmakers to avoid these features in the developing LLC statutory form. As soon as the IRS passed the check-the-box rule, LLC statutes changed to provide for more continuity by default.

Federal securities and employment discrimination laws also may have influenced organization law. These statutes are aimed at protecting relatively passive and uninformed parties such as investors or employees. In deciding whether these laws apply, the courts have tended to emphasize the plaintiff's need for protection, which may depend on whether the plaintiff participated in management. Firms therefore might have an incentive to adopt decentralized management forms such as general partnerships and member-managed LLCs and avoid centrally managed-type firms such as limited partnerships and manager-managed LLCs. This incentive in turn may have influenced the extent to which LLC statutes rely on member-management rather than manager-management default rules.

D. THE REST OF THE UNCORPORATION MENAGERIE

The following sections provide a brief overview of the evolution of variations on the partnership form other than the LLC. These can be viewed as providing part of the context for the LLC Revolution, as well as the evolution in response to this revolution. Chapter 7 presents a more complete analysis of current law that discusses each of the variations in more detail.

1. General partnership

Prior to the 1990s, general partnership law was almost totally uniform across the states, with all but one state (Louisiana) adopting the Uniform Partnership Act. The advent of the Revised Uniform Partnership Act in the early 1990s (official versions were adopted in 1994 and 1997, but drafts were available prior to 1994) then created variation. However, by 2008 uniformity was restored as nearly forty states had adopted the Revised Uniform Partnership Act.

Partnership law has been relatively uniform over the years in part because of partnership's status as the "default" business association—that is, partnership is the form a business takes when it has not deliberately chosen another form. Because partnership status can be thrust on the unwary, uniformity across the states helps enhance predictability. Also, partnership applies to the very smallest firms whose costs of shopping for partnership law may be particularly high in relation to the amount the partners have invested.

Another pressure for uniformity of general partnership laws is that the "internal affairs" choice-of-law rule that traditionally applies to corporations (and which has more recently been applied to limited partnerships and LLCs) has had less traction for general partnerships. The mechanism for applying the internal affairs rule is an official formation process in a particular state, which serves notice to the world that the particular state's law applies. However, conventional general partnerships are not limited liability firms and do not have a formal registration process. Courts now quite generally enforce contracts among the partners choosing the law of a particular state, but these contracts do not apply to non-partners, particularly regarding the partners' liability.[290]

The differences between the UPA and RUPA are not revolutionary but they are still significant. The major overall difference is that RUPA squarely accepts the *entity* view of partnership. As discussed in Chapter 3, this theory was only equivocally present in UPA. RUPA better shields the firm's property from its members and their creditors than does the UPA, explicitly provides that partnership property is owned by the entity rather than by individual partners, provides that owner dissociation does not dissolve the partnership entity, and makes it a little easier for the partners to continue the business after partner dissociation. As discussed above, however,[291] RUPA's increases in partnership continuity mainly clarify the situation that existed under the UPA. RUPA also provides for a bit more owner shielding than UPA by clarifying that for all kinds of claims

---

290. For a discussion of choice of law in partnerships see 1 Bromberg & Ribstein, *supra* note 99, § 1.04.

291. *See supra* text accompanying note 284.

partners provide only a backstop liability after partnership assets are exhausted rather than being directly liable for some partnership debts.

RUPA's second significant difference from UPA is that it more explicitly and systematically acknowledges the role of contract in partnership law. As discussed throughout this book, partnership always has been shaped by parties' agreement. The UPA acknowledges the role of contract at several points: the partners' internal governance and financial rights are explicitly "subject to any agreement between them" (Section 18), the scope of permissible partner self-benefit depends on copartner "consent" (Section 21), and a partner's power to compel liquidation of a partnership at will is "unless otherwise agreed" (Section 38(1)). However, by not expressly providing for the overall role of contract, the UPA left it open for courts to qualify or even ignore the partners' power to modify default rules by contract. By contrast Section 103 of RUPA provides for an overall set of rules on the extent to which the partnership agreement controls. All of the subsequent uniform laws on unincorporated firms followed this approach. Unfortunately (as discussed in Chapter 7), the uniform acts also introduced ambiguous restrictions on contracting that the courts had not previously recognized in applying the UPA.

2. LLP

The early history of the LLP resembles that of the LLC—an entrepreneur had the incentive to invest in an experiment, and circumstances enabled the spread of the form across the states.[292] In this case the entrepreneurs were Texas lawyers concerned about potential liability in the fallout from the government suits against law and accounting firms that had worked for failed savings and loan associations in the late 1980s. These actions for the first time threatened lawyers and other professionals with personal exposure to their firms' uninsured liabilities that they had no direct role in creating. Though professionals already could get limited liability in some states by organizing professional corporations or LLCs, in many states professionals had to be *partnerships*. The lawyers got the Texas legislature to adopt a law providing for a *limited liability partnership*. The original bill modified the partner vicarious liability of the Uniform Partnership Act to insulate a partner in a professional partnership from individual liability for another partner's professional "errors, omissions, negligence, incompetence, or malfeasance."

National law and accounting firms spurred acceptance of the LLP concept across the states because they were concerned about facing potentially firm-wide liability by having offices in states that did not recognize the LLP form. The states fell into line, and it was not long before all states had adopted LLP provisions,

---

292. This history is recounted in ALAN A. BROMBERG & LARRY E. RIBSTEIN, BROMBERG & RIBSTEIN ON LLPs, RUPA AND ULPA, § 1.01 (2009).

extending liability protection beyond errors and omissions to contract liabilities. Because LLPs formally registered in a particular state, they got the same choice of law rule as to partner liability that applies to corporations, LPs, and LLCs.[293]

However, the LLP form never became popular beyond professionals, who had particular reasons for seeking limited liability in the partnership form.[294] This is significant, because in theory the LLP would have been valuable as a way to overcome the "network" problem of creating a new business form at a time when the LLC was still in its infancy. After all, unlike with the LLC, partners could have used the LLP to simply add limited liability to the existing partnership form. This would enable partners to have limited liability while also taking advantage of the existing general partnership cases and forms. Why then was it that the LLC that became dominant?

One answer to this question is that LLP's network advantages were not important enough to outweigh the significant drawback that it did not integrate limited liability into a coherent standard form. By contrast (as discussed in more detail in Chapter 7), LLCs not only have limited liability but features such as optional centralized management that fit with limited liability. The lesson of this history for the development of uncorporate standard forms is that the network problem may not be the impediment to developing new business associations that theorists have suggested.[295]

3. Limited partnership

As discussed in Chapter 2, various versions of the limited partnership have existed throughout the history of business associations. The modern U.S. version of the limited partnership tried to maintain a clear separation between active and passive owners with the *control rule*, which provides that partners who take part in management and control are liable as general partners.

Limited partnerships have been subject to a succession of uniform laws in 1916, 1976, 1985, and 2001. Nevertheless, uniformity has played less of a role here than for general partnerships, particularly recently, as limited partnerships long have been able to make a binding choice of the applicable law by choosing the formation state, just as with corporations.[296] Limited partnerships therefore

---

293. *See id.* (describing the evolution and spread of the LLP form).

294. *See* Scott Baker & Kimberly Krawiec, *The Economics of Limited Liability: An Empirical Study of New York Law Firms* (with S. Baker), 2005 U. ILL. L. REV. 107 (2005) (empirically examining the factors relating to New York law firms' decisions to convert from general partnerships to LLPs).

295. *See* Bruce H. Kobayashi & Larry E. Ribstein, *Choice of Form and Network Externalities*, 43 WM. & MARY L. REV. 79 (2001).

296. These provisions for registration of and law applicable to limited partnerships operating outside their formation state were included in Article 9 of both RULPA and the UNIFORM LIMITED PARTNERSHIP ACT (2001) ("ULPA 2001").

do not need uniformity in order to get certainty about the applicable law. Although the 1916 and 1985 laws were widely adopted and the 2001 law is gradually spreading through the states, the states also have developed a fair amount of variation.

On the other hand, there is probably more uniformity for limited partnerships than for LLCs simply because there is a narrower possible range of variation. As discussed below, the basic point of limited partnerships, particularly now that they compete with other limited liability unincorporated entities, is to provide a clear and predictable form of centralized management. Moreover, until the 2001 uniform law, limited partnership statutes were basically an appendage to the general partnership statutes, providing mainly rules for limited liability and management by the limited partners and linking to the general partnership statute for many of the other rules. Though the 2001 statute eliminated this linkage with general partnership and made the limited partnership statute self-contained, it accomplished this by bringing over the text of many of the uniform rules from the general partnership statute.

The limited partnership has evolved recently in the shadow of the LLC. Until the LLC, the limited partnership was the most widely used form of uncorporate limited liability in the United States. Limited partnership then became a bridge to the LLC, which resembles a limited partnership except for the extension of limited liability to the managing members. Indeed, it was Georgia's recognition in 1988 of limited liability for managing members of limited partnerships that helped put on the front burner the issue of extending partnership taxation to full-fledged limited liability entities.

Now that the LLC has swept the nation, we may wonder if there is any use left for the limited partnership. In theory, there would seem to be none because (as discussed in more detail in Chapter 7), a firm can do everything through a centrally managed LLC that it can do through a limited partnership. On the other hand, a firm might gain clarity and predictability by adopting a standard form that divides the managing and nonmanaging members as clearly as does the limited partnership. The traditional version of the limited partnership *control rule*, which imposes personal liability on limited partners who participate in management, protects the general partner from excessive backseat driving and reassures creditors that the firm's managers will have the creditors' interests at heart.[297]

The distinct functions of the limited partnership have been compromised to some extent by the gradual elimination of the control rule from the LP form. Firms have long pressed for more flexibility—and state legislatures accommodated them. This was encouraged to some extent by the use of limited partnerships for

---

297. For a functional analysis of the traditional limited partnership form, see Larry E. Ribstein, *An Applied Theory of Limited Partnership*, 37 EMORY L.J. 837 (1988).

publicly traded firms regulated under the federal securities laws, which effectively import federal norms of investor voice. By 1985, the uniform law provided not only an ample safe harbor for limited partner voices that would not trigger personal liability, but that even the exercise of full-fledged management power would not trigger personal liability unless creditors reasonably believed that the limited partners are actually general partners.[298] The 2001 version now spreading across the states finally eliminated the rule.[299]

Despite the LP's loss of some of its distinctiveness, it continues to thrive alongside the LLC. While the LLC is a flexible form that tries to accommodate a wide spectrum of uses, the LP caters to a narrower clientele of investment firms (such as venture capital, private equity, and real estate partnerships) in which passive owners trust to a manager's expertise. As discussed in more detail in Chapter 8, limited partnership law provides clear recognition of several features valued by these firms: general partners' substantial discretion and significant incentive compensation, limited partners' weak voting rights, and regular distributions to the owners to offset limitations in the owners' limited governance rights, as well as generally that the terms of the partnership agreement rather than statutory defaults control the firm's management.

The LP illustrates how standard forms evolve in relation to each other. The LP was first a mechanism for importing limited liability into unincorporated firms. It reduced the need for the full-fledged "incorporated partnership" by offering limited liability to passively managed partnerships while Subchapter S catered to informal decentralized firms. When LLCs and LLPs brought full limited liability to uncorporations, the LP lost its function as a bridge to limited liability and became the ferry boat trying to stay in business after the bridge had been built. The LP then adapted to its new function as a specialized form of centralized management.

4. LLLP

The LLLP, in which the general partners have limited liability, is a seemingly inevitable phase of the recent evolution of business forms. It had already been accepted that general partnerships could simply add limited liability by becoming LLPs, that any kind of firm could have limited liability in the LLC form, and that LPs could have limited liability investors with few restraints on governance. Moreover, LPs could fashion their own version of complete limited liability by incorporating their general partners. It was obviously only a small and logical step to allowing limited partnerships to have full-fledged limited liability by registering as LLLPs.[300] This small step had the more significant ramification of cutting the liability support for the control rule and probably hastening that rule's demise.

---

298. *See* RULPA § 303(b).
299. ULPA (2001) § 303.
300. For an analysis of LLLP provisions, see BROMBERG & RIBSTEIN, *supra* note 292, Ch. 5.

E. THE EVOLVING LLC

The full tax recognition of the LLC in 1988 and the later elimination of tax barriers by the check-the-box rule only began the significant development of LLC statutes. The following is an overview of this recent history, while Chapter 7 explores the current status of LLCs in more detail.

In general, LLC statutes have evolved toward both efficiency and uniformity. A study of the first generation of LLC statutes adopted from around 1988 to 1994 showed that the statutes did not simply copy the initial Wyoming statute, which as discussed above was basically an ad hoc combination of corporate, limited partnership, and general partnership provisions. LLC statutes evolved to suit the needs of modern closely held firms. In particular, the statutes rapidly abandoned unnecessary formalities of organization and reduced restrictions on contracting, mainly regarding transferability of interests, fiduciary duties, and continuity of the firm.[301]

Early LLC statutes also evolved toward efficient uniformity.[302] Provisions that relate to third parties (such as those dealing with formalities, liabilities to creditors, and designation of who can bind the LLC in transactions with third parties) became the most uniform. This reflects the need to reduce information costs in connection with creditors' dealings in small transactions with many LLCs organized across the states. Provisions relating primarily to the members (such as those dealing with management) have shown more variation, consistent with the fact that members of closely held firms can and often do incur the costs of customized contracting.

The second stage of LLC evolution occurred once the 1996 "check-the-box" rule eliminated tax constraints on contracting. As firms now could adopt corporate-type terms such as free transferability, perpetual life, and centralized management without subjecting themselves to the corporate double tax, the statutes could include some entity-type features and eliminate restrictions on contracting intended to protect the parties and their lawyers from accidently becoming tax corporations. A key default provision of LLC statutes also changed, again for tax reasons: LLCs no longer dissolved by default because of a member's dissociation. As discussed in Chapter 7, this change was encouraged by a tax rule that placed a higher value for estate tax purposes on liquid than on illiquid interests.

As discussed in Chapter 2, the main force driving the evolution of LLC statutes appears to be lawyers who have an interest in promoting their individual reputations as experts in the area and in ensuring that the law of their home state was attractive to business formation. It is not clear how much active state competition

---

301. *See* Larry E. Ribstein, *Statutory Forms for Closely Held Firms: Theories and Evidence from LLCs*, 73 WASH. U. L.Q. 369, 412–28 (1995).

302. *See* Bruce H. Kobayashi & Larry E. Ribstein, *Evolution and Uniformity*, 34 ECON. INQ. 464 (July 1996).

there is for LLC formations. It has been shown that most LLCs forming outside their home states are relatively large (and therefore can most easily bear the costs of paying fees both to the formation and home states), and they are choosing Delaware, evidently for its sophisticated courts and lawyers.[303] Although states are continually revising their LLC statutes and coming up with innovative provisions, no correlation is shown between LLC formations and states' adoption of particular types of provisions. However, the formation data and the evolution of LLC statutes suggest that the states are keeping their statutes sufficiently current with legal developments to discourage locally based firms from forming in Delaware and elsewhere.

Three general types of LLC statutes have developed. First, as just noted, Delaware leads the competition for larger LLCs. These firms want to engage in sophisticated planning—and they expect member litigation over contract terms. They therefore want both a flexible statute that accommodates this planning and sophisticated courts and lawyers to handle the expected litigation. What they do not need are a lot of detailed default rules or restrictions on contracting.

Second, all states may compete for in-between firms that are large enough to form outside their home states, but only if the benefits of doing so outweigh high size-adjusted costs. These firms may be large enough to do sophisticated planning, and therefore might want Delaware-type flexibility. However, the state may be home to enough very small firms that it needs to offer a full set of default rules and offer more protection against improvident agreements, particularly regarding fiduciary duties. By contrast, Delaware has fewer home-based firms to worry about and can focus on the interstate market for law.

Third, some states neither compete for LLCs nor have major commercial centers. These states likely also lack the necessary legal or legislative resources for drafting sophisticated legislation. This category of states could be expected to rely on uniform laws. Indeed, there is evidence that states with smaller legislatures are generally more likely to adopt uniform laws.[304] In theory one would expect these states to prefer laws suitable for the smallest firms—that is, those heavy on detailed default rules and relatively inflexible. However, the politics of drafting uniform laws may frustrate their drafters' ability to attain coherent objectives.[305]

---

303. *See* Kobayashi & Ribstein, *supra* note 285.

304. *See* Larry E. Ribstein & Bruce H. Kobayashi, *Economic Analysis of Uniform State Laws*, 25 J. Leg. Stud. 131 (1996).

305. For a detailed analysis of the operation of the uniform lawmaking process in the LLC context, see Bruce H. Kobayashi & Larry E. Ribstein, *The Non-Uniformity of Uniform Laws*, 35 J. Corp. L. __ (forthcoming 2010).

F. EUROPEAN DEVELOPMENTS

As discussed in Chapter 5, non-U.S. countries (including those in Europe) have had an advantage over the United States in that their development of business association law has not been stunted by the dominance of the corporation or other equivalent regulated entity privileged by lawmakers. This difference might be partly attributed to history—the advent of the Industrial Revolution early in U.S. legal history and the country's immediate turn to the corporation. It also might owe something to the innate conservatism of the common law system and to the logistics of developing new rules across multiple jurisdictions. On the other hand, the U.S. common law and federal systems offer opportunities for competition, experimentation, and error correction that are unavailable in other legal systems. This is evident in comparing the rapid evolution and spread of the LLC and other unincorporated business forms in the United States with the relative stasis in European business association developments over the same period.

Europe traditionally has not had the U.S. choice-of-law rule that lets firms choose their governance law without moving their location. Europe accordingly attempted to harmonize member nations' law through European directives.[306] After almost twenty years of failure on this front, European lawmakers tried a second approach: the adoption of a new business form, the Societas Europaea (SE), which could serve as the basis of a single Europe-wide entity. This approach eschews both U.S.-style law competition and harmonization as the entity provided for under this statute would be governed mainly by the law of law of the SE's "seat."[307]

At the turn of the twenty-first century, it looked as though Europe might be moving toward a more dynamic legal environment. In 1999, the European Court of Justice (ECJ) held in the *Centros* case[308] that Denmark could not bar a company that was fully located in Denmark from incorporating in the United Kingdom and opening a "branch" in Denmark. The court relied on the "right of establishment" in what is now Article 48 of the Treaty of Rome (the European constitution), which provides that companies formed in accordance with member state law shall "be treated in the same way as natural persons who are nationals of Member States."[309] The ECJ later applied the right of establishment to give a

---

306. *See* JOSEPH A. MCCAHERY & ERIK P.M. VERMEULEN, CORPORATE GOVERNANCE OF NON-LISTED COMPANIES 59–64 (2008).

307. *Id.* at 64–65.

308. Case C-212/97, Centros Ltd. v. Erhvervs-og Selskabsstyrelsen, 1999 E.C.R. I-1459.

309. Treaty Establishing the European Community art. 8, Nov. 10, 1997, 1997 O.J. (c340) 3.

Dutch corporation the right to sue in Germany[310] and to bar the Netherlands from imposing local regulations on a company that was based locally, but incorporated elsewhere solely to avoid these regulations.[311]

These cases started a sort of European competition, but it was not like the full-scale U.S.-style legal competition that has driven the LLC Revolution. Rather, *Centros* set off a rush of formations of UK incorporations by companies based elsewhere in Europe looking for lower incorporation costs, followed by a cost-based competitive response by European countries.[312] The lack of full-fledged competition for law may be due to regulatory and tax impediments to mobility in Europe that survive *Centros*.[313] More fundamentally, it may reflect differences among European countries in law, language, and custom, the greater role of interest groups (particularly labor) in opposing changes in business association law, and lower incentives to compete by European countries as compared to U.S. states.[314] Europe's limits on chartering fees and taxes also may have reduced competition.[315] However (as discussed above), lawyers rather than fees likely have driven competition in the United States. European lawyers seem more interested in selling their expertise in complex harmonized laws.[316] This in turn may be attributable to the other factors just noted limiting the potential for interjurisdictional competition in Europe.

The result of these European developments is that business forms for closely held firms are less flexible and more regulatory than the LLC and other partnership-based business forms in the United States. Chapter 4 touched on the French and German equivalents to the LLC, which antedated the U.S. version, but that have not experienced a similar evolution. The United Kingdom, which has driven

---

310. Case C-208/00, Überseering BV v. Nordic Construction Company Baumanagement GmbH (NCC), 2002 E.C.R. I-9919.

311. Case C-167/01, Kamer van Koophandel en Fabrieken voor Amsterdam v. Inspire Art Ltd., 2003 E.C.R. I-10155.

312. *See* McCahery & Vermeulen, *supra* note 306, at 81 (noting that European competition is over reduction of incorporation costs, not changes in corporate law regimes); Marco Becht et al., *Where do Firms Incorporate? Deregulation and the Cost of Entry* 23 (Eur. Corp. Governance Inst., Working Paper No. 70, 2006) http://ssrn.com/abstract=906066 (finding that average number of European private limited companies incorporating in the U.K. increased from 4,600 firms per year before *Centros* to 28,000 firms per year afterward, totaling over 120,000 firms between 1997 and 2006, including 48,000 from Germany).

313. *See* McCahery & Vermeulen, *supra* note 306, at 91–96.

314. See Erin A. O'Hara & Larry E. Ribstein, *Rules and Institutions in Developing a Law Market: Views from the United States and Europe*, 82 Tul. L. Rev. 2147 (2008).

315. Töbias Hans Troger, *Choice of Jurisdiction in European Corporate Law—Perspectives of European Corporate Governance*, 6 Eur. Bus. Org. L. Rev. 3, 63 (2005); Marco Ventoruzzo, *'Cost-Based' and 'Rule-Based' Regulatory Competition: Markets for Corporate Charters in the U.S. and in the EU*, 3 N.Y.U. J. L. & Bus. 91, 130 (2006).

316. *See* McCahery & Vermeulen, *supra* note 306, at 87.

competition in Europe, has itself stopped short of current U.S. developments regarding closely held firms. Its LLP Act adopted in 2001 is more restrictive than U.S. LLC and limited partnership statutes; it includes prohibitions on public offerings, application of accounting regulation, and linkage to the Companies Act governing larger firms.[317]

A more dynamic process may yet emerge in Europe. The United Kingdom may take the lead driven by its "charmed circle" of international law firms. Moreover, Europe's long-standing failure to harmonize member states' law indicates that at least an aggressive competitor in Europe would not be constrained (as Delaware is in the United States) by a realistic threat of displacement by federal regulation.[318] Alternatively, competition worldwide may be driven by "entrepreneurial" jurisdictions such as Singapore, which in 2005 adopted the Singapore LLP Act as part of a deliberate effort to "accommodate current international business and commercial practices."[319]

---

317. *Id.* at 97–99.

318. As to the federal government's role in constraining state competition in the US, See Mark J. Roe, *Delaware's Competition*, 117 HARV. L. REV. 588 (2003).

319. *See* McCahery & Vermeulen, *supra* note 306, at 127–31 (including chart comparing features of various statutes around the world).

7. THE MODERN UNCORPORATION

This chapter discusses the aftermath of the LLC Revolution discussed in Chapter 6. It presents a detailed portrait of the modern uncorporation as it emerged over the last twenty years after being liberated from tax and regulation that had forced firms to accept the corporate form as the price of limited liability. This portrait includes the modern versions of the traditional general and limited partnership as well as the current version of the new LLC.

The LLC Revolution freed firms from having to incorporate in order to receive limited liability and other corporate features. But this chapter shows that the modern firms that emerged from the revolution were quite different from the very closely held partnerships that antedated the corporation. We cannot really call LLCs and their ilk partnerships even if they were derived from this form. The *uncorporation* moniker reflects that these firms are best defined in terms of their differences from corporations. Although uncorporations and corporations share the "corporate" feature of limited liability, the corporation's innate regulatory nature distinguishes it from the more flexible uncorporate forms.

The chapter demonstrates the many ways uncorporations are distinct not only from corporations, but from each other. The chapter delineates both the *vertical* variations among types of standard forms and the *horizontal* variations across jurisdictions. This combination of horizontal and vertical competition has produced at least nine types of uncorporate standard forms: UPA and RUPA general partnerships; limited liability partnerships (LLPs); RULPA and ULPA (2001) limited partnerships; limited liability limited partnerships (LLLPs); Delaware flexible LLCs; home-state flexible LLCs, and home-state inflexible LLCs. These variations enhance the uncorporation's ability to fit the needs of diverse firms and to provide a basis for continued evolution.

The analytical distinctions between these business forms emphasize the critical element of *coherence* of the various features of business association standard forms. As discussed in Chapter 2, a business association statute should offer firms the opportunity to select a *set* of default terms that fit together. Designing coherent sets of terms requires understanding the types and business needs of firms that will use each type of statute. The legislature should design statutes whose default and mandatory rules will minimize transaction costs for the statute's likely "clientele" of firms. For example, a statute that prescribes a particular type of management structure also should provide for the kinds of rules regarding transfer of interest, limited liability, fiduciary duties, and exit that firms with that management structure would prefer.

Although the concept of coherence is a useful frame of reference in analyzing uncorporations, it is important to keep in mind that this theoretical tool does not perfectly describe the reality of modern business associations. Uncorporations have evolved over time, particularly in reaction to changing tax laws and views concerning limited liability. Evolution can be inherently messy as old approaches tend to linger past their prime. Also, as discussed throughout the chapter and particularly in the last section, tax and nonbusiness association regulation can indirectly influence the shape of business associations.

In addition to examining particular standard form terms, analysis of modern uncorporation statutes illuminates some of the policy choices inherent in the architecture of business associations. For example, statute drafters need to balance the costs and benefits of flexibility against those of more rigid rules. They also need to consider the trade-offs between fully optional default rules and mandatory rules. This is not necessarily a choice between contract and regulation as long as firms can freely choose among business associations with different mixes of default and mandatory rules. Again, these choices depend mainly on the statute's likely clientele—for example, whether small, informal firms or large sophisticated ones are most likely to use the statute.

This chapter highlights the differences that have emerged between the classical partnership discussed in Chapter 3 (which had essentially endured through most of the twentieth century) and the uncorporation that has rapidly evolved over the last twenty years freed of the constraints imposed by regulatory protection of the corporate form. Uncorporate forms can now meet the needs of a wide variety of firms. The next chapter discusses the most important remaining set of issues concerning whether the uncorporate form is likely to break out of its traditional niche of small, closely held firms and embrace the larger firms the corporation was developed to serve.

In general, this chapter serves as both a detailed guide to the specific issues addressed by modern uncorporations and a theoretical overview of the fundamental characteristics of the emerging flexible uncorporation.

A. MEMBER SHIELDING: LIMITED LIABILITY

The discussion begins with the basic feature of member liability for the firm's debts—limited, that is, to the member's investment in the firm. This feature is basic because (as discussed in Chapter 5) it is the one that the parties cannot replicate by private contract. Therefore, whether a statutory form provides for limited liability therefore will dominate parties' choice of form. This in turn helps define the statute's clientele and guides the design of the rest of the statute, including provisions regarding centralization of management, fiduciary duties, owners' need to exit the firm, and rules governing exit and transfer of interests. As with other issues, we will consider how each uncorporate form differs from the corporation and from other uncorporations.

1. Corporate limited liability

Shareholders are not, in general, personally liable for the debts of the corporation merely because they are shareholders. Shareholders *are* liable for their own contracts and torts. Limited liability obviously is not intended to immunize owners from responsibility for their own acts. As we will see in the discussion of LLCs, the trick is distinguishing individual from entity liability in very closely held owner-controlled firms.

Courts also may "pierce the corporate veil" to impose liability on owners for the firm's debts when the courts find abuse of the corporate form. This doctrine recognizes the risk that owners may ignore creditors' interests in running the firm if the owners do not stake their personal wealth. However, the application of this doctrine is fuzzy because it is an umbrella for a variety of debtor misdeeds, many of which are also covered by more specific rules. For example, owners may misrepresent the corporation's assets, distribute assets to themselves and leave the firm an empty shell, or fail to make the disclosures and comply with other statute formalities the statute prescribes for incorporating the firm.

It is easy to see why this sort of misconduct should trigger owner liability to creditors. But why do we need the vague umbrella remedy of veil-piercing rather than just relying on remedies for specific wrongs? Perhaps the reason is that proof difficulties make the specific remedies an inadequate deterrent. But the loss of clarity and predictability inherent in veil-piercing may outweigh the benefits of deterring misconduct. There is some sentiment for abolishing the whole messy doctrine.[320]

As the corporate rule was the model for uncorporate limited liability, and as the basic issues are the same across different types of firms, we might not expect significant variations across firms. However, as we will see, there is surprising variation among uncorporations even regarding this standard feature.

2. The evolution of uncorporate limited liability

As discussed in Chapters 4 and 5, the evolution of uncorporations has been driven significantly by firms' search for a tax-favored alternative to corporate limited liability in the face of expanding tort and regulatory liability. Government has jealously guarded the prerogative of creating limited liability and sought to channel limited liability into the regulated corporate form.

There are also arguably reasons to be particularly concerned about limited liability in uncorporations. As discussed throughout the book, an important feature of uncorporations is the owners' greater access to the firm's cash through distributions or the power to demand liquidation or buyout. This increases the risk that the owners will simply walk away from the firm and its obligations to creditors. Also, as discussed in Chapter 6, partnership-type taxation of limited

---

320. *See* Stephen M. Bainbridge, *Abolishing Veil-Piercing*, 26 J. CORP. L. 479 (2001).

liability firms increases the risks associated with limited liability by giving the firm an extra incentive to distribute earnings to the owners rather than keeping them available in the firm for paying the firm's debts.

Notwithstanding these concerns, uncorporate law favors complete corporate-type shielding of owners from vicarious liability. This may be because (as discussed in Chapter 2) the firms' owners have more say than creditors in drafting state business association statutes. But the plight of limited liability uncorporations' tort creditors looks less ominous from another perspective. Limited liability can be seen partly as a reaction to the expansion of tort liability in the twentieth century. Tort liability once was constrained by duty rules that let manufacturers and sellers restrict their liability by controlling the terms of the contracts of the resellers with whom they dealt. As these constraints on liability weakened, limited liability emerged as an alternative way to confine tort law's reach. In other words, the LLC Revolution is at least partly a reaction to the tort revolution.

The evolution of uncorporate limited liability has not, however, been a single-minded march toward the corporate model. Rather (as discussed below) the result is an array of approaches rather than a simple choice between limited and vicarious liability.

3. General partnership: entity aspects of unlimited liability

The general partnership seemingly offers the classic version of owners' vicarious liability for the firm's debts in which each partner can be held personally liable for all of the firm's debts. However, owners' vicarious liability is not as straightforward as it seems because of the "entity" aspects of partners' liability both to the firm and directly to the creditors. With respect to the partners' liability to the firm, suppose that the creditor sues the partnership. If the partnership has more debts than assets, the partners have a duty under their agreement or the default provisions of the partnership statute to contribute toward that shortfall. Under the partnership statutes, the *partnership's* assets consist both of what the partnership owns under its name and its "accounts receivable" from the partners representing the partners' liability to contribute to the shortfall.[321] Thus, the partner's liability is handled through the partnership entity.

Even if the creditors sue the partners individually, their liability has an entity flavor. Under the *exhaustion* rule, creditors generally have to sue the partnership as well as the partners and then, on obtaining judgments against both, execute against partnership assets. The main exceptions are when the partnership is a debtor in bankruptcy, the partner agrees to be held liable without exhaustion, or a court deems exhaustion to be futile or overly burdensome.[322]

---

321. *See* UPA § 40; RUPA § 807.
322. *See* RUPA § 307(d).

The exhaustion rule has evolved over the last century. At first, exhaustion was required only in contract actions (in which the partners' liability was said to be *joint*) and not for tort liability (which was said to be *joint and several*).[323] Tort creditors got a break because they presumably were not in a position to contract for protection or compensation. However, the states gradually applied the exhaustion requirement to all partnership debts—a development that was hastened by the adoption and spread of the Revised Uniform Partnership Act.

Exhaustion is satisfied or not required if the partnership is a debtor in bankruptcy. But then the creditor has to deal with bankruptcy law. The automatic stay in bankruptcy[324] blocks actions against the debtor. Moreover, bankruptcy court injunctions might bar even actions against *non-debtor* partners as a way of protecting the partnership's bankruptcy estate, which as discussed above may include contributions from the partners.[325]

The full effect of restrictions on partners' vicarious liability becomes clearer in light of the logistical problems creditors face when loaning to partnerships.[326] Partnership creditors need to assess and monitor the credit not only of the entity, but of the individual partners. Creditors also may need to pursue actions against the partners in several states after first exhausting remedies against the partnership, which also may require actions wherever the partnership has property.

Thompson v. Wayne Smith Construction Company, Inc.[327] illustrates the burdens these rules place on plaintiffs. The plaintiff (Wayne Smith) got a judgment on a contract to build houses against the partnership in South Carolina, then tried to collect in South Carolina, Ohio, and Indiana. The South Carolina court entered judgment against the partnership but not against the individual partners, presumably because plaintiff had not exhausted its remedies against the partnership. Two years later, after plaintiff had collected only a small part of the judgment before exhausting its remedies against the partnership, plaintiff tried to collect from the partnership and individual partners in Ohio. Plaintiff got a judgment there, but the partner appealed to the Ohio Supreme Court.

Meanwhile the plaintiff sued one of the partners in Indiana where the partner resided. Plaintiff obtained a judgment against that partner, which the partner appealed. Then the Ohio Supreme Court decided that plaintiff could collect only one-third of the South Carolina judgment from each partner, which is obviously inconsistent with the partnership rule of joint and several liability for all partnership debts. Eight years after the initial judgment, the Indiana appellate court

---

323. *See* 2 BROMBERG & RIBSTEIN, *supra* note 99, at § 5.08(b).

324. Bankruptcy Code § 362, 11 U.S.C. § 362.

325. *See generally*, Larry E. Ribstein, *The Illogic and Limits of Partners' Liability in Bankruptcy*, 32 WAKE FOR. L. REV. 31 (1997).

326. *See* Larry E. Ribstein, *The Deregulation of Limited Liability and the Death of Partnership*, 70 WASH. U. L.Q. 417 (1992).

327. 640 N.E.2d 408 (Ind. App. 1994).

finally upheld the judgment against the Indiana partner against the argument that his liability was inconsistent with both the South Carolina and Ohio decisions.

Collection nightmares like the one in *Thompson* indicate that general partners' vicarious liability may not quite be the boon to partnership creditors that it seems. Given the confusion and burden of exhaustion requirements, the partners could be said to have quasi-limited liability. It is important to keep in mind that these rules developed before the LLC Revolution. Had limited liability partnership forms developed earlier, perhaps traditional general partnership liability would have remained to make available a clearer choice of liability rules. Strict vicarious liability arguably suits the nature of the general partnership as the default entity for the smallest firms. Also, there might have been less partner demand for quasi-limited liability if they could get full-fledged limited liability through the LLC or LLP. This illustrates how the structure of business forms can reflect their evolutionary path rather than strict theoretical notions of coherence.

4. Limited liability partnership

As discussed in Chapter 6, the LLP developed just as the LLC was starting to spread across the country. This business form ended up as merely a niche vehicle for professional firms rather than a dominant form of uncorporate limited liability. The seeming advantages of combining limited liability with the existing partnership framework turned out not to be what a lot of firms wanted. But at least initially the LLP form offered a potentially interesting variant on limited liability. The first LLP statutes provided for limited liability only for tort debts.[328] This inverted the traditional partnership approach of providing the most extensive form of direct joint and several liability in tort rather than contract cases. The reason for the LLP rule is that (as discussed in Chapter 6) the LLP was developed to offer professional firms a way to deal with the regulatory liability that suddenly burgeoned in the late 1980s. These firms did not need statutory relief from limited liability to handle their large contract creditors and clients.

Most state LLP statutes came to reject this rule and provide for limited liability for all debts,[329] so the rule ended up as a side road off of the LLP dead end. However, the variant actually makes sense for some firms, as it is similar in effect to the way limited liability actually comes out in closely held firms: vicarious liability for creditors who bargain for it, limited liability for the rest. The seeming anomaly of restricting limited liability to the situation in which the theoretical case for limited liability is weakest may have made the rule politically unappealing. But this reasoning ignores the fact that firms have a choice of

---

328. *See* BROMBERG & RIBSTEIN, *supra* note 292, at § 1.01.
329. *Id.* § 3.03.

forms, and that eliminating this option effectively forces firms into a form of limited liability that is worse rather than better for some creditors.

5. Limited partnership

The limited partnership offers yet another variation on limited liability. In this case, limited liability was traditionally available only to the passive owners: the limited partners. As a backup, any partner who participated in control was held liable as a general partner.[330] This addresses the risks of limited liability to creditors discussed above by giving the firm's managers (who make the critical decisions on risk and distribution of assets) a liability incentive to act in creditors' interests. It is a rule that firms cannot fully replicate just by members contractually guaranteeing *individual* debts because the incentive effect of liability depends on the general partners' being bound on *all* debts.

Although the limited partnership control rule may reduce the risks to creditors, it may increase agency costs between owners and managers. The owners, whose limited liability enables them to hold diversified portfolios of investments, may want the managers to take more risk than the personally liable managers would want to take. Also, the limited partners may want to dissolve the firm when its prospects are bleak, while general partners might want to reduce their burden by keeping the firm going.

Limited partnership statutes have reflected erosion of the control rule over the last hundred years, in which the exceptions increased until it was finally eliminated in the current version of the Uniform Limited Partnership Act (2001).[331] This may reflect that the mandatory aspect of the rule can cut against owners, who as discussed in Chapter 2 have the political advantage over many interest groups. But, as with the quasi-limited liability of the general partnership exhaustion rule, the limited partnership might have retained its limited form of vicarious liability if full-fledged uncorporate limited liability had been available earlier.

The limited partnership might seem to be ready to fade into the sunset now that the LLC offers full-fledged limited liability along with the opportunity to have limited partnership-type centralized management. However, as we will see in Chapter 8, limited partnerships still play a starring role in large firms. This may reflect the greater clarity of centralized management in limited partnerships as well as the large body of legal precedent and forms (and therefore predictability) that has built up in the limited partnership.

6. Limited liability company

As we have seen, the LLC took the significant step from the modified limited liability of the limited partnership to full-fledged limited liability of managing as

---

330. *See* RULPA § 303.
331. *See* ULPA (2001) § 303.

well as nonmanaging members. Because the LLC was the first unincorporated U.S. business association to provide for full-fledged limited liability, it posed a new question of whether this new uncorporate-type limited liability was the same as corporate-type limited liability.

The question might be best approached by turning it around and asking, why not? One answer is that (as discussed above) uncorporations present special risks for creditors because the owners can take the money and dissolve the firm. Also, the recent advent of this brand new business association itself invites a reexamination of troublesome questions concerning limited liability in closely held firms.

At least two types of cracks in limited liability have appeared in the LLC form. The first involves the concept of piercing the veil. There have been many LLC cases on this issue—perhaps more than on any other one. Most purport to apply the corporate veil-piercing test, which looks to disregard of the corporate form and whether this disregard involved fraud and harm.[332] But should veil-piercing differ between LLCs and corporations?

Some LLC statutes provide that the veil cannot be pierced for mere failure to comply with formalities. For example, the court in *Pinebrook Properties, Ltd. v. Brookhaven Lake Property Owners Ass'n*.[333] applied one such provision in refusing to pierce the veil of an LLC that had no checking account and had not filed a tax return, in which the manager signed his own name to a company letter without indicating his capacity. The idea here seems to be that as long as the LLC has complied with specific statutory rules, there is no need for an additional judicial remedy. But why should LLCs get a more lenient rule on veil-piercing than corporations? It would seem that courts should insist more firmly on LLCs following the rules because of the higher risks to creditors in partnership-type limited liability firms.

The formalities exception might indicate that courts and legislatures are taking the opportunity presented by LLCs to rethink the whole concept of veil-piercing. The real basis of veil-piercing in both corporations and LLCs is fraud, which generally occurs when creditors are misled about the nature or capitalization of the entity or value is transferred from insolvent entities to the owners. In other words (as discussed above), veil-piercing liability may be little more than a repackaging of more specific fraudulent conveyance theories.[334]

---

332. See RIBSTEIN & KEATINGE, supra note 260, § 12.03. See also O'Neal and Thompson, supra note 271, § 8.23 (noting that "courts seem oblivious to any difference [regarding veil-piercing] between a corporation and an LLC"); Robert B. Thompson, *The Limits of Liability in the New Limited Liability Entities*, 32 WAKE FOR. L. REV. 1 (1997) (predicting that LLCs will be treated like corporations for purposes of veil-piercing).

333. 77 S.W.3d 487 (Tex. App. 2002).

334. See Robert Charles Clark, *The Duties of the Corporate Debtor to Its Creditors*, 90 HARV. L. REV. 505 (1977).

Focusing on fraud might help to clarify the distinction between corporations and LLCs regarding veil-piercing. Courts may be more likely to pierce in LLCs than in corporations because the informality of LLCs leaves them more vulnerable to fraud. Also, the relative novelty of the LLC may invite creditor confusion, making it easier to pierce on the ground that creditors were misled about the limited liability of the specific firm with which they dealt.

A more specific gap in LLC limited liability may be opening in cases that purportedly respect members' liability and do not attempt to pierce the veil, but that blur the distinction between individual and vicarious liability. For example, in *Estate of Countryman v. Farmers Co-op. Ass'n*,[335] seven people tragically died in an explosion probably caused by propane gas supplied by an LLC which was co-owned by two cooperatives. The 5 percent owner provided managerial services under a management agreement, including "human resource and safety management." The court held that although the manager could not be held liable "solely by reason of being a member or manager" of an LLC, it *could* be liable for participating in torts by directing the individual manager in performing management services. The court remanded for further proceedings, noting that "we make no attempt to define the precise parameters of the participation theory of liability and the type of participation that gives rise to liability under the doctrine."[336] Along similar lines, another case held individual defendants liable for directing their LLC to make usurious loans,[337] and a Hawaii statute provides that violation of a statutory penal provision "shall be deemed to be also that of the individual members, managers, or agents of the limited liability company who have authorized, ordered, or done any of the acts constituting in whole or in part the violation."[338]

These authorities raise the question of when a manager (including a sole member-manager) can be held liable just for managing without engaging in a more specific wrongful act. Obviously no entity can do anything on its own—somebody has to act or fail to act on the firm's behalf. Is it enough that that the *firm's* act breaches a duty, or must the *particular manager* engage in specific wrongdoing in order to be held liable? Managerial liability under the former theory would seem to involve imposing liability for member or manager status, contrary to the limited liability provisions in LLC statutes.

A "negligent management" theory raises questions of its own. Should the manager's duty of care be higher to third parties than to members? Does negligent management necessarily entail an affirmative direction, or can it consist simply in failing adequately to supervise? Most importantly for present purposes,

---

335. 679 N.W.2d 598 (Iowa 2004).
336. *Id.* at n.2.
337. Gunnings v. Internet Cash Enterprise of Asheville, LLC, 2007 WL 1931291 (W.D. N.C. 2007).
338. Haw. Rev. Stat. § 480-17(b).

is there something about the LLC that invites this type of liability, or should the liability be applied equally to closely held corporations? In other words, is the rule really an end run around limited liability to address the novelty and extra risks to creditors of the LLC form?

Even if the LLC offers the potential for new liability risks, it also offers the opportunity for experimenting with ways to solve the problem. Consider the "series" LLC invented in Delaware[339] which is now spreading to several states.[340] Under these provisions of LLC statutes, an LLC can designate individual sub-entities (or series) of an umbrella LLC, each of which controls separate properties and the profits and losses associated with those properties. The statutes permit liabilities to be cabined off into particular series. So, for example, an LLC may sell interests in separate pools of assets all run by the same managers and offer investors in a particular pool the comfort of knowing that they have no exposure to the liabilities associated with the other pools.

The immediate question this peculiar device raises is: why not just use separate LLCs with common managers? Given statutory requirements for separating the series, it is not clear that using distinct LLCs would entail more formalities and record keeping. A possible answer is that using commonly managed and operated LLCs presents a risk that a court will pierce the veil and attribute the liabilities of one of the commonly managed firms to the "sister" LLCs. A series LLC statute effectively instructs courts to keep the liabilities separate as long as the members have followed the formalities and record-keeping rules. In other words, the series provisions use formalities as a shield even as the general LLC statutes provide that noncompliance with formalities cannot be used as a sword to pierce the veil.

The extra certainty provided by series provisions was a consideration in a particular situation involving conversion of a Massachusetts trust to a Delaware series LLC. The LLC planned to hold investment funds in separate series, each with different ownership interests reflecting the different investment objectives of various groups of annuity and life contract owners. The proxy statement with respect to the vote on the conversion noted that "a Delaware LLC has certain advantages over an investment company organized as a Massachusetts business trust, including greater certainty regarding the potential liability of shareholders and directors."[341]

The problem with the series provisions is that while trying to settle the veil-piercing issue, they raise a host of other issues. For example, the owner of a boat allegedly owned by a Delaware series LLC was barred from suing for breach

---

339. Del. Code Ann. § 18-215.
340. See 805 ILCS 180/37–40; Iowa Code Ann. § 490A.305; 18 Okla. St. § 2054.4; Tenn. Code Ann. § 48-249–309; Utah Code Ann. § 48-2c-606–616.
341. See John Hancock Trust, Definitive Proxy Statement (DEF14A), File No. 811-04146, Nov. 23, 2007, http://sec.gov/edgar/searchedgar/companysearch.html.

of warranty because the court could not figure out whether the series was enough of an entity to be able to sue—or whether it even had rights under the sales contract.[342] Also, does the withdrawal from a particular series of its sole member threaten the survival of the larger entity even if the other specific series still have members? What liability protection does a series LLC offer in states that do not recognize series LLCs, or in federal bankruptcy court? Perhaps most importantly, what is the effect of not following precisely the requisite series formalities? Will the court automatically pierce the veil to reach sister entities, thereby converting the series "shield" back into a sort of sword?

In short, the series LLC illustrates both the costs and benefits of new business forms: the opportunity to experiment along with the risks of uncertainty. These issues effectively replay the history of the LLC itself. Statutory innovations have to await case and regulatory law to be interpreted. Legislators can attempt to clarify the case law, but they still have to rely on the courts to interpret the statute. Moreover, one state's law may not bind courts in another state.

Series LLCs also illustrate the basic policy choice in statutory design between flexible standards and rigid rules. Veil-piercing is an open-ended standard, intended to catch all misconduct. But unpredictability has costs, which the series LLC provisions potentially address. In general, different business forms offer an opportunity to experiment with variations along this rule-standard continuum.

B. MANAGEMENT

The many permutations of management and control of uncorporations illustrate the distinctions between the flexible uncorporation and the relatively rigid corporation, as well as among different uncorporations. The spectrum of management forms extends from the centralized management model of the corporation (in which officers and directors run the firm and owners merely vote), to the decentralized partnership form (in which all owners also directly participate in the management of the firm).

Two considerations are particularly important in analyzing the various approaches to management and control. First, management comprises both power and accountability. Delegating power creates potential agency costs, as even owner-managers may have an incentive to exercise the power in their own interests rather than those of the firm or its other owners. Firms need structures or rules designed to control agency costs by making managers accountable to the owners. These include fiduciary duties, owner voting, oversight devices such as the board of directors, and owner exit rights through which owners can

---

342. *See* GxG Management LLC v. Young Bros. and Co., Inc., 2007 WL 551761 (D.Me. 2007), *clarified*, 2007 WL 1702872 (D. Me. June 11, 2007).

discipline managers by taking their money out of the firm. Managers' power cannot be fully analyzed without consideration of all of the governance rules that constrain the exercise of this power.

Second, we return to the trade-off between flexibility and rigidity of the business form. Specifically, should the business association statute lock in a particular management model (as in limited partnerships), or let firms choose their own model within a loose standard form? A flexible management structure facilitates private ordering but reduces certainty, particularly in connection with third party dealings. The more flexible the firm's structure, the easier it may be for third parties to show that the firm led them to believe that agents had more power than the firm's internal agreement gave them.

It is important to keep in mind that the third parties' costs of determining when the firm is bound by agents' acts ultimately may be borne by the firm itself because they are reflected in the price of the deal. The firm therefore has an incentive to agree to broad responsibility for its agents' acts, to make disclosures regarding the extent of the agents' power, and to adopt rigid management rules that clarify the agents' power.

These questions relate to a central concept in business association management—the agent's "positional" power. An agent's authority includes not only the authority that the firm explicitly represents the agents to have, but also the authority that customarily inhere in particular positions. This concept was perhaps most famously articulated by Judge Learned Hand in *Kidd v. Thomas A. Edison, Inc.*[343] The question there concerned the power of an agent, Fuller, to bind the company to engaging singers for series of "tone test" recitals. The company argued that Fuller lacked the power to commit to an extended engagement—and that no one had communicated on behalf of the company that he did have this power.

Nevertheless, Judge Hand held that Fuller bound the firm. The judge was at pains to point out that this was not the same sort of power that underlies apparent authority because the principal did not expressly mislead the public about the scope of the agent's power. Empowering the agent therefore seems more like endowing the agent with a "status" than basing the liability on the principal's consent as in other cases of authority. This status, said Judge Hand, was based on policy, as the firm benefits from the convenience of acting through agents without having to respond to repeated requests to clarify the agents' power. In return, the principal should be liable for acts that are at least generally within the agent's job description.

However, the summary of agency law in the *Restatement of Agency* has waffled on this concept of inherent agency power. The *Second Restatement* § 8A provided a theory similar to the one articulated in *Kidd*. Though the American Law

---

343. 239 F. 405 (S.D.N.Y.), *aff'd*, 242 F. 923 (2d Cir. 1917).

Institute took this provision out of the *Third Restatement*, the concept remains a basis for binding an *undisclosed* principal.[344] The basis of the agent's power in this situation (as articulated by Judge Hand) is a policy of enabling the principal to act through agents and the third party to rely on the agent's power to bind.

These policies relate more to the existence of positional power than to its scope in particular cases. The scope depends on the relevant statute and reflects the considerations relating to design of management provisions as discussed above. In other words, the breadth of positional power depends on the firm's ability to hold the agent accountable to the owners' interests and on the trade-off between flexibility and rigidity. The more rigid the agent's power is in a particular business association, the clearer the agent's positional power. As Judge Hand observed in *Kidd*, "[t]he scope of any authority must, of course, in the first place, be measured, not alone by the words in which it is created, but by the whole setting in which those words are used, including the customary powers of such agents."[345] This, in turn, determines the differences between the agent's internal and external authority. Where the agent has clear positional power, the principal's placing the agent in a particular position itself manifests the agent's power to bind the firm, just as did Fuller's position in *Kidd*.

In general, management provisions illustrate the role of coherence in the design of business association statutes. Determining agents' external power requires inferences from all of the elements of the contract. These inferences are easier if the elements mesh with each other rather than send conflicting signals.

1. Corporation: standardized hierarchy

As with the other issues discussed in this chapter, the initial point of comparison regarding management is the corporation. The corporate management model is designed for large firms. It is therefore not only centralized, but also standardized in order to clarify the expectations of the many people with which the corporation deals. Third parties dealing with corporations can expect that people holding certain types of corporate positions will have the particular powers custom and experience has assigned to their positions. Thus, there is relatively little difference between internal and external managerial power in a corporation. For example, the president is a general agent in charge of the business, the secretary is a functionary in charge of the formalities, the board approves significant transactions, and shareholders vote on structural changes but have no inherent power. Individual corporations generally can contract for whatever managerial powers they want, but when they do so they swim against the current of settled expectations.

---

344. AMERICAN LAW INSTITUTE, RESTATEMENT (THIRD) OF AGENCY, § 2.06 (2006).
345. *Kidd*, 239 F. at 406.

2. General partnership: direct member management

As the general partnership is the "default" business entity designed for the smallest and simplest firms, it is managed directly by the members without specialization of management and ownership. A majority of the partners must agree to ordinary transactions, each partner has one vote and can bind the firm to usual transactions within the apparent scope of the business, and all partners must agree to extraordinary transactions and amendments of the agreement. These minimal rules can be and often are altered by an infinite variety of agreements concerning partners' voting power, the vote needed for particular decisions, external power to bind the firm, and delegation of management power. The general partnership's management form therefore is at the opposite pole from the corporation along the flexibility/rigidity spectrum. This flexibility introduces uncertainty into the firm's dealings with third parties.

In the absence of an agreement to the contrary, each partner has the inherent positional power to bind the firm in ordinary transactions with third parties. This sharply contrasts with corporations in which the owners as such have no power. The partners' inherent power means that third parties can deal with individual partners in ordinary transactions and expect that the transactions will be enforceable against the firm unless the partnership has contracted around that power and the third party is aware of the contract.

Modern partnership statutes attempt to deal with questions about who can bind the firm by enabling partnerships to identify the partners and clarify their authority in a public filing.[346] However, the effect of the public filing is limited to real estate and other transactions in which third parties can be expected to check the public record. In other situations, the partnership must find some other way to notify everybody with which it deals that only certain people can bind the firm to certain types of transactions.

As with other business associations, partnership law provides mechanisms designed to hold managers accountable to the owners' interests. Partnership default rules include four such devices:

1. The owners *directly approve* the firm's decisions.
2. Owners are subject to *personal liability* for all debts of the firm regardless of whether they exercise any particular power in the firm. This not only aligns partners' interests with those of the firm's creditors but gives the owners strong incentives to watch over whoever is exercising management power.
3. *The managers are full-fledged owners*, so their fortunes and the firm's are necessarily intertwined. These are not the relatively pale incentives of corporate managers whose stock options or other forms of incentive compensation provide benefits when the firm does well, but not commensurate

---

346. *See* RUPA § 303.

detriment in bad times.[347] The partners' incentive structure is built into the firm's governance structure and can be varied only by the firm's basic governance documents with owner approval. Moreover, even optimal corporate compensation might not align managers' compensation with the firm's welfare. Corporate managers are inherently more risk-averse than the owners because they have their human capital invested in the firm while the owners typically hold diversified portfolios of shares. This misalignment of incentives could only be exacerbated by tying the managers' wealth too closely to that of the firm.
4. Each partner has a default right to be *bought out or compel a liquidation* of the firm. This enables each partner to discipline managers by reducing the assets the managers control.

Accountability may vary from firm to firm because of the range of private agreements the parties can make. For example, partnerships may provide for corporate-like durability by contracting around any buyout or liquidation right. This would dilute one of the important accountability mechanisms listed above. Conversely, corporations theoretically can approximate partner-like managerial incentives (subject in publicly held firms to the inherent conflict between risk-averse managers and diversified owners). A key difference between the two types of firms is that partnerships have more flexibility than standard form corporations to alter the default rules. Chapter 5 showed that the corporations have been converging toward partnership-type flexibility in the context of closely held firms. Chapter 8 raises the question whether this convergence will occur in the opposite direction—that is, towards less flexibility—in large and publicly held uncorporations.

3. Limited liability partnerships

LLPs simply add limited liability to the basic partnership structure. This arguably reduces the coherence of these statutes as compared to the standard version of the general partnership. Theoretically, LLP partners' limited liability should lead to more centralized management in LLPs than in standard-form partnerships. But significantly altering management in LLPs could defeat the point of these statutes, which was to give partnerships easy transition to limited liability. So LLP statutes trade coherence of member liability and other statutory features for the benefits of making the "network" of partnership cases available to limited liability firms. The fact that the LLP did not prove all that attractive may indicate that firms attached higher value to coherence than to network considerations.

---

347. For a sharp criticism of corporate compensation as resulting from abuse of managerial power, see LUCIAN BEBCHUK & JESSE FRIED, PAY WITHOUT PERFORMANCE: THE UNFULFILLED PROMISE OF EXECUTIVE COMPENSATION (2004).

4. Limited partnership: uncorporate centralized management

The limited partnership is the uncorporate approach to centralized management with passive members. In addition to the fundamental difference regarding centralized management, the limited partnership is at the opposite end from general partnership of the flexibility and internal/external power continuum. Limited partnership statutes clearly repose power in a particular group—that is, the general partners—rather than leaving allocation of power to the agreement as in the general partnership. Only the general partners can make management decisions, and these decisions bind the limited partners both as to third parties and within the firm. Limited partnerships traditionally are even less flexible than corporations by holding limited partners liable as general partners if they go too far in participating in management and control.[348]

Although the limited partnership approach to governance is comparable to corporations in many respects, it is important to emphasize that the limited partnership is not merely a partnership version of the corporation. The key difference between the two business associations lies in accountability. At first blush, the limited partnership seems to offer less accountability than the corporation despite its greater centralization of power. The limited partnership standard form does not provide for a board of directors to monitor managers or represent non-owner stakeholders, and it gives limited partners very weak voting rights. Although the current version of the Uniform Limited Partnership Act gives limited partners some power to vote on amendments and major transactions,[349] even under this statute they do not have corporate shareholders' continuous input through director elections. Indeed, the limited partnership *control rule* only gradually has been revised to even permit the partners to exercise these rights without subjecting themselves to vicarious liability. At the same time, limited partners lack the incentive to engage in management provided by personal liability. And there is no market for control built into limited partnerships because limited partners' management rights, like those of general partners, are not freely transferable in the absence of an agreement to the contrary.

So what accountability mechanisms support the nearly complete delegation of power by limited to general partners? One is general partners' personal liability for the firm's debts. But while this aligns general partners with creditors, it introduces a potential conflict of interest by potentially making general partners more risk-averse than the limited partners. In any event, general partners' vicarious liability has effectively disappeared from limited partnerships. Even if they are personally liable, general partners are often incorporated. And limited partnerships in many states now can eliminate general partners' liability by

---

348. *See* RULPA § 303.
349. *See* ULPA (2001) § 406(b)(1).

registering as limited liability partnerships and becoming "limited liability limited partnerships."[350]

A more important accountability mechanism in limited partnerships is the partners' ability to cash out of the firm. Under the traditional limited partnership default rules, limited partners could demand a buyout of their interests. This makes the general partners' hold on the investors' money more tenuous than in a corporation and forces managers to periodically face the judgment of new investors. As discussed below, the 2001 Uniform Act has eliminated default buyout rights. These tax-influenced rules arguably reduce the coherence of the form as the standard form no longer matches strong centralized management with equally strong accountability. However, exit rights remain in parties' agreements and the long-established norms of the limited partnership form.

5. Limited liability company: chameleon approach

Unlike limited partnerships and LLPs, LLCs have always provided for limited liability for all members. Early LLCs were a primitive version of this model because of their heavy reliance on limited partnership and corporate statutes. State legislatures swiftly began developing a new form after the IRS rules discussed in Chapter 6 authorizing partnership tax treatment of LLCs and "check-the-box" forms.

Management structure is an important aspect of the distinctness of LLCS, with LLC statutes generally offering two sets of default rules for centralized manager-managed firms and decentralized member-managed firms. This provides alternative approaches to positional power—the active-owner partnership model, and the passive-owner model of limited partnerships and corporations. The availability of alternative models within the same statute gives firms more flexibility than corporate and limited partnership statutes. The statutes also provide more clarity than general partnerships by enabling firms that delegate power to managers to cut off nonmanaging members' power to bind the firm in third-party transactions through a formal election (usually in the publicly filed articles).

Firms can choose not only within given LLC statutes, but from a variety of statutory approaches to addressing the costs of flexibility inherent in the LLC's dual-management structure. Most LLC statutes compromise between flexibility and clarity by offering only a binary choice between manager- and member-management. Under these statutes, internal and external power may differ if the firm's internal operating agreement delegates power in a member-managed firm or distributes it in a manager-managed firm. By contrast, the Delaware LLC statute gives all members the default power to bind the firm as in a general partnership subject to a contrary provision in the operating agreement, which is

---

350. *See* BROMBERG & RIBSTEIN, *supra* note 292, Ch. 5.

not a publicly filed document.[351] Delaware LLCs therefore get extensive flexibility plus the clarity of making the members' external power match their internal power described in the operating agreement.

Courts may reduce certainty by laying the common law of agency over the statutory categories. For example, a nonmanager may have some power to bind even a manager-managed firm if the third party can show that the nonmanager was apparently authorized.[352] However, most statutes clearly distinguish between manager-managed and member-managed firms may make it hard for a third party to establish the apparent authority of a person identified as a nonmanager. Delaware's rule explicitly making the operating agreement control would seem to make this even harder by reducing the difference between internal and externally represented authority.

LLCs offer less certainty than corporations regarding the management hierarchy apart from the general issue of managers' and members' power. As discussed above, corporations have officers whose positional authority is established by long custom. LLC statutes may *permit* LLCs to provide for corporate-type officers; however, without any provisions *defining* the authority of these officers, this authority must arise over time from case law and customs. For example, in one case the LLC's "Assistant Secretary" certified the operating agreement had been validly amended, though the amendment may not have received the unanimous consent the operating agreement required. The question was whether an "assistant secretary" has the power to bind the LLC to the authenticity of corporate documents.

The magistrate denied summary judgment in favor of a creditor who claimed that the agreement had been amended based on the secretary's certification.[353] However, the district court refused to adopt the magistrate's report and granted the creditor's motion of summary judgment based on a provision in the LLC's agreement with the creditor in which "the Members agreed that the representation in the Certificate that the attached amended LLC Agreement was valid was made on their behalf."[354] Even this opinion leaves it unclear whether the secretary's certification alone would have been enough to establish authority.

Finally, the Revised Uniform Limited Liability Company Act skips over statutory allocation of authority entirely and tries to go directly to the general law of agency. Section 301(a) provides "a member is not an agent of a limited liability company solely by reason of being a member." This seems to say that LLC members, unlike partners, have no "positional" power. But a member might be

---

351. 6 DEL. CODE § 18-402.

352. The application of agency law may be clarified by statute. *See* MD. CODE ANN. § 4A-401(b).

353. Chase Manhattan Bank v. Iridium Africa Corp., 197 F. Supp. 2d 120, 128–29 (D. Del. 2002).

354. Chase Manhattan Bank v. Iridium Africa Corp., 307 F. Supp. 2d 608 (D. Del. 2004).

an agent for a reason other than just being a member. What if the operating agreement says that each member is also a manager of the firm? Then the members would be agents not just because they are members, but because they are managers.

As it happens, that is the agreement supplied by the statutory default rule. RULLCA § 407 provides "(b) In a member-managed limited liability company . . . (1) the management and conduct of the company are vested in the members . . ." The statutory default rule would apply unless the parties agree to remove the members' managerial status.

Unfortunately, the confusion deepens. RULLCA § 301(b) provides "a person's status as a member does not prevent or restrict law other than this [act] from imposing liability on a limited liability company because of the person's conduct." This "law other than this act" probably includes agency law, per RULLCA § 107, which provides that "unless displaced by particular provisions of this act, the principles of law and equity supplement this act." The problem is that agency law itself has nothing to say about the authority of an LLC member aside from what the statutes provide, which circles back to the void on this issue in RULLCA.[355]

RULLCA's fundamental problem is that it ignores the statute's important function of determining the firm's agents' positional power to bind the firm in transactions with third parties. Indeed, RULLCA § 407 would have this effect if only § 301 did not contradict it. By contrast, Delaware § 301 clarifies the external effect of the members' internal power rather than negating it.

As with other business association statutory provisions, LLC statutes' management provisions should be analyzed in terms of their coherence—that is, whether the statutory bundle of terms suits a significant category of firms. Typical LLC statutes provide for alternative default rules. This compromise suits small and medium-sized firms by combining some management flexibility with some clarity as to agents' power. The Delaware rules make sense for the larger LLCs that are willing to incur the costs of forming outside their home states. These firms benefit from being able to custom design their management structure by choosing precisely how much to centralize management power in the operating agreement. They are also likely to engage in large transactions in which the third party's cost of checking the operating agreement is only a small part of the total amount of the deal.

---

355. *See* Larry E. Ribstein, *Are Partners Agents?* (Jan. 18, 2008), U Illinois Law & Economics Research Paper No. LE08-004, http://ssrn.com/abstract=1086745; Ideoblog, http://busmovie.typepad.com/ideoblog/2009/01/rullcas-little-agency-problem.html (Jan. 6, 2009) ("RULLCA's little agency problem"). *But see* Thomas E. Rutledge and Steven G. Frost, *RULLCA Section 301—The Fortunate Consequences (and Continuing Questions) of Distinguishing Apparent Agency and Decisional Authority*, 64 Bus. Law. 37 (2008) (advocating the RULLCA approach).

The coherence of the LLC management provisions depends on how well they work with other statutory terms. For statutes that have alternative management models, this could entail having parallel sets of provisions on other issues for each model. Most statutes do not go further in this respect than clarifying that only managers in manager-managed firms have fiduciary duties. The statutes might also give members stronger exit rights in manager-managed than in member-managed firms to adjust for managers' greater power to harm members in these firms. At the other extreme, Delaware does not correlate type of management with any other provisions. This is consistent with Delaware's general approach of letting the large and sophisticated firms that are likely to be forming in Delaware provide for these matters in the operating agreement.

Although RULLCA is offered as a model for state statutes, is not a model of coherence. As discussed above, RULLCA is incoherent in the most direct sense that §§ 301 and 407 contradict each other. More generally, the statute appears designed to suit smaller firms without extensive planning and agreements for whom flexibility is less important than the need for certainty in transactions with third parties. Yet even apart from the confusion discussed above, RULLCA § 301 attempts to take a more open-ended Delaware-type approach to agency. This incoherence results from the general drafting approach of uniform laws in which the drafters seek compromises among policy makers rather than a product that can be sold to particular firms.[356] Each provision represents a victory by a particular faction rather an attempt to form a coherent whole.

C. MEMBERS' FINANCIAL RIGHTS

Uncorporate statutes provide several types of provisions relating to members' financial rights. The differences between uncorporations are not as significant here as with the topics discussed above, so the following discussion is organized around some important issues concerning financial rights.

1. Noneconomic members

There is an initial question whether a firm can have members who do not have a right to share in the firm's profits. At first blush the answer would seem to be *no*. Recall from Chapter 2 that profit sharing matters to the economic definition of the firm as it motivates owners to monitor the other parties to the firm. Not surprisingly then, profit sharing is a basic element of the statutory definition of partnership.[357] Moreover, profit sharing is coherent with other partnership statutory provisions. For example, why give non-profit sharers management

---

356. *See* Kobayashi & Ribstein, *supra* note 305.
357. *See* UPA § 6 and 7; RUPA §§ 101, 202.

rights if they do not have the incentive to use these rights? Why give them buyout and dissolution rights if they have no interest to cash out? Why should managers owe fiduciary duties to people who have not invested anything that managers can misappropriate?

Despite these questions, business association statutes do not explicitly *require* all owners to be profit sharers or to have any other type of economic interest. The partnership law provisions referred to above *presume* that a profit sharer is a partner and define a partnership as carrying on a business for profit, but do not explicitly demand that a person be a profit sharer in order to be a partner. Delaware uncorporation statutes now explicitly provide that a person may be admitted as a partner or member without acquiring an economic interest in the firm.[358]

Should firms be allowed to have noneconomic owners, or should profit sharing be mandatory in the sense that one cannot be an owner without it? Even if the resulting contract arguably would be incoherent, who would be hurt by allowing these contracts? One answer is that permitting noneconomic owners undermines the formation of a coherent body of business association law, and that idiosyncratic arrangements such as those involving noneconomic owners may dilute the standard form's value for the usual contracts as well as the idiosyncratic ones. Noneconomic "owners" might get or be denied rights because of their noneconomic status where the case might have been decided differently if the "owner" had had financial rights. If the courts do not clarify the basis for their decisions, we may end up with cases applying to all owners that make sense only for "owners" who do not have economic rights.

The problem with this argument is that any theoretical cost to the purity of business association law is easily counterbalanced by the real benefits of enforcing agreements. The parties expect to realize benefits through these idiosyncratic arrangements—and in the absence of tangible harm, the law should accommodate these expectations. Also, mandatory rules of this sort create unpredictability at the edges. For example, would a prohibition on noneconomic ownership sweep in nominal economic interests? If so, how do we define *nominal*? Finally, there is a potential payoff from promoting the evolution of business forms.

Still, one might wonder if people who organize firms with noneconomic owners are up to some mischief. After all, the fact that this type of interest does not fit with the other terms of the statute creates risks in terms of how courts will apply business association law and provisions of the operating agreement to these idiosyncratic arrangements. Why not then drop the member or owner label? Perhaps the status conferred by the partner or member label is a perk even

---

358. *See* 6 DEL. CODE § 15-205 (general partnership); *id.* § 17-301(d) (limited partnership); *id.* § 18-301(d) (LLC).

if it does not bring the usual economic rewards. If so, the firm's benefit from providing this low-cost compensation might outweigh the costs of confusion about the "partner's" status. On the other hand, if the reason for noneconomic owners is simply to mislead third parties as to the "partner's" status (particularly in professional firms), this should give us pause on the policy front.

2. One-owner firms

An additional complication as to owners' financial rights concerns uncorporations that not only have some owners without profit interests, but only one owner with such an interest. This is particularly a problem for partnerships. The partnership statutes *define* a partnership as having *two or more* owners.[359] Indeed, the idea of multiple owners is inherent in the partnership standard form and coherent with partnership's other provisions. Among other things, partnerships are based on contracts, which seemingly require two or more people: they are associations involving sharing of financial and management rights among the members, and the important partnership concepts of dissociation and dissolution necessarily imply a relationship from which to dissociate. Moreover, multiple owners distinguish partnership from another standard form—that of agency, which is based on a single party (the principal) getting all of the benefit (i.e., profit) and having all of the control.[360]

A high profile example of a "partnership" that seemingly had only one economic owner is the law firm of Marc Dreier, which spectacularly flamed out in late 2008.[361] The firm billed itself as *Dreier LLP*—that is, a limited liability partnership. But the firm could not be a limited liability partnership under any LLP statute unless it was actually a partnership. The firm had only one profit-sharer: Dreier himself, who not only got all the profits but also had exclusive management rights. The other lawyers shared the firm's *revenues* (the fees they helped generate) but not its *profits*, a critical distinction for the definition of partnership.[362] So this seems to have been an agent-principal relationship between Dreier and his lawyer-employees.

Yet the Dreier Web site identified some of these lawyers as "partners" of the firm. If these other "partners" were not partners (note that the firm, such as it was, probably was governed by New York law, which has a standard version of the Uniform Partnership Act), then the Dreier firm could not be a partnership because it would not have two or more co-owners. The lawyers identified as "partners" probably intended to be partners (though the firm's Web site cryptically

---

359. *See* U.P.A. § 6, R.U.P.A. § 101(6), 202(a).
360. *See* AMERICAN LAW INSTITUTE, RESTATEMENT (THIRD) OF AGENCY, § 1.01.
361. *See* Ideoblog, http://busmovie.typepad.com/ideoblog/2008/12/dreier-economic-and-legal-ramifications.html (Dec. 10, 2008) ("Drier: Economic and Legal Ramifications").
362. *See* U.P.A. § 7(3), R.U.P.A. § 202(c)(2).

described it as "not just an association of attorneys but a collaboration of attorneys"), but as this was not a Delaware firm that intent might not be enough.

This raises the question whether the law should permit one-owner partnerships. Similar considerations apply to this issue as to noneconomic partners. Although one-owner "partnerships" are incoherent, maybe the owners should be able to take the risks of incoherence. Moreover, there is no concern about misleading third parties except to the extent that the non-owners are represented as partners (as in Dreier). Indeed, prohibiting one-owner partnerships might have the perverse effect of encouraging misrepresentations of ownership.

Uncorporation statutes take various positions on one-owner firms. After some state resistance to the notion, every LLC statute permits one-member LLCs.[363] On the other hand, limited partnerships have to have at least one general partner and one limited partner,[364] though it is not clear these have to be separate individuals or entities.[365] A limited liability partnership (such as Dreier's) is defined as a partnership.[366]

Perhaps partnership statutes, like LLC statutes, should explicitly permit one-owner firms. To be sure, there is a lot to be said for insisting on multiple owners as a matter of coherence and as a way to reinforce the contractual basis of all of these firms. This is clearest for general partnerships because these informal firms are *defined* as associations of multiple owners. The other uncorporations do not involve the same problem because they require formalities that at least reduce the uncertainty as to whether the firm exists and who its members are. But even in partnerships there are the same sorts of concerns about mandatory rules as apply to noneconomic owners.

The problems caused by mandatory rules start to loom large when the parties see a benefit to pushing the contractual envelope in partnerships and business associations, which in turn forces the barriers to crumble. Letting partnerships have noneconomic owners permits a holder of any package of rights to be a partner, effectively nullifying the multiple owner requirement. So would a ban on one-member partnerships imply a ban on noneconomic owners?

The general lesson from all this is that, while coherence of business association statutes is a good objective for crafting default rules, reality is messier. Real coherence can be maintained only by mandatory rules. These in turn are vulnerable to the inherent flexibility of uncorporations, which encourages continual evolution through private agreements. The evolutionary process might

---

363. *See* Ribstein & Keatinge, *supra* note 260, at § 4:3.
364. *See* ULPA (2001), § 102(11).
365. *Id.* § 102(11) requires that the limited partnership be "formed" by two or more persons, but apparently can exist without multiple owners.
366. *See* BROMBERG & RIBSTEIN, *supra* note 292, § 2.02. This suggests that if Dreier's firm is *not* a "partnership," it is not an LLP and therefore nobody gets the LLP liability shield.

reach a temporary coherent equilibrium, but it first has to go through a stage of incoherence—and it remains vulnerable to entropy.

3. No-owner and nonprofit firms

What if *nobody* has a right to the firm's profits? This seems odd because (as discussed in Chapter 2) a firm in the economic sense inherently produces some kind of surplus over and above what is allocated to the contributors. Recall that Alchian and Demsetz argued that there has to be somebody who gets this surplus and thereby has the incentive to monitor the firm's other inputs. To be sure, an entity without an owner would produce a joint benefit for the participants in terms of lower prices (in the case of a buyers' cooperative) or distribution to the society or some community at large. For example, a public radio station may have supporters who contribute money in exchange for good music. But can this be a firm if it operates directly for the participants rather than having a firm-level objective to earn a profit?

A nonprofit relationship currently cannot be a partnership because partnership statutes define the partnership as carrying on a business for profit.[367] As with noneconomic owners, this limitation makes sense as a matter of the coherence of the standard form. If the firm has no owners entitled to the profits, then it would want very different financial and dissolution provisions than a standard form partnership. Without economic owners who have incentives to protect their interests in profits, the firm also would need devices to protect donors from misconduct by managers. That is why nonprofit corporations have to form under special statutory provisions and are subject to special state supervision.

Yet here again we meet the question whether the development of business associations should be constrained by a mandatory rule. Indeed, while a not-for-profit firm cannot be a partnership, it *may* be an LLC under many statutes[368] or a limited partnership under the current uniform law.[369] The factors that make nonprofit partnerships incoherent—the unsuitability of financial and other rights—also apply to LLCs and limited partnerships.

But does it follow that the statute should prohibit these firms? Perhaps so because (as indicated above), allowing the firms involves potential costs to noncontracting parties—that is, the donors. However as discussed below, nonprofit LLCs do not involve a threat to the general public because, unlike charities, they are formed for the benefit of contracting parties who can protect themselves. This illustrates the general tension between the beneficial flexibility of the uncorporate form on the one hand and the need on the other to constrain this flexibility to preserve the effectiveness of efficient regulation.

---

367. *See* UPA § 6, RUPA § 101(6), 202(a).
368. *See* Ribstein & Keatinge, *supra* note 260, § 4:10, nn. 8–9.
369. *See* ULPA (2001), § 102(11).

A variation on a *non*profit LLC is a "*low*-profit limited liability company," or L3C. Vermont, which enacted the first such statute,[370] describes the entity as

> a cross between a nonprofit organization and a for-profit corporation. The entity is designated as low-profit with charitable or educational goals * * * The basic purpose of the L3C is to signal to foundations and donor directed funds that entities formed under this provision intend to conduct their activities in a way that would qualify as program related investments.[371]

The statute requires the L3C, among other things, not to have a "significant purpose" of producing income or property appreciation.

L3C provisions raise issues as to the costs of flexibility and tradeoffs between flexibility and coherence. To be sure, it is not clear what parties can do under these provisions that they could not do under a standard LLC statute, particularly if the statute permits non-profit LLCs. However, any additional flexibility the statutes permit would seem to raise the same coherence issues as a nonprofit LLC. The L3C provisions also involve uncertainty as to which firms satisfy the statutory requirements and the consequences of not meeting those requirements (e.g., does the firm lose its liability shield?).

4. Contributions

In general, uncorporations like other firms exist to raise money for firms and distribute the money to the owners. These issues normally are covered in the parties' agreement as well in statutory mandatory and default rules.

Contribution rules serve two functions: protecting the owners from co-owner opportunism and protecting creditors from owner misconduct. With respect to rules protecting owners, closely held firms may have high costs of borrowing or raising new equity capital. It is harder for these firms to communicate reliable information about themselves than it is for large firms whose shares are traded in information-rich public securities markets. These information costs increase risks for investors and therefore the firm's cost of raising capital. Also, newer firms are risky because they do not have a track record, and new outside investors may be leery of trusting the entrepreneurs with their loans or minority equity stakes.

Given these problems of attracting outside capital, the owners themselves may be the best source of additional funding. However, it is very difficult for the firm to determine at the outset how much capital it will need over time. At the same time, the owners may not be able to trust their co-owners to come up with the money when the firm needs it without exacting a high price for the contribution (such as a much bigger piece of the firm). Because it is difficult to design

---

370. *See* Vt. Code, title 11, ch. 21, § 3001(27).
371. Low Profit Limited Liability Company, http://www.sec.state.vt.us/corps/dobiz/llc/llc_l3c.htm.

default rules that efficiently balance the firm's need for cash against the potential for abuse, and because the owners should be able to design provisions appropriate for their firm, these concerns are best left to be dealt with in the firms' agreements.

Therefore, firms may want to contract for a right to assess existing owners if owners or managers determine that the funds are needed. The agreement might provide that contributions by owners who meet the capital call would dilute the shares of those who do not. The owners would need protection from abuse of the power to make assessments (e.g., managers or majority owners might make capital calls even when the firm does not need the cash solely in order to dilute the minority holders). Disclosure and good faith requirements along with imposition of fiduciary duties could fill gaps in the agreement.[372]

The business association statute may include contribution provisions designed to protect creditors from the owners' incentive to impose risks on the creditors. Creditors, like owners, generally can contract for protection. But tort victims and creditors in small and routine transactions might benefit from baseline statutory protections. These protections are not necessary in general partnerships because partners are not only directly liable to partnership creditors, but also for contributions to the partnership necessary to pay the partnership's debts. Thus, partnership law in a sense provides for an "ex post" contribution obligation assessed when the partnership is wound up.

Conversely, creditors of limited liability firms might want the owners to make some contributions to ensure that the latter are not speculating entirely with the creditors' money. The problem is that, given wide differences among firms, it is impossible to design such an obligation so that it both meaningfully protects creditors and avoids unduly burdening the smallest firms. Moreover, requiring contributions on formation is unlikely to provide much protection for creditors of the ongoing firm years after formation.

Instead of minimum capital contributions, the statutes might require the owners to clearly disclose the contributions they are making and to leave the contributed funds in the firm as a capital cushion. Alternatively, the statute might restrict the form of the contribution—that is, require cash or tangible property rather than intangible property or promises that might do the creditors little good in a crunch. Although these requirements would impose a lower burden on members than minimum capital requirements, they do not help creditors much because an ongoing firm's overall solvency at any given time has more to do with the firm's earning capacity than with the members' contributions.

---

372. *See, e.g.,* Walter v. Holiday Inns, Inc., 985 F.2d 1232 (3d Cir. 1993) (involving claim that joint venture misrepresented the firm's prospects in making a capital call that diluted co-venturer's interest).

Accordingly, modern uncorporation statutes put little constraint on the form and amount of initial contributions.[373]

So although there is some benefit in statutory contribution obligations, the costs of these rules outweigh their benefits in most situations. The elimination of these requirements from uncorporation statutes is an example of efficient statutory evolution. The emphasis from the standpoint of creditor protection has been on distributions (discussed below) as well as the veil-piercing rules discussed above.

5. Profits, losses, and distributions

Business association statutes must provide for rules regarding the owners' rights to share the firm's earnings. Specifically, these rules would specify when the owners can get distributions from the firm and how these distributions are allocated among the owners. In designing these rights, lawmakers have to balance the owners' individual and collective interests in having control over the firm's cash against the interests of owners and other claimants in promoting the long-term management of the firm's assets. As discussed throughout this book, corporate law stresses the managers' power to run the firm, which includes the power to determine whether to distribute earnings or use them to grow the firm. By contrast, uncorporate law emphasizes the members' rights to distributions as a complement to or substitute for corporate-type monitoring of managers through voting, directors, and fiduciary duties.

As with members' duties to make contributions to the firm, the significant variations among firms make it very difficult for lawmakers to prescribe default rules. Thus, the statutes limit members' rights to distributions to buyout of their entire interest and liquidation of the firm. The owners generally have no statutory default rights to distributions from the ongoing firm.

The parties can and often do provide for a right to distributions in their governance agreements. These customized agreements sharply contrast with corporations in which common shareholders' rights to distributions normally are within the directors' discretion. This difference between uncorporations and corporations regarding distributions has particular significance for the governance of large firms (as discussed below in Chapter 8).

While uncorporation statutes are similar to corporate statutes in not specifying member rights to receive distributions, they diverge from corporate statutes in three general respects. First, uncorporation statutes vary regarding whether they provide for allocation of profits and losses. The general partnership acts[374]

---

373. *See, e.g.,* ULPA (2001) § 501 (providing that "a contribution of a partner may consist of tangible or intangible property or other benefit to the limited partnership, including money, services performed, promissory notes, other agreements to contribute cash or property, and contracts for services to be performed").

374. UPA § 18(a); RUPA § 401(b).

and the 1985 Uniform Limited Partnership Act[375] provide by default for sharing of profits and losses, while the 2001 Limited Partnership Act[376] and the 1996[377] and 2006[378] Uniform LLC Acts provide only for sharing of distributions.

Focusing on distributions rather than profits and losses arguably makes sense for all business associations. As discussed above, the key issue is the extent to which owners can take assets out of the firm. Profits and losses, by contrast, are merely accounting items that do not necessarily determine the timing and amount of distributions. The main practical reason for allocating profits and losses is to determine the partners' tax on partnership income and losses irrespective of distributions. But this arguably should be left to the parties' tax accounting rather than dealt with by statutory default rule.

The difference between the partnership statutes (which allocate profits and losses), and the corporation, LLC, and more modern limited partnership statutes (which do not) reflects the different uses of these statutes—and therefore provides another illustration of differentiation among standard forms. The partnership statutes are intended to provide rules for unintentional and informal firms that may not have specific agreements. Allocation of profit and loss enables computation of both taxes and distributions to the partners if the agreement does not provide for any other basis. Thus, the Revised Uniform Partnership allows creation of partner capital accounts based on the profit and loss allocation and for settling of accounts by distribution of the excess of credits over charges or contribution of the excess of charges over credits.[379] By contrast, LLC and modern limited partnership statutes generally are designed for firms that are expected to have an operating agreement and therefore some agreed mechanism for creating accounts and determining distributions. The statutes assume the parties have figured out a way to determine when and how much will be distributed, and therefore only add rules for determining how the distributions are allocated among the members.

General partnerships also differ from other business associations with regard to the method of allocating financial items among the members. Here the difference is justified more by the members' limited or vicarious liability than by the level of informality. The general partnership statutory default rule is equal sharing of profits and losses (or, more precisely, equal sharing of profits and sharing of losses in proportion to profit share). This reflects the assumption that the vicariously liable partners will be contributing comparable totals of capital, credit, and labor. Rather than trying to compute the precise value of each contribution,

---

375. RULPA § 503.
376. ULPA (2001), § 503.
377. UNIFORM LIMITED LIABILITY COMPANY ACT, § 405 (1996) ("ULLCA").
378. REVISED UNIFORM LIMITED LIABILITY COMPANY ACT, § 404 (2006) ("RULLCA").
379. See RUPA §§ 401, 807.

the statute leaves any variations to the agreement. By contrast, limited liability business associations generally allocate financial rights pro rata by contributions or the value of members' interests because LLC members' contributions may be mostly financial and can be easily computed.

Most limited liability business associations restrict distributions by insolvent firms as a way of addressing the conflict of interest between creditors and limited liability owners.[380] These are essentially fraudulent conveyance rules that prevent owners from taking cash out of a failing firm just as it is most needed to pay creditors. Also (as discussed above), veil-piercing fills the gaps in these rules.

However, most LLP statutes do not provide for liability to creditors for excessive distributions.[381] This reflects both the balance of costs and benefits of these liabilities and the special function of LLP statutes, which are primarily designed for and used by professional firms whose partners may rely on the firm's distribution as their regular compensation. Moreover, it may be particularly difficult to value the assets of service firms for purposes of determining whether the firms are insolvent.

A final issue relating to financial rights in uncorporations concerns the use of these firms to hide assets from creditors. This is not conventional limited liability but rather an aspect of what was identified in Chapter 2 as *entity shielding* rules, which protect the entity's continuity from owners and those claiming through them. This makes sense to the extent that it facilitates ongoing firms. However (as discussed below), entity shielding may become a form of backdoor asset protection device to the extent that the "entity" doing the shielding is not a real business, but just a repository for holding assets that the owners want to protect from their creditors.

D. FIDUCIARY DUTIES: GENERAL PRINCIPLES

Fiduciary duties raise three important questions for statutory design. First, what should be the default fiduciary duty? Second, to what extent may the members contract around this default? And, third, what should be the remedy for breach? The following discussion summarizes general principles that apply to all business associations. The next section discusses applications to specific uncorporations.

Fiduciary duty in its most precise formulation refers to the duty of those who manage property on behalf of others to refrain from selfish behavior.[382] The owner of the property, who is the beneficiary of the fiduciary relationship,

---

380. *See, e.g.,* ULPA (2001), §§ 508–509; RULLCA §§ 405–406.
381. *See* Bromberg & Ribstein, *supra* note 292, at § 4.04(d).
382. *See* Larry E. Ribstein, *Are Partners Fiduciaries?* 2005 Ill. L. Rev. 209.

wants the fiduciary to manage the property so that it produces the maximum benefit for the owner. Though the fiduciary might not be as attentive to the owner's interests as the owner would like her to be, the beneficiary still entrusts property to the fiduciary in order to take advantage of the latter's skill and expertise.

However, the delegation will not be worthwhile to the beneficiary if the fiduciary can run amok with the latter's money. Thus, the fiduciary's discretion must be constrained by legal duties together with other accountability mechanisms, including the beneficiary's power to replace fiduciaries and the fiduciary's desire to protect her reputation. The duty is designed to be administered by a court with limited business expertise. Rather than scrutinizing the fiduciary's actions in detail, courts insist only that managers refrain from self-dealing and assume managers who are not self-dealing have adequate incentives to serve the firm.

1. Fiduciaries vs. non-fiduciaries

Fiduciary duties should be applicable only when a firm's owners delegate substantial power to managers. If the duty extends further, the costs of forcing parties to act unselfishly and to refrain from protecting their own interests may exceed the benefits in terms of constraining agency costs. Because the fiduciary duty is strong medicine, it is justified only when the potential for harm demands it.

More specifically, controlling shareholders should not have *fiduciary* duties to noncontrolling shareholders. Controlling shareholders are entitled to act in their self-interest—that it, as they bought and paid for the power, they should be able to use it. Unlike fiduciaries, controlling shareholders have not undertaken to act unselfishly on behalf of the beneficiary. Here the law need only constrain opportunism by holding the controller to its express or implied contractual obligations, including the duty of good faith (as discussed in Chapter 2 and further below).

2. Due care

Courts often purport to extend fiduciary duties beyond the strict duty of loyalty and recognize a duty of care. However, this additional liability requires a completely different theory from the one underlying fiduciary duties. The duty of loyalty is designed to provide a check on managers' conduct in the limited situation in which the managers are conflicted and the courts may do a better job than the managers. However, when managers are not conflicted, the costs of judicial second-guessing are likely to outweigh the benefits. Although the duty of care might be conceived as involving a conflict of interest regarding time and effort, this does not avoid the problem of judicial second-guessing. The manager is not a slave who belongs to the firm 24/7. The court would have to determine how not only how much effort the manager owes the firm, but how any lack of effort hurt the firm. It is therefore not surprising that courts go no further than imposing liability for decisions that are so bad or ill-considered that it seems those who made them almost must have been conflicted.

3. Misappropriation

Courts also impose liability for misappropriating the firm's property. This duty is not really fiduciary in the sense of being a constraint on the manager's exercise of discretion, but follows from the owner's joint rights in the property. A manager or owner has no more right to take the firm's property without the firm's consent than does a third party. To be sure, the fiduciary relationship matters in defining a taking. Third parties are entitled to enjoy the fruits of anything they can learn about a firm by their own efforts. However, in the absence of a contrary agreement, owners and managers may not use their special access to the firm's information for other than a corporate purpose.

4. Business opportunities

The duty not to usurp business opportunities is closely related to the misappropriation duty. The opportunities might be considered firm property, and usurpation is often facilitated by misappropriation of the firm's information.[383] The business opportunities duty connects with the duty of loyalty to the extent that fiduciaries are liable for appropriating opportunities that would be fair game for non-fiduciaries. For example, in the classic *Meinhard* case discussed in Chapter 3, Salmon was liable for taking an opportunity that the court said he should have shared with Meinhard. Like the duty of loyalty, the business opportunities duty disciplines self-interest—in this case by ensuring that the fiduciary does not let self-interest dilute his vigorous pursuit of these opportunities for the firm's benefit.

5. Good faith

In non-fiduciary situations courts may apply an "implied covenant of good faith and fair dealing." Under this approach, the court looks beyond the literal contract language and attempts to interpret the contract in light of the parties' expectations. Courts can tailor this approach to the type of firm, hewing most closely to the contract language where the parties are the most sophisticated and therefore most likely to have meant what they said. Delaware's Chancellor Allen provided a concise statement of this duty in a case involving a firm's (Oak's) non-fiduciary duty to its bondholders:

> It is this obligation to act in good faith and to deal fairly that plaintiff claims is breached by the structure of Oak's coercive exchange offer. Because it is an implied contractual obligation that is asserted as the basis for the relief sought,

---

383. The classic case on this is Guth v. Loft, Inc., 5 A.2d 503 (Del. 1939), which involves the early history of Pepsi-Cola.

the appropriate legal test is not difficult to deduce. It is this: is it clear from what was expressly agreed upon that the parties who negotiated the express terms of the contract would have agreed to proscribe the act later complained of as a breach of the implied covenant of good faith—had they thought to negotiate with respect to that matter. If the answer to this question is yes, then, in my opinion, a court is justified in concluding that such act constitutes a breach of the implied covenant of good faith.[384]

In a sense, this is just contract interpretation, albeit in the special context of the very open-ended contracts that comprise a firm.

6. Opt-out

It is important to keep in mind that the standard-form fiduciary duty courts apply is only a rough cut based on a generalization of when the strong medicine of a duty to act unselfishly is justified despite the costs of judicial second-guessing. The fiduciary duty may be unwarranted in some situations in which the general conditions for imposing a fiduciary duty exist. For example, the firm may have special reasons not to constrain the expert fiduciary's discretion, or may believe that other mechanisms for controlling the fiduciary's discretion (such as the owners' power to remove errant managers) are likely to be effective. Because the relevant circumstances are likely to vary from firm to firm, there is a value in enforcing contracts that opt out of or customize default duties. On the other hand, courts may hesitate to enforce broad opt-outs because of a concern that the beneficiaries may not have freely and knowingly consented to waive this important protection.

Several factors are likely to be relevant to the courts in differentiating among types of firms regarding enforceability of fiduciary waivers. Business association forms used by the smallest firms—that is, the ones that firms choose when they have done the least sophisticated planning—arguably require the most protection against improvident waivers. At the other end of the scale, business association forms used by large firms with many owners who have not negotiated directly with the fiduciaries involve the same sort of potential danger as other types of "standard form" contracts. But if the firm's shares are widely traded or if the terms otherwise become widely known in the investment community, even unsophisticated and uninformed owners may get what they pay for.

7. Remedy

It seems straightforward that the firm ought to have a remedy, but who decides whether the firm should sue? The conflicted managers, who usually would make litigation decisions, obviously cannot be trusted to decide whether to sue themselves. On the other hand, putting the decision directly in the owners' hands

---

384. Katz v. Oak Industries, Inc., 508 A.2d 873, 880 (Del. Ch., 1986).

arguably runs counter to their reasons for delegating management to expert agents. As we will see, corporate law has worked out a compromise—the derivative remedy, which carried over to limited but not to general partnerships. Determination of the appropriate rule for LLCs turns out to be a critical choice in defining the nature of that entity.

E. FIDUCIARY DUTIES IN SPECIFIC BUSINESS ASSOCIATIONS

This section applies the above principles to fiduciary duties in corporations and uncorporations.

1. Corporation

Default duties: Corporate managers have the usual fiduciary duty of loyalty described above. The corporate statute does not automatically invalidate conflict-of-interest transactions, but instead requires review of these transactions by the court, independent board members, or shareholders.[385] Moreover, even if the transaction has been approved by the appropriate body, the court may step in to review the transaction's substance and procedure.[386]

The corporate business judgment rule has been specifically identified with publicly held corporations in which the discipline provided by the market for control enables courts to avoid second-guessing director decisions.[387] But as discussed above, the qualifications on the duty of care follow from the courts' inherent limitations in judging fiduciaries' conduct rather than from any particular aspects of the manager's role in the corporate context. Thus, in corporations as in other business associations, in the absence of an agreement to the contrary, managers are not liable for their exercise of discretion if they are not conflicted or grossly negligent. In the corporation, the business judgment rule protects managerial decisions that do not fall into either of these categories.[388]

Opt-out: Corporate statutes do not authorize waiver of the duty of loyalty. However, Delaware pioneered the idea of permitting waiver of the duty of care following the notorious Delaware decision in *Smith v. Van Gorkom*.[389] In that case, unlike others involving duty of care, the Delaware Supreme Court imposed liability for what it viewed as a grossly negligent board decision despite there being little evidence of a conflict of interest and despite its finding that the

---

385. *See* DEL. G. C. L. § 144.
386. *See* Cinerama v. Technicolor, Inc., 663 A.2d 1156 (Del. 1995).
387. *See* Henry G. Manne, *Our Two Corporation Systems: Law and Economics*, 53 VA. L. REV. 259 (1967).
388. *See* Aronson v. Lewis, 473 A.2d 805 (Del. 1984).
389. 488 A.2d 858 (Del. 1985).

board's selling the firm for a significant premium over the current market price did not wear the badge of disloyalty.

To correct this evident error in applying the duty of care, the Delaware legislature authorized a charter provision

> eliminating or limiting the personal liability of a director to the corporation or its stockholders for monetary damages for breach of fiduciary duty as a director, provided that such provision shall not eliminate or limit the liability of a director: (i) For any breach of the director's duty of loyalty to the corporation or its stockholders; (ii) for acts or omissions not in good faith or which involve intentional misconduct or a knowing violation of law; (iii) under § 174 of this title; or (iv) for any transaction from which the director derived an improper personal benefit.[390]

This provision left confusion in its wake over the exceptions, particularly concerning what might be an act or omission "not in good faith"—a term the Delaware courts had not previously defined. More than twenty years after *Van Gorkom*, the Delaware Supreme Court held in *Stone v. Ritter* that this phrase might embrace a board's conscious failure to adopt a compliance program in the face of a known duty to act.[391] The decision appeared to restore to non-waivability what had been recognized as a breach of the duty of care prior to *Van Gorkom*—that is, very careless acts that might be badges of conflict. In other words, following *Stone* it seems that corporations can opt out of only *Van Gorkom*'s misreading of the duty of care rather than what the duty had been prior to *Van Gorkom*.

Remedy: Corporate statutes have been enacted to respond to the dilemma of how to get the corporation to sue the very people who are supposed to be in charge of its litigation by providing for the derivative suit, which authorizes a single shareholder to sue in the name of the corporation. However, this procedure solves one problem only by creating another: how to ensure that the volunteer derivative plaintiff is acting in the corporation's interests. Because the suit is on the firm's cause of action, the plaintiff has to share any recovery with the corporation. Then of course, to motivate a shareholder to come forward and sue, the plaintiff must be allowed to recoup the costs and fees of the action out of the recovery. But this fee award only puts the plaintiff back where she started, without enough potential for gain to motivate the suit.

In fact, the real motivation is that of the plaintiff's lawyer, who earns a fee that is typically based on the corporation's recovery. The lawyer is interested only in successful litigation and may not care about the firm's direct and indirect litigation costs. Corporate law attempts to deal with this incentive problem through devices for monitoring the derivative plaintiff's lawyer (who, in turn, is supposed to be monitoring the managers). The plaintiff may have to first ask the board to

---

390. DEL. G.C.L. § 102(b)(7).
391. 911 A.2d 362, 370 (Del. 2006).

take action,[392] and the board is empowered to seek dismissal of even meritorious derivative suits on the ground that the action's overall costs exceed its benefits.[393] However, these procedures can be very costly and time-consuming.

So although the derivative suit might be a way around the conflict of interest inherent in fiduciary litigation, it is hardly a panacea. Indeed, the main thing it has going for it is that there is no obviously better way to solve the problem in the large, publicly held firm for which corporate statutes are primarily designed. One theoretical alternative is to empower shareholders to directly authorize litigation. However, in a firm with thousands of shareholders, this would require an expensive meeting called and run by the conflicted managers themselves. The shareholders also might bring a class action on their own behalf. But then the court would have to figure out precisely who was hurt and by how much, which involves a daunting determination of when shares traded and how news of the fraud and the suit affected their trading prices.

2. General partnership

Default duties: The theory underlying fiduciary duties discussed above does not seem to fit the "default" partnership. Recall that the fiduciary duty of loyalty addresses the specific problem that arises when an owner delegates power over property to a non-owner agent. The standard form partnership calls for coequal joint managers who equally split management and financial rights and who can force the liquidation of the firm and the distribution of its assets if they do not like how things are going. Moreover, partners' personal liability for partnership debts gives them strong incentives to monitor their copartners. The partners' power in this relationship to protect themselves hardly seems to justify strong judicial supervision under the duty of loyalty.

Although partners in a default partnership ought to have duties to each other and to the firm, these duties need not rise to the level of the fiduciary duty of unselfishness. Partners should not be able to appropriate for themselves the partnership's property, but remember this is a violation of the partners' joint property rights rather than an aspect of the duty of self-abnegation. Partners also have specific duties under the partnership agreement and the statute. Courts might expand these duties in particular cases through the implied covenant of good faith and fair dealing. An example is the *Page* case (discussed in Chapter 3) in which a partner arguably used his contractual liquidation power to frustrate his brother's legitimate expectation to gain from the relationship. But again, this is simply a marginal constraint on selfish conduct, not a broad prohibition on self-gain.

---

392. This demand requirement is articulated in Aronson v. Lewis, 473 A.2d 805 (Del. 1984).

393. *See* Zapata Corp. v. Maldonado, 430 A.2d 779 (Del. 1981).

Notwithstanding these theoretical limits on fiduciary duties in partnerships, Justice Cardozo said in *Meinhard v. Salmon* (discussed in Chapter 3) that partners owe each other "the punctilio of an honor." Salmon arguably did owe Meinhard a fiduciary duty in the strict sense discussed here because Salmon fully controlled the day-to-day management of the firm. However, we saw that Justice Cardozo applied the duty in particularly sweeping fashion despite several reasons this might have pushed the edges of the partners' deal.

Courts often cite Justice Cardozo's language in applying fiduciary duties. Although the partnership statutes do not explicitly embrace the Cardozo fiduciary standard, they at least leave room for it to operate. UPA § 21 requires partners to "account to the partnership for any benefit, and hold as trustee for it any profits derived by him" from partnership transactions. RUPA § 404 provides explicitly for fiduciary duties of loyalty and care.

While the logic behind imposition of fiduciary duties does not seem to justify their broad application to partnerships, there is nevertheless an argument for Justice Cardozo's sweeping articulation of joint venturers' duties. The general partnership standard form, as the "default" business relationship, must accommodate parties who have fallen into a business association without entering into a comprehensive agreement. It is therefore reasonable to put the contracting burden on the fiduciary, whose expertise the nonmanaging owners trusted. The strong normative flavor of Justice Cardozo's language ensures that the fiduciary duty will be read into the smallest gaps left in the parties' agreement. Strong duties also fit with the partners' opportunity to escape these duties through buyout and dissolution, as discussed below. Partnership fiduciary duties therefore mesh with the other elements of the general partnership standard form and the needs of the general partnership's clientele of firms. Moreover, partnership rules permitting opting out of fiduciary duties (discussed immediately below) are consistent with the rationale for Cardozian norms of motivating fiduciaries to articulate their duties in the agreement.

Opt-out. General partnership law long has explicitly permitted contractual alteration of default fiduciary duties—and the courts have broadly enforced these contracts.[394] The waiver rule is built into UPA § 21, which provides that "every partner must account to the partnership for any benefit, and hold as trustee for it any profits derived by him without the consent of the other partners."

The Revised Uniform Partnership Act is somewhat more restrictive, but at least has the virtue of providing a clear basis for waiver of duties. RUPA § 404 provides that the partners' "only" fiduciary duties are those specified in the section: the duties of loyalty and care. The parties need to deal only with these

---

394. *See* Larry E. Ribstein, *Fiduciary Duty Contracts in Unincorporated Firms*, 54 WASH. & LEE L. REV. 537 (1997).

duties in their agreement without having to worry about what other duties courts will suddenly impose.

The Act also provides a specific roadmap for opting out of these duties: The agreement cannot "eliminate" the duty of loyalty, but can provide for partner voting rules to authorize self-benefiting transactions or "identify specific types or categories of activities that do not violate the duty of loyalty, if not manifestly unreasonable." Also, the agreement cannot "unreasonably reduce the duty of care."[395] Although these limitations are potentially troubling because their application by courts is unpredictable, the basic intuition underlying the limitations comports with the general notion that courts will apply Cardozian norms to partnerships only to the extent that the agreement does not explicitly negate fiduciary duties.

Remedies: The statutory remedy for fiduciary breach in general partnerships is the rather odd one of an "accounting."[396] In contrast to the corporate derivative suit, an accounting is an individual action by one or more partners. The extraordinary derivative remedy, which bypasses the firm's managers and lets a volunteer shareholder sue on behalf of the firm, is not necessary in a context in which where partners presumably have vicarious liability, substantial stakes in the firm, and the power to institute litigation on the firm's behalf. Most strikingly, the common law goes beyond the statute in making the accounting remedy not only available but exclusive. This forces partners to sue not just for a specific harm, but for a comprehensive review of partnership affairs, adjudication of all pending disputes, and determination and allocation among the partners of all of the firm's profits and losses.[397]

The exclusivity rule is rooted in an extreme aggregate view of partnership, bygone procedural distinctions between law and equity, and outmoded restrictions on adjudication of multiple claims.[398] Accordingly, the rule seems anachronistic,[399] and RUPA expressly disowned it.[400] But despite its seeming anachronism, the accounting rule still has the very modern function of deterring costly litigation among partners by making this litigation very costly for the plaintiff. Contentious litigation is more than just a nuisance in the informal, close-knit firm for which partnership default rules are designed.[401]

---

395. *See* RUPA § 103(b). The section also provides that the parties cannot "eliminate the obligation of good faith and fair dealing," which makes sense since this is really a rule of judicial interpretation rather than a specific duty.

396. *See* UPA § 22.

397. *See* 2 Bromberg & Ribstein, *supra* note 99, at § 6.08.

398. *See* Sertich v. Moorman, 162 Ariz. 407, 783 P.2d 1199 (1989).

399. *See id.*

400. *See* RUPA § 405.

401. *See* Saul Levmore, *Love It or Leave It: Property Rules, Liability Rules, and Exclusivity of Remedies in Partnership and Marriage*, 58 J.L. & Contemp. Prob. 221 (Spring 1995).

The accounting rule also meets the coherence criterion of fitting with other aspects of the general partnership standard form. As already discussed throughout this book and emphasized below, one of a partnership's most important features is the ease with which individual members can exit the firm by compelling its liquidation. This liquidation power may be a more efficient remedy for copartner misconduct than litigation over fiduciary breach. The full accounting normally occurs on dissolution or dissociation, though the statute technically lets partners bring it at other times. In larger partnerships designed to survive disputes and departures, the partners may contract for remedies that suit these relationships. Also (as discussed below), other types of uncorporations restrict partner exit by eliminating dissolution at the will of an individual partner and limiting buyout of individual partners. The "nuclear" option of blowing up the firm and having an accounting does not fit these firms. The accounting remedy is designed specifically to fit the default partnership that dissolves at will.

A little-noted element of partnership remedies for fiduciary breach is the role of criminal law, specifically the crime of embezzlement. One might suppose, particularly given strict Cardozian norms, that if an agent's theft from an individual or a corporation is a crime, a fortiori it should be a criminal act in a partnership. Yet some state embezzlement statutes explicitly apply only to embezzlement in the former situations and not the latter.[402] Although this seems like an unseemly loophole, the rule fits with the contractual nature of partnership duties. Whether a particular partner benefit is theft or an allocation of rights to partnership property authorized by the partnership agreement may be a close call given partnership informality and flexibility. Only clear breaches of social norms should give rise to criminal penalties.

3. Limited partnership

Default duties: General partners in limited partnerships exercise the sort of open-ended management power that is appropriate for classic fiduciary duties. Although limited partners traditionally can exit the firm through buyout, they are more likely than general partners to be passive given their limited liability for the debts of the firm. In any event, if a managing general partner should have fiduciary duties imposed in *Meinhard,* the same certainly should be true for a general partner in a limited partnership. Indeed, until recently limited partnership statutes did not even provide separately for general partner fiduciary duties, instead linking to general partnership law.[403] The ULPA (2001) essentially cuts and pastes RUPA-type duties into the statute.[404]

The main question about fiduciary duties in limited partnerships concerns the duties of limited partners. It would seem that they should have none because

---

402. *See* Champluvier v. State, 942 So.2d 145 (Miss., 2006).
403. *See* RULPA § 403.
404. ULPA (2001) § 408.

they are not managers. On the other hand, the demise of the limited partnership "control rule" means that limited partners no longer may have general partner liability for participating in control, and therefore they might exercise significant power either de facto or de jure under the partnership agreement. This raises the question whether general partner-type fiduciary duties automatically accompany the limited partners' increased power, at least in the absence of an agreement to the contrary. Some cases have in fact recognized fiduciary duties in this situation.[405] This introduces potentially costly unpredictability as to when a limited partner has enough power to be a fiduciary. It would be better to have a clear rule distinguishing general and limited partners, leaving it to the partners to add the appropriate duties to the agreement when they adjust partner power. The ULPA (2001) clarifies the situation a bit by providing that a limited partner acting solely as such does not have fiduciary duties.[406]

However, limited partners who are acting in their more traditional roles of contributing money and voting on partnership transactions should also be subject to duties. Limited partners might behave opportunistically by blocking or approving limited partnership transactions or refusing to meet their contribution obligations based on their selfish interests rather than those of the firm. However, as they are not fiduciaries unless they are exercising management power, limited partners ought to be able to act selfishly unless they are breaching the contract interpreted in the light of the implied covenant of good faith and fair dealing. This is clarified by ULPA (2001).[407]

Opt-out. Until 1990, it might have been thought that opting out of fiduciary duties, as with the default duties themselves, was the same in limited as in general partnerships. But that year Delaware amended its limited partnership act to provide that "the partner's duties and liabilities may be expanded or restricted by provisions in a partnership agreement."[408] This provision strikingly contrasts with the corporate post-*Van Gorkom* provision quoted above and adopted only a few years earlier which provided for opt out only of the duty of care and not the duty of loyalty.

During the decade or so following this provision's enactment, Delaware courts held that the agreement could reduce fiduciary duties or substitute contractual duties for default fiduciary duties.[409] For example, the court in *Sonet v. Timber Co., L.P.*[410] held that an agreement giving the general partner "sole discretion"

---

405. *See* 4 BROMBERG & RIBSTEIN, *supra* note 99, § 16.07(a)(1).
406. ULPA (2001), § 305(a).
407. *Id.* § 305(b) and (c).
408. *See* 6 DEL. CODE § 17-1101. Several states have adopted similar provisions. These provisions are discussed in 4 BROMBERG & RIBSTEIN, *supra* note 99, at § 16.07(h)(5).
409. *See* Larry E. Ribstein, *Fiduciary Duties and Limited Partnership Agreements*, 37 SUFFOLK U. L. REV. 927 (2004).
410. 722 A.2d 319 (Del. Ch. 1998).

preempted a fiduciary duty remedy in connection with a merger transaction. Often the agreements at issue merely tweaked default duties, providing for similar safeguards against disloyalty—substantive fairness standards, review by disinterested directors, and shareholder voting. Thus, it was unclear how the courts would react to a full-fledged waiver of duties.

The Delaware Supreme Court's first case interpreting the waiver provision, *Gotham Partners, L.P. v. Hallwood Realty Partners, L.P.*[411] attempted to answer that question with dictum rebuking the chancery court for suggesting that fiduciary duties could be eliminated in a Delaware limited partnership. The court noted that the statute did not explicitly permit elimination, and

> the historic cautionary approach of the courts of Delaware that efforts by a fiduciary to escape a fiduciary duty, whether by a corporate director or officer or other type of trustee, should be scrutinized searchingly.

The court also disagreed with the lower court that the implied covenant of good faith and fair dealing was relevant in filling any gaps.

Two years after *Gotham*, the Delaware legislature reversed the court's dictum by amending the above statute to explicitly provide that fiduciary duties may be "eliminated" by the partnership agreement. Then in a speech which was later published, Delaware Chief Justice Steele admonished his fellow Delaware judges to enforce the parties' agreements in Delaware noncorporate cases.[412] In general, Delaware's fiduciary duties for uncorporations amount to a sophisticated legal technology that has helped provided a foundation for the large uncorporations discussed in Chapter 8.

We may wonder why limited partnerships get so much more freedom of contract than either general partnerships or corporations. As always, the answer lies in the structure and function of the particular business association. Although general partnerships may be very informal, limited partnerships almost always are the product of detailed bargaining. As for corporations (as discussed more fully in Chapter 8) the limited partnership substitutes other constraints on managers for fiduciary duties, particularly high-powered owner-like incentives of managers and the owners' greater access to the firm's cash.

Remedies: The accounting remedy (particularly the accounting exclusivity rule) is clearly an inappropriate default rule for the modern limited partnership. The partnership rules are designed for very closely held firms in which litigation among the members occurs only at the end of the relationship. Moreover, the accounting remedy fits relationships with extensive mutual rights and duties. A limited partnership involves a more arms'-length relationship between the

---

411. 817 A.2d 160, 167–68 (Del. 2002).

412. *See* Myron T. Steele, *Judicial Scrutiny of Fiduciary Duties in Delaware Limited Partnerships and Limited Liability Companies*, 32 DEL. J. C. L. 1 (2007).

general and limited partners. The relationship is also asymmetrical in that limited partners have rights but few default obligations.

The corporate solution of letting a volunteer owner sue for the firm makes as much sense in limited partnerships as in corporations. It is not surprising then that the corporate derivative suit eventually made the jump to limited partnerships. At first, limited partnership law required partners to proceed via accounting,[413] and the original ULPA did not authorize derivative suits. However, the law changed after an influential federal decision in New York implied the existence of a derivative remedy under New York law,[414] and New York and Delaware adopted the first statutory provisions.[415]

4. Limited liability company

Default rule: Consistent with their "chameleon" management structure, most LLC statutes provide default fiduciary duties for managers of manager-managed firms and for all members of member-managed firms, but not for members of manager-managed firms, therefore effectively merging general and limited partnership fiduciary rules. Delaware builds on its flexible management structure by letting courts decide the members' and managers' fiduciary duties without clear statutory guidelines. However, LLCs forming under the Delaware statute generally will have detailed agreements that often provide customized fiduciary duty provisions.

Opt-out: Should LLCs be treated like general partnerships or limited partnerships for purposes of permitting opt-out? Unlike general partnerships, LLCs must be intentionally formed, suggesting that they will have explicit agreements that provide a good basis for waiving duties.

Notably, the Delaware LLC statute includes the same provision for wide-open opt-out as the Delaware limited partnership statute.[416] Indeed, one of the strongest applications of Delaware's freedom of contract approach is in the LLC case of *R & R Capital, LLC v. Buck & Doe Run Valley Farms, LLC*, in which the court enforced an operating agreement provision waiving the right to bring an action for judicial dissolution.[417] The court emphasized Delaware's strong public policy favoring freedom of contract, observing that this freedom is important to "[t]he allure of the limited liability company,"[418] and the "legitimate business reasons

---

413. *See* 2 BROMBERG & RIBSTEIN, *supra* note 99, § 5.05(b).
414. Klebanow v. New York Produce Exch., 344 F.2d 294, 296 (2d Cir. 1965).
415. 6 DEL. CODE, § 1732; N.Y. PARTNERSHIP LAW §§ 115-a, 115-b, 115-c.
416. *See* 6 DEL. CODE § 17-1101.
417. *R & R Capital, LLC v. Buck & Doe Run Valley Farms, LLC*, No. 3803-CC, 2008 WL 3846318, at *8 (Del. Ch. Aug. 19, 2008). For a discussion of this case, see Ideoblog, http://busmovie.typepad.com/ideoblog/2008/08/waiving-judicia.html (Aug. 23, 2008) ("Waiving Judicial Dissolution: Our Remedies Oft in Ourselves Do Lie").
418. *R & R Capital*, at 8.

why members of a limited liability company may wish to waive their right to seek dissolution or the appointment of a receiver," such as to avoid default in loan agreements.[419] As discussed below, this case is notable in allowing waiver of a remedy that has been considered in both uncorporations and close corporations as a backstop to express provisions of the operating agreement.

The question is whether the courts will continue to be permissive in LLC cases. As LLCs increasingly become the new default entity, many undoubtedly are being formed with plain-vanilla certificates and no detailed agreements. LLC statutes may come to reflect this state of affairs by including restrictions on contracting for fiduciary duties similar to those in partnerships. However, the Delaware statute likely will remain an option for sophisticated LLCs. This illustrates how distinctiveness can be as important among different statutory versions of the same business associations as it is among different types of business associations.

Remedy: We have seen two types of remedies in uncorporations. The general partnership model emphasizes direct partner litigation through the accounting proceeding. This fits the very closely held default firm, in which members easily can take the decision to sue into their own hands and litigation is the end of the relationship rather than a routine event. By contrast, limited partnerships are closer to the corporate model where derivative suits are the default remedy for injuries to the firm.

What litigation model fits LLCs, which have elements of both general and limited partnerships? Limited partnership-type derivative suit provisions are now common in LLC statutes.[420] The judicial attitude is indicated by a New York Court of Appeals decision applying the derivative remedy to LLCs even though the legislature had explicitly declined to provide for the remedy.[421] The majority stressed the two hundred-year history of derivative suits in corporations and limited partnerships and expressed concern that the alternative result would leave "no remedy when corporate fiduciaries use corporate assets to enrich themselves."[422] It responded to a strong dissent complaining that the court was engaging in judicial legislation with the argument that legislators might have assumed that courts would supply the missing remedy.

Consistent with the analysis throughout this chapter, the appropriateness of the derivative remedy depends on its coherence with the overall structure and function of the statute. Legislatures and the *Tzolis* court have been misled by the limited liability of the LLC into assuming that the corporate-limited partnership

---

419. *Id.* at 7.
420. *See, e.g.*, RULLCA, Art. 9.
421. Tzolis v. Wolff, 10 N.Y.3d 100, 855 N.Y.S.2d 6, 884 N.E.2d 1005 (2008).
422. *Id.*, 10 N.Y.3d at 105, 855 N.Y.S. 2d at 8, 884 N.E. 2d at 1007.

litigation analogy was appropriate.[423] Because LLC statutes permit direct member participation, LLC members are likely to play a greater role in management than limited partners. Accordingly, it is less necessary in this context than in limited partnerships and corporations to provide an extraordinary mechanism for bypassing conflicted managers in making the decision to sue. The costs of delegating the decision to a volunteer member therefore are likely to exceed the benefits.

It follows that LLC statutes should not make derivative suits the default remedy for fiduciary misconduct affecting the LLC. Rather, the members should be able to decide the issue directly through a suit authorized by a majority of the members[424] or a direct action joined by all of the members.[425] In any event, given the flexibility and variability of the LLC form, no specific set of statutory remedies is likely to suit many LLCs, which likely will provide for customized remedies (including arbitration) in their operating agreements.

F. DISSOCIATION AND DISSOLUTION

Business associations must balance protecting the firm's continuity by locking in owners' investments against protecting the owners from co-owner opportunism and manager agency costs by enabling them to cash in their investments. Corporate law lets owners leave only if they can find somebody to buy their shares, while uncorporations generally let members exit via buyout or liquidation. As discussed in Chapter 5, corporate law accommodated closely held firms by providing for judicial dissolution and buyout. However, attempts to create partner-like exit within the corporate form can lead to unpredictability and confusion. The advent of the modern uncorporation and its liberation from tax classification paved the way for coherent limited liability uncorporation statutes.

Uncorporations did not, however, reach the promised land of coherence because "family limited partnership" tax rules swiftly replaced tax classification as a force for incoherence. Family-owned firms often form a limited partnership or LLC and make the owner's potential heirs limited partners or nonmanaging LLC members. This not only facilitates succession but also gives the children's

---

423. For criticism of the LLC derivative remedy, *see* Larry E. Ribstein, *Litigating in LLCs*, 64 BUS. LAW. 739 (2009).

424. This is the approach of the Prototype LLC Act, § 1102, promulgated by a Working Group of the Partnerships and Unincorporated Business Organizations Committee of the Business Law Section in 1992.

425. This is the approach for close corporations in the American Law Institute's PRINCIPLES OF CORPORATE GOVERNANCE: ANALYSIS AND RECOMMENDATIONS § 7.01(d) (1992).

shares a lower value for estate and gift tax purposes as long as they cannot cash in their interests whenever they want when their mother or father dies.

Theoretically, business owners could contract to lock in the interest on the parent's death. But tax law provides that a limitation on liquidity does not count for tax valuation purposes unless it is legally imposed.[426] State legislatures responded to this rule by taking buyout rights out of limited partnership statutes even though these rights can provide valuable liquidity for passive members of closely held firms.[427] Most LLC statutes also now provide either that LLC members have no default right to dissociate or no right to be paid for their interests when they do dissociate.[428] The latter statutes treat dissociated LLC members as guests who have overstayed their welcome: mere assignees of their own interests, with financial but no management rights.

The no-dissociation default rule is less coherent for LLCs than for limited partnerships. Limited partnerships are a suitable vehicle for family firms because the founder and head of the family probably wants the sort of near-total control that general partners of limited partners have by default. If most family firms used limited partnerships, the tax-induced exit rule would work for the smaller ones that are most likely to use the default rule. The larger and more sophisticated investment limited partnerships probably would draft customized dissolution and dissociation provisions regardless of the default rule, and default LLCs are likely to be used by many different types of firms that do not have the same tax needs as family firms. If the tax rules made LLCs unsafe for family firms, this would have the beneficial effect of channeling these firms into the more appropriate limited partnership.

Removal of default buyout rights from LLCs has the perverse secondary effect of forcing lawmakers to provide a backup exit right. Therefore, judicial dissolution, which had brought so much unpredictability to close corporations, now haunts the LLCs that replaced them. These provisions come in two varieties. One type, represented by the ULLCA and RULLCA, uses the term *oppressive*.[429] It encourages application of the open-ended case law from the close corporation context, which as discussed in Chapter 5 may or may not reach results consistent with what the parties contemplated under their agreement.

The other variety, represented by Delaware,[430] permits judicial dissolution when it is "not reasonably practicable to carry on the business in conformity with a limited liability company agreement," or similar language. This language has the advantage of inviting the court to analyze the parties' expectations under

---

426. *See* IRC (26 U.S.C.) § 2704; Treas. Reg. (26 C.F.R.) § 25.2704-2.
427. *See* 4 BROMBERG & RIBSTEIN, *supra* note 99, § 17.13(a)–(c).
428. *See* RIBSTEIN & KEATINGE, *supra* note 260, app. 11-2 (tabulating statutes).
429. *See* ULLCA § 801(4)(v); RULLCA § 701(a)(5)(B).
430. 6 DEL CODE § 18-802.

the agreement. For example, the court in *Fisk Ventures, LLC. v. Segal*[431] ordered dissolution only after determining that the agreement left the parties no way to resolve their bitter deadlock over the future of the LLC.[432] Here it was relatively easy to reconcile the remedy with the agreement because the latter explicitly contemplated the possibility of judicial dissolution. Moreover, the connection with the agreement is reinforced by authority letting LLCs substitute contractual arbitration for dissolution[433]—or even wholly contracting out of the remedy.[434]

The *R & R Capital* case discussed above permitting contractual elimination of the judicial dissolution remedy[435] is particularly significant. If this case had involved a close corporation or a general partnership, the court likely would have held that judicial dissolution is an indispensable safety valve when the rest of the agreement fails to provide for exit or some alternative form of dispute resolution. But the court held here that in an LLC, given the Delaware statute's freedom-of-contract provisions,[436] the waiver was enforceable unless the act explicitly makes the relevant statutory provision mandatory. The only "safety valve" the court recognized was judicial interpretation of the agreement applying the implied contractual covenant of good faith and fair dealing. The court stressed the rationale for enforcing this agreement:

> [T]here are legitimate business reasons why members of a limited liability company may wish to waive their right to seek dissolution or the appointment of a receiver. For example, it is common for lenders to deem in loan agreements with limited liability companies that the filing of a petition for judicial dissolution will constitute a noncurable event of default. In such instances, it is necessary for all members to prospectively agree to waive their rights to judicial dissolution to protect the limited liability company. Otherwise, a disgruntled member could push the limited liability company into default on all of its outstanding loans simply by filing a petition with this Court.

It is not clear the extent to which other courts, particularly those outside of Delaware, will apply this extra flexibility to LLCs if they replace close corporations and general partnerships as the default entity. The more unsophisticated the LLC's clientele, the more courts might decide they need a judicial escape valve.

---

431. 2009 WL 73957 (Del. Ch., Jan. 13, 2009).

432. For an analysis of the case, see Ideoblog, http://busmovie.typepad.com/ideoblog/2009/01/reconciling-oppression-with-an-llc-agreement.html (January 27, 2009) (" Reconciling Oppression With An LLC Agreement").

433. *See* Ribstein & Keatinge, *supra* note 260, § 11:5, n. 27; Larry E. Ribstein, *Ideoblog*, "Avoiding Judicial Dissolution through Arbitration," http://busmovie.typepad.com/ideoblog/2006/03/avoiding_judici.html (Mar. 19, 2006).

434. *See* R & R Capital, LLC, discussed *supra* note 417.

435. *See supra* text accompanying note 417.

436. *See* 6 DEL. CODE § 18-1101.

Ironically, the popularity of LLCs could undercut some of what the *R & R Capital* court referred to as the LLC's "allure."[437]

G. TRANSFERRING INTERESTS

Business association statutes include provisions for acquiring and transferring ownership rights in the entity. The statutes distinguish between *entity* rights that the owners may not transfer for individual purposes and *individual* rights that the owners can transfer separate from the entity. This distinction is vital to the central role of business association law of protecting the entity's viability and continuity.

In all business associations, transfers of interests convey no direct rights to the firm's property. These rights can be conveyed only by the members collectively exercising their management rights. Corporate shareholders can freely transfer both their economic and management interests in the firm. As discussed in Chapter 3, partners can transfer only their economic rights and not management rights. This limitation reflects the close-knit nature of partnerships.

All modern uncorporations have adopted the partnership approach restricting transferability of management rights. It may seem odd that statutes do not treat limited partners and members in manager-managed LLCs like corporate shareholders in this respect. This approach carried over from general to limited partnerships where it was reinforced by tax classification rules that made free transferability a "corporate" tax characteristic. Also, uncorporations are designed for closely held firms in which there is a limited market for the firm's shares. As noted in Chapter 8,[438] publicly held firms contract to lift the restriction.

Restricted transferability of management rights has special application to creditors. As discussed in Chapter 3, partners' creditors, as with voluntary transferees, can access the members' financial rights through a device called a charging order. Also as with voluntary transferees of partners' interests, they do not have a default right to acquire the members' management rights. Partnership rules on charging orders have been applied to modern limited liability uncorporations. In a strange tale of business association statutory design gone awry, the rules have become a way for parties to use LLCs to protect the members' assets from their individual creditors.[439]

---

437. See *supra* text accompanying note 418.
438. See *infra* note 550 and accompanying text.
439. For an analysis of these charging order rules and a discussion of how they developed into an asset-protection device, see Larry E. Ribstein, *Reverse Limited Liability and the Design of Business Associations*, 30 DEL. J. CORP. L. 199 (2005).

The development of LLCs as asset protection vehicles involves the unexpected conjunction of three rules. First, creditors of limited partners[440] and LLC members[441] do not have the right of partners' creditors[442] to seek a judicial dissolution of the firm. As a result, if the member's debt cannot be paid out of the distributions to which the member is entitled under the partnership or operating agreement, the creditor is out of luck. Second, LLC statutes came to provide that LLCs could be organized for any purpose, not just to engage in business.[443] This lets LLCs be set up to passively hold the members' property without generating distributions that creditors might grab through a charging order. By contrast, traditional general partnerships can be used only by a "business for profit."[444] Third, as discussed above, unlike general and limited partnerships, LLCs may have only one member. This eliminates the possibility that members other than the debtor will insist on making distributions that the debtor's creditors may reach. Also, it is important to keep in mind that creditors cannot easily resolve this problem by contract or credit terms as they may be unaware of the details of how the owners' assets are held—and the transfer to the LLC may even occur after the extension of credit.

Courts have tried several ways to restrict the use of LLCs as asset-protection vehicles, with none being fully effective. If the debtor was insolvent when it transferred assets to the asset-protection LLC, the court might reach the transfer as a fraudulent conveyance. However, a debtor who is concerned about litigation can avoid this result through careful planning by transferring the assets when the entity is still solvent.

A court might try "reverse veil-piercing" to redress injustice in this situation. For example, in *Litchfield Asset Management v. Howell*,[445] a creditor obtained a $657,000 judgment against the operator of an interior design firm in Texas. The debtor had organized two LLCs in Connecticut while the creditor was trying to enforce its judgment. She contributed $144,679 to one of the LLCs in return for a 97 percent interest (family members had the rest for a nominal contribution), and this LLC contributed $102,901 for a 99 percent interest in another, plus 1 percent to the debtor for a $10 payment. The court pierced the LLCs' veils to get at their assets to pay the owner's debts based on evidence at trial that the debtor controlled the LLCs and commingled the LLCs' funds and expenses with personal expenses. Note that a member probably could avoid piercing on this

---

440. *See, e.g.*, ULPA (2001) § 802 (requiring application by a partner).
441. *See, e.g.*, RULLCA § 701(5) (same).
442. RUPA § 801(6) (permitting judicial dissolution on application of a partner's transferee).
443. *See* RIBSTEIN & KEATINGE, *supra* note 260, at § 4:10, nn. 5–7.
444. *See* UPA 6(1), RUPA 101(6).
445. 70 Conn. App. 133, 799 A.2d 298 (2002).

ground by being careful not to commingle assets and by maintaining appropriate formalities.

Another judicial tool may be available in bankruptcy court. A bankruptcy court held that a sole member's trustee in bankruptcy could exercise the member's management rights because there were no non-consenting members. The court reasoned that:

> [T]he charging order, as set forth in Section 703 of the Colorado Limited Liability Company Act, exists to protect *other* members of an LLC from having involuntarily to share governance responsibilities with someone they did not choose, or from having to accept a creditor of another member as a co-manager. A charging order protects the autonomy of the original members, and their ability to manage their own enterprise. In a single-member entity, there are no non-debtor members to protect. The charging order limitation serves no purpose in a single member limited liability company, because there are no other parties' interests affected.[446]

So far this case stands alone in its willingness to disregard state restrictions on the rights of LLC's members' creditors solely on the ground that the LLC has only one member. But even if other bankruptcy courts follow this case, members theoretically can avoid the holding simply by having other nominal members, as the debtor did in *Litchfield*.

The basic problem is that business association statutes should not have allowed nonbusiness and one-member LLCs because the statutes were not designed for these situations. The charging order provisions exist to protect ongoing businesses with multiple members. Opening up the statutes to relationships that do not fit the rules of the business association rendered them incoherent. It should not be surprising that this led to unintended consequences.

H. TAXES, REGULATION, AND BUSINESS ASSOCIATION DESIGN

This chapter has applied general theoretical considerations to explain the design of business association statutes. We have seen that business associations should be—and generally are—coherent in the sense that their bundles of terms fit with each other and serve distinct types of firms. But the coherence is not perfect. In part this naturally results from the way these statutes have developed by evolution and experimentation rather than as the work of a master planner. The coherence theory predicts that more coherent statutes will survive or gradually evolve toward coherence because business associations will demand coherent features.

---

446. *In re* Albright, 291 B.R. 538, 541 (Bankr. D.Colo. 2003) (emphasis in original).

However, it does not predict that business association statutes will be perfectly coherent at any given time.

The main exceptions to coherence have been caused by tax and regulation. It is not surprising that lawmakers take these factors into account in designing the statutes along with other transaction cost considerations. Business association statutes that take tax and regulation into account may be efficient in the sense that they reduce the overall costs of forming firms. However, the statutes may be less coherent than they would be if the tax and regulatory statutes were designed with a view to their effects on business association statutes. This suggests that lawmakers could minimize total social costs by designing tax and regulatory statutes that take into consideration business association coherence as well as other statutory objectives.

A clear example of the effect of tax rules on business association design is tax classification, which as we have seen constrained uncorporation statutory evolution for the early history of the uncorporation. The obvious way this effect could be avoided is what the IRS ultimately did: adopt the "check the box" rule discussed in Chapter 6. This rule let firms choose their governance (and therefore let legislators design default rules) without having to take tax into account. Of course Congress had to consider that allowing firms to avoid the corporate tax might be inconsistent with the revenue, fairness, and other objectives of the tax laws. But it turned out that there was a better way to do this than trying to classify corporations and partnerships—that is, by taxing publicly traded partnerships.[447] This rule perversely constrains choice of form (as discussed below in Chapter 8). But the combination of check-the-box and the publicly traded partnership provision had the virtue of interfering less with coherence than the prior classification test.

As discussed above in this chapter, estate and gift tax provisions also have undermined statutory coherence. Those drafting the tax statutes seemingly should care only about the valuation of the recipient's interest, which with business association interests should depend on the partnership or operating agreement. However, the statute and rule focus on the terms of state law, which has distorted LLC default rules.

Statutes and rules may have more subtle effects on governance forms. For example, some types of regulation that protect firms' owners and employees arguably should not apply to those who are directly involved in management and therefore can protect themselves. In particular, the underlying policies of the employment discrimination and securities laws apply to asymmetric relationships in which the statute deems protected parties (employees and investors) to need protection from the regulated parties (employers and promoters). The flexibility of uncorporate structures discussed throughout this chapter significantly complicates the lawmakers' task.

---

447. *See* IRC (26 U.S.C.) § 7704.

To prevent evasion of regulation, Congress and the courts may use general standards rather than narrow rules in determining the application of the statute. But lawmakers must balance business needs for certainty and predictability against the need to reduce evasion of the statute. Congress, courts, and administrative agencies may temper vague and inclusive standards with rules. However, clear rules give firms an opportunity for regulatory *arbitrage*—that is, engaging in behavior that technically complies with the statute, but raises the policy problems the statute was intended to cover. One way to do this is by manipulating flexible business association rules under state law. State business association rules may facilitate this manipulation even if this compromises the coherence objectives of the statute. The following subsections discuss some situations that present these issues.

1. Securities regulation

The federal Securities Act of 1933 and Securities Exchange Act of 1934 include anti-fraud and mandatory disclosure rules protecting investors in connection with the purchase or sale of a "security." A security includes an "investment contract." Under the leading case of *Securities & Exchange Commission v. W.J. Howey Co*,[448] whether a transaction involves an investment contract depends on whether the investor needs the protection of the disclosure laws, including whether she is relying on "the efforts of others." This assumes that one who has invested in another's ability to deliver profits needs the information required by the securities laws in order to evaluate the entrepreneur's abilities. This test is easily met in a standard publicly traded corporation that clearly separates management and ownership. But what about partnerships and other unincorporated firms whose owners both directly participate in governance and delegate some management functions?

Searching for some certainty in the vague policy, statutory language, and case law, the court in *Williamson v. Tucker*[449] held that a general partnership is presumptively not an investment contract because the partners typically are managers. In *Rivanna Trawlers Unlimited v. Thompson Trawlers, Inc.*,[450] retired Justice Lewis Powell sitting by designation held that a general partnership formed by twenty-three parties to acquire, own, lease, and operate multipurpose fishing vessels and engage in the commercial fishing business was not a security under the *Williamson* test. Justice Powell wrote:

> [O]nly under certain limited circumstances can an investor's general partnership interest be characterized as an investment contract. A court must examine

---

448. 328 U.S. 293 (1946).
449. 645 F.2d 404, 422 (5th Cir.), *cert. denied*, 454 U.S. 897, 102 S.Ct. 396, 70 L.Ed.2d 212 (1981).
450. 840 F.2d 236 (4th Cir. 1988).

the partnership agreement and circumstances of a particular partnership to determine the reality of the contractual rights of the general partners. When, however, a partnership agreement allocates powers to the general partners that are specific and unambiguous, and when those powers are sufficient to allow the general partners to exercise ultimate control, as a majority, over the partnership and its business, then the presumption that the general partnership is not a security can only be rebutted by evidence that it is not possible for the partners to exercise those powers.[451]

On the other hand, the court in *Securities & Exch. Comm. v. Merchant Capital, LLC*[452] held that a scheme to raise $20 million from more than 350 investors to invest in a debt pool did involve the sale of a security. Although the partners had the power under the partnership statute and agreement to dissolve the firm and actively participate in management and control, the particular facts of the case cut in favor of the investors needing securities-type disclosures. For example, the investors had no independent experience in the debt-purchase business, they could remove the general partner only for cause by unanimous vote, and they were geographically dispersed with no connections to each other.[453]

In contrast to general partnerships, limited partnerships are presumptively securities because the limited partners do not participate in management.[454] Then what about LLCs? Should manager-managed LLCs be treated like limited partnerships (presumptive securities) and member-managed LLCs be treated like general partnerships (presumptive non-securities)? Or should *all* LLCs be entitled to the partnership non-security presumption because they have flexible management and clearly are not corporations?

The court in *Robinson v. Glynn*[455] addressed this question by engaging in a fact-specific inquiry, holding that an LLC interest was not a "security" where plaintiff had the power to appoint two of the seven members (including himself as vice-chairman) of the firm's "board of managers," was one of four members of the executive committee to which the board delegated substantial responsibility, served as treasurer with extensive powers over financial matters, and had the power to approve extraordinary indebtedness and consult on financing that

---

451. *Id.* at 241.
452. 483 F.3d 747 (11th Cir., 2007).
453. Apart from the details of the partnership relationship, the partnership had no contractual right to get control of the assets from a third party firm with which the general partner had contracted to manage them. This suggests that, even if the partners could be deemed to have control over their own firm, they did not control the entire enterprise. It is not clear how relevant this fact was to the court's decision.
454. *See* BROMBERG & RIBSTEIN, *supra* note 99, at § 12.14(a).
455. 349 F.3d 166 (4th Cir. 2003).

would dilute his interest. The court refused to hold that LLCs should be generally classified as either securities or non-securities:

> Precisely because LLCs lack standardized membership rights or organizational structures, they can assume an almost unlimited variety of forms. It becomes then exceedingly difficult to declare that LLCs whatever their form either possess or lack the economic characteristics associated with investment contracts. Even drawing firm lines between member-managed and manager-managed LLCs threatens impermissibly to elevate form over substance. Certainly the members in a member-managed LLC will often have powers too significant for them to be considered passive investors under the securities laws. And yet even members in a member-managed LLC may be unable as a practical matter to exercise any meaningful control, perhaps because they are too numerous, inexperienced, or geographically disparate. By the same token, although interests in manager-managed LLCs may often be securities, their members need not necessarily rely on the efforts on their managers.[456]

Consider the implications of the above cases for a firm engaging in planning or choice of business form. The disclosure burdens and liabilities of the securities laws may be quite substantial. If the firm believes that drafting the agreement in a particular way or choosing a particular form will help it avoid the securities laws, it may do so even if the drafting or choice has other costs. It may, for example, choose to be an LLP rather than an LLC and hope that it thereby gets the anti-"security" presumption that *Williamson* gives general partnerships. Or it may choose to be a member-managed LLC even if it is going to delegate significant power to managers, thereby creating potential confusion vis-à-vis third parties dealing with the firm.[457]

Consider also the implications for statutory drafting. If firms want flexible management that can bend both ways (superficially decentralized but outwardly centralized), state lawmakers may serve this need even if the statute reduces clarity and predictability among the members and in the firm's dealings with third parties. Also, the securities laws may create a clientele for a particular standard form based on the insulation this form provides from the securities laws. This clientele may differ significantly from the form's non-securities clientele, which then makes it difficult to provide a coherent set of rules that suits both clienteles. For example, promoters of investment schemes may use the LLP form, which is generally suited to small or professional firms, to lend a partnership aura to a scheme to raise funds from widely disseminated investors.

These issues might be resolved by a rule that provides some predictability and clarity without inviting the arbitrage that compromises coherence. For example,

---

456. *Id.* at 174.
457. *See* Carol Goforth, *Continuing Obstacles to Freedom of Choice for Management Structure in LLCs*, 1 J. SMALL & EMERGING BUS. LAW 165 (1997).

a pure general partnership with vicarious liability probably does not implicate the policy problems addressed by the securities laws because vicariously liable owners are likely to be at least somewhat involved in management. Thus, the securities laws might exempt general partnerships.[458]

The resolution is trickier for LLCs given the wide range of firms this form accommodates. One possible response is to apply the *Williamson* anti-security presumption to LLCs as well as partnerships.[459] Alternatively, the securities laws might be phrased or interpreted to apply only to centrally managed firms, regardless of business form, as this would "catch" the firms that are most appropriate for securities regulation. It would also encourage state lawmakers to offer firms clear management alternatives rather than a muddy option that combines centralized and decentralized management.

2. Employment discrimination

The employment discrimination laws are supposed to protect employees from a firm's discriminatory hiring and firing decisions. Members of management do not generally need this protection. What about partners? In a concurring opinion in *Hishon v. King & Spalding*,[460] Justice Powell (again as in *Rivanna* the promoter of certainty) observed that the employment discrimination laws probably do not regulate employment decisions involving *bona fide partners*. This triggered case law defining this term.

The basic question is similar to that in the securities cases: regulate by a specific rule and encourage both arbitrage and incoherent business association statutes, or regulate on a fact-specific policy basis and leave a lot of unpredictability? Courts or lawmakers applying the first approach would hold that a partner of any firm that is a partnership under state law is a "bona fide partner." But we have seen how much leeway there is in the state definition of partnership. Application of the second approach might involve ignoring whether the firm is a partnership and force firms to roll the dice as to which decisions are subject to the federal discrimination laws. For example, the court in *Strother v. Southern California Permanente Medical Group*[461] reversed a trial court determination that the plaintiff was not an employee. The agreement labeled plaintiff and 2500 or so others as "partners" and gave them partner-like rights to serve on the firm's board of directors and vote on various matters, but little control over the board while their compensation was based on performance rather than the firm's profits.

---

458. *See* Larry E. Ribstein, *Private Ordering and the Securities Laws: The Case of General Partnerships*, 42 Case West. L. Rev. 1 (1992).

459. *See* Larry E. Ribstein, *Form and Substance in the Definition of a "Security": The Case of Limited Liability Companies*, 51 Wash. & Lee L. Rev. 807 (1994); Mark Sargent, *Are Limited Liability Company Interests Securities?*, 19 Pepp. L. Rev. 1069 (1992).

460. 467 U.S. 69, 79 (1984).

461. 79 F.3d 859 (9th Cir. 1996).

As in the securities cases, firms can respond to this law by making their members "partners" and endowing them with enough partner rights to pass the courts' form-based test even if the "partners" are in substance employees for purposes of the policies under the employment discrimination laws. However, this will encourage law firms to create a confusing quasi-"partner" status that would not exist but for the employment discrimination laws. Such contracts could undermine partnership law's coherence as quasi-partners would not expect to have the rights and responsibilities of standard-form partners, and third parties dealing with the firm would not expect them to have these rights and powers. Employment discrimination laws may be one reason law firms have pushed the envelope in creating noneconomic partners (as discussed in Section C above).

Perhaps the most interesting law firm employment discrimination case is *Equal Employment Opportunity Commission v. Sidley Austin Brown & Wood*,[462] which held there was enough doubt as to whether the thirty-two equity partners in a law firm demoted to "counsel" or "senior counsel" were covered by the age discrimination laws that the Equal Employment Opportunity Commission (EEOC) was entitled to seek documents on the partners' status. Age discrimination is an increasingly important context for this issue to arise as many large firms facing economic pressures are seeking to trim senior partners whose business production does not match their pay.

In this case, Sidley was controlled by a self-perpetuating executive committee. Partners who were not members of the committee had some power over hiring, firing, promotion, and compensation of their subordinates, a power to vote on a specific merger (with Brown & Wood) that the firm allowed after the EEOC began its investigation, rights to share in the firm's profits, substantial capital accounts, and liability for the firm's debts in proportion (but only in proportion to their capital investments). The court concluded that the demoted partners' classification under state law did not control their treatment under federal antidiscrimination law. Judge Posner, writing for the majority, reasoned:[463]

> The law does not allow firms to obtain the benefits or avoid the costs associated with particular forms of doing business by simple redesignation. Of course firms have broad freedom of election among the different forms of doing business, such as the corporate, partnership, LLC, and so forth. Their freedom is not unlimited; there is, for example, the "substance over form" rule of tax law. [Citation omitted.] * * * The question is whether, when a firm employs the latitude allowed to it by state law to reconfigure a partnership in the direction of making it a de facto corporation, a federal agency enforcing federal antidiscrimination law is compelled to treat all the "partners" as employers.

---

462. 315 F.3d 696 (7th Cir. 2002).
463. *Id.* at 705, 707, 709–10.

* * * We are not ruling that the 32 demoted partners were in fact employees within the meaning of the age discrimination law. Such a ruling would be premature. Sidley has respectable arguments on its side, not least that the functional test of employer status toward which the EEOC is leaning is too uncertain to enable law firms and other partnerships to determine in advance their exposure to discrimination suits—that it would be better if the courts and the Commission interpreted the employer exclusion to require treating all partners as employers, with perhaps a narrow sham exception. These issues will become ripe when Sidley finishes complying with the coverage part of the subpoena. We hold only that there is enough doubt about whether the 32 demoted partners are covered by the age discrimination law to entitle the EEOC to full compliance with that part, at least, of its subpoena.

Judge Easterbrook, concurring in part, wrote:

No one believes that a bona fide partner is in a master-servant relation with the partnership, or that the partner "is employed by" the partnership. The qualification "bona fide" is important; as Justice Powell observed in *Hishon*, an employer may not evade obligations under federal law by plastering the name "partner" on someone whose legal and economic characteristics are those of an employee. . . . It is neither our duty, nor our privilege, to invent a federal law of employment relations, as my colleagues appear to believe. . . .

. . . [I]t makes both linguistic and economic sense to say that someone who is liable without limit for the debts of an organization is an entrepreneur (a principal) rather than an "employee" (an agent). Unlimited liability and profit-sharing give each partner an interest in monitoring (and if need be expelling) those other partners who are shirking or otherwise not carrying their part of the load. Their actions in this respect are those of owners. . . .

Judge Easterbrook offered a solution similar to the one suggested above for securities cases—let the partners' vicarious liability determine the issue at least in that type of firm. This would provide predictability while doing little violence to the standard form because partners who have chosen to be vicariously liability probably are not so powerless that they need the protection of the employment laws. But this would be only an incomplete solution as it does not do much for the many cases involving limited liability firms.[464]

---

464. In 2006, Judge Posner held that the EEOC could seek damages although individual partners had not filed claims with the EEOC and therefore could not pursue claims on their own behalf. EEOC v. Sidley Austin LLP, 437 F.3d 695 (7th Cir. 2006). The case was finally settled by the firm's paying $27.5 million to thirty-two fired former partners and consenting to an injunction barring certain discriminatory practices. *See* WALL ST. J. LAW Blog, http://blogs.wsj.com/law/2007/10/05/in-age-bias-suit-sidley-to-pay-ex-partners-275-million (Oct. 5, 2007) ("In Age-Bias Suit, Sidley To Pay Ex-Partners $27.5 Million").

The Supreme Court ultimately threw a monkey wrench into this issue by applying a general agency test based on control in determining who should be deemed to be an employer.[465] This test seems to eschew predictability in favor of policy. But note that a factor in the Supreme Court's test is "[w]hether the parties intended that the individual be an employee, as expressed in written agreements or contracts"[466] This may let employers argue that an individual who is clearly a partner by statute and agreement meets the Court's test, in which case we would be back with the "bona fide partner" test.

3. General thoughts on tax and regulation

The discussion of these tax and regulatory issues could be extended almost endlessly, but the above examples should be enough to indicate the problems and suggest potential solutions. However, these solutions may not be feasible in the real world because it may be too much to expect that Congress and regulators will focus on business association coherence amid more pressing demands of competing interest groups.

We might be tempted to argue that, to the extent the confusion is caused by having multiple flexible uncorporate forms, this flexibility is more trouble than it is worth. But it is important to keep in mind that although using standard forms to "arbitrage" tax and regulation may cause complications, this also helps to mitigate the costs of tax and regulatory statutes. The more costs these statutes impose on firms, the more the firms will be willing to spend on arbitrage, even at the sacrifice of coherence. This system may be messy in practice, but it also facilitates evolution toward efficient rules. For example, the tax classification rules set off a round of manipulating business association statutes to fit firms' tax needs. Although this triggered some statutory incoherence, the ultimate result was the more efficient check-the-box regime.

---

465. Clackamas Gastroenterology Associates, P. C. v. Wells, 538 U.S. 440 (2003).
466. *Id.* at 450.

8. UNCORPORATING THE LARGE FIRM

So far we have seen how the corporate form initially rose to prominence in the United States to serve the needs of the large firms that arose during the nineteenth-century Industrial Revolution. Large firms chose the corporate form over partnership-type alternatives such as the joint stock company that they might have adapted to their purposes. By the mid-twentieth century, the corporation dominated for closely held firms as well. Then, in the late twentieth century, the LLC Revolution pushed the close corporation aside. So at this point in the story corporations and uncorporations seem to neatly divide between large publicly held and smaller closely held firms.

This chapter shows that the big-small equilibrium is being threatened as uncorporations invade the modern corporation's large firm turf.[467] This seems odd at first glance. After all, whether or not the corporation initially was the best choice for big firms, the corporate form has developed over more than a century to suit the needs of the large, integrated, and durable firm whose shares are held by passive owners and traded on public securities markets.

The modern corporation, however, is far from ideal. A key problem lies in how the corporate form deals with the agency costs of delegating control to powerful managers. Corporations address passive owners' vulnerability to mismanagement through such devices as monitoring of management by independent directors, shareholder voting backed by federal proxy and disclosure rules, fiduciary duties, and takeovers. These devices not only cannot make managers perfectly loyal to owners' interests, but also could generate their own costs. For example, strict fiduciary duties may make managers more risk-averse than owners want them to be and allow judges' unsophisticated judgments to be substituted for those of expert managers.

The important question is not whether the corporation falls short of a hypothetical ideal, but whether there are better governance structures for large firms. This chapter shows that the uncorporation provides potentially more efficient ways to control the agency costs of centralized management. Moreover, uncorporations already have shown that they can play an important role in governing large firms. Private equity, hedge fund, and venture capital firms have controlled operating firms organized as corporations. Jonathan Macey observes that these firms "fill the governance gap created by the passive credit-rating agencies, the

---

467. Some of the ideas presented in this chapter were summarized in Larry E. Ribstein, *Partnership Governance of Large Firms*, 76 U. CHI. L. REV. 289 (2009).

moribund market for corporate control, the rational ignorance in shareholder voting, and . . . captured directors and self-interested management."[468] More directly, publicly traded firms have been organized as publicly traded partnerships (PTPs) and real estate investment trusts (REITs).

Many commentators have extensively discussed the benefits of uncorporate governance. This chapter develops these observations into a general theory of uncorporate governance in large firms. It shows how uncorporations substitute high-powered owner-like managerial incentives and owner access to the firm's cash (which rely heavily on the objective market measures) for subjective evaluation of managerial performance by directors, shareholders, and courts. Those using uncorporate governance technologies are proving more adept than corporations at handling the modern challenges of running large and complex firms.

It is important to emphasize the role of business forms in these new governance technologies. These are not discrete terms, but parts of business associations that have evolved over centuries. As discussed throughout the book, standard forms are coherent *sets* of terms that provide a basis for norms, gap-filling, and regulation. Corporations cannot easily contract around strong corporate norms emphasizing the managers' power over corporate assets and the roles of shareholder voting, board of directors, and fiduciary duties in constraining this power. This inflexibility is at least partly attributable to the corporation throughout its history having been a mechanism for political control of governance, particularly in large firms. The government accordingly has used tax and regulation to channel large firms into the corporate form.

By contrast, uncorporations, like the partnerships they are derived from, traditionally eschew the mainstays of corporate governance while relying on devices that are alien to corporations, particularly including the owners' right to exit the firm. Modern uncorporations also continue the partnership's emphasis on the parties' agreement.

Here is an obvious question about the rise of uncorporate governance in large firms: why is this happening now? Both uncorporations and the problems with corporations have been around for a long time. Why is the uncorporation only now managing to overcome the political forces that have so long aligned in favor of the corporation?

One answer is that corporate agency costs became particularly salient as corporate governance collapsed under the weight of the millennial tech bust of 2000–2001 and the financial crisis of 2008–2009. Other factors include increasing financial complexity that demands better governance and the ingenuity of financial pioneers in developing the private equity format.

The large uncorporation's story is still unfolding. Courts, regulators, and tax authorities may decide that large firms should be subject to corporate rules

---

468. Macey, *supra* note 46, at 248.

whatever business form they have chosen. On the other hand, policy makers may see that the crisis in the governance of large firms demands a fresh approach rather than just tinkering with an increasingly unsatisfactory model. Understanding the distinct mechanisms of uncorporations and giving them room to operate may be a key to this fresh approach.

A. THE TROUBLES WITH CORPORATE GOVERNANCE

In the fall and winter of 2008–2009 large firms, particularly financial firms, dramatically crumbled in the United States and throughout the world. Companies that seemed to be pillars of strength one day were in or approaching insolvency the next. Some of these failures revealed striking governance problems, particularly including failure to understand and manage risk. For example, some financial firms apparently bet their assets on the dubious proposition that real estate prices would rise forever. As the firms should have known, these prices were fueled (among other things) by accommodating credit policies and lax credit controls. Financial assets predictably evaporated when the underlying assumptions proved faulty.

Lehman Brothers was one of the most spectacular of these financial busts. Lehman flamed out in bankruptcy on September 15, 2008. Yet Lehman's annual report issued earlier in the year contained this statement:

> Lehman Brothers continues to be committed to industry best practices with respect to corporate governance. Below you will find links to the Firm's corporate governance guidelines and code of ethics, as well as charters for the Audit, Compensation and Benefits, and Nominating and Corporate Governance Committees of the Firm's Board of Directors.

If Lehman was a paragon of *corporate* governance, its flameout was as much a failure of the corporate model as it was of Lehman in particular. The following discussion analyzes the gaps in corporate agency cost control mechanisms that could lead to a failure like Lehman's. It shows that corporate governance's failure results not simply from a few mistakes by policy makers or corporate agents, but rather from inherent attributes of corporate structure.

1. Shareholder voting

While firms like Lehman were crumbling, where were the owners? They had an interest in preserving their investments and the legal power to do something about it. They annually elected the directors who oversaw the managers and voted on the important transactions that shaped their firms. Yet shareholder voting rights are not as potent a constraint on management as many believe. Individual shareholders in publicly held firms generally own small bits of many companies in diversified portfolios. Indeed, corporations are designed to enable shareholders to be rationally ignorant about what is happening in their firms. Moreover, most investors own firms only indirectly through mutual and pension funds and other institutions. These institutions act as agents of the owners and may have little to gain from aggressively monitoring portfolio firms.

Given these facts, we might question whether shareholders should have a power to vote. One answer has a political flavor—that shareholder voting adds legitimacy to corporate management. Without a shareholder vote on at least major transactions and electing directors, corporate managers would wield huge power over resources comparable to those of a significant-sized country seemingly without any accountability to the governed. But this political analogy is flawed.[469] Managers can do nothing to shareholders other than lose their money, and shareholders can protect themselves from mismanagement in specific firms by diversifying their portfolios. Shareholders get all the legitimacy they need when they make or accept a governance contract upon investing in the firm.

An alternative and more satisfying answer to why shareholders have voting rights turns on the vote's role in protecting the firm from managerial agency costs. Shareholders have a unique interest in the overall financial health of the firm because of their right to what is left after all of the non-shareholder claimants are paid. Shareholders' profit interest motivates them to ensure the other claimants perform efficiently. Giving non-shareholders voting rights could lead to chaos because instead of trying to maximize the firm's wealth, these other claimants would squabble over their shares of the pie.

In short, shareholders have a vote because they are supposedly well-suited to monitor the firm's management. Thompson and Edelman refer to this as the "error-correcting" role of shareholders, and show how this function explains various features of shareholder voting rights, including why only shareholders and not other corporate constituencies may vote.[470] Shareholder powers are designed to operate in situations where shareholders can most effectively prevent or correct mistakes by the agents who are supposed to be watching over the firm.

However, although shareholders may be the appropriate monitors in theory, in practice they are not very effective in playing this role. Consider a few of the problems with shareholder voting rights:

1. The costs of the shareholders' franchise necessitates that it be limited to a few major corporate acts and electing directors, with the directors themselves exercising significant control over the voting agenda.[471]

---

469. *See* Henry G. Manne, *The "Higher Criticism" of the Modern Corporation*, 63 COLUM. L. REV. 399 (1962).

470. Robert B. Thompson & Paul H. Edelman, *Corporate Voting*, 62 VAND. L. REV. 129 (2009).

471. *See* Macey, *supra* note 46 at 201–02; Stephen M. Bainbridge, *The Case for Limited Shareholder Rights*, 53 UCLA L. REV. 601 (2006).

2. Small shareholders typically lack incentives to do much with their rights because they would have to share the fruits of governance activities and information-gathering with thousands of other shareholders, who would free ride on their efforts. Even mutual funds and other institutional holders are discouraged by regulatory and tax rules from owning big enough stakes to make significant governance initiatives worthwhile.[472]
3. Many active shareholders have interests that divert them from disciplining managerial agency costs. For example, labor unions and public pension funds may use their power as shareholders to pursue political and other concerns that their passive co-owners do not necessarily share.[473]
4. Shareholders who do not value their voting rights may sell them, thereby enabling those without economic interests to exercise significant voting rights for strategic purposes that may or may not be consistent with those of the owners.[474]
5. Controlling shareholders may seek to extract private benefits rather than maximize corporate wealth.
6. Large shareholders may have inherently different incentives from smaller shareholders because their stakes in individual firms make them more risk-averse than shareholders with broadly diversified portfolios.

---

472. *See* Roe, *supra* note 38.

473. *See* Bainbridge, *supra* note 471, at 634 n.88 (2006) (noting that "the most activist institutions—union and state and local employee pension funds—may have interests that diverge substantially from those of other investors"). For discussions of the incentives of activist shareholders see Edward B. Rock, *The Logic and (Uncertain) Significance of Institutional Shareholder Activism*, 79 GEO. L.J. 445, 479–81 (1991); Roberta Romano, *Public Pension Fund Activism in Corporate Governance Reconsidered*, 93 COLUM. L. REV. 795, 801–19 (1993); Stewart J. Schwab & Randall S. Thomas, *Realigning Corporate Governance: Shareholder Activism by Labor Unions*, 96 MICH. L. REV. 1018, 1033–34 (1998). For direct evidence that shareholders' union affiliation affects voting for directors, see Ashwini K. Agrawal, *Corporate Governance Objectives of Labor Union Shareholders: Evidence from Proxy Voting*, NYU Working Paper No. FIN-08-006 (Feb. 2009), http://papers.ssrn.com/sol3/papers.cfm?abstract_id=1354494.

474. For discussions of the policy implications of these structures see Bruce H. Kobayashi & Larry E. Ribstein, *Outsider Trading as an Incentive Device*, 40 UC-DAVIS L. REV. 21 (2006); Henry T. C. Hu & Bernard Black, *The New Vote Buying: Empty Voting and Hidden (Morphable) Ownership*, 79 S. CAL. L. REV. 811 (2006) (showing how shareholders and corporations can separate economic ownership and voting rights in ways that are not evident to other shareholders and proposing greater disclosure); Henry T.C. Hu & Bernard Black, *Hedge Funds, Insiders, and the Decoupling of Economic and Voting Ownership: Empty Voting and Hidden (Morphable) Ownership*, 13 J. CORP. FIN. 343 (2007); Shaun P. Martin & Frank Partnoy, *Encumbered Shares*, 2005 ILL. L. REV. 775 (2005); Thompson & Edelman, *supra* note 470.

7. Logistical problems infect corporate voting, including delayed delivery of disclosures, defective vote counting, and incidental discrepancies between ownership and voting rights.[475]

Commentators long have recognized the potential problems with shareholder voting, particularly the weak incentives most shareholders have to participate in governance. In the wake of the 1929 stock market crash, Berle and Means published their important 1932 book, *The Modern Corporation and Private Property*, which documented the individual shareholders' small stakes in the country's biggest firms and lamented the extent to which this left non-owner managers effectively in control.

The Securities Exchange Act of 1934 addressed the problems identified by Berle and Means in trying to ensure that shareholders are informed about the matters to be voted on at meetings before they give the corporate managers their proxy to vote so that they can effectively direct the proxy holder to vote their shares. These rules assume that shareholders could be a stronger force in corporate governance if only they received more information about their companies. It apparently did not occur to policy makers that shareholders who lack incentives to participate in governance also would not read boring technical disclosure documents. Thus, seventy-five years later, a leading commentator described shareholder voting as a "myth" because of the sparse record of shareholder successes in challenging incumbent managers.[476]

Although the proxy rules have done little to make shareholders more effective monitors, they have bolstered the misguided notion of the corporation as a political rather than purely market institution. In particular, the SEC promulgated its "shareholder proposal" rule that enables any small shareholder to use the corporation's proxy statement to propose a topic for shareholder action.[477] Many of these proposals have more to do with society at large than the corporation. Prominent litigated examples include proposals dealing with the Vietnam war and health care.[478] The proxy disclosure rules also have responded to various hot-button governance issues that arise from time to time. Accordingly, the shareholders now get extensive disclosure about such things as executive compensation and environmental compliance, which may not be much help in enabling them to monitor managers.

---

475. *See* Marcel Kahan & Edward B. Rock, *The Hanging Chads of Corporate Voting*, 96 Geo. L.J. 1227 (2008).

476. *See* Lucian Bebchuk, *The Myth of the Shareholder Franchise*, 93 Harv. L. Rev. 675 (2007).

477. SEC Rule 14a-8, Fed. Reg. § 240.14a-8.

478. New York City Employees' Retirement System v. Dole Food Company, Inc., 795 F. Supp. 95 (S.D.N.Y.), *dismissed as moot*, 969 F.2d 1430 (2d. Cir. 1992); Medical Committee for Human Rights v. SEC, 432 F.2d 659 (DC Cir. 1970), *vacated*, 404 U.S. 403 (1972).

All of this is not to say that corporate shareholder voting is useless. Even shareholders with relatively small stakes may have an incentive to vote on some issues (such as takeover defenses) that arise repeatedly over time in similar ways in many firms in their portfolios.[479] Also, if a proposed transaction will transfer wealth from one class of owners to another, the benefits of objecting may outweigh the costs. Most importantly, individual shareholders can sell their shares to somebody who is accumulating enough shares to make it economical to participate actively in control. Shareholder voting rights need to be evaluated in relation to this "market for control,"[480] which is discussed further below. It turns out a key benefit of shareholder voting has been to give corporate shareholders the power to turn over control to uncorporations.

2. Board of directors

Directors initiate and approve important corporate transactions. Indeed, Stephen Bainbridge sees directors rather than shareholders as the primary corporate governance institution.[481] Given the problems we have just seen, it is logical to empower a small group of experts rather than the passive, fractious, and conflicted shareholders. However, on a closer look, the corporate board is a dubious candidate for a central decision making.

To begin with, it is not obvious why corporations need to divide management power between executives and boards of directors rather than giving all management power to executives. As discussed in Chapter 4, the board originated in the government nature of early corporations. Early boards of directors were intended as ways to provide direct participation in governance by different constituencies. In the modern corporation, the board has turned into a device for overseeing managers on the shareholders' behalf. But it has never been clear how the board should be designed to serve this role.

The problem begins with the way the board is chosen. If the directors oversee the managers, the shareholders ought to select them. But because the shareholders of publicly held corporations are generally passive holders of diversified portfolios, why assume they would be in a position to choose and supervise the board? Obviously somebody must nominate specific candidates for the job. Taking suggestions from thousands of shareholders would be chaotic and unworkable. So the board itself has to nominate candidates for board positions.

At one time this process rendered the board almost useless as a monitoring device because strong managers in effect hand selected nominees who were then pro forma proposed by the management-selected board and elected by the

---

479. *See* Macey, *supra* note, at 200–01, 204, 207–08.
480. *See* Henry G. Manne, *Mergers and the Market for Corporate Control*, 73 J. POL. ECON. 110 (1965).
481. *See* Stephen M. Bainbridge, *Director Primacy: The Means and Ends of Corporate Governance*, 97 NW. U. L. REV. 547 (2003).

passive shareholders. The managers could, in effect, appoint baby birds to the board and keep them quiet by feeding them the right worms. For example, a popular book about the RJR Nabisco takeover tells how Ross Johnson, Nabisco's powerful CEO, controlled his board with lucrative services and consulting contracts, corporate money to endow faculty chairs (one named after the director), high directors' fees, and use of corporate jets.[482]

Commentators thought this problem could be solved by procedural rules that made directors more independent of corporate executives. A leading advocate of this approach has been Professor Melvin Eisenberg of the University of California at Berkeley, who recommended that nonexecutive members of corporate boards serve on an *audit* committee that works with the corporation's auditing firm and is responsible for seeing that the board has accurate information about the company, and a *nominating* committee that is responsible for nominating director candidates.[483] Many influential organizations have pushed these ideas over the years, including the American Bar Association,[484] the Securities and Exchange Commission (through consent decrees in the 1970s[485] and in rules requiring disclosures regarding audit committees),[486] the New York Stock Exchange,[487] and the *Principles of Corporate Governance* promulgated by the prestigious American Law Institute.[488]

Despite all these moves to bolster the monitoring board, there have been repeated meltdowns in corporate governance, including the collapses of Enron and WorldCom. A class action complaint for securities fraud sought damages from WorldCom directors for being "utterly derelict in fulfilling the most basic functions of a true board."[489] The complaint alleged that the "Audit Committee was reckless by failing to become sufficiently familiar and involved with the Company's internal financial workings, to see the weaknesses in the Company's internal control structure, and to appreciate or detect the true corporate culture at WorldCom"; that although WorldCom was "a complicated company in

---

482. Bryan Burrough & John Helyar, Barbarians at the Gate (1990).

483. Melvin A. Eisenberg, The Structure of the Corporation (1976).

484. American Bar Association Committee on Corporate Law, Corporate Directors Guidebook, 33 Bus. Law. 1595, 1607–10 (1978); 1994 Edition, 49 Bus. Law. 1243 (1994).

485. *See* Lewis A. Solomon, *Restructuring the Board of Directors: Fond Hope–Faint Promise?* 76 Mich. L. Rev. 581 (1978).

486. Securities & Exchange Commission, *Standards Relating to Listed Company Audit Committees*, 17 CFR Parts 228, 229, 240, 249 and 274, Release 33-8220; 34-47654 (Apr. 25, 2003).

487. *See* NYSE Guide, CCH Fed. Sec. L. Rep. ¶ 2501 (1988).

488. *See* American Law Institute, Principles of Corporate Governance, Part III-A, Recommendations of Corporate Practice (1994).

489. *See* Complaint, Alan G. Havesi, New York State Comptroller on behalf of New York State Retirement Funds, http://www.worldcomlitigation.com/courtdox/WorldCom8.03cplt.pdf, at 11.

a fast-evolving industry" which was expanding quickly, the "Audit Committee only met for three to five hours a year"; and that the Committee did not understand what was going on either at the company's outside auditor, now-defunct Arthur Andersen, or in WorldCom's own internal audit department.[490] The outside directors settled by agreeing to pay $24.75 million out of their own pockets in addition to $36 million contributed by insurers. Nineteen ex-Enron directors also agreed to add $13 million of their own money to $155 million in insurance money.[491]

Congress reacted to these scandals by adopting the Sarbanes-Oxley Act of 2002, which among other things strengthened the role of the audit committee.[492] But Sarbanes-Oxley and other post-Enron moves clearly did not solve corporate governance problems. As noted at the beginning of this section, another meltdown in 2008–2009 took with it much of Wall Street and the financial community, including firms such as Lehman, whose good governance standards were quoted above.

The reasons for the ineffectiveness of corporate boards are not difficult to understand. Indeed, they were detailed almost forty years ago by Miles Mace of Harvard Business School,[493] who showed that outside directors lack *time*, *information*, and *inclination* to participate effectively in management.

With respect to *time*, the corporation naturally wants the best people, who are already busy, including serving on other boards or working full time for other companies. Stringent independence and diversity increase the demand for particular people. The three-to-five hours a year the WorldCom audit committee could spare for the enormously complex affairs of WorldCom indicates this problem. The law can require board members to spend more time on their firms and impose liability for failure to monitor. Indeed, as already noted, Sarbanes-Oxley increased duties of audit committees in response to the failure of those committees in Enron and WorldCom. Also, the Delaware Supreme Court held in *Stone v. Ritter*[494] that a total monitoring failure might trigger director liability even in the face of a charter provision opting out of the duty of care. But as discussed below, fiduciary duties are significantly weakened by the business judgment rule. In any event, directors themselves have the last word because

---

490. *See id.* at 151–72 (laying out the audit committee's failings).

491. *See* http://www.worldcomlitigation.com/.

492. *See* Sarbanes-Oxley Act of 2002, § 301, adding Securities Exchange Act of 1934, 15 U.S.C. § 10A(m) (requiring securities exchanges and associations to amend listing standards to require issuers' audit committees to be responsible for hiring and supervising the firm's auditor and restricting members from receiving fees from or being affiliated persons of the issuer).

493. *See* MILES MACE, DIRECTORS: MYTH AND REALITY (1971).

494. 911 A.2d 362 (2006).

they can simply decide not to serve, which may deprive corporations of the most experienced and qualified people.

Information is a problem not just because there is a lot the board has to know, but because what gets to the board is controlled by the managers the board is supposed to be monitoring. The directors can demand more, but they need to know what to ask for as well as have the time to read and understand it.

Most importantly, directors lack the *inclination* to second-guess managers. This is true even after the advent of independent nominating committees. Even the most independent directors will rationally trust managers who have turned out to be right in the past. This is one reason CEOs such as Michael Eisner of Disney and Steve Jobs of Apple became so powerful. Moreover, numerous pressures and behavioral biases lead even the most honest, dedicated, and independent directors to reach judgments that do not square with a purely rational and dispassionate analysis of the facts. These problems were first summarized more than twenty years ago in a pathbreaking article.[495] Directors are likely to share cultural and social origins and work experience and therefore to naturally sympathize with managers. The sort of successful business people who become directors have been socialized to be collegial and cooperative and therefore unwilling to spearhead uncomfortable questions or a revolt against corporate managers or fellow board members. Even more fundamentally, board members are called upon to question as monitors the same decisions they helped make in their managerial role, including their selection of managers.[496]

Because directors are inherently tempted to go along with managers, the courts face serious problems in deciding precisely where to draw the line on independence. This is particularly true of the courts' attempts to discern bias in "special litigation committees" of directors that are called on to screen fiduciary litigation against managers (a procedure discussed in the next section). For example, in a case involving Oracle Corporation, the court denied a motion by the company's SLC to terminate an action against its directors and officers for insider trading where two SLC members were Stanford professors and the defendants included a Stanford professor, a Stanford alumnus who made or directed substantial contributions to Stanford Law School, and Oracle CEO Lawrence Ellison who was a big Stanford contributor.[497] The court said nonindependence could be shown by:

> [M]otives like love, friendship * * * Nor should our law ignore the social nature of humans. To be direct, corporate directors are generally the sort of

---

495. *See* James D. Cox & Harry L. Munsinger, *Bias in the Boardroom: Psychological Foundations and Legal Implications of Corporate Cohesion*, LAW & CONTEMP. PROBS. (Summer 1985) at 83. This article has been discussed in approximately 170 articles on Westlaw. For a more recent discussion, see Macey, *supra* note 46, at 59–64.

496. *Id.* at 53–54.

497. *In re* Oracle Corp. Derivative Litigation, 824 A.2d 917 (Del. Ch. 2003).

people deeply enmeshed in social institutions. Such institutions have norms, expectations that, explicitly and implicitly, influence and channel the behavior of those who participate in their operation. Some things are "just not done," or only at a cost, which might not be so severe as a loss of position, but may involve a loss of standing in the institution. In being appropriately sensitive to this factor, our law also cannot assume—absent some proof of the point—that corporate directors are, as a general matter, persons of unusual social bravery, who operate heedless to the inhibitions that social norms generate for ordinary folk. [footnotes omitted] * * *

The court noted the special ties of collegiality, friendship, and obligation between SLC members and their Stanford colleagues and the sense of obligation to large donors felt by professors loyal to their institution. It said the committee's independence should be judged in light of the fact that "by any measure this was a social atmosphere painted in too much vivid Stanford Cardinal red for the SLC members to have reasonably ignored it." Indeed, the court went all the way to the city limits in observing that "[t]he notion that anyone in Palo Alto can accuse Ellison of insider trading without harboring some fear of social awkwardness seems a stretch."[498]

Even if independent directors do serve some purpose, there is little basis for *requiring* firms to have independent directors as a panacea for corporate governance problems. Indeed, the empirical evidence as a whole shows no correlation between director independence and firm performance.[499] Moreover, any correlation would face the question of causation: does board independence cause corporate performance, or vice versa? There is theory and evidence that board independence arises "endogenously" from the manager's performance in the sense that, as managers perform more poorly, the board gets more independent.[500]

3. Fiduciary duties

In enforcing corporate managers' fiduciary duties to the shareholders or corporation, judges are among the monitors that corporations rely on to constrain agency costs. But judges have less expertise than independent directors and

---

498. The SLC nevertheless ultimately prevailed in getting dismissal on summary judgment. See In re Oracle Corp., 867 A.2d 904 (Del. Ch. 2004), aff'd, 872 A.2d 960 (Del. 2005).

499. See Sanjay Bhagat & Bernard Black, *The Non-Correlation Between Board Independence and Long-Term Firm Performance*, 27 J. CORP. L. 231 (2002); Sanjay Bhagat & Bernard Black, *Uncertain Relationship between Board Composition and Firm Performance*, 54 BUS. LAW. 921 (1999); Roberta Romano, *The Sarbanes-Oxley Act and the Making of Quack Corporate Governance*, 114 YALE L.J. 1530 (2005).

500. See Benjamin E. Hermalin & Michael S. Weisbach, *Endogenously Chosen Boards of Directors and their Monitoring of the CEO*, 88 AM. ECON. REV. 96 (1998).

weaker incentives than the shareholders. Excessive liability can make managers too gun-shy and deter them from taking the sort of risks that the diversified shareholders would prefer them to take.

Fiduciary law deals with the problem of judges making business decisions through the *business judgment rule,* which protects managers from liability for decisions. For example, in the famous *Disney* case, Michael Eisner decided to hire his close friend Michael Ovitz as president of Disney under an extremely lucrative contract that entitled to Ovitz to $140 million in pay despite being fired after only fourteen totally ineffectual months. The compensation committee had approved this contract, along with more than one hundred other compensation deals and option grants, in a meeting lasting only an hour. The trial court said the case "clarified how ornamental, passive directors contribute to sycophantic tendencies among directors and how imperial CEOs can exploit this condition for their own benefit, especially in the executive compensation and severance areas."[501] Yet after ten years of litigation in the Delaware courts, the Delaware Supreme Court upheld dismissal.[502] The courts have been similarly tolerant of boards' failure to monitor risk. One case dismissed claims against the Citigroup board despite allegations that it ignored mounting evidence of a meltdown in credit markets that ultimately wiped out the company's value.[503]

Although directors are rarely liable for breach of fiduciary duty, litigation against them consumes significant corporate resources. The problem lies in the procedures for managing the litigation given that corporate managers are themselves the defendants and the shareholders face the same coordination and incentive problems in litigation as in voting. Corporate law's solution is to let a volunteer shareholder sue for the company in a so-called *derivative* suit. Obviously a lone shareholder has little incentive to expend the money and effort to prosecute the suit if he has to share recovery with the other shareholders. The real incentives are those of the derivative plaintiff's lawyer, who typically gets a fee from any recovery. The problem is that the lawyer is focused on this fee rather than on a good result for the company. The lawyer can get her fee by getting the defendants to agree to a settlement paid by the company's directors' and officers' liability insurer. This could uncharitably be characterized as the defendants paying the lawyer a ransom with the insurer's money, which comes back to the shareholders in the form of higher rates. Meanwhile, the corporation may suffer the disruption of lost executive time and energy defending the case. The plaintiff's lawyer sees these costs mainly as a lever to induce the corporation to pay the "ransom."[504]

---

501. *In re* The Walt Disney Company Derivative Litigation, 907 A. 2d 693, 741, n.373 (Del. Ch. 2005).
502. Brehm v. Eisner, 906 A. 2d 27 (Del. 2006).
503. *In re* Amer. Intern. Group, Inc., 2009 WL 366613 (Del. Ch., February 10, 2009).
504. *See generally,* John C. Coffee, Jr., *Understanding the Plaintiff's Attorney: The Implications of Economic Theory for Private Enforcement of Law Through Class and Derivative Actions,* 86 COLUM. L. REV. 669 (1986).

Given the potential problems with derivative suits, Delaware and other states have established procedures by which the board can screen the suit. The main procedure is for the board to set up a special litigation committee of independent directors. The committee studies the suit and (almost invariably) moves to dismiss it on the ground that it would harm the corporation. This procedure can be long and call for a close judicial judgment on, among other things, the committee's independence (as discussed above). Moreover, the outcome of the process is usually a settlement, which results in another court hearing about, among other things, the fees for the plaintiff's lawyer. Indemnification and insurance generally cover the defendants' payments and attorneys' fees.

This process is so protracted and costly compared to what it yields for the shareholders that a cynic would conclude that it was set up more for the lawyers than for the firm. Indeed, in most states (particularly including Delaware) lawyers have the most direct interest in corporate law and therefore are the dominant interest group to which state judges and legislators cater.[505] Although Delaware does not want to make corporate litigation so costly that firms will not incorporate there and pay the franchise fees that the tiny state relies on,[506] Delaware's dominance of the corporate market is sufficiently entrenched that it can leave a lot for the lawyers before corporations move elsewhere.

One might think that at least some shareholders would want their corporations to opt out of this costly system. Indeed, many corporate statutes -including Delaware's- permit waiver of the duty of care.[507] However, fiduciary duties are firmly entrenched in corporate norms. Thus it is not surprising that neither Delaware nor any other state permits a general opt-out of all fiduciary duties. Delaware has held that the non-waivable duty of loyalty encompasses a good faith duty, which might be breached by a board's complete failure to adopt a compliance program.[508] Although this theory is unlikely to result in liability,[509] it can still give rise to costly litigation.

4. Takeovers

Despite the problems with shareholder voting discussed above, shareholder voting rights do play an important role as the foundation of a market for corporate control. A bidder for control can aggregate voting rights into an effective block that overcomes the free-rider problem.[510] Thus, voting rights that are weak or inconsequential when held by dispersed shareholders can become valuable

---

505. *See* Jonathan R. Macey & Geoffrey Miller, *Toward an Interest-Group Theory of Delaware Corporate Law*, 65 TEX. L. REV. 469 (1987).

506. *See* Roberta Romano, *Law as Product: Some Pieces of the Incorporation Puzzle*, 1 J.L. ECON. & ORG. 225 (1985).

507. *See* DEL. GEN. CORP. L., § 102(b)(7).

508. Stone v. Ritter, 911 A.2d 362, 365 (Del. 2006).

509. *See supra* note 503 and accompanying text.

510. *See* Manne, *supra* note 480.

when the gap between the firm's actual and potential value becomes big enough to justify the costs of a bid for control.

A problem with this mechanism for addressing corporate agency costs is that corporate agents necessarily have some say in how the market for control operates. The board and managers can protect their incumbency by enacting powerful anti-takeover devices that make a takeover prohibitively costly. The Delaware Supreme Court, in its notable *Moran* decision,[511] held that even without shareholder approval, the board had the power to issue a new class of shares containing a *poison pill*, which powerfully deters takeovers by diluting the bidder's investment in the target.

Although *Moran* might seem to have greatly increased directors' power, the opinion was fully consistent with fundamental corporate architecture and norms of corporate governance that give significant power to powerful managers with little effective scrutiny by shareholders, directors, or courts.[512] It is hardly surprising that hostile takeovers triggered both powerful defenses and judicial approval. Moreover, one bad case could not resist the dynamic processes of corporate governance. Legislatures could have amended their statutes to forbid poison pills. In fact, there is evidence that the competition runs the other way—firms' home states compete with Delaware by offering more takeover protection.[513] Shareholders might have demanded pro-takeover charters in buying shares or by reversing anti-takeover moves in the firms they own. But there is evidence that anti-takeover protections are common in the charters of firms going public.[514] And shareholders might not have the legal power to take the initiative to vote down or prohibit poison pills or other anti-takeover defenses.[515] Clearly managers' insulation from takeovers cannot be attributable simply to one judicial mistake.

In any event, despite takeover defenses, the market for control lives as long as the shareholders can vote and sell their shares. Bad management can cause shareholders to sell—and this can drive down share price.[516] When the gap

---

511. Moran v. Household International, 500 A. 2d 1346 (Del. 1985).

512. For a review of cases under the Delaware test for managers' fiduciary duties in defending against takeovers, see Stephen M. Bainbridge, *Unocal at 20: Director Primacy in Corporate Takeovers*, 31 DEL. J. CORP. L. 769 (2006).

513. *See* Lucian Bebchuk & Alma Cohen, *Firms' Decisions Where to Incorporate*, 46 J. L. & ECON. 383 (2003).

514. *See* Robert Daines & Michael Klausner, *Do IPO Charters Maximize Firm Value? Antitakeover Protection in IPOs*, 17 J. LAW, ECON. & ORG. 83 (2001).

515. *See* Lawrence A. Hamermesh, *Corporate Democracy and Shareholder-Adopted By-Laws: Taking Back the Street?*, 73 TUL. L. REV. 409 (1998). For a contrary view, see Jonathan R. Macey, *The Legality and Utility of the Shareholder Rights Bylaw*, 26 HOFSTRA L. REV. 835 (1998).

516. One mechanism for accomplishing this is significant contemporaneous sales by relatively informed and sophisticated holders of blocks of shares. *See* Alex Edmans &

between a firm's actual and potential value is big enough, courts might intervene, or managers might be induced to cooperate, perhaps by a rich severance package or a position in the post-takeover firm.

Although takeover defenses have not prevented takeovers, they have shaped the market for control. For a generation, the takeover market has been dominated by uncorporations: private equity firms and hedge funds. This means that takeovers have become largely a way to change corporations into uncorporations. As discussed below, uncorporations' organizational innovations enabled them to squeeze enough profits out of target firms to make even powerful takeover defenses worth penetrating. Indeed, these restrictions on takeovers might even be said to have played a role in the development of private equity. Thus, there is a sort of symbiotic relationship between corporations and uncorporations: Uncorporations discipline corporate managers and help maintain the viability of the corporate form despite the problems detailed above, while corporate takeover defenses have spurred the evolution of the uncorporation.

B. INCENTIVES AND DISCIPLINE IN THE LARGE UNCORPORATION

Since this chapter began with a quote about the failure of corporate governance in the 2008–2009 financial meltdown, it is appropriate to start this discussion of uncorporate governance with another quote about the meltdown, this time from Michael Lewis, drawn from the same episode:

> No investment bank owned by its employees would have levered itself 35 to 1 or bought and held $50 billion in mezzanine C.D.O.'s. I doubt any partnership would have sought to game the rating agencies or leap into bed with loan sharks or even allow mezzanine C.D.O.'s to be sold to its customers. The hoped-for short-term gain would not have justified the long-term hit.[517]

In other words, large financial firms melted down because they were no longer partnerships. The whole costly corporate monitoring structure discussed above did little to prevent the meltdown of these firms.

This part of the chapter discusses how uncorporations can fill the gaps in corporate governance. As stressed throughout the book, the uncorporation is about the gap-filling and norm-providing role of standard-form business associations rather than specific devices and contracts. Uncorporate standard forms (particularly limited partnerships and LLCs) have two general advantages that

---

Gustavo Manso, *Governance Through Exit and Voice: A Theory of Multiple Blockholders,* (Jan. 19, 2009), U of Penn, Inst for Law & Econ Research Paper No. 08-09, http://ssrn.com/abstract=1102730.

517. Michael Lewis, *The End,* Portfolio (Dec. 2008), http://www.portfolio.com/news-markets/national-news/portfolio/2008/11/11/The-End-of-Wall-Streets- Boom?.

have enabled them to compete successfully with corporations in the current business environment. First, they tend to rely on objective measures, including market judgments of the firm's outputs. They eschew forms of governance such as boards of directors that attempt to monitor and second-guess managers' judgments. Second, because of the flexibility they inherited from their partnership origins, uncorporations have been able to evolve structures to meet business, tax, and regulatory challenges, including the increasing costs of acquiring corporate assets.

The discussion begins by surveying uncorporate governance mechanisms and what might be called *ungovernance*—how uncorporations eschew the corporate-type monitoring devices discussed above in this chapter. We then look more closely at how these general approaches are applied in specific types of uncorporations.

1. Managerial compensation

Although corporate managers and directors typically own only a small fraction of the firm's shares, managers of general and limited partnerships and LLCs are partners who participate fully in the firm's profits and losses. This may not seem much different from corporate executives' stock and stock option compensation, but equity-compensated corporate managers are quite different from full-fledged partners. Consistent with the general uncorporate strategy of tying discipline to markets, partners have both upside opportunity *and* downside risk.

Although general partners' traditional vicarious liability is negated or remote in most modern uncorporations, these firms carry on the partnership approach of forcing managers to bear losses as well as gains. For example, the general partner of a hedge fund limited partnership usually makes nothing unless the firm's earnings cross a specified hurdle, and the firm has to make up any losses before fees to the partners resume. Many hedge funds liquidated in the financial collapse of 2008 as their losses mounted to the point that general partners saw only a dim prospect of fees. By contrast, corporate executive' compensation insulates them from declines in their firms' fortunes even as they get full credit for good years.[518] Investors have to make up for the bad times, but the executives may not.

We might ask whether there is anything specifically *corporate* or *uncorporate* about these modes of compensation. Hurdles and other uncorporate compensation techniques are contractual provisions that are not legally bound to the form of business association. However, compensation is affected by features that inhere in the standard form. First, uncorporations make partners' compensation part of the governance agreement, while corporate managers' compensation is subject to board discretion. Even if a corporate board chooses at a particular

---

518. *See* Bebchuk & Fried, *supra* note 347, at 7.

point in time to follow a partnership model, whether it sticks to this approach depends on whether the board is truly independent of the executives whose pay they supposedly control. As we have seen, they are not.

Second, it is not even clear that corporations *should* give managers partner-like high-powered financial incentives. Compensation must be coherent with other elements of the business association. Forcing corporate managers to bear downside risks as well as upside rewards would introduce a conflict of interest between them and the firm's owners, who can mitigate their exposure to corporate risks by holding diversified portfolios. Although managers theoretically could be full-fledged owners, they cannot be full-fledged *diversified* owners without diluting their incentive to maximize their employer's wealth. Owner-like managers might have an incentive to avoid risks that owners want them to take, as by having the firm hold excessive amounts of cash against rainy days. Of course the same is true of managers of uncorporations whose owners hold diversified portfolios. But the next section shows how the uncorporate form guards against excessive cash retention by forcing managers to make distributions or providing for liquidation or buyout of the firm after a preset amount of time.

2. Distributions

As discussed in Chapter 4, scholars have asserted that a critical element of the corporation's success as a vehicle for large firms is its ability to lock capital in the firm under the managers' control. The cash remains in the corporation to further its interests, rather than being available to individual owners to serve theirs. This works as long as the firm has structures in place to ensure that the cash does, indeed, serve the firm. However, delegation of control entails agency costs, and we have seen that there are gaps in corporate mechanisms for dealing with these costs. Instead of passing corporate cash onto the owners, corporate managers might prefer to grow the firm because their pay depends on the amount of assets under their control or because a bigger firm is harder to take over.

One way to deal with this problem is to limit managerial discretion to retain earnings. This would force managers who want to fund new projects to raise the cash from the capital markets rather than using the corporate piggy bank. Markets will price these investments based on how they think managers will use the money. This in effect bolsters the role of the efficient stock markets as monitors of management.[519] The stock market can be a much more discerning critic of management than shareholders, directors, or courts. In addition, the markets do not need special incentives to price a company's stock. Market participants have their own reasons for trading that keeps stock prices in line with corporate values. Corporate managers cannot influence market forces in the same way

---

519. *See* Frank Easterbrook, *Two Agency-Cost Explanations of Dividends*, 74 Am. Econ. Rev. 650 (1984); Henry J. Manne, *Review of Livingston, The American Stockholder*, 5 St. Louis U. L.J. 309, 316 (1958).

they can influence directors. And unlike the market for control (which needs control purchasers ready to take the heavy risks of a takeover), forcing distributions brings the stock market automatically into play whenever the managers need to fund their plans.

Partnerships and other uncorporations typically mandate or encourage distributions. Partnership law explicitly contemplates agreements requiring managers to periodically distribute the cash.[520] For example, publicly traded partnership agreements commonly require partners to distribute net cash less reserves, restrict specific actions such as issuance of additional equity that might reduce distributions, and give the general partners significant financial incentives to make distributions, as by increasing their distributions depending on how much the firm distributes to the limited partners.[521] The Internal Revenue Code encourages uncorporations to contract for distributions as tax partnerships must pay tax on all earnings whether or not they are distributed to the owners.[522] Courts also may be wary of managers using the tax on retained earnings to squeeze out partners.[523]

Corporate shareholders also might contract for rights to distributions. However, distribution agreements, like compensation, may collide with the plenary power vested in the board of directors. Although (as also discussed in Chapter 5) corporate statutes now let corporations completely eliminate board functions, these provisions only apply to closely held corporations.[524] Even if corporate law does not proscribe distribution agreements, courts may narrowly interpret and apply these agreements in light of corporate norms favoring managerial control of distributions.[525] For example, recall that in *Clark v. Dodge* (discussed in Chapter 5), an agreement requiring the payment to a shareholder of a quarter of the firm's net income was valid only if "net income" was interpreted

---

520. *See, e.g.*, RULPA § 601, which provides that a partner is entitled to receive distributions before dissolution or withdrawal "to the extent and at the times or upon the happening of the events specified in the partnership agreement."

521. *See* John Goodgame, *Master Limited Partnership Governance*, 60 BUS. LAW. 471 (2005).

522. *See* IRC § 701 (providing that partnerships are not subject to corporate income tax).

523. *See* Labovitz v. Dolan, 189 Ill. App. 3d 403, 136 Ill. Dec. 780, 545 N.E.2d 304 (1989) (finding breach of fiduciary duty where withholding distributions enabled a squeezeout of partners); Alloy v Wills Family Trust, 944 A2d 1234 (2008) (same, relying on *Labovitz*).

524. *See, e.g.*, DEL. G.C.L. §§ 341–356. The Delaware statute expressly provides that its close corporation subchapter does not invalidate provisions authorized under other sections (*see id.* § 356). However, interpreting this provision to give full power to alter the board's power would seem to undermine the statute's explicit distinction between closely held and publicly held firms.

525. *See* Steven A. Bank, *Tax, Corporate Governance, and Norms*, 61 WASH. & LEE L. REV. 1159, 1218–19, 1223–28 (2004).

to mean what was left after the directors had "set aside whatever they deemed wise." Also, in interpreting dividend provisions in preferred share contracts, courts have let directors refuse to distribute dividends to noncumulative preferred shareholders even where this effectively prevented the shareholders from ever getting any cash.[526]

Baron v. Allied Artists Pictures Corp.[527] colorfully illustrates this approach. The court gave a board installed by preferred shareholders discretion as to when to resume dividends and thereby return control to the common shareholders. The board had returned the firm to profitability by emphasizing classy pictures such as *Cabaret* and *Papillon* over the more plebian fare produced under common shareholder control (such as *Attack of the 50 Foot Woman*). The chancery court held that the board's discretion was subject only to the very loose scrutiny of the business judgment rule.[528]

Corporations might achieve some of the effects of partnership-type distributions by using alternative types of contracts. But each of these alternatives has drawbacks. Corporations might borrow a lot of money and deduct the interest payments, giving them some of the tax advantages of partnership. However, debt increases the risk of a potentially costly liquidation or reorganization in bankruptcy. Corporations also might contract for preferred or common shares with *cumulative* dividend rights, which prod managers to distribute cash to the preferred because the common shareholders (who vote on the directors) get nothing until the firm pays all of the missed preferred dividends. However, a class of preferred shares with limited dividend rights does not substitute for a partnership-type obligation to distribute earnings to all of the owners as the managers could pay out the preferred percentage while not paying off the common shareholders—or even deny dividends to both classes of holders.

A corporation theoretically could go all the way to partnership-type distribution rights by mandating distributions on its shares. The corporation would, in effect, have a single class of preferred shares. But a corporation without common stock may become incoherent in the sense that its corporate features are at war with its uncorporate features. Here, again, is the *All of Me* problem discussed with regard to close corporations in Chapter 5. For example, a duty to

---

526. *See* Guttman v. Illinois Central Railroad Co., 189 F.2d 927 (2d Cir.), *cert. denied*, 342 U.S. 867 (1951); Kern v. Chicago & Eastern Illinois Railroad Co., 6 Ill. App. 3d 247, 285 N.E.2d 501 (1972); L.L. Constantin & Co. v. R.P. Holding Corp., 56 N.J. Super. 411, 153 A.2d 378 (1959).

527. 337 A.2d 653 (Del. Ch. 1975), *app. dismissed*, 365 A.2d 136 (Del. 1976).

528. Perhaps a court deciding the case today would have given less deference to the incumbent board because of its control by a single preferred shareholder (who owned only 7 percent of the total equity) and the decision's effect of entrenching management. (The author is indebted to Stephen Bainbridge for this observation.) On the other hand, we might view it as notable that *Baron* let the board hang onto control despite these considerations.

make distributions increases the impact of the corporate tax on earnings at the corporate level plus distributions to the owners. More generally, reducing managers' control over the cash would make costly corporate-type monitoring redundant. In other words, as with compensation, changing a critical element of the corporation triggers the need for other changes. A corporation with uncorporate features may need to become an uncorporation in substance. If it is in substance an uncorporation, it would be better off adopting an uncorporate standard form to mesh its features with the norms, signaling and gap-filling aspects of the standard form in which these features belong. Again, standard forms matter.

3. Buyout and liquidation

Firms can reduce capital lock-in and give the owners access to earnings not only through periodic distributions but by letting owners cash in their interests, enabling an individual or a minority of owners to compel dissolution and liquidation of the firm, or setting a time for termination and liquidation of the firm. As with forcing distributions, any of these alternatives would force managers periodically to face the judgment of the capital markets as to their past stewardship and future plans by having to raise cash from new investors.

The most drastic of these provisions—unilateral dissolution and buyout—are consistent with the partnership standard form. As discussed in Chapters 3 and 4, partners also can provide for any amount of continuity of the firm they want in their partnership agreement. Limited partnership and LLC statutes now do not generally provide for dissolution or buyout at will. This recognizes the need to enable managers to formulate strategy without being subject to individual owners' demands for cash based on their personal needs or preferences. The trade-off is that these firms usually have a definite time limit by which managers must show their strategy has paid off or liquidate. This has roots in the traditional limited partnership rule requiring the partnership certificate to specify the date by which the partnership is to dissolve.[529]

Corporations can contract for all these terms, just as they can for the other uncorporate terms discussed above. However, as with these other contracts, buyout and liquidation provisions do not mesh with other corporate terms and are inconsistent with corporate norms. The owners' access to the cash would both undermine the board's power and reduce the need for costly monitoring. Even if the corporation adjusted its other terms to mesh with buyout and dissolution rights, it would still be subject to corporate norms, which could affect the interpretation and application of these provisions. Provisions compelling buyout, dissolution, and termination would conflict with the managers' plenary power to decide when to initiate dissolution and make distributions.[530] Courts also may

---

529. *See* ULPA § 2(1)(a)(V); RULPA (1985), § 201(4). There is no such provision in the most recent uniform act, ULPA (2001).

530. *See, e.g.,* DEL. G.C.L. § 275(a) (board initiates vote on dissolution).

hesitate to interpret the provisions to eliminate board discretion to run the firm, as they have with such matters as takeover defenses and distributions. For example, the board likely could prevent distributions or breakup that might endanger the firm's long-term plans. The firm might try to explicitly remove any board discretion. However, even if firms were willing to go that far, these provisions are subject to the same argument as those requiring distributions—that they are permitted only in close corporations.

Specialized types of corporations may arise with partnership-type provisions for liquidation and buyout. For example, special purpose acquisition corporations (SPACS) explicitly commit to either finding a target or liquidating within a set period.[531] This type of firm, while technically taking the statutory form of a corporation, differs so much from the standard corporation as to actually be a distinct standard form. Nevertheless, by technically adopting the corporate form, these firms remain vulnerable to the application of corporate norms. Thus, even a SPAC was subjected to corporate-type shareholder activism by a hedge fund that did not want to wait until the preset time for liquidation.[532]

4. Supplementary monitoring mechanisms

The discussion so far has focused on the monitoring mechanisms built into corporate law. But corporate law operates in the context of other devices that supplement the "official" corporate governance structure. For example, products markets (enhanced by market intermediaries such as ratings services) ensure that profits will decline when managers shirk on quality or overcharge for products. Shareholder advisors and credit rating services monitor firms' financial health.

While markets and advisors make it cheaper and easier for official corporate monitors do their jobs, this may not be enough if these monitors are inadequate. For example, a likely cause of the market meltdown in 2008–2009 was the poor performance of bond-rating firms.[533] Shareholder advisory services give their institutional investor customers general recommendations that enable these shareholders to vote on certain types of governance improvements across their large portfolios.[534] However, voting consistent with this standardized advice may not make much difference to specific portfolio firms' performance. If shareholders demanded more specific and costly advice, the market would supply it. But as explained above, individual shareholders do not want to shoulder this burden because they have to share the benefit with other shareholders.

---

531. *See* Steven M. Davidoff, *Black Market Capital*, 2008 COLUM. BUS. L.J. 173.

532. *See* Harvard Law School Corporate Governance Blog, http://blogs.law.harvard.edu/corpgov/2009/02/01/hedge-fund-activism-extends-to-spacs/ (Feb. 1, 2009) ("Hedge Fund Activism Extends to SPACs").

533. *See infra* text accompanying note 627.

534. *See* Paul Rose, *The Corporate Governance Industry*, 32 J. CORP. L. 187 (2006).

214 THE RISE OF THE UNCORPORATION

In general (as explained throughout this section), the problem with the corporate monitoring system is that the various elements of corporate governance insulate managers from direct exposure to market forces. Markets cannot fill gaps in a system designed to ignore them.

C. UNCORPORATE UNGOVERNANCE

Courts, commentators, and policy makers long have lamented the flaws of corporate governance discussed above. Yet these flaws generally have been put in the same category as death and taxes—unfortunate but inevitable problems that have to be accepted along with the benefits of large corporations. This section shows that there is another way: uncorporations can participate in or even take over the governance of large firms without exposing them to governance costs such as those discussed above. The following are some uncorporate features that can give many types of firms a reasonable alternative to the corporation.

1. Undirectors

Given the manifest problems with the corporate-type board of directors discussed above, it is easy to see how other management models might work better. As with everything else in governance, it is a matter of trade-offs. Again, the relevant trade-off in uncorporations can be described as one between an objective, self-executing mechanism that relies on general market forces and one that relies on monitors' close observation of managers. Although these relationships can yield better information, they also involve a higher probability that the monitors (including the board of directors) will not be truly independent of the managers.

Partnership and LLC agreements may provide for boards of directors. However, these boards are not outside monitors, but rather insiders who advise and consult with the full-time managers. Consider, for example, the role of the board of directors in the publicly traded limited partnership arm of Blackstone Group, L.P. The registration statement for the public offering states:

> As a public company, we intend to continue to employ our current management structure with strong central management by our founders and to maintain our focus on achieving successful growth over the long term. This desire to preserve our current management structure is one of the principal reasons why we have decided to organize The Blackstone Group L.P. as a limited partnership that is managed by our general partner and to avail ourselves of the limited partnership exception from certain of the New York Stock Exchange governance rules, which eliminates the requirements that we

have a majority of independent directors on our board of directors and that we have a compensation committee and a nominating and corporate governance committee composed entirely of independent directors. * * *[535]

The Blackstone Group partnership agreement provides:

The General Partner shall conduct, direct and manage all activities of the Partnership. Except as otherwise expressly provided in this Agreement, all management powers over the business and affairs of the Partnership shall be exclusively vested in the General Partner[.][536]

Compare this language to the Delaware General Corporation Law, which provides for management of a corporation "by or under the direction of a board of directors."[537] The only "board of directors" the agreement provides for is that of the general partner—not the limited partnership whose interests are being sold to the public.[538]

Even publicly held uncorporations have been freed from some of the rules discussed above imposing monitoring boards on publicly held corporations. For example, as the above excerpt indicates, the New York Stock Exchange exempts limited partnerships from many of its independent director rules because of limited partnerships' "unique attributes."[539]

2. Undemocracy

One might surmise from the uncorporation's classic form, the general partnership, that owner voting rights would be more intense in uncorporations than in corporations. As discussed in Chapter 3, general partnership statutes (which are primarily designed for very closely held firms) give partners a right to vote on all of the firm's decisions, and require unanimity on the important ones.[540] However, the *large* uncorporation is based primarily on the limited partnership. These firms typically have all-powerful general partners and relegate their limited partners to the status of glorified creditors. Although limited partners may have a

---

535. The Blackstone Group LP, Amendment No 9 to Form S-1, 11 (June 21, 2007), online at http://files.shareholder.com/downloads/BX/245990728x0xS1047469-07-5100/1393818/filing.pdf.
536. Amended and Restated Agreement of Limited partnership of The Blackstone Group L.P. ("Blackstone agreement"), § 7.1(a), http://ipo.nasdaq.com/edgar_conv_html%5C2007%5C03%5C22%5C0001047469-07-002068.html.
537. Del. G. C. L. § 141(a).
538. *See* Blackstone agreement, *supra* note 536, § 1.1.
539. New York Stock Exchange Listed Company Manual. *Id.* ¶303A.00.
540. *See* UPA § 18(e), (h); RUPA § 401(f), (j).

default right to vote on fundamental transactions,[541] they generally do not participate in regular meetings to elect directors.[542]

Limited partners' voting rights might not seem strikingly different from those of corporate shareholders, which as we have seen are also very weak. However, there are two critical differences. First, limited partners' statutory voting rights are clearly subject to any agreement to the contrary, though courts may interpret the agreement to favor these rights.[543] By contrast, corporate norms preserve what prominent commentators have called a "sacred space" for shareholder voting.[544]

Second, although the market for control helps make the corporate shareholders' voting rights effective, this market is generally unavailable in uncorporations because of the usual nontransferability of management rights discussed in the next section.

Third, owners have little ability to exercise even the weak voting rights they do have. Uncorporations typically do not provide for regular meetings of owners as with corporations. The limited partners may have to somehow coordinate to meet the agreement's provisions (if any) for calling a special meeting,[545] and then to assemble the typically high percentage of votes necessary to remove the general partner.[546] Moreover, removal of the general partner is a drastic action as the

---

541. See ULPA (2001) § 406. The 1985 version of RULPA provides for default limited partner voting rights to admit new general or limited partners (§§ 301(b)(1) and 401, requiring consent of the partners, which is defined in § 101(8) to include both limited and general partners); continue the partnership following dissolution by general partner withdrawal (§ 801); and consent to general partner self-dealing (through linkage with UPA § 21 and RUPA § 404(b)).

542. Note, however, that uncorporations are subject to many of the member voting rules in the New York Stock Exchange Listed Company Manual, the main exception being the rules for owner approval of securities issuances (¶312.03).

543. For an example of this interpretation approach, see *In re* Nantucket Island Associates Ltd. Partnership Unitholders Litigation, 810 A.2d 351 (Del. Ch. 2002).

544. *See* Robert B. Thompson & D. Gordon Smith, *Toward a New Theory of the Shareholder Role: "Sacred Space" in Corporate Takeovers*, 80 Tex. L. Rev. 261 (2001).

545. For example, the Blackstone agreement provides that "Special meetings of the Limited Partners may be called by the General Partner or by Limited Partners owning 50% or more of the voting power of the Outstanding Limited Partner Interests of the class or classes for which a meeting is proposed." See Blackstone agreement, *supra* note 536, § 13.4.

546. For example, the Blackstone agreement permits general partner removal only on a vote by "at least 66²/3 % of the voting power of the Outstanding Voting Units (including Voting Units held by the General Partner and its Affiliates). Any such action by such Unitholders for removal of the General Partner must also provide for the election of a successor General Partner by the Unitholders holding a majority of the voting power of Outstanding Voting Units (including Voting Units held by the General Partner and its Affiliates)." *Id.* § 11.2.

limited partners likely invested based on the general partner's special expertise. Unless they designate a new general partner, disgruntled owners likely would have no way to propose transactions on their own. They could only reject the limited types of transactions proposed by the general partner that are subject to limited partner approval.[547]

To be sure, corporations also can sharply reduce or eliminate the power of nonmanagement shareholders. Many corporations, including prominent media firms such as the New York Times, the Washington Post, and Google have multiple classes of stock that effectively give most control to the founders or founding family. This may not seem much different in effect from a limited partnership as the power to vote is not worth much if a powerful and cohesive group controls the outcome. But again, as with other devices discussed above, whenever corporate terms imitate those of uncorporations they face the problem of incoherence or failure to mesh with other aspects of the corporate standard form. Elimination of corporate monitoring can leave the managers free to harm the owners *if* the firm does not substitute uncorporate incentive and disciplinary devices such as giving owners exit rights or access to the cash.[548] Also, this assumes that the corporate voting bloc remains cohesive. Control can shift as long as the owners retain the technical voting power. Dow, Jones used to be a family-controlled media firm until Rupert Murdoch came along and made the dispersed family members an offer they could not refuse.

3. Takeover proofing

We have seen that the market for control plays a central role in corporate governance. Dispersed shareholders' voting rights are made valuable by the combination of efficient securities markets and transferable management rights.

---

547. For example, the Blackstone agreement requires a limited partner vote only on sale, exchange or other disposition of all or substantially all of the partnership's assets. See id. § 7.3.

548. For evidence that firm value negatively correlates with separation of insider control from cash-flow rights in corporations, see Stijn Claessens et al., *Disentangling the Incentive and Entrenchment Effects of Large Shareholdings*, 58 J. FIN. 81 (2002); Harry DeAngelo & Linda DeAngelo, *Managerial Ownership of Voting Rights: A Study of Public Corporations with Dual Classes of Common Stock*, 14 J. FIN. ECON. 33 (1985); Alexander Dyck & Luigi Zingales, *Private Benefits of Control: An International Comparison*, 59 J. FIN. 537 (2004); Paul A. Gompers et al., *Extreme Governance: An Analysis of Dual Class Firms in the United States* (2006). There is also evidence that insiders who control voting rights extract private benefits. See Ronald C. Lease et al, *The Market Value of Control in Publicly-Traded Corporations*, 11 J. FIN. ECON. 439 (1983); Cong Wang et al., *Agency Problems at Dual-Class Companies*, http://ssrn.com/abstract=961158 (Feb. 12, 2007); Tatiana Nenova, *The Value of Corporate Voting Rights and Control: A Cross-Country Analysis*, 68 J. FIN. ECON. 325 (2003); Cong Wang et al., *Agency Problems at Dual-Class Companies* http://papers.ssrn.com/sol3/papers.cfm?abstract_id=1080361 (Jan. 1, 2008).

Shares trading in efficient securities markets indicate firms' value under current management. Free transferability of voting rights enables market participants to buy control when they see an opportunity to increase the firm's stock price by changing its management.

By contrast to corporations, uncorporations' default rules do not let owners freely transfer management rights.[549] Economic rights may be freely transferable, but the transferee would have no vote. This obviously eliminates any possibility of a market for control. This rule originated in general partnerships, where members need to screen who will exercise partners' significant management rights. As discussed in Chapter 7, the rule also has been applied to limited partnerships and LLCs although these firms have passive, limited liability members who would not seem to be very concerned about the wealth and expertise of their co-owners.

Restrictions on transfer of management rights in passively managed limited liability uncorporations might initially have been a way to ensure that the firms would be treated as partnerships for tax purposes. However, the rule has stuck even after check-the-box replaced tax classification. In publicly held limited partnerships, the limited partners' voting rights are transferable,[550] but as discussed above are so minimal that the partners cannot transfer much control. These firms rely on incentive and disciplinary devices rather than on monitoring by owners or purchasers of control. Managers disciplined by high-powered compensation who must distribute cash to the owners have less need for the additional discipline of the market for control. Corporate shareholders have to hope that a third party purchaser for control will identify situations in which managers are misusing the firm's cash. This discipline operates more automatically in uncorporations, as managers with a looser grip on the firm's cash need to continually seek the market's endorsement of how they are running the firm.

Although uncorporations do not rely on the market for control to constrain their own agency costs, they are a critical part of the *corporate* market for control.[551] As discussed above, the uncorporate role in large firm governance was arguably created or at least significantly boosted by the tightening of takeover defenses in corporations. As the costs of hostile takeovers rose, successful bidders could

---

549. *See, e.g.,* RUPA § 502 (1997) (defining a partner's transferable interest as the partner's share of profits and losses and right to receive distributions); § 503 (permitting transfer of transferable interest); Revised ULLCA § 502 (permitting transfer of economic rights).

550. For example, the Blackstone agreement, *supra* note 536, defines "limited partners interest" to include voting rights (§ 1.1), and provides that these interests are freely transferable (§ 4.5(c)).

551. *See* Karen Hopper Wruck, *Private Equity, Corporate Governance, and the Reinvention of the Market for Corporate Control,* http://papers.ssrn.com/sol3/papers.cfm?abstract_id=1273308.

sustain their activity only by showing greater potential profits from changing control. Private equity and hedge funds met this challenge, most strikingly in KKR's victory in the hard-fought battle to take over RJR Nabisco.[552] Private equity also can offer incumbent managers a graceful exit either through a lucrative buyout or job in the restructured firm.[553]

4. Fiduciary unduties

As we have seen, fiduciary duties are a corporate fixture despite their high litigation costs and relatively small benefits in controlling agency costs. By contrast (as discussed in Chapter 7), substantial authority supports enforcement of fiduciary duty opt-outs in uncorporations. This discussion left open whether courts would be as receptive to contracts in large firms. Some of these cases did arise in larger firms. For example, the *Gotham* case, the Delaware Supreme Court's first involving Delaware's broad fiduciary opt-out provision, applied the contract rather than default duties to a general partner's buyout of limited partnership interests in a publicly traded limited partnership. That case stopped short of allowing firms to eliminate fiduciary duties—a gap the legislature swiftly filled.

The court in *Wood v. Baum*[554] clarified that the Delaware courts would give significant contractual freedom regarding fiduciary duties to large, publicly held uncorporations. Plaintiff had alleged that the managers of a publicly traded LLC breached their duties by "fail[ing] properly to institute, administer and maintain adequate accounting and reporting controls, practices and procedures" which resulted in a "massive restatement process, an SEC investigation, and loss of substantial access to financial markets."[555] The Delaware Supreme Court held that the managers could be held liable under the operating agreement only for "fraudulent" or "illegal" conduct or a "bad faith" breach of the covenant of good faith and fair dealing. Thus, in contrast to the corporate case of *Stone v. Ritter*,[556] even a strong allegation of a breach of monitoring duties could not

---

552. *See generally*, Burrough & Helyer, *supra* note 482.
553. *See* Jana P. Fidrmuc et al., *Do Private Equity Investors Crowd Out Management Buyouts?* (Feb. 2008), http://papers.ssrn.com/sol3/papers.cfm?abstract_id=913362 (evidence based on UK buyouts showing that private equity offers an alternative to management buyouts and is more likely to be chosen when managers own a small fraction of the firm, and the firm is large and lacks the cash to finance a management deal).
554. 953 A.2d 136 (Del. 2008). For an analysis of this case, see Harvard Law School Corporate Governance Blog, http://blogs.law.harvard.edu/corpgov/2008/08/05/delaware-enforces-a-fiduciary-opt-out-in-a-publicly-held-firm (Aug. 5, 2008) ("Delaware enforces a fiduciary opt-out in a publicly held firm").
555. 953 A. 2d at 139.
556. *See supra* text accompanying note 494.

withstand dismissal in a case involving an LLC.[557] The court reasoned that the implied covenant:

> is a creature of contract, distinct from the fiduciary duties that the plaintiff asserts here. The implied covenant functions to protect stockholders' expectations that the company and its board will properly perform the contractual obligations they have under the operative organizational agreements. Here, the Complaint does not allege any contractual claims, let alone a "bad faith" breach of the implied contractual covenant of good faith and fair dealing.[558]

In short, the Delaware Supreme Court in *Wood* clearly articulated a contract-based theory of fiduciary duties in a publicly held LLC.

The Blackstone Group, L.P. limited partnership agreement discussed above takes full advantage of the contractual flexibility authorized by the Delaware statute. In contrast to corporate conflict-of-interest transactions (which necessarily are subject to review by the court, shareholders, or independent board members),[559] the Blackstone agreement provides that in the event of a potential conflict between the general partner and the partnership:

> [A]ny resolution or course of action by the General Partner or its Affiliates in respect of such conflict of interest shall be permitted and deemed approved by all Partners, and shall not constitute a breach of this Agreement, or any agreement contemplated herein or therein, or of any duty hereunder or existing at law, in equity or otherwise, if the resolution or course of action in respect of such conflict of interest is (i) approved by Special Approval, (ii) on terms no less favorable to the Partnership than those generally being provided to or available from unrelated third parties or (iii) fair and reasonable to the Partnership, taking into account the totality of the relationships between the parties involved (including other transactions that may be or have been particularly favorable or advantageous to the Partnership).[560]

In other words, the agreement purports to preclude any judicial review of a conflict transaction that has been through the contractually prescribed hoops. "Special approval" may be granted by the "conflicts committee," which the agreement defines as a committee of independent directors of the *general partner's* board of directors. The prospectus for the public offering clarifies that "[c]ommon unitholders will, as a practical matter, not be able to successfully challenge an

---

557. *Id.*
558. *Id.* at 143 (footnotes omitted).
559. Del. G. C. L. § 144.
560. Blackstone agreement, *supra* note 536, at § 7.9(a).

informed decision by the conflicts committee." Notably, even if the partner does *not* get this approval:

> [I]t shall be presumed that, in making its decision, the Board of Directors acted in good faith, and in any proceeding brought by or on behalf of any Limited Partner, the Partnership or any other Person bound by this Agreement challenging such approval, the Person bringing or prosecuting such proceeding shall have the burden of overcoming such presumption.

This is roughly the standard of judicial review of corporate decisions reviewed by an *independent* board elected by the members. Despite these provisions, the public snapped up units for as much as $7 more than the offering price (though the market meltdown later gave them reason to regret their investment).

We might ask why the same fiduciary standards should not apply to both corporate and uncorporate centrally managed, publicly held firms. As should be apparent from the discussion so far in this chapter, the answer is that a firm's standard form matters. Uncorporations can afford to do without fiduciary duties because they let firms substitute other, possibly more cost-effective mechanisms for ensuring that fiduciaries act in the owners' interests, including strong incentive compensation and owner exit and distribution rights.

Uncorporate flexibility extends to the remedy for fiduciary breach. As discussed above, the corporate derivative suit gives shareholders a costly mechanism for suing conflicted managers on the firm's behalf. In uncorporations the members only need remedies adequate to ensure the viability of contractual protective devices such as managerial incentives, distributions, and liquidation. Thus, one court let hedge fund limited partners sue directly rather than derivatively for general partner acts that reduced the value of their interests.[561] The court noted that the limited partners were protected by the managers' disclosure duty and their ability to withdraw from the fund.[562] The uncorporate approach of limiting managers' control of the firm's cash substituted for a corporate remedy for fiduciary breach. In another case, the Delaware Supreme

---

561. Anglo American Security Fund, L.P. v. S.R. Global International Fund, L.P., 829 A. 2d 143 (Del. Ch. 2003).

562. 829 A. 2d at 154. The court's other distinctions between the hedge fund and standard-form corporations were less persuasive. The court emphasized that any diminution of value affected current rather than later partners, so that paying damages to the fund would be a windfall to the later partners and fail to redress the injured. But this problem generally affects corporate derivative suits, where courts nevertheless permit derivative suits in recognition of the difficulty of apportioning injury among the shifting group of shareholders, and in order to deter wrongful behavior. Similarly, the court observed that the fund "operates more like a bank" because the partners have individual accounts and the fund has no going concern value. But since the partners' accounts depended on the overall value of the fund, it is not clear how these facts distinguish the fund from a corporation.

Court enforced a contractual provision mandating arbitration of disputes.[563] The court relied on Delaware's freedom-of-contract policy and its "strong public policy in favor of arbitration."

D. EXAMPLES OF UNCORPORATE GOVERNANCE OF LARGE FIRMS

Large firms use uncorporate business forms in two different ways. Some uncorporations (particularly private equity, venture capital, and hedge funds) have significant or controlling investments in large firms, while others (including publicly traded partnerships and REITs) are themselves operating firms. As we will see, tax considerations are the major constraint on large uncorporate operating firms, just as they once were in closely held firms. The following discussion briefly describes the main uncorporate devices for managing large firms. It reveals not only the uncorporation's governance functions but the significant flexibility of the uncorporation in accommodating the needs of a wide variety of firms.

Before we analyze these firms, an important caveat is in order. Much of the learning about these uncorporations is based on the finance booms of the late 1980s and early 2000s. This book is being completed in early 2009, as financing has dried up, private equity firms are retrenching, hedge funds are liquidating, the real estate business is miserable, and venture capital firms have little prospect for taking their portfolio firms public. The firms that emerge from this environment are likely to look different from those that entered it. But the theory discussed in the first part of this chapter likely will guide these new firms just as it has the development of uncorporations until this time. The main changes will result from these theories interacting with a new financial and regulatory environment. Accordingly, the following discussion should be viewed as a basis for an educated projection of the future.

1. Private equity

Private equity buyouts provide a leading example of the use of partnership mechanisms in governing large firms. Uncorporate features appear at three different levels: the umbrella private equity firm, the individual funds used to finance the buyouts, and the portfolio firm that is the subject of the buyout.

Buyout firms such as Kohlberg Kravis or Blackstone usually are organized as general partnerships or limited liability companies. The firm's partners and the network of experts it employs provide overall guidance, expertise, and reputational backing in selecting and managing targets. The buyout firm in effect

---

563. Elf Atochem North America, Inc. v. Jaffari, 727 A.2d 286 (Del. 1999).

substitutes active and engaged managers for agents who typically work for publicly held corporations.[564]

The buyout partnership, in turn, sponsors buyout funds (generally organized as limited partnerships) to provide the financing for the buyouts. These funds have several features that substitute strong incentives and discipline for corporate-type monitoring:

(1) Fund managers have significant upside and downside incentives designed to align managers' and owners' interests.[565] Fund partners traditionally earn an average two percent fee based on assets under management plus 20 percent of the fund's profits, or "carry," over a threshold amount, as well as a significant equity share in the fund. The fund managers typically get nothing until they have at least repaid the limited partners' investments and then "catch up" with the limiteds by getting all of the profits, after which the general partners are reduced to the standard 20 percent split.

(2) The fund automatically cashes out investors on expiration of its term. The general partner therefore has only a limited time to produce results and a strong incentive to improve the fund's portfolio companies enough to resell them privately or take them public through a so-called *reverse LBO*.

(3) The fund's finite life requires it to be structured to discourage managers from taking too much risk toward the end of the fund's term. The fund pools investments from several buyouts and subtracts losses of failed buyouts from the profits of successes. Also, the fund investors do not fully finance the fund's buyouts, forcing managers to borrow from third parties rather than simply drawing from the fund. As with the general uncorporate discipline of forcing the managers to make distributions or to buy out members, this exposes the managers to the capital markets' unbiased judgment. The combination of finite life and mechanisms designed to mitigate the agency costs of finite life distinguish the private equity structure from that of a standard corporation. Permanent financing enables corporate managers to invest for the long term and to react to changing circumstances by reallocating funds between projects. By contrast, uncorporate devices force managers periodically to face the judgment of the capital markets. The increased agency costs of permanent capital may be worth bearing if the firm gets a big benefit from giving the managers long-term power. Where long-term management has

---

564. *See* Michael C. Jensen, *The Economic Case for Private Equity* (Feb. 15, 2007), http://papers.ssrn.com/abstract=963530.

565. For a useful discussion of these devices, see Ulf Axelson, Per Strömberg and Michael S. Weisbach, *Why are Buyouts Leveraged? The Financial Structure of Private Equity Funds* 13 (Dec. 14, 2007), http://ssrn.com/abstract=676546.

fewer benefits, as with the sort of mature firms that have attracted private equity investment, investors may be better off holding the managers' feet to the fire.

(4) The funds' limited partnership agreements give investors some assurance of distributions rather than giving managers free rein to invest earnings in new projects. As with the limited term and the managers' need to seek additional funding of deals, this forces managers to face ongoing capital market evaluation.

(5) As illustrated by the Blackstone provisions quoted above, buyout fund owners typically have only minimal voting rights and managers have only limited fiduciary duties.

Uncorporate features also appear in portfolio firms' management. The fund uses borrowed money to buy out the public shareholders, which reduces agency costs by uniting management and ownership. The post-buyout firm's substantial debt forces managers to produce cash in order to repay the loans rather than being able to play with *free cash flow*—that is, cash that the firm does not need for debt repayment and other current expenses. The post-buyout firm's managers own a significant share of their firm's equity, making them more like partners than corporate executives. The private equity firm also imposes important structural changes on the portfolio firm, including new incentives, decision-making structures, and performance measures.[566]

A press account of the Hertz buyout illustrates some effects of this newly incentivized ownership structure.[567] Ford had sold Hertz in 2005 for $14 billion to private equity investors. It went public again eleven months later at a value of $17 billion after adding $12 billion in debt and taking out a billion-dollar dividend. Hertz's post-buyout president invested $6 million of his own money. He and the other owner-employees made several profit-increasing operational changes such as reducing how long it took to refuel and clean cars and get them to where they were needed, devising better purchasing methods, and allowing for quicker sales of cars.

A study of buyout transactions in the United Kingdom between 1996 and 2004 provides more systematic evidence of the potential advantages of private equity governance.[568] The authors documented general differences between post-buyout firms and publicly held firms in similar industries, including smaller

---

566. For analyses of the incentive mechanisms of post-buyout firms, see GEORGE P. BAKER & GEORGE DAVID SMITH, THE NEW FINANCIAL CAPITALISTS (1998); Allen Kaufman & Ernest J. Englander, *Kohlberg Kravis Roberts & Co. and the Restructuring of American Capitalism*, 67 THE BUS. HISTORY REV. 52 (Spring, 1993); Wruck, *supra* note 551.

567. *See* Andrew Ross Sorkin, *Is Private Equity Giving Hertz a Boost?*, N.Y. TIMES, Sept. 23, 2007, http://www.nytimes.com/2007/09/23/business/23hertz.html?ref=business.

568. Viral V. Acharya et al., *Corporate Governance and Value Creation: Evidence from Private Equity* (Jan. 2, 2009), http://papers.ssrn.com/sol3/papers.cfm?abstract_id=1324016.

boards populated by more company insiders, greater equity ownership, more frequent meetings, and active engagement of the buyout firms' general partners in management. The authors also found that the most successful deals had the most active ownership and governance.[569]

Because all levels of the private equity structure combine to make buyouts work, a firm cannot necessarily achieve the same results as a buyout simply by mimicking aspects of the structure, as by borrowing money to buy back some shares. It needs the discipline imposed by the umbrella firm and the buyout fund—and perhaps also a closely held structure that replaces the public shareholders with creditors.

It should be clear by now that private equity relies significantly on uncorporate business forms. Although corporations technically could replicate all of private equity's financial features, for the reasons discussed above only uncorporate business forms can ensure proper judicial interpretation and enforcement of such devices as pre-agreed liquidation dates and distribution obligations. Perhaps more importantly, uncorporations accommodate governance tradeoffs such as minimal voting rights and modified managerial fiduciary duties essential to the efficient operation of these devices.

Private equity, as the name implies, entails turning the target into a privately held firm, which reduces the agency costs inherent in publicly held firms by unifying management and ownership and replacing shareholders' weak monitoring with debt's high-powered obligations. At the same time, concentration of ownership reduces owners' ability to diversify risk, which increases financing costs. This means private equity firms generally need to go public again after they have been restructured. Also, constraining managers' power to retain earnings makes sense mainly in firms with reliable cash flows.

Private equity comes in several flavors. For example, although the public offering of the restructured target firm is generally regarded as an important form of exit from private equity, it might also be viewed as an additional phase of the private equity cycle. *Reverse LBO* firms retain some elements of their private equity structure, including significant manager ownership.[570] Also, an investment known as a *PIPE*, or "private investment in public equity," involves a private equity firm investing in financially distressed companies that remain

---

569. The authors measured success in terms of what they called "alpha"—that is, the excess of the buyout firms' returns, separated from the effect of leverage, over equivalent returns of similar non-buyout firms.

570. *See* Jerry X. Cao & Josh Lerner, *The Performance of Reverse Leveraged Buyouts* (Oct. 15, 2006), http://papers.ssrn.com/sol3/papers.cfm?abstract_id=937801, at 11 (showing that the buyout group retains on average a 38 percent stake, while its managers and directors retain an average 36 percent share).

publicly held.[571] Given the challenges facing today's publicly held firms, one or more of these variations might emerge as models for the "private" equity of the future.

2. Venture capital

Venture capital involves investments in start-up or early-stage firms. In contrast to the private equity buyout firms discussed above, venture capital portfolio firms are growing. Instead of having too much "free cash" that managers can waste (which needs to be addressed by compelling distributions or taking on debt that must be repaid), these firms are hungry for cash. The main agency cost that investors have to worry about here is entrepreneurs rolling the dice in an unrealistic expectation of success.[572]

As with private equity firms, venture capital involves three levels of uncorporations. Once again, there is an umbrella firm (such as Kleiner Perkins) that provides reputational capital. Again as with private equity, the umbrella firm establishes limited partnerships to raise investment funds to invest in start-up businesses.[573] These firms need mechanisms for reducing agency costs between the venture capitalist and its investors. The general partner exercises substantial discretion, incentivized by partner-like profit sharing but constrained by limited partners' power to exit the firm, contractual covenants, and obligations to distribute cash to the limited partners.

VC funds' limited partners traditionally have two kinds of exit rights. First, as with private equity funds, VC funds typically liquidate after set terms. These terms usually are longer than those for private equity (ten years), reflecting the uncertainty inherent in start-up financing. Another important type of investor exit is their ability to walk away from contribution obligations. This power depends on the penalty investors have to pay for failing to make an agreed contribution. In other words, investors may have significant flexibility to take their contributions "out" by refusing to follow through on a commitment to put them in. There is evidence that the extent of VC investors' "walkaway" rights is negatively correlated with the firms' adoption of governance devices such as

---

571. For descriptions and analyses of PIPEs, see Susan J. Chaplinsky, *PIPES: Private Equity Investments In Distressed Firms*, http://ssrn.com/abstract=909741; Hsuan-Chi Chen et al., *The Choice of Equity Selling Mechanisms: PIPES versus SEOS* (May 2008), http://papers.ssrn.com/sol3/papers.cfm?abstract_id=1139887; William K. Sjostrom, Jr., *Pipes*, 2 ENTREPRENURIAL BUS. L.J. 381 (2007); Wruck, *supra* note 551.

572. *See* George G. Triantis, *Financial Contract Design in the World of Venture Capital*, 68 U. CHI. L. REV. 305 (2001).

573. *See generally*, PAUL GOMPERS & JOSH LERNER, THE VENTURE CAPITAL CYCLE 8 (1999) (discussing the limited partnership structure of venture capital investments).

advisory boards.[574] This indicates that VC partnerships trade conventional monitoring type devices for uncorporate-type exit rights.

Another substitute for corporate-type monitoring in venture capital limited partnerships are covenants forbidding particular behavior that potentially involves a high risk of conflicts of interest between the managers and the investors. For example, the fund's general partner might be tempted to reinvest funds rather than distribute them to the investors, "shoot the moon" by investing in risky firms, or increase its management fees by raising money for new funds and neglecting the ones to which the investors are already committed. Covenants accordingly may require distributions or restrict particular types of investments or raising money for new funds. There is evidence that larger and riskier funds that involve the most potential agency costs also have more covenants.[575] Unlike conventional corporate-type monitoring, the covenants are automatically triggered by specific, objectively observable behavior, and therefore are not susceptible to the incentive and information problems of directors, shareholders, courts, and other traditional corporate monitors.

Venture capital portfolio firms typically are organized as corporations.[576] These corporations have several features that approximate uncorporate-type discipline. The venture capitalist's active role on the board of directors mitigates the usual corporate separation of management and ownership.[577] While the corporate form generally locks in minority investments, venture capitalists contract for various types of exit. Just as investors in venture capital funds can "exit" by foregoing contributions, so the funds themselves often invest in stages with the right to forego later stages.[578] Because the funds buy preferred shares providing for rights to compel liquidation, redeem, or compel a public offering,[579] they can

---

574. See Kate Litvak, *Firm Governance as a Determinant of Capital Lock-In* at 6–7 http://ssrn.com/abstract=915004, University of Texas Law School Law and Economics Research Paper No. 95 (2007). As discussed below, VC fund boards appear to function more as advisors than monitors.

575. See Gompers & Lerner, *supra* note 573.

576. See Joseph Bankman, *The Structure of Silicon Valley Start-Ups*, 41 UCLA L. REV. 1737 (1994).

577. See D. Gordon Smith, *The Exit Structure of Venture Capital*, 53 UCLA L. REV. 315 (2005) (analyzing agreements providing that board representation increases with investments); William W. Bratton, *Venture Capital on the Downside: Preferred Stock and Corporate Control*, 100 MICH. L. REV. 891, 921 (2002); Steven N. Kaplan & Per Strömberg, *Financial Contracting Theory Meets the Real World: An Empirical Analysis of Venture Capital Contracts*, 70 REV. ECON. STUD. 281 (2003). VC-backed boards also include independent directors, who may play advisor or mediator roles. See Brian J. Broughman, *The Role of Independent Directors in VC-Backed Firms* (July 17, 2008), http://ssrn.com/abstract=1162372.

578. See Ronald J. Gilson, *Engineering a Venture Capital Market: Lessons from the American Experience*, 55 STAN. L. REV. 1067 (2003).

579. See Phillippe Aghion et al., *Exit Options in Corporate Finance: Liquidity Versus Incentives*, 8 REV. FIN. 327 (2004); Douglas J. Cumming & Jeffrey G. MacIntosh, *Venture-Capital*

cash out if they are not impressed by the entrepreneur's performance.[580] These uncorporate-type rights and the closely-held nature of VC-startups arguably would mesh better with the uncorporate form. This suggests that venture capital firms' choice of the corporate form may be at least partly attributable to tax considerations.[581]

3. Activist hedge funds

Both private equity and venture capital firms invest for the medium term to aim for significant structuring or restructuring of the firm. Uncorporations also may be useful for shorter term investments in firms that retain the conventional publicly held corporate form. Hedge funds traditionally make money by exploiting market anomalies—for example, by short selling what they view as overpriced stock. "Activist" hedge funds stretch that model by buying significant stakes in firms and triggering a profitable asset sale or other restructuring. The hedge fund thereby "arbitrages" the difference between the value of assets under current management and their value if sold or managed differently.[582]

Exits in Canada and the United States, 53 U. Toronto L.J. 101 (2003); Smith, *supra* note 577, at 345–56.

580. Venture capital portfolio firms also use debt financing, which has been partly explained as a mechanism for controlling agency costs by reducing managers' control over the cash. See Darian M. Ibrahim, *Debt as Venture Capital*, Univ. of Wisconsin Legal Studies Research Paper No. 1081, http://papers.ssrn.com/sol3/papers.cfm?abstract_id=1418148 (June 12, 2009). VC firms' Moreover, preferred shares provide a right to convert into common stock that offers the VC fund an opportunity to actively participate in the business. See Douglas Cumming & Sofia Johan, *Advice and Monitoring in Venture Capital Finance*, forthcoming *Financial Markets and Portfolio Management*, http://ssrn.com/abstract=939338 (showing evidence that VCs take a more active interest in the firm the more equity ownership their convertible preferred provides).

581. These firms' choice of the corporate form may have something to do with the complex tax implications for the tax-exempt investors in venture capital funds of structuring the portfolio firms as partnerships. See Bankman, *supra* note 576 at 1741–47; Victor Fleischer, *The Rational Exuberance of Structuring Venture Capital Start-Ups*, 57 Tax. L. Rev. 137, 158–59 (2004). Also, VC funds generally take their portfolio firms public, and therefore may prefer to start them as corporations rather than having to change forms at the time of the IPO.

582. For data and analyses of activist hedge funds' role in corporate governance see William Wilson Bratton, *Hedge Funds and Governance Targets*, 95 Geo. L.J. 1375 (2007); Nicole M. Boyson & Robert M. Mooradian, *Hedge Funds as Shareholder Activists from 1994–2005* (July 31, 2007), http://papers.ssrn.com/sol3/papers.cfm?abstract_id=992739; Alon Brav et al., *Hedge Fund Activism, Corporate Governance, and Firm Performance*, 63 J. Fin. 1729 (2008); Christopher Clifford, *Value Creation or Destruction? Hedge Funds as Shareholder Activists*, http://ssrn.com/abstract=971018; Robin Greenwood & Michael Schor, *Investor Activism and Takeovers*, 92 J. Fin. Econ.362 (2009); Jiekum Huang, *When Bad Stocks Make Good Investments: The Role of Hedge Funds in Leveraged Buyouts* (May 2008), http://papers.ssrn.com/sol3/papers.cfm?abstract_id=1086687; Marcel Kahan &

Activist hedge funds fill gaps in the traditional corporate monitoring mechanisms discussed above. By taking significant positions, these investors avoid the free rider problem that impedes effective shareholder voting.[583] On the other hand, the size and undiversified nature of hedge fund investments limits the governance role of activist hedge funds. Unlike VC and private equity firms, these funds traditionally do not seek to fundamentally restructure their targets. Rather, they are looking for a quick fix.[584]

Most analyses of hedge funds take their internal structure for granted and focus on their external activities. However, hedge funds' uncorporate structure affects their role in corporate governance.[585] In general, hedge funds' structure helps motivate their managers to achieve the funds' goal of obtaining above-market risk-adjusted returns by spotting value others miss. As with private equity and VC funds, hedge funds are commonly organized as limited partnerships and include provisions limiting managers' control over the cash by providing for distributions and termination.[586]

Because hedge fund managers have to execute strategic decisions, they have more power over the investors' cash than do conventional mutual fund managers who are bound to give the investors their money back anytime they ask for it. To be sure, hedge fund investors generally have to lock up their money for up to two years and are subject to notice, lockups, and gates that limit when and how much the investors can withdraw. But hedge fund investors generally get quicker

---

Edward Rock, *Hedge Funds in Corporate Governance and Corporate Control*, 155 U. Pa. L. Rev. 1021 (2007); April Klein & Emanuel Zur, *Entrepreneurial Shareholder Activism: Hedge Funds and Other Private Investors*, 64 J. Fin. 187 (2009). There is evidence that hedge funds play an analogous role in enforcing bondholder rights. See Marcel Kahan & Edward Rock, *Hedge Fund Activism in the Enforcement of Bondholder Rights*, 103 Nw U. L. Rev. 281 (2008).

583. See Kahan & Rock, *supra* note 582.

584. See Clifford, *supra* note 582 (showing evidence that hedge funds earn excess returns mostly resulting from divestiture of underperforming assets); Greenwood & Schor, *supra* note 582 (showing evidence indicating that hedge funds are better suited for identifying undervalued targets and prompting takeovers than for improving long-term governance or operation); Scott Thurm, *When Investor Activism Doesn't Pay*, Wall St. J., Sept. 12, 2007 at A2, http://online.wsj.com/article/SB118956349313624707.html?mod=todays_us_page_one (suggesting that hedge funds are successful only at selling rather than running firms).

585. For a comprehensive analysis of hedge fund governance mechanisms, see Houman B. Shadab, *The Law and Economics of Hedge Funds: Financial Innovation and Investor Protection*, 6 Berk. Bus. L.J. __ (2009). For analyses of hedge fund governance focusing on their incentive compensation structures, see Robert C. Illig, *The Promise of Hedge Fund Governance: How Incentive Compensation Can Enhance Institutional Investor Monitoring*, 60 Ala. L. Rev. 41 (2008); Robert C. Illig, *What Hedge Funds Can Teach Corporate America: A Roadmap for Achieving Institutional Investor Oversight*, 57 Am. U. L. Rev. 225 (2007).

586. These terms of hedge fund agreements are summarized in Shadab, *supra* note 585.

access to their cash than private equity or VC investors, reflecting the shorter-term nature of what hedge funds seek to accomplish.[587]

Hedge fund managers also have general partner-type incentives. These include a 15 to 20 percent profit share above a specified hurdle rate.[588] So hedge fund managers do not make money unless the investors do. Hedge fund managers also make substantial investments in their firms.[589]

Given their uncorporate discipline, hedge funds can shed corporate-type monitoring devices as by contracting out of strong manager fiduciary duties and making takeovers difficult.[590] Courts are particularly likely to enforce these agreements in hedge funds because the funds sell only to wealthy or sophisticated investors as a way to avoid registering with the SEC.[591]

Hedge funds critically differ from mutual funds. Indeed, the effectiveness of activist hedge funds in governance is due substantially to their not being subject

---

587. The financial crisis of 2008–2009 tested hedge fund exit restrictions as illiquidity and pessimism drove investors to the exits, which the managers sought to block. *See* Louise Story, *Hedge Funds, Unhinged*, N.Y.TIMES, BU1 (Jan. 18, 2009), http://www.nytimes.com/2009/01/18/business/18hedge.html?_r=1. These exit-blocking moves arguably frustrated hedge fund governance structure by forestalling the market's judgment on hedge fund managers' strategy.

588. *See* Robert C. Illig, *supra* note 585 (describing hedge fund manager compensation and analyzing its effect in motivating better monitoring). These hurdle rates became significant during the market collapse of 2008–2009, when managers liquidated many hedge funds that had declined to the point that managers would never get over their hurdles. *See* Story, *supra* note 169.

589. One study estimates the average investment by managers to be 7.1 percent of fund assets, with the median manager owning 2.4 percent of the fund. Vikas Agarwal et al., *Role of Managerial Incentives and Discretion in Hedge Fund Performance*, (Centre for Financial Research Working Paper No. 04-04, Mar. 1, 2007), http://ssrn.com/abstract=889008. This paper shows a correlation between the level of manager co-investment and the performance of the fund. Note, however, that this data on the amount and effect of co-investment and compensation does not separate activist hedge funds from those that generate returns through investment and trading strategies.

590. *See* M. Corey Goldman, *Mutiny? Good Luck*, ALPHA (Feb. 24, 2009), http://www.iimagazine.com/Alpha/Articles/2113458/FEATURES/Mutiny?_Good_Luck.html (noting investors' difficulty in some hedge funds of calling meetings and the fact that management may hold most of the voting power).

591. *See* Investment Company Act §§ 3(c)(1) and (7), 15 U.S.C. § 80a-3(c)(1), (7) exempting from registration funds whose securities are owned by not more than one hundred persons and funds whose securities are owned exclusively by qualified purchasers. *Anglo American*, *supra* note 561 noted that "[t]he plaintiff limited partners each appear to be sophisticated parties that understood and voluntarily accepted the terms of the Agreement and assumed the risks of investing in the Fund in order potentially to reap the rewards of undertaking such risks."

to the same regulatory and tax constraints that apply to mutual funds.[592] Because mutual funds diversify their holdings in response to these tax and regulatory requirements, they cannot be used for taking large and active positions in portfolio firms.[593] Also, hedge fund managers are not subject to Investment Adviser Act limits on fees, which lets them be paid high-powered incentive compensation.[594]

The distinction between mutual and hedge funds suggests a potential role for standard forms to preserve distinctions between types of firms. Most mutual funds are organized as statutory business trusts.[595] The business trust form is useful precisely because it has no structural limitations and therefore can occupy niches created by federal bankruptcy, securities, and tax law.[596] The business trust is essentially a purely "contractual entity"—that is, a business association based entirely on the parties' customized contract with no default rules other than limited liability.[597] Structural regulation of business trusts comes mostly from nonbusiness-association law. By contrast, the limited partnership or LLC provides a self-contained governance structure for hedge funds. Consistent with the general function of business associations discussed throughout this book, firms can choose among these business forms depending on their business objectives and regulatory environment.

4. Publicly traded partnerships

The uncorporations discussed above invest and exercise important governance power in operating firms. The operating firms may or may not be organized as uncorporations. This section discusses large, publicly traded firms that are themselves uncorporations.

Tax law restricts this structure's use. The Internal Revenue Code permits partnership-type "flow-through" taxation in publicly traded firms that mostly earn "qualifying income," defined to include (among other things) interest,

---

592. *See* William Fung & David A. Hsieh, *A Primer on Hedge Funds*, 6 J. EMPIRICAL FIN. 309 (1999); Alan L. Kennard, *The Hedge Fund v. the Mutual Fund*, 57 Tax. L. 133 (2003); Larry E. Ribstein, *Do the Mutuals Need More Law?* REGULATION MAGAZINE (Spring 2004) at 14 (contrasting regulation of hedge funds with that of mutual funds).

593. *See generally*, Mark J. Roe, *Political Elements in the Creation of a Mutual Fund Industry*, 139 U. PA. L. REV. 1469 (1991).

594. *See* Investment Advisers Act Rule 205-3, 17 C.F.R. § 275.205-3 (exempting advisors to hedge and private equity funds from limitations on performance fees).

595. Robert H. Sitkoff, *The Rise of the Statutory Business Trust* (estimating that around 75 percent of the firms in the $10 trillion mutual fund industry are business trusts).

596. *Id*; Robert H. Sitkoff, *The Trust as "Uncorporation": A Research Agenda*, 2005 U. ILL. L. REV. 31.

597. *See* Larry E. Ribstein, *Limited Liability Unlimited*, 24 DEL. J. CORP. L. 407 (1999).

dividends, rents, and capital gains.[598] Publicly traded partnerships (PTPs) generally fall within these categories to take advantage of flow-through taxation.

PTPs, like other uncorporations, substitute incentive devices and partner access to the cash for corporate-type monitoring. PTP agreements traditionally promise to distribute net cash less reserves and restrict actions such as issuance of additional equity that might reduce distributions. They also incentivize the general partners, for example by linking their compensation to how much the firm distributes to the limited partners. At the same time, PTP agreements reduce corporate-type voting rights and fiduciary duties and make hostile takeovers very difficult.[599]

Real estate investment trusts (REITs) resemble PTPs, but are formally organized as corporations.[600] These firms receive flow-through tax treatment if they invest at least 75 percent in real estate-related assets and receive at least 75 percent of their income from these assets, with the rest in and from cash or government securities.[601] As with PTPs, REITs substitute uncorporate-type access to the cash and incentives for corporate-type monitoring. The Internal Revenue Code requires REITs to distribute 90 percent of their income.[602]

As in PTPs, the trade-off for uncorporate discipline is less corporate-type monitoring. Hostile takeovers are limited to costly proxy contests. The Internal Revenue Code effectively limits the potential for aggressive shareholder monitoring by restricting the five largest shareholders of a REIT to no more than 50 percent ownership.[603] REITs' uncorporate features raise the question (as with venture capital portfolio firms) of whether they would be more coherently packaged as corporations if tax law did not drive the choice of form.[604]

It is not clear whether publicly traded uncorporate operating companies eventually will break out of the relatively small category to which tax law so far confines them. As discussed throughout this chapter, a critical feature of uncorporations is the extent to which they constrain managers' power over the firm's cash. There is therefore some sense in limiting flow-through tax treatment to firms that mainly collect rents and royalties from natural resources, real estate, and other properties as these firms can commit to making distributions without compromising long-term business plans.

---

598. *See* IRC §§ 7704(c)–(d) (defining passive and "qualifying" income).
599. For a general analysis of PTP governance, see Goodgame, *supra* note 521.
600. *See* MD. CORP. & ASSOC. CODE, § 8-101 *et seq.*
601. *See* IRC §§ 856(c)(3), (c)(4)(A), 857(b)(2).
602. *Id.* § 857(a) (excluding real estate trusts from REIT tax treatment unless 90 percent of the trust's income is distributed as dividends).
603. *Id.* §§ 856(h), 542(a)(2).
604. *Id.* § 856(a) defines a "real estate investment trust" as "a corporation, trust, or association."

The tax code's flow-through tax category is, however, probably smaller than the set of firms that would seek to commit to distributions and that therefore in the absence of tax restrictions could benefit from flow-through taxation. For example, this category might include some mature operating firms with stable earnings, such as the firms that are often private equity targets. If these firms lack significant new business opportunities, they may want to reduce the amount of cash with which managers can play by committing to distributions. Yet most of these firms could not be PTPs or REITs because they operate ongoing businesses. Their only route to tax-advantaged commitment to distributions is through debt, which has the drawback of increasing bankruptcy costs.

Private equity firms have sought to, in effect, expand the traditional PTP category by publicly selling shares in the entity that manages and receives fees and profits from the private equity firm.[605] These "privlic equity" firms challenge the tax restrictions on publicly held uncorporations.[606] As with uncorporations generally, these firms substitute uncorporate incentives and discipline for corporate-type monitoring such as corporate-type voting rights and fiduciary duties. Also, the managing general partner gets the strong-form incentive compensation that typifies the private equity structure.[607] Although the firms do not

---

605. *See, e.g.,* Apollo Global Management, LLC, Form S-1 Registration Statement, 198–204 (April 8, 2008), http://www.sec.gov/Archives/edgar/data/1411494/000119312508077312/ds1.htm; Fortress Investment Group, LLC (http://www.fortressinv.com/site_content.aspx?s=16); Blackstone Group, L.P., S-1A, (filed June 21, 2007), http://files.shareholder.com/downloads/BX/245990728x0xS1047469-07-5100/1393818/filing.pdf; KKR & Co., L.P. S-1 (filed July 3, 2007), http://www.sec.gov/Archives/edgar/data/1404912/000104746907005446/a2178646zs-1.htm (visited Sept 8, 2008). *See* Larry E. Ribstein, "Going Privlic," *American.com,* Mar. 27, 2007, http://www.american.com/archive/2007/march-0307/going-privlic (discussing the Blackstone IPO and its private control characteristics). The proposed KKR and Apollo offerings were strictly mechanisms for existing owners to have publicly traded shares rather than for the firms to raise capital. *See* Steven M. Davidoff, "Plumbing the K.K.R. Un-IPO" (July 31, 2008), *Dealbook,* http://dealbook.blogs.nytimes.com/2008/07/31/plumbing-the-kkr-un-ipo/. Although the privlic equity offerings died down with the market bust, as of the summer of 2009 it appeared that the KKR offering was being revived through a proposed European offering that eventually could lead to a public offering in the United States. *See* Peter Lattman, *KKR Stock is Coming, via Europe,* WALL ST. J., June 25, 2009 at C1, http://online.wsj.com/article/SB124586313350748445.html.

606. Blackstone, for example, avoids corporate taxation by qualifying its income under the publicly traded partnership provision as capital gains from the funds (i.e., the carried interest), and as dividends from the management LLC out of management fees paid by the funds. Although this technically comes under the PTP tax exception, it is arguably inconsistent with the purpose of the exception because the fees are the product of Blackstone's active management of the fund, in contrast to the passive rent-collection of most PTPs. *See* Victor Fleischer, *Taxing Blackstone,* 61 TAX L. REV. 89 (2008).

607. *See* Blackstone Form S-1A, cited in note 605 at 14–19.

commit to a particular level of distributions, the application of flow-through taxation gives the owners a strong expectation of distributions—and managers who frustrate this expectation are likely to face problems when they make future offerings. In general, because private equity firms rely on uncorporate discipline and incentives rather than owner monitoring, they should be able to scale their ownership up from a few to many owners.

Privlic equity shares have melted down with the rest of the market in the bleak winter of 2009, dimming prospects for more such offerings and even raising the possibility that the firms will repurchase their newly cheap shares and become private again. It is not clear whether the privlic model ultimately will be seen as a short-lived fad of the financial boom, will make a comeback when the market does, or be seen as a transitional structure that will give rise to the publicly held uncorporation of the future. The last section of this chapter speculates on this possibility.

E. WHY UNCORPORATE NOW?

Although the agency costs inherent in public corporations and the alternatives available through partnerships have been recognized for a long time, firms have long thought the corporation's benefits worth the costs. Why, then, did uncorporations start playing a bigger role in this arena over the last twenty years? The possible answers illustrate the general idea that business associations evolve under pressure from political, technological, and economic developments. Together these developments led many large firms to conclude that the high costs of corporate governance were no longer worth bearing.

1. The demand for capital lock-in

As discussed throughout the book (and particularly in Chapter 4), theorists attribute the rise of the corporation to its ability to lock in capital, thereby freeing managers to engage in long-term business planning. But big firms' need for lock-in depends on whether they need to own substantial property for factories and the like. Having to meet investors' demand for return of their cash could threaten a firm's viability by forcing it to sell critical assets. Compelling liquidation is especially costly where the costs of selling assets and restructuring are high, as when the firm's employees have training or expertise connected with specific types of assets and the firm cannot easily buy what it needs on the open market.[608]

---

608. *See* Chris Parsons & Sheridan Titman, *Capital Structure and Corporate Strategy*, http://ssrn.com/abstract=983553. *See also* Thomas H. Noe et al., *Activists, Raiders, and Directors: Opportunism and the Balance of Corporate Power*, http://ssrn.com/abstract=983748 (relating the need for board control to the degree of illiquidity and opacity of the firm's assets).

The question as always comes down to tradeoffs. Capital lock-in prevents effective market discipline by making it hard for investors to pry their capital loose from inept managers. This cost may loom large if the benefits of capital lock-in decline. One important factor driving this decline is a firm's ability to outsource its needs from a broad market of independent suppliers.

The benefits of capital lock-in also depend on a firm's growth prospects. Mature firms with few growth prospects can set specific financial targets and time-frames for incentive compensation and cash distributions to investors. Not surprisingly, these are the firms that private equity firms have tended to buy, using their revenues to repay the new debt.[609] Thus, even if capital lock-in remains important for many firms, private equity firms found a way to carve out a category of firms for which the costs of lock-in outweigh the benefits.

2. New governance technologies

Private equity, venture capital, and hedge funds differ significantly from the traditional partnerships discussed in Chapter 3. The modern version is based on new technologies for addressing agency costs developed by innovators such as Henry Kravis of Kohlberg, Kravis and Stephen Schwarzman of Blackstone. The success of these technologies depends to some extent on legal structures such as the Delaware legislature's enactment of its freedom-of-contract provision and the Delaware courts' willingness to enforce fiduciary opt-outs under this provision (as discussed in Chapter 7). Although it is not clear the extent to which these financial and legal innovations responded to or spurred the other developments discussed in this part, they clearly played a role in the rise of the uncorporation.

3. Fleeing Sarbanes-Oxley

The uncorporation's increasing role in large firm governance may be partly due to a decline in the net benefits of public ownership of large firms. Private equity's rise has been attributed at least partly to the costs of complying with the Sarbanes-Oxley Act (SOX) adopted in 2002.[610] As with governance technologies, the direction of causation is unclear. After all, private equity firms arose in the 1980s, a full generation before SOX. The scope of the SOX effect is also unclear. While there is evidence suggesting that *small* firms went private post-SOX to avoid SOX's burdens,[611] *large* firms actually *chose* to go private with debt financing

---

609. *See* Baker & Smith, *supra* note 566, at 60.
610. *See* INTERIM REPORT OF THE COMMITTEE ON CAPITAL MARKETS REGULATION (Dec. 5, 2006), http://www.capmktsreg.org/pdfs/11.30Committee_Interim_ReportREV2.pdf.
611. Ehud Kamar et al., *Going-Private Decisions and the Sarbanes-Oxley Act of 2002: A Cross-Country Analysis*, 25 J. L. ECON. & ORG. 107 (2009) (showing that U.S. firms subject

that was subject to SOX.[612] This suggests that, despite SOX's costs, large firms might get net benefits from the quality signal and bond provided by compliance with SOX,[613] and therefore that factors other than SOX caused the firms to go private. Alternatively, uncorporate structures might enable large firms to comply with SOX. The implications of this interaction between regulation and uncorporations are discussed further below.

4. Credit costs and the role of debt

Debt has been perceived as critical to the success of private equity.[614] Tax deductibility of debt and government policies that decreased the cost of credit therefore bolstered private equity. Not surprisingly, the private equity market shrank with the credit supply in the summer of 2007,[615] even before the financial meltdown of 2008–2009.

Debt matters to private equity because it helps shape the incentives that drive value increases in restructured firms. First, debt disciplines deal selection. We have seen that the buyout funds have been structured so as to force the general partner to borrow for individual buyouts rather than raising all of the money up front in equity. This keeps the manager from taking too much risk when the fund is close to termination.

Second, debt constrains agency costs between investors and the post-buyout firm's managers. A highly leveraged capital structure enables the managers to own a significant chunk of the remaining equity, thereby uniting management and control and reducing manager-investor agency costs as compared to the pre-buyout firm.[616] Also, debt forces managers to distribute cash in interest and principal payments rather than wasting it internally.[617]

---

to the Act went private at a greater rate than otherwise comparable foreign firms not subject to the Act).

612. *See* Robert P. Bartlett, III, *Going Private but Staying Public: Reexamining the Effect of Sarbanes-Oxley on Firms' Going-Private Decisions*, 76 U. CHI. L. REV. 7 (2009).

613. Because SOX compliance costs are not completely scalable, SOX compliance costs smaller firms more per dollar of capitalization than larger firms. *See* Kamar et al., *supra* note 611.

614. *See* Robert P. Bartlett, III, *Taking Finance Seriously: How Debt-Financing Distorts Bidding Outcomes in Corporate Takeovers*, 76 FORD. L. REV. 1975 (2008).

615. *See, e.g.*, Dennis K. Berman, *Game Theories: Calling the End of Cheap Debt*, WALL ST. J., June 5, 2007, at C1; Henny Sender & Serena Ng, *Market Pressures Test Resilience of Buyout Boom Higher Interest Rates Raise Financing Costs; Signs of Fatigue Appear*, WALL ST. J., June 8, 2007, at A1, http://online.wsj.com/article/SB118549929176179833.html?mod=todays_us_money_and_investing; Henny Sender et al., *Debt Crunch Hits Deals, Deal Makers and Key IPO KKR May Find It Hard to Launch Stock Offer, Let Alone Its Financings*, WALL ST. J., July 27, 2007, at C1, http://online.wsj.com/article/SB118549929176179833.html?mod=todays_us_money_and_investing.

616. *See* Wruck, *supra* note 551.

617. *See* Jensen, *supra* note 564 (discussing the role of debt in "unlocking" investor funds).

Third, debt covenants can be designed to keep managers from substituting agency costs to creditors for those formerly borne by the shareholders. For example, the covenants may prohibit managers from "rolling the dice" by purchasing riskier assets to keep a foundering firm afloat.[618] In general, a highly leveraged capital structure replaces shareholders' weak monitoring powers with automatically triggered contractual obligations that the managers and shareholders must obey if they want to keep control of the company.[619]

These explanations for debt's importance are incomplete, however, because uncorporate contracts theoretically could replicate most or all of debt's incentive effects. For example, venture capital preferred stock resembles private equity debt, down to the covenants that constrain agency costs.[620] More generally, uncorporations have termination and distribution provisions that give the investors access to the cash and force the managers to face the judgment of the capital markets. Such provisions in the PTP contracts discussed above provide the incentive effects of debt without triggering the high costs of bankruptcy when cash flow falters. In short, debt and uncorporations are just types of contracts whose terms the parties theoretically can alter or shuffle at will.

Given the theoretical availability of debt-like contracts, tax considerations ultimately explain why debt matters to private equity. Publicly traded firms can avoid the corporate tax only by fitting into a relatively narrow rent-collecting category. Imposing the second-level corporate tax on distributions penalizes distributions, thereby burdening an important element of the uncorporate incentive structure. Debt provides tax consequences similar to partnership because interest payments are tax deductible. A large firm that wants to avoid the incentive problems of passive ownership but cannot fit into the tax cubbyhole for publicly traded partnerships therefore has to use debt instead of uncorporate contracts.

The problem is that tax considerations aside, bankruptcy risk may make debt more costly than equivalent uncorporate mechanisms. Taxes therefore may not only force a shift to debt, but also may reduce the number of workable deals. We will discuss below the implications of this analysis for tax policy.

F. THE FUTURE OF THE LARGE UNCORPORATION

Although the uncorporation has made broad inroads into large firm governance, the corporation remains dominant in this area. Private equity, venture capital,

---

618. *See* Stephen F. Diamond, *Beyond the Berle and Means Paradigm: Private Equity and the New Capitalist Order*, DISSENT—FOUNDATION FOR STUDY OF INDEPENDENT IDEAS (Winter, 2007), http://ssrn.com/abstract=1004234 (noting that detailed provisions in debt contracts are part of the incentive structure of private equity).

619. *See* Baker & Smith, *supra* note 566, at 98(noting importance of the debt constraint).

620. *See supra* text following note 575.

and hedge funds are really just temporary governance vehicles aimed at setting up or restructuring firms that then expect to be turned loose as conventional publicly held firms. The PTP is a more permanent governance form but is restricted by tax rules to a limited class of firms. Moreover, the market crash has raised serious questions about the future of private equity and other uncorporations in governing large firms. The crash not only has temporarily dried up debt financing (which has been the lifeblood of the uncorporation), but in the long term may have dampened investor enthusiasm for innovative finance and significantly changed the business landscape in which uncorporations have operated. This suggests that this chapter's discussion of the large uncorporation may be largely of only historical significance. However, this section considers several factors that may actually increase the uncorporation's role in large firm governance in the post-meltdown era.

1. Financial engineering

The large uncorporation's horizons could expand if changes in business practices increase the costs of the standard publicly traded corporation. The financial crisis unfolding in late 2008 and early 2009 indicates that could be happening. What occurred with major financial institutions indicated a serious and widespread breakdown in corporate governance. As Michael Lewis colorfully described in his chronicle of the 2008–2009 meltdown, financial firms apparently bet their futures on trillions of dollars of securities the value of which ultimately depended on the simple-minded proposition that real estate prices would always go up.[621] This was not the first outbreak of delusional thinking, as similar problems surfaced in the previous bust only seven years before. For example, widespread misunderstanding of Enron's use of derivatives was a significant factor in allowing insiders to essentially turn the firm into a house of cards.[622]

These problems have been laid at the door of derivatives such as mortgage-backed securities, collateralized debt obligations, and credit default swaps. These securities have been said to have created:

> opacity—an inability of any but a few analysts to get a clear sense of what happened. And the creation of arcane financial instruments made effective supervision virtually impossible, both by superiors in the firm, and by outside regulators.[623]

---

621. *See* Lewis, *supra* note 55.
622. *See* William C. Powers, Jr. et al., REPORT OF INVESTIGATION BY THE SPECIAL INVESTIGATIVE COMMITTEE OF THE BOARD OF DIRECTORS OF ENRON CORP. (Feb. 1, 2002) 2002 WL 198018 at 67–71 (describing LJM and Raptor transactions that were presented as hedges but were actually bets on Enron's future stock price); Frank Partnoy, *Enron and Derivatives*, http://ssrn.com/abstract=302332.
623. *See* Jerry Z. Muller, "Our Epistemological Depression," *American.com* (Jan. 29, 2009), http://american.com/archive/2009/our-epistemological-depression.

It is, however, misleading to blame the financial instruments themselves. Michael Lewis aptly quotes a friend as saying, "[T]he problem isn't the tools. It's who is using the tools. Derivatives are like guns."[624] Even this is not quite accurate: the problem is not the people but the standard corporate incentive structure under which they were operating. Several commentators have suggested that the severe problems that led to the meltdown would not have happened if the Wall Street investment firms had remained partnerships instead of incorporating in the 1990s, as then the partners' personal liability would certainly have focused their attention on potential risks.[625]

Although this may be true, it is not clear that investment firms need to turn back the clock to the partnership era. Managers' personal liability may deter beneficial risk-taking because there is a lot of uncertainty that even the most intense monitoring cannot eliminate. Modern uncorporate business forms may be a better approach because they combine limited liability with partnership-like mechanisms for addressing agency costs.

It is worth noting that hedge funds apparently did a better job than corporations in generally avoiding investing in overpriced subprime securities.[626] The incorporated Wall Street firms involved in the meltdown had managerial compensation structures that excessively rewarded risk-taking, including stock options rather than full-fledged ownership. Managers were subject to weak monitoring by outside directors and public shareholders. Managers and directors

---

624. *See* Lewis, *supra* note 55.

625. *See* James K. Glassman & William T. Nolan, *Bankers Need More Skin in the Game; Partnerships may be a more trustworthy business model than corporations*, WALL ST. J., Feb. 25, 2009, at A15; Lewis, *supra* note 55; Muller, *supra* note 623. *See also* Steven M. Davidoff, *A Partnership Solution for Investment Banks* (August 20, 2008), http://dealbook.blogs.nytimes.com/2008/08/20/a-partnership-solution-for-investment-banks/ (noting that the firm that best avoided the problems with subprime – Goldman Sachs – "retained the most partnership-like attributes" of all the investment banking firms, but that "all partnerships were not created equal").

626. *See* Richard A. Posner, A FAILURE OF CAPITALISM, 99–100 (2009) (noting that the fact that hedge funds have not done as badly as large publicly held financial firms is partly due to their being "less plagued by conflicts between owners and managers" and indicates "that the incentive to take risks that is created by executive overcompensation in publicly held companies has been a factor in the financial crisis"); Alan S. Blinder, *Crazy Compensation and the Crisis*, WALL ST. J., May 28, 2009 at A15, http://online.wsj.com/article/SB124346974150760597.html (arguing that hedge funds have less leverage than investment and commercial banks because their senior partners "almost always have significant shares of their own personal wealth tied up in the funds"); Charles W. Calomiris, *The Subprime Turmoil: What's Old, What's New, And What's Next*, http://www.voxeu.org/index.php?q=node/1561 (Aug. 22, 2008) (linking hedge funds' relative success in subprime to their governance structure and incentives of hedge fund managers); Larry E. Ribstein, "Governance, the uncorporation and subprime," *Ideoblog*, (Aug. 23, 2008), http://busmovie.typepad.com/ideoblog/2008/08/governance-the.html.

were willing to defer critical risk decisions to bond rating firms that had agency problems of their own.[627] Managers might have been more attentive to owners' interests if they had to distribute cash rather than earnings statements, if they had to return to the capital markets periodically for cash, if their investors had been a few large institutions rather than thousands of dispersed individuals,[628] or if their compensation depended on their firms' basic financial health rather than short-term prosperity. Perhaps more importantly, the managers would have had strong incentives (as did Hertz's new managers discussed above)[629] to scrutinize their firms' risk profiles and the actual value of their investments rather than simply being able to sell a story to Wall Street that would boost the value of their stock options.

Firms might respond to the governance risks inherent in derivatives by simply avoiding sophisticated financial instruments. Indeed, regulators may force this response. However, derivatives in the right hands can be a powerful way to reduce risk-bearing costs. Firms need to adjust their governance to suit their business needs rather than vice versa. If complex financial instruments can reduce firms' costs of doing business but are dangerous for conventional corporations, this should drive a move toward the uncorporation rather than one away from derivatives.[630]

In fact, there are indications that uncorporations' use of derivatives may increase. Hedge funds' basic strategies depend on these instruments. Private equity and venture capital funds may need to emulate hedge funds in this respect to manage the increased investment risks connected with hanging onto portfolio firms longer in depressed securities markets.[631] If that happens, the various categories of uncorporations discussed above in this chapter may start to merge.

2. Financial regulation

We have seen that SOX may have helped boost the private equity industry by encouraging firms to leave the public securities markets. SOX's greatest effect is on small firms because SOX's requirements are not perfectly scalable—there is a minimum cost to setting up a SOX compliance system even for the

---

627. For a good discussion of these problems, see Macey, *supra* note 46.

628. *See* Ronald Masulis & Randall Thomas, *Does Private Equity Create Wealth? The Effects of Private Equity and Derivatives on Corporate Governance*, 76 U. CHI. L. REV. 219 (2009).

629. *See supra* text accompanying note 567.

630. Moreover, the use of derivatives may indirectly increase the attractiveness of uncorporate governance by increasing firms' ability to handle debt. *See* Ronald J. Gilson & Charles K. Whitehead, *Deconstructing Equity: Public Ownership, Agency Costs, and Complete Capital Markets*, 108 COLUM. L. REV. 231 (2008).

631. *See* Houman B. Shadab, *Coming Together after the Crisis: The Global Convergence of Private Equity and Hedge Funds*, 29 NW. J. INT. L. & BUS. 603 (2009) (noting that private equity funds may begin to use credit default swaps to reduce credit exposure).

smallest firms. Although SOX also increases costs for larger firms, these firms may find it easier to bear even substantial compliance costs than to avoid SOX by going offshore or private.

Ironically, some large firms might adopt the uncorporate form not because they want to avoid SOX by going private, but because uncorporate governance (particularly higher-powered managerial incentives) may help public firms deal with SOX's risk-reporting requirements. This is supported by evidence that some large firms are staying private but voluntarily opting to comply with SOX.[632]

These observations about the effect of SOX have obvious implications for increasing financial regulation. Stricter financial regulation increases both the need to escape public securities markets and the need for better governance to reduce regulatory costs. But if firms adopt better governance, including the uncorporate form, do we *also* need more financial regulation? At the same time, increased regulation of the uncorporation (discussed next) may make general financial regulation more costly or less effective.

3. Regulation of uncorporations

The above subsections discuss the factors affecting market demand for uncorporate governance of large firms. It is also important to consider the possible impact of regulation and taxation of uncorporations (discussed in this and the next subsection).

Uncorporations are particularly vulnerable to regulation, especially as they move into the large firm realm. As discussed throughout this book, uncorporations have had to swim against the tide of legal efforts to channel firms (particularly large firms) into the corporate form. This tide likely will become even stronger as corporate managers, labor unions, and other influential interest groups confront the threat to their power represented by the substitution of uncorporate discipline for corporate monitoring. Moreover, this substitution is effective only if courts and regulators enforce contracts providing for the critical trade-off. It is not clear that other state lawmakers will follow Delaware's lead in enforcing opt-outs from fiduciary duties.[633]

In particular, other states may fail to consider the firm's entire bundle of rights and obligations in deciding whether to enforce elimination or extensive modification of traditionally important monitoring devices such as owner voting and fiduciary rights. Nonenforcement and regulation may become particularly likely if a breakdown in uncorporate governance gives pro-regulatory forces an easy target. And such a breakdown will become particularly likely as uncorporate

---

632. *See supra* note 612 and accompanying text.
633. *See supra* text accompanying note 554.

governance of large firms spreads. In other words, the large uncorporation may become the victim of its own success.

Legislatures and administrative agencies also may react to the financial meltdown by increasing regulation of some of the specific mechanisms discussed in this chapter, particularly private equity and hedge funds.[634] Proponents of this legislation and regulation may argue that hedge funds increase the market's "systemic risk" by employing financial engineering to link market actors into a huge bubble that could suddenly pop. However, a big problem with this argument is that hedge funds seek to succeed by making bets against the accepted wisdom and by using secret business methods that do not spread to wide swaths of the market.[635] Proponents of regulation also might argue that investors in these funds do not fully understand their risks. These arguments may acquire more weight if these funds continue to be opened up to public investors—a possibility that is discussed further below.

Whether the arguments for regulation make sense from a policy standpoint or have political support, there are at least three important reasons they are unlikely to put uncorporations out of business. First, we have seen that an important feature of the uncorporate form is its flexibility and ability to mutate under regulatory pressure. The uncorporation will survive because, for the reasons discussed in this chapter, firms will continue to demand a viable alternative to corporate governance—and the uncorporation will continue to be able to meet this demand.

Second, populist criticism of the corporate form provides a significant political counterweight to managers and other interest groups seeking to constrain the corporation. This force was perhaps best expressed by Justice Brandeis, writing in the shadow of the Great Depression. In *Louis K. Liggett Co. v. Lee*,[636] in dissenting from an opinion striking down a Florida law against chain stores, Justice Brandeis argued that the law could be upheld as a reasonable constraint on large corporations:

> The typical business corporation of the last century, owned by a small group of individuals, managed by their owners, and limited in size by their personal wealth, is being supplanted by huge concerns in which the lives of tens or hundreds of thousands of employees and the property of tens or hundreds of thousands of investors are subjected, through the corporate mechanism, to the control of a few men. Ownership has been separated from control; and this separation has removed many of the checks which formerly operated to curb the misuse of wealth and power. And, as ownership of the shares is becoming continually more dispersed, the power which formerly accompanied

---

634. *See* Story, *supra* note 587.
635. *See* Macey, *supra* note 46, at 265–72.
636. 288 U.S. 517, 564–67 (1933) (footnotes omitted).

ownership is becoming increasingly concentrated in the hands of a few. The changes thereby wrought in the lives of the workers, of the owners and of the general public, are so fundamental and far-reaching as to lead * * * scholars to compare the evolving 'corporate system' with the feudal system; and to lead other men of insight and experience to assert that this 'master institution of civilised life' is committing it to the rule of a plutocracy. * * * Such is the Frankenstein monster which states have created by their corporation laws.

Justice Brandeis prominently cited Berle and Means[637] among the academic critics of the large corporation. Brandeis was echoing an often-expressed concern with the illegitimacy of reposing vast power in unaccountable corporate managers.[638] At least some modern critics of the corporate "Frankenstein" might welcome the idea of a form of business in which managers were subject to tighter constraints. To be sure, at least some of these critics might simply shift their concerns to the impersonal markets that provide these constraints. But the general point is that public pressure against uncorporations is unlikely to be monolithic.

Third, people across the political and ideological spectrum are likely to have in mind for some time to come the revelations of bad governance both in Enron and in the corporate meltdown of 2008–2009, as well as uncorporations' successes in governing large firms over the last twenty years. Even if some of these people mistrust the uncorporations or financial innovation generally, they will be forced to choose between this vague unease and the practical need to find some way to fix the governance of large firms.

4. The corporate tax

We have seen that the corporate tax is now applied to most publicly traded firms. Taxing distributions burdens an important aspect of the uncorporate approach to governance. Yet the only way large firms can be publicly held is to fit into a small exception from the rule treating publicly traded firms as corporations. Large firms that want the discipline provided by owner access to the cash need to end-run the tax on distributions by using tax-deductible debt, thereby increasing the risk of costly bankruptcy. This encourages firms to continue to use the corporate form even as the costs of this form increase.

Apart from the general preference for incorporating large firms, powerful interest groups gain from the corporate status quo and might be threatened by the rise of the uncorporation. Corporate managers support laws that enhance

---

637. ADOLF A. BERLE, JR. & GARDINER C. MEANS, THE MODERN CORPORATION AND PRIVATE PROPERTY (1932).

638. For more contemporary examples of this criticism, see JOEL BAKAN, THE CORPORATION: THE PATHOLOGICAL PURSUIT OF PROFIT AND POWER (2004); RALPH NADER ET AL., TAMING THE GIANT CORPORATION (1976).

their power.[639] This includes the tax on corporate distributions, which gives managers an excuse to retain earnings rather than distributing them to shareholders. Indeed, there is evidence that corporate managers promoted double taxation in 1936 as part of a deal to avoid an undistributed profits tax.[640] Managers of large firms could be expected to continue to resist any effort to significantly curb or eliminate the tax on distributions.

The factors discussed above in this chapter pointing to more use of the uncorporation for publicly held firms eventually might encourage a change in tax policy. As discussed above, the current exception from the corporate tax on publicly traded firms is limited essentially to passive rent collectors such as natural resource and real estate firms. This is probably narrower than the class of firms that could benefit from flow-through partnership taxation and that would seek this taxation under a more flexible rule. For example, mature, slow-growth firms that get fairly predictable earnings from established brands might derive comparable benefits from a tax rule that encouraged regular distributions to owners.

Congress might accommodate this need for flexibility by drawing the corporate-partnership tax border with a view to encouraging governance structures that mitigate agency costs. Firms arguably should be able to balance the costs and benefits of the tax as they do with other governance devices. In other words, firms' governance choices should determine the application of the tax rather than vice versa. At the same time, as long as the corporate tax remains, Congress has to restrict firms' ability to opt out of it. Lawmakers could let firms choose to be taxed as partnerships on the condition that they have substantially adopted partnership-type governance, including committing to making distributions. This would be analogous to the tax code's approach to REITs in which the application of partnership-type tax turns to some extent on the firms' distribution of earnings.[641] It also would be consistent with the goal of making statutory standard forms coherent because it would enable firms to mesh tax consequences with their choice of business association.

Other changes in tax policy could reduce use of the uncorporate form. In particular, raising personal income tax rates and holding other factors (including capital gains rates) constant may increase firms' benefit of retaining earnings. This could reverse the LLC Revolution, which as we saw in Chapter 5 was triggered by the significant reduction of personal tax rates during the 1980s.

---

639. See Roe, supra note 38.
640. See Steven A. Bank, *Corporate Managers, Agency Costs, and the Rise of Double Taxation*, 44 WM. & MARY L. REV. 167, 183–98 (2002); Steven A. Bank, *The Story of Double Taxation: A Clash over the Control of Corporate Earnings*, in BUSINESS TAX STORIES 153 (Steven A. Bank & Kirk J. Stark eds., 2005).
641. See supra text accompanying note 602.

5. The future of publicly held uncorporations

The private equity boom spurred the rise of "privlic" equity firms in which private equity firms opened themselves to public investors.[642] This may prove to be a short-lived fad and casualty of the collapse of the securities markets. On the other hand, dismal financial markets have sent private equity investors searching for an exit. This could spur experimentation with and evolution of quasi-public markets in uncorporations open only to institutional and other large investors, along the lines of the PORTAL market created in 2007.[643]

The quasi-public form could be particularly useful for firms that are tiptoeing into markets for outside capital. This could include law and other professional firms that are seeking new forms of financing.[644] These firms may want to give control shares to the insiders and noncontrol shares to the outside investors. This may call for uncorporate controls on agency costs that are not provided for in conventional dual class corporate stock. At the same time, these firms may face regulatory and other problems in making full-fledged public offerings.

If conventional public markets for uncorporate interests ultimately develop, this could lead to convergence of corporate and uncorporate forms or some sort of reconfiguration of the divisions among large firms. As noted above, maintaining the trade-off between corporate monitoring and uncorporate discipline is critical to the preservation of the uncorporation. The political pressure to impose corporate duties on uncorporations may prove irresistible if these firms come to look too much like conventional publicly traded corporations and to be owned by the same type of individual investors.

---

642. See supra text accompanying note 605.

643. See The PORTAL Alliance to Create Industry-Standard Facility for 144A Equity Securities, http://ir.nasdaq.com/releasedetail.cfm?ReleaseID=275224 (Nov. 12, 2007). It has also been argued that the shift toward public markets may occur in debt rather than equity markets. See Charles K. Whitehead, The Evolution of Debt: Covenants, the Credit Market, and Corporate Governance, Boston Univ. School of Law Working Paper No. 08-26 CLEA 2008 Meetings Paper (Jan. 26, 2009), http://papers.ssrn.com/sol3/papers.cfm?abstract_id=1205222. These developments arguably are fundamentally equivalent in light of debt's uncorporate features discussed above.

644. State law currently prohibits law firms from having non-lawyer owners. See MODEL RULES OF PROFESSIONAL CONDUCT, Rule 5.4. However, the initial public offering of an Australian law firm suggests this barrier may eventually fall. See Slater & Gordon Ltd Prospectus 8, 10–11 (Apr. 13, 2007), http://www.slatergordon.com.au/docs/prospectus/Prospectus.pdf). With respect to potential business justifications for publicly traded law firms, see Larry E. Ribstein, Want to Own a Law Firm?, AMERICAN.COM (May 30, 2007), http://www.american.com/archive/2007/may-0507/want-to-own-a-law-firm (visited Sept. 8, 2008); Larry E. Ribstein, On My Mind: Lawyers Don't Make Enough, 180 FORBES 40 (Oct. 29, 2007), http://members.forbes.com/forbes/2007/1029/040.html (suggesting possible merger of private equity and law firms). For a general discussion of issues concerning publicly owned law firms, see Milton Regan et al., Law Firms, Ethics and Equity Capital: A Conversation, 21 GEO. J. LEG. ETHICS 61 (2008).

6. The corporate/uncorporate partnership

We have seen that uncorporations have significant potential governance advantages over corporations. However, the uncorporation is unlikely to push the corporation off the main stage. Rather, this chapter suggests that corporate governance will function in partnership with uncorporations, with the latter providing discipline to fill the governance gaps in conventional corporations.

In general, firms early and late in their life cycles are the best candidates for uncorporate governance. Venture capital-type firms likely will continue to incubate young firms, while private equity-type firms will swoop in to restructure mature firms that can commit to making regular cash distributions.

Beyond these best candidates, there is a large swath of growing, entrepreneurial firms in the middle that need to give their managers substantial power over the cash. but also need to be watched by hedge fund-type activist shareholders. Moreover, all types of firms are potentially subject to mismanagement and are therefore candidates for the market for control. We have seen that uncorporations have evolved governance structures designed to squeeze value out of takeovers even in the face of strong takeover defenses.

In other words, all types of corporations will need help from uncorporations in controlling agency costs. The extent of the uncorporate role will depend on balancing the costs and benefits of capital market discipline against those of insulating managerial discretion to formulate and execute long-term business plans from day-to-day market pressures.

9. NEW DIRECTIONS

This book has a theory and history of business forms from early partnerships through the modern uncorporation. This chapter builds on this foundation in considering where the corporation and uncorporation might be headed.

A. CONVERGENCE OR DIVERGENCE OF BUSINESS FORMS

We have focused on the major uncorporate forms: general and limited partnerships and limited liability companies. But there are many more where these came from, some of which we have touched on, including business or statutory trusts,[645] limited liability partnerships (discussed in Chapter 7) and limited partnership associations and joint stock companies (discussed in Chapter 3).

As discussed in Chapter 2, there are costs and benefits to all these business associations. They provide different standard form contracts to suit the many different types of firms and help them avoid the costs of customized terms. The availability of many kinds of statutory business associations therefore can help firms reduce contracting costs. This is especially important for smaller firms for which drafting and planning costs loom large in relation to total capitalization.

However, a given standard form is only as good as the network of cases, forms, advice, and so forth that interpret it. More standard forms means that other things being equal, there will be on average fewer interpretations of each form. But this may not be much of a problem as long as the more useful standard forms quickly become prominent and acquire substantial interpretive networks. Perhaps the best way to decide on the optimal number is just to let the market for state laws work it out.

The main question for present purposes is where the law is heading. The rapidly increasing popularity of the LLC suggests that form is likely to be the main one for closely held firms. Limited partnerships also fill a significant niche, particularly for larger and publicly held uncorporations (as discussed in Chapter 8). General partnerships likely will remain the default entity that firms get when they have not chosen a particular firm and become a niche entity for the relatively small set of firms that are still comfortable with personal liability.

---

645. *See* Robert H. Sitkoff, *The Trust as Uncorporation: A Research Agenda*, 2005 ILL. L. REV. 31.

This prognosis is complicated by the fact that LLCs are popular partly because of their flexibility and chameleon-like nature. Indeed, it is hard to nail down precisely what characterizes the LLC because it can so easily morph between manager-managed/limited partnership and member-managed/general partnership varieties. Cases and forms that apply to the manager-managed LLC do not necessarily provide much guidance for member-managed firms and vice versa. The overriding importance of the operating agreement also prevents strong generalizations within the categories. Add to that the variation among LLC statutes as to a large swath of terms that apply between members and we get something close to an all-purpose form with few clear guideposts.

Perhaps as the LLC evolves, it might spawn variations that are embodied in distinct statutes. For example, these statutes might provide for separate manager-managed and member-managed forms. Should it make a difference whether these variations are in separate statutes? Why not a "Chinese menu" of features, which firms get to mix and match? Or legislatures might compromise by putting certain features as a statutory "hub" for all business associations and separating other features into the "spokes" of specific business associations. This is the approach taken by the Texas Business Organizations Code (see Chapter 2) that puts all of Texas's business association laws into a single thousand-page behemoth.

Evaluating these proposals raises the question discussed throughout this book of the functions of separate business association statutes. We have seen there are significant potential advantages to separate statutes. First, a complete set of provisions encourages statutory drafters to think through all the rules needed for a particular type of firms. Standard forms need to be *coherent*, where all features are matched to particular types of firms. For example, fiduciary duties obviously differ between manager-managed and member-managed firms, and the choice of management modes arguably has implications for continuity or capital lock-in. In Chapter 5, we discovered that it was the absence of coherence that did in the close corporation.

Second, a coherent statutory set of provisions gives courts a clearer basis to fill contractual and statutory gaps with common law rules or clarifications. The parties' decision to form a limited partnership implies that they want the general partner to have significant power and duties. In a marginal case where it is unclear whether the parties intended to delegate power to the manager, the parties' choice of form may guide the court's decision.

Third, a separate statute for centrally managed firms clarifies the agency power the managers have to bind the firm. Parties dealing with firms can learn a lot from the standard form rather than having to delve into the particular firm's management structure.

Despite these considerations favoring separate manager-managed and member-managed forms, the LLC "chameleon" approach may have staying power. The approach provides a flexible compromise between statutory centralized management like that in limited partnerships and a completely contractual version like that in general partnerships. Many firms may want to centralize power while giving nonmanaging members significant input. These firms would want third parties to inquire into authority, and would not necessarily want to allocate all power and duty to one particular group of participants.

Regulatory considerations also may favor the flexible LLC approach. In Chapter 7, we discussed how choice of form may matter on the margin in applying regulatory statutes such as securities or employment discrimination laws. Some firms therefore may trade more regulatory certainty for management flexibility. However, firms that do not face significant regulatory constraints may prefer the flexible LLC approach. In other words, rather than reducing the number of standard forms, combining the member-managed and manager-managed modes in the LLC provides a distinct "flexible management" approach. The general and limited partnership forms remain available for firms that do not like chameleons.

Regulation might have the opposite effect of pushing business forms toward convergence. As discussed below in Section C, some regulation might be imposed on all firms, or at least on all publicly held firms, regardless of choice of form. This might blur distinctions between business forms, particularly concerning the decree of flexibility, and reduce or eliminate the underlying business rationale for maintaining separate forms.

B. THE LONG-TERM FUTURE OF THE UNCORPORATION

As we move beyond the future of distinct standard forms, there is a further question concerning the respective roles of *uncorporate* versus *corporate* forms. Why should we not simply have a variety of standard forms offering a spectrum of features?

This question obviously goes to the heart of this book's thesis that the uncorporation is an identifiable type of business association. As discussed throughout, uncorporations have two important features. First, they offer an alternative to the corporation in mitigating agency costs. Rather than relying on monitoring of managers by courts, shareholders, and the market for control, uncorporations give members access to the firm's cash and managers higher-powered incentives.

Second, uncorporations provide more flexibility than the hardwired corporate form. This feature may be attributable partly to the inherently regulatory nature of the corporate form—that is, as a device expressly designed to constrain choice. It is also partly due to the fact that the corporation evolved to suit firms traded in public securities markets, which favor the clarity of relatively inflexible rules. By contrast, uncorporations evolved primarily to suit closely held firms. For reasons discussed at the end of Chapter 8, even large firms may no longer need public markets.

The uncorporation's flexibility and default rules work together, and therefore may remain distinctive. Financial economists might object that there is no reason why firms could not mix corporate and uncorporate features and thereby blur the distinctions between the two categories of firms. However, the coherence of standard forms discussed above supports maintaining a clear separation between corporate and uncorporate features. Also, the inflexibility of the corporate form implies that a particular set of features is locked in place, including strong managerial power, shareholder voting, weak shareholder powers to directly participate in management, independent directors, fiduciary duties, and the market for control. Inflexibility implies that uncorporations may evolve more rapidly than corporations, thus enhancing the distinctions between the two categories.

However, the corporate/uncorporate equilibrium may be upset by the advent of the publicly held uncorporation. As discussed in Chapter 8, at least some types of publicly held firms may be able to use the uncorporate form. Assuming this form is not taxed or regulated out of existence, it might become as inflexible as the publicly held corporation. For example, regulators may insist that firms adopt uncorporate discipline before they can waive such important corporate features as shareholder voting and fiduciary duties. Also, publicly traded uncorporations arguably have the same need for inflexible rules as publicly held corporations. Regulators therefore might mandate features such as limited terms or regular distributions for firms that seek to opt out of standard corporate features. In short, the publicly traded partnership could become a distinct type of firm that straddles the corporate-uncorporate boundary.

C. THE UNCORPORATION AND MANDATORY RULES

The uncorporation's future is both a result and cause of the general structure of business association law. Business associations have been produced by state competition against the backdrop of federal law, primarily the federal securities laws. How might the rise of the uncorporation—and particularly of the uncorporation's role in large firms—affect this structure? More specifically, will the uncorporation provide at least a partial exit from federal and state regulation of corporate governance?

So far the answer to that question is a qualified yes. States (led by Delaware) have let even publicly traded uncorporations opt out of fiduciary duties and other rights that are locked into corporate governance. Moreover, publicly traded limited partnerships have been able to avoid some federal proxy rules that are built on the corporate structure, particularly those relating to independent directors. However, as discussed above, it is not clear how far this flexibility will go if publicly traded uncorporations became more prevalent. The SEC and Congress likely will be unwilling to allow partnerships to create a broad exit from federal regulation of governance. If the federal government is waiting in the wings to regulate partnerships, Delaware probably would be unwilling to challenge Congress with flexible uncorporations, just as it has been careful with its corporate law.[646]

On the other hand, tax restrictions on the types of firms that can profitably use the uncorporate form might facilitate weaker securities regulation of these firms. As discussed in Chapter 8, current tax law effectively restricts use of the uncorporation to relatively stable firms that can promise distributions and limited life. This type of firm inherently gives managers less leeway to harm owners than does a corporation. Also, the tax restriction helps ensure against significant erosion of the corporate tax base through increased use of uncorporations that can elect a single-level tax.

These built-in limits on the uncorporation might make it a suitable vehicle for deregulation of governance in response to international competition. In the wake of the adoption of SOX, there was some indication firms were avoiding U.S. securities markets either by going abroad[647] or by going or remaining privately held.[648] This led to proposals for lightening the regulatory and litigation burden on publicly held firms, and to at least one important rule change facilitating exit from U.S. markets.[649] However, there has been significant resistance to more aggressive deregulation. The uncorporation could open a more moderate deregulatory path that is open to a specific category of firms that have less need than standard corporations for traditional corporate governance.

There is therefore some chance that uncorporations might lead to a lower total level of business governance regulation. Moreover, even without immediate regulatory changes, in the long run the availability of alternative business forms that firms can select merely by choosing their state of organization creates an opportunity for regulatory "arbitrage" that inherently limits the potential for federal regulation of governance. There always has been a tension between mandatory federal securities laws and enabling state rules. Mandatory rules suit standard corporations managed by boards of directors that have particular rules for shareholder voting. Governance variations enabled by flexibility at the state level challenge federal regulators to redesign their rules. The rise of the uncorporation threatens to unleash a flood of variations with which federal

---

646. *See* Mark J. Roe, *Delaware's Competition*, 117 HARV. L. REV. 588 (2003).

647. *See* Joseph D. Piotroski & Suraj Srinivasan, *Regulation and Bonding: The Sarbanes-Oxley Act and the Flow of International Listings* (January 1, 2008), Rock Center for Corporate Governance at Stanford University Working Paper No. 11, http://ssrn.com/abstract=956987 (showing that small foreign firms were less likely to list in the US following the enactment of Sarbanes-Oxley).

648. *See* Ehud Kamar et al., *supra* note 611; Ehud Kamar et al., *Sarbanes-Oxley's Effects on Small Firms: What is the Evidence?* forthcoming in IN THE NAME OF ENTREPRENEURSHIP? THE LOGIC AND EFFECTS OF SPECIAL REGULATORY TREATMENT FOR SMALL BUSINESS (Susan M. Gates & Kristin Leuschner, eds. June 2007), http://ssrn.com/abstract=993198.

649. *See* SEC Rule 12h-6, Fed. Reg. § 240.12h-6.

regulators and Congress cannot easily cope. Just as LLC statutes forced the IRS to abandon the Kintner classification rules and adopt check-the-box for closely held firms (see Chapter 6), so the increased use of uncorporations by large firms could provoke a loosening or material reshaping of the federal regulation of corporate governance.

The financial crisis that is happening at the time this book is being written and the calls for regulation it has engendered are likely to affect these developments. Lawmakers are threatening tighter scrutiny of hedge and private equity funds and may dig in against a potential onslaught of free markets.[650] Moreover, there have been recent moves toward mandating disclosure of ownership of all types of firms, suggesting that the regulatory tide might wash over even the smallest uncorporations as well as large firms.[651] These moves could force retrenchment of the uncorporation and harden traditional lines between publicly held and closely held firms.

D. TOWARD THE DISAPPEARANCE OF THE CLOSE CORPORATION?

As discussed in Chapter 6, the close corporation was the LLC Revolution's first major casualty. The close corporation always was a misbegotten compromise, in which the corporate tax or the restrictions of Subchapter S was accepted as the price of limited liability. In the wake of check-the-box, there is seemingly very little need for firms to adopt the close corporation. Yet they continue to do so.

There are at least two potential explanations for the stubborn persistence of the close corporation. The first is simple laziness. Lawyers and accountants who advise clients on choice of form are familiar with the close corporation form and do not want to have to learn a whole new governance technology. They also may be concerned about malpractice liability for mistakes and conclude that this potential outweighs any risk of liability for mistaken choice of form advice. Law professors also may have little incentive to learn to teach a whole new uncorporate area when they can comfortably continue to teach the same corporations material for which they already have notes.

---

650. This is indicated by the recommendation for hedge fund disclosure and registration contained in the Treasury Department's white paper for financial regulatory reform. See Department of the Treasury, FINANCIAL REGULATORY REFORM: A NEW FOUNDATION at 37, http://www.financialstability.gov/docs/regs/FinalReport_web.pdf.

651. See S. 569, 111th Congress (March 11, 2009) (proposed Incorporation Transparency and Law Enforcement Assistance Act applying to corporations and LLCs with provision for studying application to other types of entities); National Conference of Commissioners on Uniform State Laws, Uniform Law Enforcement Access to Entity Information Act (Discussion Draft, April 22, 2009) (uniform state law proposal applying to all types of business entities).

A less cynical explanation is that the close corporation still has an edge over the relatively new LLC in case law, interpretations, and the rest of the network of materials that impart critical certainty. All of the features that give LLCs an advantage over existing forms also make the form less settled and riskier to use. For example, as discussed in Chapter 7, the LLC's "chameleon" management raises questions for both the firm and third parties as to when a member binds the LLC, and particularly as to the relationship between the LLC default rules and the general law of agency. These questions will only intensify in impact if states adopt the confusing RULLCA agency provisions discussed in Chapter 7. Finally, LLCs present some still-unresolved tax issues that may be more troubling than those applying to close corporations under Subchapter S.

However, it is not clear that the uncertainty under LLC law actually increases risks for lawyers and their clients. For example, although there is still some confusion about the application of corporate-type standards in much-litigated veil-piercing cases, the analysis in Chapter 7 shows that it is at least clear that veil-piercing is not more likely in LLCs than in corporations given comparable facts. Also, although it may not be clear whether courts will fully enforce fiduciary duty opt-outs in LLCs, at least they are more likely to do so in LLCs than in corporations. On balance, these considerations suggest that the close corporation will disappear over time as LLC law becomes more detailed and certain and as a new generation of lawyers and law professors learns to deal with LLCs.

Although LLCs may come to dominate small firms, they are not necessarily for everybody. The LLC's flexibility may make it unsuited for some firms even as other firms find this feature attractive. Small firms may prefer the comfort of corporate restrictions on opting out of fiduciary duty and mandatory remedies for majority shareholder oppression. Although they could contract for protection, the costs of these detailed contracts may outweigh the benefits for small firms. The mantle of protection that cases such as *Meinhard v. Salmon* throw over general partners (see Chapter 3) limits the risks people inevitably face when going into business with strangers, friends, or family.

It is important to keep in mind that close corporations have evolved toward flexibility that is now only slightly less than that available to LLCs. As discussed in Chapter 5, firms can contract in many states for all partnership or LLC features while adopting the corporate form. Although LLC law may give firms many of these features by default, LLCs often have detailed operating agreements. The parties might conclude that even a slight risk with the LLC form is not worth its marginal benefits.

Finally, the regulatory developments discussed above[652] might affect the survival of the close corporation. Adopting regulation applicable to all business

---

652. *See supra* note 651 and accompanying text.

entities could reduce the attractiveness of the flexible uncorporation and revive the popularity of the traditionally more regulated close corporation.

E. THE SOCIALLY RESPONSIBLE UNCORPORATION

This book emphasizes how uncorporate forms of governance can reduce the costs of delegating discretion by aligning managers' and owners' interests. A potential problem with these mechanisms is that they reduce managers' flexibility to use corporate resources to benefit non-owner corporate constituencies, including employees, creditors, and society as a whole. This point reveals the schizophrenia inherent in criticisms of the modern corporation: do the critics really want managers to be more loyal to shareholders?

The debate about corporate social responsibility is actually less important than it seems to be. As discussed throughout this book, the basic problem with corporate governance—and an important reason for uncorporate governance—is that current law gives corporate managers significant leeway to deviate from shareholders' interests. Moreover, it is difficult to define the sphere of "social" responsibility as managers have to cater to a wide range of corporate constituencies to serve their firms' long-run interests. It follows that it is not obvious what proponents or opponents of corporate social responsibility want to change about current law. Few social responsibility proponents advocate laws *requiring* managers to serve society's interests, and opponents need to explain how managers can be prevented from doing so without fundamentally altering current corporate law.[653]

The uncorporation enters this debate by providing a potential way to reduce managers' leeway to be socially responsible. Managers who have to meet stringent requirements to distribute cash to owners (and whose compensation depends closely on profits) may have less power or incentive to serve society. Yet it is not clear whether well-disciplined managers would shortchange customers or neglect local communities as such behavior could reduce long-term profitability. Nor is it clear that managers use any extra discretion to help society rather than themselves. In any event, uncorporations' inherent flexibility discussed throughout this book may give them *more* freedom than corporations to diverge from corporate profit-maximization norms.[654]

Uncorporations' critics may ignore these nuances and focus on the uncorporation's potential for reducing managers' discretion to help society. Even if corporate managers are not paragons of compassion, social responsibility advocates

---

653. For a more detailed version of this analysis of the corporate social responsibility debate, see Ribstein, *supra* note 201.

654. One indication of this flexibility is the move toward "low-profit" LLC provisions. *See supra* text accompanying note 370.

may prefer them to the soulless capitalists in private equity and hedge funds. Therefore, the concern for social responsibility of firms is a factor that could continue to make the uncorporation a target of tax and regulation, as it has been throughout its history.

F. SMALL VERSUS LARGE FIRMS?

The modern uncorporation's move into the large firm domain might not only risk the application of mandatory rules (as discussed above) but more fundamentally could threaten the uncorporation's suitability for its traditional small firm clientele.[655]

In some respects, the uncorporation already has fallen down on the task of providing suitable default rules for small firms. As discussed in Chapter 7, estate tax rules have led state legislatures to provide corporate-type durability for LLCs and limited partnerships. Owners of minority stakes may be left without adequate tools to deal with oppression by controlling owners. Though sophisticated firms can craft agreements that deal with all parties' concerns, uncorporation statutes need to provide suitable default rules for the smallest firms that cannot easily bear the costs of customized drafting. This tendency to neglect the problems of smaller firms also infected corporation statutes (as discussed in Chapter 5).

The rise of the large uncorporation might exacerbate these problems of small uncorporations. The leading state of Delaware, and particularly its lawyers, reaps the biggest rewards from catering to the needs of large firms, as these firms are the most likely to shop for law outside their home states.[656] Though the home states of the smallest firms can be expected to continue to provide default rules for stay-at-home firms, states that do not want to lose their more mobile firms may want to emulate Delaware. This may diminish closely held firms' options for well-crafted provisions and increase the costs of forming firms.

The solution is for state legislators to follow this book's lessons in crafting distinct and coherent uncorporate business associations suited to small, closely held firms. For example, states might enact Delaware-type LLC statutes for larger LLCs and partnership-type LLC statutes for smaller firms. Alternatively, states might recognize that they cannot easily compete with Delaware's sophisticated legal infrastructure for larger firms and focus on catering to the smaller firms that are likely to stay at home.

---

655. The author is indebted to Robert Thompson for the raising the issues discussed in this section.

656. *See* Kobayashi & Ribstein, *supra* note 285 (showing that largest LLCs are mostly likely to form outside their home states, specifically in Delaware).

G. THE FUTURE OF THE BUSINESS ASSOCIATION

One possible future is that statutes may make possible the fully customized firm. In other words, firms may go beyond the uncorporation to the *un-business association*. Some firms may not want any of the business association's baggage, including the vestige of fiduciary or good faith duties left by even the most flexible statutes or inherent authority rules that courts derive from general statutory default rules rather than particular circumstances. These firms now can enter into a detailed contract without deliberately forming a particular type of firm. However, a court might characterize them as partnerships and saddle them with rules they do not want, particularly including vicarious liability to creditors.

In short, although the default rules of business associations may be useful in filling gaps, some parties may want to be able to avoid these rules. They may prefer to fill their contracting space with their own terms and not leave gaps for courts and legislatures to fill. For example, two firms forming a joint venture to develop a specific product or joint business plan may want their arrangement covered entirely by the contract, subject to the general rules of interpreting contracts. They may not want their arrangement to be characterized as a general partnership and subject to rules such as imposition of fiduciary duties they never intended. These parties might take advantage of a statute that lets them enter into a customized contract, but still have limited liability—a sort of "contractual entity."[657] This type of statute could signal a new approach to the concept of a business association. At the same time, these contractual entities could spawn new business associations as idiosyncratic contracts harden over time into types and accrete appropriate default rules. The popularity of this approach may depend to some extent on the developments discussed above in this Chapter. The convergence of business associations or regulation of all firms irrespective of their chosen business form may reduce the value of distinct standard forms and encourage firms to move toward customized contracts.

H. WHY THE UNCORPORATION MATTERS

Finally, it is worth reflecting briefly on why society should care about the issues raised in this book—that is, on why this is not just for legal technicians immersed in the fine points of business of law.

First, consider the implications for the biggest firms that drive the economy's performance. The recent financial meltdown demonstrates clearly the importance of governance to firms' success. Big financial firms lost control of their risks and made dubious bets on their futures—most importantly, the big bet on

---

657. *See* Larry E. Ribstein, *Limited Liability Unlimited*, 24 Del. J. Corp. L. 407 (1999).

real estate prices. The result was a disastrous loss of shareholder wealth and jobs and a threat to the retirement funds of millions of Americans. How could this have happened, despite the broad range of federal regulations, state laws, and good governance practices? As discussed in Chapter 8, the explanation might lie in the architecture of corporate law. This suggests that it might be time for a fundamental reevaluation of governance and, perhaps, recognition that the uncorporation offers a better way. The rise of the uncorporation could play a significant role in the rebuilding of the economy.

That is not to say that all of the damage has been done by corporations. In recent years sophisticated financial vehicles have proliferated, some of which use uncorporate governance forms. Whether misuse of these forms was driven by corporations (such as Enron), the fact remains that their availability arguably invited abuse. Some might argue for mitigating these risks by sticking with tried-and- true corporations, but this would be throwing the baby out with the bathwater. It would be better to understand the appropriate uses of business associations than to truncate the evolution of business.

Finally, although the biggest firms may drive the economy at any given time, smaller firms are the source of future growth—the vehicles that today's entrepreneurs use to develop tomorrow's big firms. Whether entrepreneurs can find capital depends importantly on the contractual structures available to solve agency cost and opportunism problems. Statutory business associations are a crucial aspect of these contractual structures. Business people cannot be expected to bear the entire burden of drafting new forms and taking on the risks as to how new business associations will be interpreted and enforced. Unless states develop appropriate business associations, firms may be stuck in costly contracts—or on the margin may not form at all. Business associations in general, and the flexible uncorporation in particular, therefore are an important aspect of economic development.

TABLE OF CASES

Abercrombie v. Davies, 130 A. 2d 338 (1957).................107, 107n241
Allegheny Tank Car Co. v. Culbertson, 288 F. 406
   (N.D. Tex. 1923) 81n185
Alloy v. Wills Family Trust, 944 A.2d 1234 (2008).................210n523
Anglo American Security Fund, L.P. v. S.R. Global
   International Fund, L.P., 829 A.2d 143 (Del. Ch. 2003)...........221n561
Aronson v. Lewis, 473 A.2d 805 (Del. 1984)...............169n388, 171n392
Austin v. Michigan Chamber of Commerce, 494
   U.S. 652 (1990) 66n137

Baron v. Allied Artists Pictures Corp., 337 A.2d 653
   (Del. Ch. 1975), *app. dismissed*, 365 A.2d 136 (Del. 1976).......211, 211n527
Bauer v. The Blomfield Company/Holden Joint Venture,
   849 P.2d 1365 (Alaska 1993)....................................52n91
Bloodworth v. Bloodworth, 226 Ga. 898, 178 S.E.2d 198 (1970).........42n60
Brehm v. Eisner, 906 A.2d 27 (Del. 2006)..........................204n502

Carden v. Arkoma Associates, 494 U.S. 185 (1990)...................73n152
Centros Ltd. v. Erhvervs-og Selskabsstyrelsen,
   Case C-212/97, 1999 E.C.R. I-1459.....................133, 133n308, 134
Champluvier v. State, 942 So.2d 145 (Miss., 2006)................174n402
Chase Manhattan Bank v. Iridium Africa Corp.,
   197 F. Supp. 2d 120, 128–29 (D. Del. 2002)......................154n353
Chase Manhattan Bank v. Iridium Africa Corp.,
   307 F. Supp. 2d 608 (D. Del. 2004)..............................154n354
Cinerama v. Technicolor, Inc., 663 A.2d 1156
   (Del. 1995)...169n386
Clackamas Gastroenterology Associates, P.C. v. Wells,
   538 U.S. 440 (2003).....................................192n465, 192n466
Clark v. Dodge, 269 N.Y. 410, 199
   N.E. 641 (1936)..........................105, 105n239, 110, 210–211
Cranson v. International Business Machines Corp.,
   234 Md. 477, 200 A.2d 33 (1964)...............................83n195
CTS Corp. v. Dynamics Corp. of America,
   481 U.S. 69 (1980)..75, 75n160

Donahue v. Rodd Electrotype Co., 367 Mass. 578,
328 N.E. 2d 505 (1975) 111–112, 111n254, 115

Edgar v. MITE Corp., 457 U.S. 624 (1982) 75, 75n161
EEOC v. Sidley Austin LLP, 437 F.3d 695 (7th Cir. 2006) 191n464
Elf Atochem North America, Inc. v. Jaffari, 727
A.2d 286 (Del. 1999) 222n563
Equal Employment Opportunity Commission v. Sidley Austin
Brown & Wood, 315 F.3d 696 (7th Cir. 2002) 190–191, 190n462
Estate of Countryman v. Farmers Co-op, Ass'n, 679
N.W.2d 598 (Iowa 2004) 145, 145n335

Fisheries Co. v. McCoy, 202 S.W. 343 (1918) 81n187
Fisk Ventures, LLC. v. Segal, 2009 WL 73957
(Del. Ch., Jan 13, 2009) 181, 181n431

Gardstein v. Kemp & Beatley, 64 N.Y.2d 63, 484
N.Y.S.2d 799, 473 N.E.2d 1173 (1984) 110, 110n250, 111, 116
Giles v. Vette, 263 U.S. 553 (1924) 89n207
Gotham Partners, L.P. v. Hallwood Realty Partners,
L.P., 817 A.2d 160, 167–68 (Del. 2002) 176, 176n411, 219
Gunnings v. Internet Cash Enterprise of Asheville,
LLC, 2007 WL 1931291 (W.D.N.C. 2007) 145n337
Guth v. Loft, Inc. 5 A.2d. 503 (Del. 1939) 167n383
Guttman v. Illinois Central Railroad Co., 189 F.2d 927
(2d Cir.), *cert. denied*, 342 U.S. 867 (1951) 211n526

Hishon v. King & Spalding, 467 U.S. 69, 79 (1984) 189, 189n460

In re Albright, 291 B.R. 538, 541 (Bankr. D.Colo. 2003) 184n446
In re Amer. Intern. Group, Inc., 2009 WL 366613
(Del. Ch., February 10, 2009) 204n503
In re Oracle Corp. Derivative Litigation, 824 A.2d 917
(Del. Ch. 2003) 202–203, 202n497
In re Pace Photographers, 71 N.Y.2d 737, 530 N.Y.S. 2d 67,
525 N.E.2d 713 (1988) 111, 111n253, 116
In re The Walt Disney Company Derivative Litigation,
907 A.2d 693, 741, n.373 (Del. Ch., 2005) 204, 204n501

Jackson v. Hooper, 75 A. 568
(N.J.Err. & App. 1910) 103, 103n235, 104, 105

Kamer van Koophandel en Fabrieken voor Amsterdam
   v. Inspire Art Ltd, Case C-167/01, 2003 E.C.R. I-10155............134n311
Katz v. Oak Industries, Inc., 508 A.2d 873, 880
   (Del. Ch., 1986) 167–168, 168n384
Kern v. Chicago & Eastern Illinois Railroad Co., 6 Ill.
   App. 3d 247, 285 N.E.2d 501 (1972) 211n526
Kidd v. Thomas A. Edison, Inc., 239 F. 405 (S.D.N.Y.),
   aff'd, 242 F. 923 (2d Cir. 1917)................148, 148n343, 149, 149n345
Kintner v. United States, 216 F.1d 418 (9th Cir. 1954)...........100, 100n231
Klebanow v. New York Produce Exch., 344 F.2d 294,
   296 (2d Cir. 1965) 177n414

Labovitz v. Dolan, 189 Ill. App. 3d 403, 136 Ill. Dec. 780,
   545 N.E.2d 304 (1989) 210n523
Lake River Corp. v. Carborundum Co., 769 F.2d 1284,
   1290 (7th Cir. 1985) 25n27
Litchfield Asset Management v. Howell, 70 Conn.
   App. 133, 799 A.2d 298 (2002)...................... 183, 183n445, 184
L.L. Constantin & Co. v. R.P. Holding Corp., 56 N.J. Super.
   411, 153 A.2d 378 (1959) 211n526
Louis K. Liggett Co. v. Lee, 288 U.S. 517,
   564–67 (1933) 242–243, 242n636

Martin v. Peyton, 246 N.Y. 213, 158 N.E. 77 (1927).............58–59, 58n111
Matter of Radom & Neidorff, Inc., 307 N.Y. 1, 119
   N.E.2d 563 (1954)......................................109, 109n246
Medical Committee for Human Rights v. SEC, 432
   F.2d 659 (DC Cir. 1970), vacated, 404 U.S.
   403 (1972)...198n478
Meinhard v. Salmon, 249 N.Y. 458, 164 N.E. 545 (1928)........ 48–50, 48n81,
                                                49n83, 68–69, 167, 172, 174, 253
Minute Maid Corp. v. United Foods, Inc., 291 F.2d 577 (5th Cir.),
   cert. denied, 368 U.S. 928 (1961) 57–58, 57n110, 59
Moran v. Household International, 500 A.2d 1346
   (Del. 1985).. 206, 206n511

New York City Employees' Retirement System v. Dole Food
   Company, Inc., 795 F. Supp. 95 (S.D.N.Y.), dismissed as moot,
   969 F.2d 1430 (2d Cir. 1992) 198n478
Nixon v. Blackwell, 626 A.2d 1366, 1379–81
   (Del. 1993)..115, 115n270

Paciaroni v. Crane, 408 A.2d 946 (Del. Ch. 1979) 47n79
Page v. Page, 55 Cal. 2d 192, 359 P.2d 41, 10
    Cal. Rptr. 643 (1961) 54–55, 54n101, 97, 109, 171
Pinebrook Properties, Ltd. v. Brookhaven Lake Property
    Owners Ass'n, 77 S.W.3d 487 (Tex. App. 2002) 144, 144n333

Rafe v. Hindin, 29 A.D.2d 481, 288 N.Y.S. 2d 662, *aff'd mem.*,
    23 N.Y.2d 759, 244, N.E.2d 469, 296 N.Y.S.2d 955 (1968) 108n242
Ringling v. Ringling Brothers-Barnum &
    Bailey Combined Show, Inc., 49 A. 2d 603 (1946)........... 107, 107n240
Rivanna Trawlers Unlimited v. Thompson Trawlers, Inc.,
    840 F.2d 236 (4th Cir. 1988)........................186–187, 186n450
RKO-Stanley Warner Theaters, Inc. v. Graziano, 67
    Pa. 220, 355 A.2d 830 (1976).....................................82n191
Robinson v. Glynn, 349 F.3d 166 (4th Cir. 2003)........... 187–188, 187n455
R & R Capital, LLC v. Buck & Doe Run Valley Farms,
    LLC, No.3803-CC, 2008 WL 3846318, at *8
    (Del. Ch., Aug. 19, 2008)....................... 177, 177n417, 181–182

Securities & Exchange Commission v. Merchant Capital,
    LLC, 483 F.3d 747 (11th Cir., 2007)..................... 187, 187n452
Securities & Exchange Commission v. W. J. Howey Co., 328
    U.S. 293 (1946) 186, 186n448
Sertich v. Moorman, 162 Ariz. 407,783 P.2d 1199 (1989) 173n398
Smith v. Van Gorkom, 488 A.2d 858 (Del. 1985) 169–170, 169n389
Sonet v. Timber Co., L.P., 722 A.2d 319 (Del. Ch. 1998) 175–176, 175n410
State v. Morales, 256 La. 940, 240 So. 2d 714 (1970)..................42n58
Stone v. Ritter, 911 A.2d 362 (Del. 2006) 69n141, 170, 170n391, 201,
                                                  201n494, 205n508, 219
Strother v. Southern California Permanente Medical Group,
    79 F.3d 859 (9th Cir. 1996)............................ 189, 189n461

Thompson v. Schmitt, 115 Tex. 53, 274 S.W. 554 (1925) 81n186
Thompson v. Wayne Smith Construction Company, Inc,
    640 N.E.2d 408 (Ind. App. 1994)..................... 141–142, 141n327
T-K Distributors, Inc. v. Soldevere, 704 P.2d 280
    (Ariz. App. 1985)..83n194
Toner v. The Baltimore Envelope Co., 498 A.2d 642
    (Md. 1985).. 115, 115n269

Trustees of Dartmouth College v. Woodward, 17 U.S. (4 Wheat.)
518, 636 (1819) 74
Tzolis v. Wolff, 10 N.Y.3d 100, 855 N.Y.S.2d 6, 884
N.E.2d 1005 (2008) 178n421

Überseering BV v. Nordic Construction Company
Baumanagement GmbH (NCC), Case C-208/00, 2002
E.C.R. I-9919 ....134n310

Walter v. Holiday Inns, Inc., 985 F.2d 1232 (3d Cir. 1993)............162n372
Watteau v. Fenwick, 1 Q.B. 346 (1892) 82, 82n189
Williamson v. Tucker, 645 F.2d 404, 422 (5th Cir.),
cert. denied, 454 U.S. 897, 102 S.Ct. 396, 70 L.Ed.
2d 212 (1981)................................. 186, 186n449, 188, 189
Wood v. Baum, 953 A.2d 136 (Del. 2008) 219–220, 219n554

Zapata Corp. v. Maldonado, 430 A.2d 799 (Del. 1981)............... 171n393
Zion v. Kurtz, 50 N.Y.2d 92, 428 N.Y.S.2d 199, 405
N.E.2d 681 (1980) 115, 115n268

INDEX

accountability of management, 147
  in general partnerships, 150–51
  in limited partnerships, 152–53
accounting proceeding, 53–54, 173–74, 178
  inappropriateness for modern limited partnership, 176
agency costs, 18–19
  debt as constraint, 236
  help from uncorporations in controlling corporate costs, 246
  judges as monitors of, 203–4
  in modern corporations, 193, 194
  shareholder voting and, 196
  uncorporations, mitigation of, 249–50
agency rules in partnership, 46
agents. *See* management
aggregate. *See also* entity
  partnership as, 73
Alchian, Armen, 16, 160
Allen, William T., 167–68
American Bar Association, 200
American Express as joint stock company, 63
American Law Institute, 200
Ames, James Barr, 41, 42
Andrews, William S., 50, 60
anti-takeover devices, 206–7
asset protection, LLCs and, 183
associations, corporate tax on, 100
audit committees, 200
  role strengthened by Sarbanes-Oxley Act, 201

Bainbridge, Stephen, 199
Baldwin Locomotive as partnership, 78
bankruptcy
  court on charging order, 184
  debt financing and, 211, 233, 237, 243
  exhaustion rule and, 141
  of partner
    and dissolution of partnership, 53, 98
    RUPA on, 122n284

  of partnership, 140–41
Berle, Adolf, 198, 243
Blackstone Group, L.P., 222, 235
  avoidance of corporate taxation, 233n606
  general partner removal, 216n546
  preclusion of judicial review of conflict transaction, 220–21
  role of board of directors, 214–15
  special meetings, 216n545
  vote of limited partner, 217n547
Blair, Margaret M.
  on capital lock-in, 71, 76
  on dissolution, 77–78
  on role of the board of directors, 67–68
board of directors
  accountability of managers and, 147
  corporate governance and, 87, 199–203
  of corporations, 67–68
  firm performance and independence of, 203
  ineffectiveness of, 201–2
  litigation against directors, 204
  special litigation committees, 202, 205
  in uncorporations, 214–15
  partnerships, 79
Brandeis, Louis D., 242
Bubble Act (U.K., 1720), 84, 91
business association law
  advantages of separate statutes for different forms, 26–27, 248
  reasons for, 25–26
  relationship with non-organization law, 124–25
business associations
  convergence versus divergence of forms, 247–49
  evolution of, 31–36
  flexibility versus rigidity of forms, 148
  future of, 256
  importance of distinct and coherent statutes on, 26–27, 248
  modular approach to construction of, 30

business judgment rule, 69, 169, 204
business opportunities, duty not to usurp, 167
business trusts, 84
  as contractual entity, 231
buyout
  firms organized as general partnerships, 222
  funds organized as limited partnerships, 223
buyout rights
  elimination of default rights by Uniform Limited Partnership Act (2001), 153
  in large uncorporations, 212–13
  removal from LPs and LLCs, 180

capital lock-in
  closely held firms and, 97–98
  in corporations, 71–72, 209
  development of uncorporation and, 234–35
  partnerships and, 76
capital markets
  buyout managers and, 223
Cardozo, Benjamin N., 48, 172
care, duty of. *See* duty of care
Carnegie Steel Company as limited partnership association, 64, 78
Carney, William, 120
Chandler, Alfred, 71
charging order, 51, 182–83
Chayes, Abram, 109
"check-the-box" rule, 121, 252
  effect on business association design, 185
  effect on LLC statutes, 131
choice-of-law rules
  corporations (*See* internal affairs choice-of-law)
  limited liability companies and, 123
  limited liability partnerships and, 128
  partnerships, 74
Citigroup, 204
civil law
  on partnership as entity, 42
  responsiveness to need for uncorporate forms, 35
close corporations, 95–117, 103
  breakdown and exit, 108–12, 113
  compared to limited liability companies, 253
  defined in statutes, 114
  director control agreements, 106
  entity shielding in, 122
  failure of, 116–17
  fair value on an interest in, 111
  future of, 252–54
  ratios to total corporations by states, 116n271
  rejecting treatment as, 115–16
  shareholder voting arrangements, 106–7
  share transfer restrictions, 107–8
  statutory authorization of, 113–16
  tax accommodation, 112–13
closely held firms
  avoidance of corporate tax through Subchapter S, 11
  creditors of, 96–97
  impact of corporate tax on, 99
coherence, 26–27, 137
  accounting proceeding and, 174
  compensation provisions and, 209
  derivative suit for LLCs and, 178–79
  effect of estate and gift tax provisions on, 185
  flexibility versus, 161
  importance in statutes, 31
  in LLC statutes, 155–56
  in LLP statutes, 151
  in LP statutes, 153
  management provisions and, 149, 155–56
  necessity in standard forms, 194, 244, 248
  as objective of business association statutes, 159
  one-owner partnerships and, 159
  RULLCA and, 156
  separation of corporate and uncorporate features and, 250
  tax rules effect on, 179–80
  theory, 138, 184–85
commenda as origin of limited partnership, 61
common law
  contracting for governance and, 88

impeding acceptance of
  uncorporations, 35
 of partnership, 40
compagnia as origin of general
  partnership, 40
Congress, 250
 possible tax policies, 244
contracts
 choice and design of, 31–32
 on distributions, 210
 evolution of business association law
  and, 8
 limited liability not established by, 138
 uncorporation reliance on, 6–7, 37–38
contributions, 161–63
control rule in limited partnerships, 25,
  57, 128, 129, 143, 152
 demise of, 175
corporate governance. *See* governance of
  corporations
corporate law, 65–66
 on corporation by estoppel, 83
 jurisdictional competition for, 74
 mandatory terms of, 6
 supplementary monitory mechanisms,
  213–14
corporate tax, 99–101, 243–44. *See also*
  taxation
 corporate features triggering, 99–100
corporate/uncorporate partnership, 246
corporation by estoppel, 83–84
corporations. *See also* board of directors;
  corporate tax; governance of
  corporations
 buyout and liquidation provisions
  inconsistent with other norms,
  212–13
 centralized management, 67–68, 78–79
 closely held firms as, 95
 compared to
  limited partnerships, 60–61
  partnerships, 66
 creditors of, 10–11
 distributions in, 163, 209–10, 210–12
  taxes on, 244
 as entity, 41, 73–75
 fiduciary duties, 68–69, 169–71
  opt-out, 169–71
  remedy, 170–71

governance regulation, 85–90
 inflexibility of, 194, 250
 internal affairs choice-of-law, 74, 85,
  86–87
 limited liability, 72
 management and standardized
  hierarchy, 149
 owner voting, 69–70
 politics and development of, 37
 problems with modern, 193
 rise of, 65–94
 role of general partnership
  in rise of, 39
 state-creation, 66, 74
 suitability for publicly held firms, 96
 transferable shares, 72
courts. *See also* judicial dissolution
 application of partnership law, 59–60
 application of regulations influenced by
  choice of business association, 27
 closely held corporations and, 103,
  104–12
 dissolution of close corporations,
  109–10
 judges as monitors of agency costs,
  203–4
covenants. *See also* implied covenant of
  good faith and fair dealing
 debt, 237
 in venture capital limited partnerships,
  226, 227
creditors
 business association law and, 25–26
 of closely held firms, 96–97
 contributions and protection of, 12
 of corporations, 10–11
 of general partnerships, 161–62
 of limited liability firms, 161–62
 of limited liability partnerships, 165
 of owners, 22, 52
 protection against excessive
  distributions, 22, 165
 restricted transferability of
  management rights and, 182
 risks of uncorporations for, 144, 165
credit rating services as monitoring
 mechanism, 213
culture and business, 36
cumulative dividend rights, 211

debt
  deduction of interest payments, 211
  private equity and, 236, 237
  role in development of
    uncorporation, 236
debt financing, 228n580, 235, 238
debtor-creditor law effect on business
    form, 33
Delaware
  catering to large firms, 255
  fiduciary duties
    in limited liability company, 177
    in limited partnership act, 175–76
    in publicly held LLC, 220
  freedom to contract out of
    corporate-type duties, 12
  General Corporation Law, 215
  on judicial dissolution, 180
  LLC statute, 153–54, 155
    on noneconomic members, 157
  new governance technologies and, 235
  role of bar association, 34n41
  Supreme Court
    on duty of care, 69
    on implied covenant of good faith
      and fair dealing, 219–20
Demsetz, Harold, 16, 160
derivatives, 240
derivative suit, 178
  board of directors and, 205
  in corporations, 170–71, 204–5
  limited liability company and, 178–79
  limited partnerships and, 177
  uncorporate limits to managers' control
    of the firm's cash substituting
    for, 221–22
Dill, James, 104
directors. *See* board of directors
dissociation. *See* dissolution
dissolution, 179–82, 212. *See also* judicial
    dissolution
  accounting and, 174
  of close corporations, 109–10
  of limited liability companies, 131, 212
  of partnerships
    compared to corporate capital lock-in, 71
    dispute resolution and, 53–54
    judicial, 78
    RUPA on, 126

distributions, 163–65
  contracting for, 210
  creditor's access to through charging
    order, 52
  debt and, 236
  in hedge funds, 229
  incentives and, 209–12
  protection of creditors against
    excessive, 22, 165
  restriction for insolvent firms, 165
  taxes on, 100, 244
  transfer of rights to, 51
Dooley, Michael, 112
Dreier, Marc, 158
due care. *See* duty of care
durability
  of closely held firms, 97–98, 97n226
  of corporations, 108 (*See also* capital
    lock-in)
  effect of estate tax rules on, 255
  of joint stock companies, 63
  of partnerships, 74, 77, 151
duty of care, 166–67
  contracting out of, 69
  in corporations, 169
  waiver of, 169–71, 205
duty of loyalty, 166–67
  in corporations, 169

Easterbrook, Frank H., 191
East India Company, 63
Edelman, Paul H., 196
Eisenberg, Melvin, 200
Eisner, Michael, 202, 204
Ellison, Lawrence, 202–3
embezzlement, 174. *See also*
  misappropriation of firm's property
employment discrimination laws and
  business association design, 33, 125,
  189–92
English Partnership Act (1890), 40
Enron, 200, 201, 238
entity. *See also* aggregate
  corporation as, 10–11, 73–75
  individual rights versus rights of, 182
  partnership's features of, 73
  shielding, 25, 77, 78, 122
    Revised Uniform Partnership Act
    and, 126

estate and gift tax provisions
    effect on business form, 33
    effect on LLCs and limited
        partnerships, 255
    undermining of statutory
        coherence, 185
estoppel, corporation by, 83–84
European Court of Justice, 133
executives, corporate, 208
exhaustion rule, 140–41
exit rights
    accountability of managers and, 147
    of investor in venture capital funds, 226
    of partners, 53–55, 151

family-owned firms and dissolution,
    179–80
federal securities laws
    influence on business association
        law, 125
    in tension with enabling state rules, 251
federal system
    contracting for governance and, 88
    effect on evolution of business
        forms, 35
fiduciary duties
    accountability of managers and, 147
    contracting out
        of default fiduciary duties in
            partnership, 50–51
        in hedge funds, 230
    controlling shareholders and, 166
    in corporations, 68–69, 169–71
        governance and, 87, 203–5
    defined, 165–66
    general principles, 165–69
    good faith duty versus, 48–49
    monitoring of management and, 193
    opting-out and customizing default, 168
    in publicly traded uncorporations
        opt out, 250
        reduction in PTP agreements, 232
    in uncorporations, 219–22
        mechanisms substituting for, 221
        opt-outs, 219
financial engineering, 238–40
financial regulation, 240–41
financial rights of members, 156–65.
    See also distributions

contributions, 161–63
    losses, 163–164
    noneconomic members, 156–58
    in nonprofit firms, 160–61
    in no-owner firms, 160–61
    in one-owner firms, 158–60
    profits, 163–65
financial vehicles, abuse of, 257
firms
    cash
        uncorporate members'
            access to, 249
        uncorporate constraints over
            management's power over,
            221–22, 232
    as competitors of lawmakers
        for power, 87
    size as distinction in the United
        Kingdom, 83
firms, large
    corporate form
        as prerequisite for, 65
        suitable for, 8, 67–75
    decline in net benefits of public
        ownership, 235
    future of uncorporation in, 237–46
    private equity's use of partnership
        mechanisms in governing, 222
firms, small
    choice of uncorporate form for
        flexibility, 8
    providing default rules for, 255
    source of future growth, 257
flexibility
    of close corporations, 253
    of limited liability companies, 248
    of management structure
        in limited liability companies, 153
        uncertainty in third party dealings
            and, 148, 150
    trade-off with coherence, 161
    of uncorporate forms, 7–8, 37, 208
        compared to corporate form, 249
        mutation under regulatory
            pressure, 242
Florida LLC statute, 120
France
    limited liability company, 93
    limited partnership in, 61

fraud as basis of veil-piercing, 144
French Commercial Code (1807), 61

general agency test, 192
general incorporation statutes, 6
general partnerships
   allocation of financial items among members, 164
   buyout firms organized as, 222
   creditors of, 161–62
   default entity, 247
   direct member management, 150–51
   entity aspects of unlimited liability, 140–42
   fiduciary duties, 171–74
      accounting as remedy, 173–74
      opt-out, 172–73
   impossibility of one-owner firm, 159
   law on, 5, 39, 126–27
Georgia, limited partnership act in, 121, 129
Germany, limited liability company in, 93
Gevurtz, Frank, 68
gift tax provisions. *See* estate and gift tax provisions
good faith duty, 49, 167–68, 205. *See also* implied covenant of good faith and fair dealing
governance, 36–38
   contracting for, 2, 88
   new technologies, 235
governance of corporations, 38
   board of directors and, 199–203
   breakdown in, 238–40
   fiduciary duties and, 87, 203–5
   regulation of, 85–90
      means, 87–90
      reasons for, 86–87
   shareholder voting, 195–99
   takeovers, 205–7
governance of uncorporations, 1–2, 38, 214–22
   advantages of, 246
   board of directors and, 214–15
   fiduciary duties and, 219–22
   hedge funds, 229–31
   owner voting rights, 215–17
   partners' compensation part of agreement, 208

   private equity, 222–26
   publicly trade partnerships, 231–34
   takeovers, 217–19
   venture capital, 226–28
Gower, L. C. B., 83
gross revenues, sharing of, 57

Hand, Learned, 148, 149
Hansmann, Henry, 77, 122
hedge funds, 219, 238, 246
   governance of, 229–31
   regulation of, 242
   subprime securities and, 239
Hertz buyout, 224
Hetherington, John A.C., 112

implied covenant of good faith and fair dealing, 38, 49, 167–68, 171, 175, 181
   Delaware Supreme Court on, 219–20
incentives
   and discipline in large uncorporations, 207–14
   buyout and liquidation, 212–13
   distributions, 209–12
   managerial compensation, 208–9
   supplementary monitoring mechanisms, 213–14
   to managers of uncorporations, 249
   in ownership structure of post-buyout firms, 224
   in publicly traded partnerships, 232
incorporated partnership, 96
inflexibility of corporations, 194, 250
internal affairs choice-of-law, 85
   in corporations, 74
   regulation of corporate governance and, 86–87
Internal Revenue Code
   on distributions in uncorporations, 210
   flow-through tax category, 232–33
   on REITs, 232
   restrictions on use of publicly traded partnership, 231–32
   Subchapter S, 11, 112–13
Internal Revenue Service
   difficulty of distinction between tax partnerships and tax corporations, 120–21

Wyoming LLC as partnership for tax purposes, 121
Investment Adviser Act, 231
investment firms as limited partnerships, 130

Jobs, Steve, 202
Johnson, Ross, 200
joint and several liability, 141
joint liability, 141
joint management, 47
joint stock company, 39, 62–63, 85
　transferability, 79
　in the United Kingdom, 91, 92
judges as monitors of agency costs, 203–4
judicial dissolution, 180–81
　contractual elimination of, 181
jurisdiction competition. *See* state competition
jurisdictions, multiple, 88–89

Kintner Rules, 100, 101, 120–21
　effect of LLC statutes on, 252
Klein, William, 59, 59*n*112, 60
Kohlberg Kravis, 222, 235
Kraakman, Reinier, 77, 122
Kravis, Henry, 235

L3C (low-profit limited liability company), 161
Lamoreaux, Naomi, 85
lawmakers
　limited liability partnerships and, 39, 79, 84–85
　political favors and changes in general incorporation statutes, 87
　restriction of partnership alternatives to the corporation, 66, 88
　restriction of partnership alternatives to the regulated corporate form, 90
lawyers
　catering to large firms, 255
　derivative suits and, 170–71, 204
　evolution of LLCs and, 131–32
　pressure for competitive state laws, 34, 34*n*41
legal system. *See also* civil law; common law
　flexibility and response to business needs, 26

legitimacy of corporate management, 70, 196
Lehman Brothers, 195
Lewis, Michael, 207, 238, 239
Lewis, William Draper, 41, 42
liability
　of managers in LLC, 145
　of promoters, 82–83
　limited liability, 138–47
　　as basis for corporate tax, 100–101
　　closely held firm and, 96–97
　　contractual approaches to, 80–85
　　corporate shareholders versus partners, 79–80
　　in corporations, 72, 139
　　general partnerships and, 140–42
　　in joint stock companies, 63
　　lawmakers' restrictions on noncorporate, 66
　　in limited liability companies, 143–47
　　in limited liability partnerships, 142–43
　　in limited partnership associations, 64
　　in limited partnerships, 50, 143
　　problems of adding to noncorporate business forms, 85
　　uncorporate, 139–40
Limited Liability Act (U.K., 1855), 92
limited liability companies (LLCs), 84, 119–23
　board of directors of, 214–15
　buyout and dissolution, 212
　buyout firms organized as, 222
　charging order and, 182
　closely held firms as, 247
　compared to limited partnership, 129
　evolution of, 131–32
　fiduciary duties, 177–79
　　opt-out, 177–78
　　remedy, 178–79
　flexibility of, 248–49
　growth of, 28
　limited liability in, 143–47
　management, 153–56
　no default right to dissociate, 180
　not-for-profit firms as, 160
　with one-member, 159
　statutes
　　influenced by tax rules, 125
　　uniformity of, 131
　veil-piercing in, 144–45

limited liability firms
  allocation of financial rights, 165
  creditors of, 161–62
limited liability limited partnerships
    (LLLPs), 130
limited liability partnerships (LLPs), 28,
    84, 127–28
  limited liability in, 142–43
  management in, 151
  no provision for liability to creditors for
    excessive distributions, 165
limited partners
  fiduciary duties of, 174–75
  limited liability of, 143
  rights of, 61
    voting rights, 215–17, 218
Limited Partnership Act (2001), 164
limited partnership associations,
    63–64, 89
limited partnerships, 39, 60–62, 84,
    85, 128–30
  buyout and dissolution, 212
  buyout funds organized as, 223
  centralized management, 152–53
  common law federal system and
    creation of, 89
  fiduciary duties in, 174–77
    opt-out, 175–76
    remedy, 176–77
  form for larger and publicly held
    uncorporations, 247
  hedge funds as, 229
  history of, 84
  impossibility of one-owner
    firm, 159
  limited liability in, 143
  no buyout rights, 180
  not-for-profit firms as, 160
  in the United Kingdom, 92
  in venture capital, 226
limited tort liability, 84
liquidation, 212–13. *See also* buyout rights;
    dissolution; term expiration
litigation. *See also* derivative suit
  against directors, 204
  entity nature and, 73
  special litigation committees, 202, 205
LLC. *See* limited liability companies
    (LLCs)

LLLP. *See* limited liability limited
    partnerships (LLLPs)
LLP. *See* limited liability partnerships
    (LLPs)
LLP Act (U.K.), 135
losses, allocation of
  equal share of partners, 44–45
  in general partnership acts, 163–64
low-profit limited liability
    company (L3C), 161
loyalty, duty of, 205. *See* duty of loyalty

Mace, Miles, 201
Macey, Jonathan, 193–94
Mahoney, Paul, 84, 87
management, 147–56. *See also*
    monitoring of management
  of buyout funds, 223
  centralized
    in corporations, 78–79, 149
    as default in limited liability
      companies, 153
    in limited partnerships, 129, 152–53
    in partnerships, 78–79
  compensation in large uncorporations,
    208–9
  decentralized, 153
  delegation of power to, 5
    in closely held firms, 98
  ensuring responsibility of in
    partnerships, 40
  in general partnerships, 150–51
  of hedge funds
    general partner-type incentives, 230
    no subject to Investment Adviser Act
      limits on fees, 231
  hierarchy of
    in corporations, 149
    in LLCs, 154
  liability in limited liability
    company, 145
  in limited liability companies, 153–56
  in limited liability partnerships, 151
  in limited partnerships, 152–53
  nontransferability of rights in
    partnerships, 52
  portfolio firms, 224
  positional power, 148
  power

divided between executives and
boards of directors, 199
over firm's cash constrained in
uncorporations, 221–22, 232
restricted transferability of rights in
uncorporations, 182, 218
market for control, 246
in corporate governance, 217–18
role of uncorporations in, 218–19
no role in uncorporations, 218
shareholder voting and, 70, 205–6
Marshall, John, 74
Means, Gardiner, 198, 243
Michigan, limited partnership
association in, 63
Miller, Geoffrey, 49–50
misappropriation of firm's property, 167.
See also embezzlement
Mitchell, William, 63
Model Business Corporation Act, 115
Model Registered Agents Act, 30
*Modern Corporation and Private Property,
The* (Berle and Means), 198
monitoring of management
in modern corporations, 70, 193
replaced by incentives and
discipline, 241
in buyout funds, 223–24
shareholders votes and, 70
shareholder voting and, 196
monopolies, government, corporations
created for, 65
moral hazard as justification for
regulating governance, 86
Murdoch, Rupert, 217
mutual funds, 230–31

National Conference of Commissioners
for Uniform State Laws, 123–24
negligent management theory, 145–46
New Jersey, limited partnership
association in, 63
New York
dissolution of close corporations, 110
general incorporation law, 68
New York Stock Exchange, 200, 216n542
no-dissociation default rule, 180
nominating committees, 200
noncorporate limited liability firms, 84–85

non-organization law, importance of,
124–25. *See also* estate and gift tax
provisions; securities regulation;
taxation
non-recourse contracts, 81
North Carolina, statute on closely held
corporations in, 114

Ohio, limited partnership association
in, 64
Oracle Corporation, 202
Ovitz, Michael, 204
owners. *See also* limited partners; partners;
shareholders
contributions and protection of,
161–62
shielding, 25, 77
RUPA on, 126–27
voting
accountability of managers and, 147
in close corporation, 106–7, 113
in closely held firms, 98
of partners, 69
in standard form corporations,
69–70
in uncorporations, 215–17

partners. *See also* limited partners
agency power of, 46–47
in buyout funds, 223
cashing out of partnership, 5,
53–55, 153
creditors of, 52
equal share of profits and losses, 44–45
general versus limited, 152
limited ability to transfer rights, 51–53
management by, 46, 150
personal liability for the firm's debts,
40, 43, 150, 152
veto power of, 47
vicarious liability, 40, 43–44
voting of, 69
partners' equities, doctrine of, 42
partnerships, 39–64. *See also* general
partnerships; limited liability
limited partnerships; limited liability
partnerships; limited partnerships;
publicly traded partnerships (PTPs)
as aggregate, 41–43

partnerships (cont.)
  as basic form of business association, 36, 126
  board of directors of, 214–15
  break up, 77–78
    unilateral dissolution and buyout, 212
  closely held firms and, 98
  corporate features adoption, 76–80
  definition in statutes, 55
  distributions, 210
  early history, 40–41
  exit of partner, 53–55
  fiduciary duties and remedies, 48–51
  formation, 55–60
    unintentional, 81
  management, 46–48
    centralized, 78–79
  nonprofit firms and, 160
  owners' financial rights, 44–46
  property rules, 41
  suitability for closely held firm, 96
  transfer of rights, 51–53
    economic, 182
  vicarious liability, 40, 43–44
Pennsylvania, limited partnership association in, 89
piercing of the veil. *See* veil-piercing
PIPE (private investment in public equity), 225–26
PORTAL market, 245
portfolio firms
  of buyouts, 224
  of venture capital, 227
Posner, Richard, 190–91, 191n464
post-buyout firms, 224
Powell, Lewis, 186–87, 189
power
  allocation of, 5, 154–55
  centralization in partnerships, 47
  internal versus external
    in corporations, 149
    in limited liability companies, 153
  management and, 147
  positional, RULLCA and, 155
Principles of Corporate Governance (American Law Institute), 200
private equity, 219, 237–38, 246
  governance of, 222–26
  regulation of, 242

  reliance on uncorporate business forms, 225
privlic equity, 233–34, 245
products markets as monitoring mechanism, 213
profits
  allocation of, in general partnerships, 163–64
  sharing as element of partnership agreement, 56
profits and losses, defined, 45–46
promoter liability, 82–83
property
  of corporations (*See* capital lock-in)
  of partnerships, 41
    RUPA on, 43, 126
    UPA on, 42–43
  statutes necessary for enforcement of rules concerning, 25
proxy rules, 198
PTPs. *See* publicly traded partnerships
publicly held uncorporations
  equilibrium corporate/uncorporate and, 250
  future of, 245
publicly traded partnerships (PTPs), 194, 238
  distributions, 210
  exception from the corporate tax, 244
  governance of, 231–34
  taxation, 185

quasi-limited liability, 141
quasi-public markets, 245

real estate investment trusts (REITs), 194, 232
regulations
  application by courts influenced by form of business association, 27
  business association design and, 184–92
  of business governance
    effect of uncorporations on, 251
  effect on divergence or convergence of business associations, 249
  evolution of uncorporate structures and, 207
  hedge funds and, 242

private equity and, 242
uncorporations and, 241–43
REITs. *See* real estate investment trusts
remedy, fiduciary duties and, 168–69
 in corporations, 170–71
 in general partnerships, 173–74
 in limited liability companies (LLCs), 178–79
 in limited partnerships, 176–77
Restatement of Agency, 148–49
reverse LBO, 223, 225
reverse veil-piercing, 183–84
Revised Uniform Limited Liability Company Act (RULLCA)
 on allocation of authority, 154–55
 on judicial dissolution, 180
Revised Uniform Partnership Act (RUPA), 6, 126
 compared to Uniform Partnership Act, 126–27
 continuity of partnerships and, 122
 on creation of partner capital accounts, 164
 on dissolution of partnership, 53, 126
 exclusivity of accounting disowned by, 173
 exhaustion rule and, 141
 on fiduciary duties, 172
  default, 51
  waiver of, 172–73
 on partnership as entity, 74, 126
 on partnership property, 43, 126
 on role of contract in partnership law, 127
risk, failure to understand and manage, 195
RJR Nabisco, 200

Sarbanes-Oxley Act (2002), 201
 development of uncorporation and, 235–36
 effect on markets, 251
 private equity industry and, 240–41
Schwarzman, Stephen, 235
Securities Act (1933), 186
Securities and Exchange Commission, 200, 250
Securities Exchange Act (1934), 186
 on shareholder information, 198

securities regulation
 disclosure burdens and liabilities, 188
 effect on business association design, 186–89
Seitz, Collins J., 107
"series" LLC, 146–47
shareholder advisers as monitoring mechanism, 213
shareholders
 classes of stock and, 217
 numbers in close corporations, 114
 reduction of power of nonmanagement, 217
 in Subchapter S, 113
 transfer of economic and management interests, 182
 voting of, 69, 185–99
  monitoring of management and, 193
  problems with, 196–98
  securities markets and, 70
shielding. *See* entity: shielding; owner: shielding
Sixteenth Amendment, 41
social responsibility, 254–55
societas as origin of general partnership, 40
Societas Europaea (SE), 133
South Sea Company, 90
special purpose acquisition corporations (SPACs), 213
Squire, Richard, 77, 122
standard form contracts
 interpretations, 247–49
 multiplicity of, 247–49
state competition
 evolution of business association law and, 8, 34
 pressure by lawyers, 34, 34n41
 for regulation of corporate governance, 7
 uncorporations and, 123
state laws
 coordinating, 123–24
 on incorporation, 7, 65–66
 recognition of closely held corporations, 11
Statute of the Staple (UK, 1343), 40

276 INDEX

statutes
  advantage of standard form created by, 25
  architecture of, 28–31
    flexibility, 31
    hub-and-spokes approach, 30–31
    menu approach, 29–30
    short all-purpose, 29
  policy choices and modern uncorporation, 138
  practical limits on variations of business associations, 123
  variations on limited liability companies, 248
Steele, Myron T., 176
stock markets as monitors of management, 70, 209
Stout, Lynn A., 67–68
structure of the uncorporation, 4–6
Subchapter S corporations, 11, 112–13
Supreme Court
  corporate political expenditures and, 66
  on corporate tax, 100
  on effect of state formation of corporations, 74

takeovers
  corporate governance and, 205–7
  difficulty in hedge funds, 230
  difficulty in PTPs, 232
  monitoring of management and, 193
  RJR Nabisco, 200
  uncorporations and, 217–19
taxation. *See also* corporate tax
  business association design and, 184–92
  of closely held corporations, 112–13
  on corporate distributions, 244
  effect on structure of firms and choice of form, 32–33
  evolution of uncorporate structures and, 207
  influence on business association, 125–33
  restriction of uncorporation to relatively stable firms, 251
  Subchapter S corporations, 11
Tax Reform Act (1986), 120

tax-reporting entities, uncorporations' percentage of, 3
term expiration
  of buyout funds, 223
  of hedge funds, 229
  of venture capital funds, 226
Texas
  Business Organizations Code, 248
  limited liability partnership law, 127
  multiple entity statute, 30
third parties. *See also* creditors
  dealing with corporations, 149
  dealing with partnerships, 46
  effect of partners' equal-sharing rule on, 45
Thompson, Robert B., 196
timing of development of uncorporations, 234–37
tort liability
  expansion of, 101
  LLC Revolution as reaction to, 140
  limited liability partnerships and, 142
transferring rights, 182–84
  Bubble Act (U.K.) on, 92
  in close corporations, 107–8
  in corporations, 72
  in partnerships, 72, 79
  restrictions
    in closely held corporations, 114
    in uncorporations, 182
Treaty of Rome, 133

un-business association, 256
uncorporations. *See also* specific forms of uncorporations
  advantages of standard forms, 207–8
  large
    financial engineering, 238–40
    financial regulation, 240–41
  long-term future, 249–50
  need to end-run the tax on distributions by using tax-deductible debt, 243
undisclosed principals, 81–82
Uniform Limited Liability Company Acts (1996, 2006)
  on judicial dissolution, 180
  on sharing of distributions, 164
Uniform Limited Partnership Act (1985)
  on fiduciary duties, 174, 175

on sharing of profits and losses, 164
Uniform Limited Partnership Act (2001)
    elimination
        of control rule, 143
        of default buyout rights, 153
    on limited partners, 152
    on voting rights, 216n541
Uniform Partnership Act (UPA),
    6, 40–41, 126
    compared to Revised Uniform
        Partnership Act, 126–27
    on dissolution of partnership, 53
    on fiduciary duties
        in partnership, 50
        waiver rule, 172
    limited partnership, 89
    on partnership property, 42–43
United Kingdom
    buyout transactions in, 224–25
    corporation, rise of, 90–93
    large firm governance in, 94
    limited partnership in, 61, 62
    LLP Act, 135
    partnership law in, 40
    regulation based on number
        of owners, 85

veil-piercing, 139, 144
    distinction between corporations and
        LLCs, 145

venture capital, 237–38, 246
    funds as limited partnerships, 226
    governance of, 226–28
Vermont, 161
veto power of partners, 47
vicarious liability, 40, 43–44
    restrictions on, 140, 141
Virginia, limited partnership
    association in, 63
voting rights
    of limited partners, 215–17
    transferability of, 218
    of owners
        accountability of managers and, 147
        in close corporation, 106–7, 113
        in closely held firms, 98
    of partners, 69
    in standard form corporations,
        69–70
    in uncorporations, 215–17
    reduction in PTP agreements, 232
    of shareholders, 69, 185–99
        monitoring of management and, 193
        problems with, 196–98
voting trusts in close
    corporations, 107, 113

Warren, Edward, 63
WorldCom, 200–201
Wyoming, LLC statute in, 119–20